ActiveX™ and VBScript™

VOLUME 3 OF THE

Web Publishing & Programming

Resource Kit

201 West 103rd Street
Indianapolis, IN 46290-1097
317-581-3500

MW01170335

Publisher and President	*Richard K. Swadley*
Publishing Manager	*Dean Miller*
Director of Editorial Services	*Cindy Morrow*
Managing Editor	*Mary Inderstrodt*
Director of Marketing	*Kelli S. Spencer*
Assistant Marketing Managers	*Kristina Perry*
	Rachel Wolfe

Acquisitions Editor
Cari Skaggs

Development Editor
Brian-Kent Proffitt

Software Development Specialist
Patricia J. Brooks

Production Editor
Mary Inderstrodt

Copy Editors
Cheri Clark
Marilyn Stone

Indexer
Ben Slen

Technical Reviewers
Brett Bonnenberger
Mark Butler

Editorial Coordinator
Katie Wise

Technical Edit Coordinator
Lynette Quinn

Editorial Assistants
Carol Ackerman
Andi Richter
Rhonda Tinch-Mize

Cover Designer
Jay Corpus

Book Designer
Louisa Klucznik

Copy Writer
Peter Fuller

Production Team Supervisors
Brad Chinn
Charlotte Clapp

Production
Jeanne Clark
Brad Lenser
Carl Pierce
Mark Walchle

Overview

Contents

About the Authors

Weiying Chen is a developer at Microsoft and has been leading the development of various technologies and platforms, including Windows NT custom server applications, ActiveX controls, and numerous Internet applications. Her current technology focuses are OLE and ActiveX. Weiying is a contributing author for *Windows NT 4.0 Server Unleashed* and *Designing and Implementing Internet Information Server,* by Sams Publishing. Weiying can be reached via e-mail at v-weiyc@microsoft.com.

Sanjaya Hettihewa is an accomplished Webmaster and a consultant specializing in integrating Windows NT–based information systems on the Internet. He has been living in the Washington, D.C. area for the past six years and has done extensive research in setting up Internet information systems utilizing various powerful and unique features of Windows NT. Sanjaya is the author of *Windows NT 4 Web Development*, and he co-authored *Designing and Implementing Internet Information Server, Windows NT 3.51 Unleashed, FrontPage Unleashed, Internet Explorer Unleashed*, and *Internet Information Server Unleashed*, all by Sams and Sams.net Publishing. You can reach Sanjaya at http://www.NetInnovation.com (or, if you prefer the old-fashioned way, at sanjaya@NetInnvation.com).

Daniel Leeks has been programming Windows applications for the past six years. He graduated from Purdue University in 1993, from the Department of Computer and Electrical Engineering. He is currently employed at Monolith Productions, Inc., in Kirkland, WA, where he is working on the video game Blood. When not sitting at his desk programming or writing articles, Daniel can be found mountain biking or hiking in the Cascades with his wife Tamara.

Lois Patterson lives in Vancouver, British Columbia, Canada. She is a freelance writer and Web consultant, and has a law degree. She authored the *HTML* volume in the *Web Publishing and Programming Resource Library,* by Sams.net. When not busy writing, surfing the Internet, or trying new software, Lois spends her time with her husband Paul and their two delightful home-schooled children, Anne Marie and Andrew. Visit Lois on the Web at http://www.greatstar.com/lois/ or e-mail her at lpatter@greatstar.com.

Vincent (Vinny) W. Mayfield lives in Navarre, Florida, with his faithful, yellow Labrador Retriever named Gunner. He is a Senior Software Engineer and a Microsoft Certified Professional with more than ten years of experience developing software and more than five years developing Windows-based applications with C and C++. He has been in the U.S. Army Reserves and the U.S. Air Force. Currently, Vinny is a Senior Software Engineer and Project Manager for Delta Research Corporation, a BTG Company, in Niceville, Florida, developing Visual C++, MFC, and Oracle applications. Vincent has also done freelance technical consulting with his own company, V Max Technical Solutions, and has done technical editing on numerous books for Macmillan Publishing. Vinny is an FAA Commercial Instrument-rated pilot, and when not punching holes in the sky or pounding the keyboard, Vinny enjoys spoiling his two nieces, Kaitlyn and Mary, and his nephew Anthony. In addition, Vinny is a *Star Trek* fanatic, an aviation enthusiast—and he loves military history and roughing it in the great outdoors. Vinny holds a B.S. in Mathematics with minors in Computer Science and Aerospace Science as well as an M.S. in International Relations.

Thomas Fredell is the consulting manager for the Atlanta Office of Brainstorm Technologies, a leading provider of groupware tools and consulting services. Thomas has the distinction of being the first graduate with a degree in Cognitive Science from the University of Virginia. His interests include software development using C, C++, and Java, and he has written chapters in books about Java and Lotus Notes. He can be contacted via e-mail at `tfredell@braintech.com`.

Mahendra Palsule is a software professional born and raised in Mumbai, India. With an engineering diploma in computer technology from Bombay in 1991, he is also a Microsoft Certified Professional in Windows Operating Services and Architecture. He has worked as a software consultant for the last four years and has experience in software development, networking, and multimedia authoring on Windows and Macintosh platforms. He has contributed to multimedia projects in Europe and the Middle East. He is currently involved in Web publishing at Radan Multimedia Limited, Mumbai. Apart from his obsession with computers and the Internet, he has diverse interests ranging from astronomy to epistemology. He loves to work on multimedia projects in which he can synthesize his creative and technical skills. You can reach him at `mahendra@radanmedia.com`.

James Mohler is Assistant Professor of Technical Graphics at Purdue University. He has produced interactive titles for national and international publishers and provides technical training and media services to the industry through Sunrise Productions. James can be reached at `jlmohler@tech.purdue.edu`. Technical Graphics at Purdue University prepares graphics professionals for electronic publication, illustration, modeling and animation, and engineering documentation specialties. You can visit the department at `http://www.tech.purdue.edu/tg/main.html`.

Daniel Wygant is a Senior Software Analyst with Intergraph Corporation in Huntsville, Alabama, where he has been employed for 12 years. He received his B.S. in Pure Mathematics from Florida State University. His development experiences include Windows NT, Windows 95, UNIX, and VMS. Daniel is currently working on an ActiveX Document Viewer for IGR files, the file format for Intergraph's new Imagineer Technical 2D CAD drawing product. His interests include OLE and Internet programming, such as ActiveX DocObjects, ISAPI, and Java. His publications include articles in *Windows NT Magazine* and two chapters in a Sams.net book, *Presenting ActiveX*. Daniel's e-mail address is `dfwygant@ingr.com`.

Laurent Poulain is a French computer engineer who has been working on Windows NT for a couple years (since NT 3.5 beta 2). On the Web, he maintains the gcc4ms FAQ (GCC for Microsoft), for people who are looking for a free C++ compiler on their Microsoft platforms. Besides computing, Laurent is interested in Asia, with a strong appreciation for Chinese/Hindu art, mangas, and aikido. Laurent used to work for companies such as Third Wave France on an international project or the Banque de France (the French equivalent of the U.S. Federal Reserve). He now works at Object Design, Inc., the world leader in object databases.

Tell Us What You Think!

As a reader, you are the most important critic of and commentator on our books. We value your opinion and want to know what we're doing right, what we could do better, what areas you'd like to see us publish in, and any other words of wisdom you're willing to pass our way. You can help us make strong books that meet your needs and give you the computer guidance you require.

Do you have access to CompuServe or the World Wide Web? Then check out our CompuServe forum by typing GO SAMS at any prompt. If you prefer the World Wide Web, check out our site at http://www.mcp.com.

---

note

If you have a technical question about this book, call the technical support line at 317-581-3833.

As the publishing manager of the group that created this book, I welcome your comments. You can fax, e-mail, or write me directly to let me know what you did or didn't like about this book—as well as what we can do to make our books stronger. Here's the information:

Fax: 317-581-4669

E-mail: opsys_mgr@sams.samspublishing.com

Mail: Dean Miller
          Sams.net Publishing
          201 W. 103rd Street
          Indianapolis, IN 46290

Conventions Used in This Book

The following conventions are used in this book:

---

note

A note box presents interesting pieces of information related to the surrounding discussion.

---

tip

A tip box offers advice or shows you an easier way to do something.

---

warning

A warning box advises you about potential problems and helps you steer clear of disaster.

HTML/path/
www.hrHTML/
path/www.hr
Chapter 8

This icon tells you where on the CD-ROM you can locate the file, or code, being discussed.

All code, filenames, and directory names appear in `monospace`. Placeholders (words that stand for what you actually type) in regular text appear in *`italic monospace`*.

When a line of code is too long to fit on only one line of this book, it is broken at a convenient place and continued to the next line. The continuation of the line is preceded by a code continuation character (➥). You should type a line of code that has this character as one long line without breaking it.

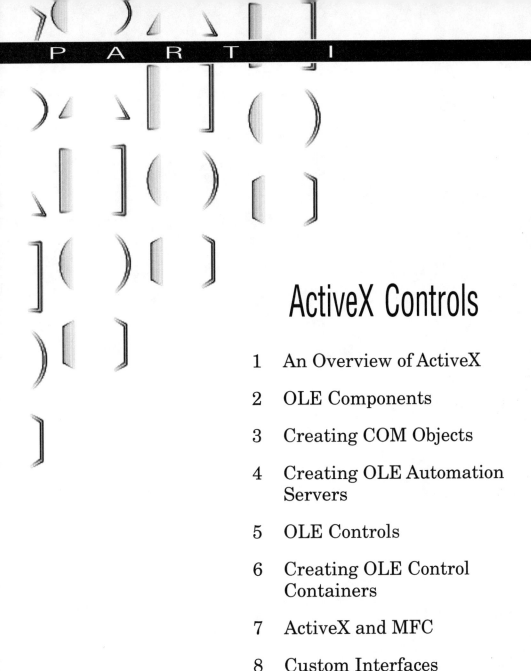

ActiveX Controls

An Overview of ActiveX

by Weiying Chen

Microsoft has unveiled an extensive new solution technology for the Internet called ActiveX. Microsoft ActiveX is a broad and powerful abstraction for Microsoft Internet Solutions.

Content providers and Internet application developers now have a robust and extensible framework that enables them to develop a new generation of Internet applications.

Microsoft is aggressively adding features to the Win32 Application Programming Interfaces (APIs) that will let developers "Internet-enable" their applications. These new features are based on object linking and embedding (OLE) technology so that developers who have made investments into Win32 and OLE applications can leverage their investments.

ActiveX exposes a set of APIs that enables developing a new generation of client/server applications for the Internet. ActiveX has interfaces to integrate almost every media technology within an application. It provides extensive support for animation, 3D virtual reality, real-time audio, and real-time video.

ActiveX gives developers an open framework for building innovative applications for the Internet. ActiveX technologies form a robust framework for creating interactive content using reusable components, scripts, and existing applications. Specifically, ActiveX technologies enable content providers and application developers to create powerful and dynamic Web content and Web server extensions quite easily. This feat is achieved by using ActiveX controls, active client- and server-side scripts, and the active document interfaces and ISAPI (Internet Server Application Programming Interface).

COM: The Fundamental Object Model for ActiveX and OLE

COM (Component Object Model) is the technical cornerstone for the ActiveX technology; it defines how objects expose themselves for use within other objects and how objects can communicate between processes and across a network. You can easily integrate COM objects for use in many languages, such as Java, BASIC, and C++. COM objects are reusable binary components.

The following concepts are fundamental to COM:

- Interface: The mechanism through which an object exposes itself.
- IUnknown interface: The interface on which all others are based. It implements the reference-counting and interface-querying mechanisms required for COM objects.
- Reference counting: The technique by which an object keeps track of its reference instance count. The instance of the object class should be deleted when there is no reference to this instance.
- QueryInterface method: This is called with the Interface ID (IID) to which the caller wants a pointer. IID can be generated by Guidgen.exe by choosing the DEFINE_GUID(...) format. QueryInterface enables navigation to other interfaces exposed by the object.
- IClassFactory interface: This interface must be implemented for every object class. It provides functionality to create an instance of the object class with CLSID and locks the object server in memory to allow creation of objects more quickly.
- Marshaling: The mechanism that enables objects to be used across process and network boundaries, allowing interface parameters for location independence by packing and sending them across the process boundary. Developers have to create a proxy/stub DLL, for the custom interfaces if they exist. The custom interface has to be registered in the system registry.
- Aggregation: A COM object supports an interface by including another object that supports that interface. The containing object creates the contained object as part of its own creation. The result is that the containing object exports the interface for the contained object by not implementing that interface.

- Multiple inheritance: A derived class may inherit from multiple interfaces.

ActiveX Object Model

There are two primary pieces to the ActiveX Object Model: the Microsoft Hypertext Markup Language (HTML) Viewer component (`MSHTML.dll`) object and the Web browser control (`shdocvw.dll`). Both are in-process (DLL-based), COM `objects.classes`.

All interfaces defined in the ActiveX Object Model are "dual" interfaces. A "dual" interface means that the objects inherit from `IDispatch` and `IUnknown`. They can be used by client applications at "early bind" via Vtable and at "late bind" via the OLE automation controller by using `IDispatch::GetIdsOfNames` and `IDispatch::Invoke.vtable`.

MSHTML is the HTML viewer part of Microsoft Internet Explorer 3.0. It is an in-process COM server and a Document object. It can be hosted in OLE Document object containers.

MSHTML implements the OLE Automation object model described in the HTML Scripting Object Model. With this object model, you can develop rich multimedia HTML content. VBScript running inline in the HTML and Visual Basic 4.0 running external to the HTML can use the object model.

The Web browser control object is an in-process COM server. It also serves as a Document object container that can host any Document objects, including MSHTML, with the added benefit of fully supporting hyperlinking to any document type.

The Web browser control is also an OLE control. The `IWebBrowser` interface is the primary interface exposed by the Web browser control.

The Web browser control is the core of what customers see as "the Internet Explorer 3.0 product." Internet Explorer 3.0 also provides a frame to host this control. Internet Explorer 3.0 supports the following HTML 3.x0 extensions:

- Frame: Creates permanent panes for displaying information, supporting floating frames or borderless frames.
- NOFRAMES: Content that can be viewed by browsers not supporting frames.
- OBJECT: Inserts an OLE control.
- TABLE: Fully compliant with HTML 3.x0 tables with cell shading and text wrapping.

- Stylesheet: Font size, intra-line space, margin, highlighting, and other features related to styles can be specified in the HTML by the user.
- In-line sound and video.

ActiveX Controls

An ActiveX control (formerly known as an OLE control) has a broader definition. It refers to any COM objects. For instance, the following objects are considered ActiveX controls:

- Objects that expose a custom interface(s) and the IUnknown interface
- OLE automation servers that expose the IDispatch/Dual interfaces
- Existing OLE controls (OCX)
- OLE objects that make use of monikers
- Java applets with the support of COM

> **note**
>
> A moniker acts as a name that uniquely identifies a COM object. It is a perfect programming abstraction for Uniform Resource Locator (URL).

ActiveX controls used inside scripting languages make binary reusable components in the Internet world. Almost any type of media wrapped into an ActiveX control can be seamlessly integrated into your Web page. Sound, video, animation, or even credit-card approval controls can be used within your Web page.

ActiveX Scripting

ActiveX Scripting is the interface for script engines and script hosts. Following this interface specification, the script vendors can use their custom script engine in any script host, such as IE 3.0. What's more, with its infrastructure, developers can choose any script language they prefer. A script is some executable block, such as a DOS batch file, Perl script, or an EXE file.

ActiveX Scripting components can be grouped into two major categories: an ActiveX Scripting Engine and an ActiveX Scripting host. A host creates a script engine so that scripts can run against the host.

Here are some examples of ActiveX Scripting hosts:

- Microsoft Internet Explorer

- Internet Authoring tools
- Shell

The ActiveX Scripting Engine is an OLE COM object that supports the IOLEScript interfaces, with at least one of the IPersist interfaces and an optional IOleScriptParse interface.

ActiveX Scripting Engines can be developed for any language, such as

- Microsoft Visual Basic Script Edition (VBScript)
- JavaScript
- Perl

Microsoft ActiveX Scripting Languages products, such as Visual Basic Script and JavaScript, can be used to "glue" together the functionality exposed in ActiveX controls to create rich Web-based applications.

Active Documents

Active Documents are based on the OLE Document objects (DocObjects, for short). The DocObjects technology is a set of extensions to the OLE Compound Document technology. It is the core technology that makes Microsoft Office Binder work. Active Document also refers to any document that contains ActiveX controls, a Java applet, or a Document object.

One other obvious application for this technology is "Internet browsers." You can open richly formatted documents, such as Microsoft Word and Excel spreadsheets, directly in the browser.

Figure 1.1 shows how seamlessly the Word document can be placed in IE 3.0. The word *toolbar* is added to the browser, enabling you to work on the document while surfing the Internet.

The following describes the general criteria for the Document object container and the Document object.

A Document object container must implement the following objects and interfaces:

- Document Site objects with IOleClientSite, IAdviseSink, and IOleDocumentSite interfaces exposed.
- View Site objects with IOleInPlaceSite and IContinueCallBack interfaces exposed.
- Frame objects with IOleIPlaceFrame and IOleCommandTarget interfaces exposed.

- `IOleDocumentSite` to support the DocObjects.
- `IOleCommandTarget` on the Frame object.
- `IOleClientSite` and `IAdviseSink` for "site" objects.
- `IPersistStorage` to handle object storage.
- `IOleInPlaceSite` to support in-place activation of embedded objects.
- `IOleInPlaceFrame` for a container's Frame object.

Figure 1.1.
Active document.

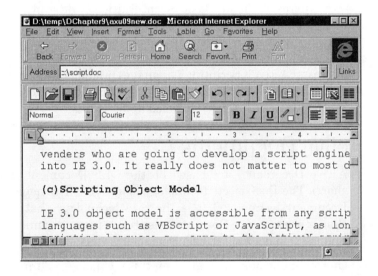

Similarly, Document objects must implement the following objects and interfaces:

Objects

- Document object with `IDataObject`, `IPersistStorage`, `IPersistFile`, and `IOleDocument` interfaces exposed.
- View object with `IOleInPlaceObject`, `IOleInPlaceActiveObject`, `IOleDocumentView`, `IPrint`, and `IOleCommandTarget` interfaces exposed.

Containers

- `IPersistStorage` for storage mechanism.
- `IOleInPlaceObject` and `IOleInPlaceActiveObject` for in-place activation extension of OLE documents.
- `IPersistFile`, `IOleObject`, and `IDataObject` to support the basic embedding features of OLE documents.
- `IOleDocument`, `IOleDocumentView`, `IOleCommandTarget`, and `IPrint` to support the Document objects' extensions interface.

ActiveX Server and Server-Side Scripting Framework

The ActiveX Server Framework, another component of ActiveX technologies, is based on the Microsoft Internet Information Server (IIS). IIS is built on the Windows NT 3.51 Advanced Server or greater. This framework enables developers to take advantage of the powerful Microsoft BackOffice family of products, such as Microsoft SQL, SNA, Management, and Exchange Server.

Server support consists of ActiveX server-side scripting and the usage of Aside, Batch, or JavaScript.

The Common Gateway Interface (CGI) is also supported under the ActiveX Server Framework. Common Gateway Interface is a protocol used to communicate between your HTML forms and your program so that your program can extract the information from the form. A lot of languages can be used to write your program, as long as the language has the capability to read the STDIN, write to the STDOUT, and read the environment variables.

An HTTP server responds to a CGI execution request from a client browser by creating a new process, reading the input from the form through the environment variable, doing some processing with the form data, and writing the HTML response to the STDOUT.

The server creates one process for each CGI request received. However, creating a process for every request is time-consuming and takes a lot of server resources. Using too many server resources can starve the server itself.

One way to avoid this is to convert the current CGI executable file into a dynamic link library (DLL) so that the DLL can be loaded into the same address space as the server. The server can load the DLL the first time it gets a request. The DLL then stays in memory, ready to service other requests until the server decides it is no longer needed. There are two types of DLLs that can be created for this purpose: one is the Internet Server Application (ISA), and the other is the ISAPI filter.

An ISA is also known as the Internet Server Extension. There are two entry points for this DLL: `GetExtensionVersion` and `HttpExtensionProc`.

HTTP Server first calls the ISA at the entry point of `GetExtensionVersion` to retrieve the version number of the ISAPI specification on which the extension is based. For every client request, the `HttpExtensionProc` entry point is called. Interaction between an HTTP server and an ISA is done through extension control blocks (ECBs). The ISA must be multithread-safe because multiple requests can be received simultaneously.

An ISAPI filter is a replaceable DLL that sits on the HTTP server to filter data traveling between the Web browser and HTTL server. Figure 1.2 shows the relationship between the HTTP server, ISA, and ISAPI filter.

Figure 1.2.
*HTTP server, ISA, and
ISAPI filter.*

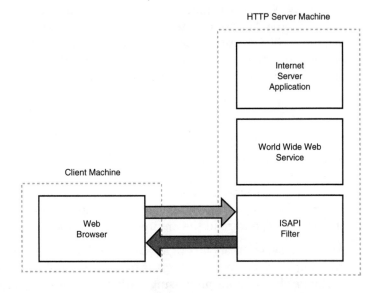

The ISAPI filter has the same entry point as the ISA. When the filter is loaded, it tells the server what sort of notifications it will accept. After that, whenever a selected event occurs, the filter is called and is given the opportunity to process the event.

ISAPI filters are very useful to provide the following functions:

- Authentication
- Compression
- Encryption
- Logging of HTTP requests

You can also install multiple filters on the server. The notification order is based on the priority specified by the filter, and then the load order in the registry. The registry key for the filter is under `\HKEY_LOCAL_MACHINE\SYSTEM\CurrentControlSet\ Services\W3SVC\parameters\Filter DLLs\`. After you install the filter, IIS must be restarted.

To ease the development of the server-side application, Microsoft also provides an Internet Personalization System (IPS) on top of the IIS. It provides a server-side VBScript, a set of server components, and a system installed with IIS on a Web server computer to make the server-side scripting available. With this system installed, you can integrate VBScript commands and expressions into the HTML files, and calls out to server-side OLE automation objects. When you point your browser to a script file, this system will process the script and return HTML to the browser. This allows developers to create more elaborate content with less effort. Server-side scripting will make the server-side development a piece of cake.

Active Animation and Movies

Active Animation (formally known as ActiveVRML; VRML stands for Virtual Reality Modeling Language) is an advanced markup language and a viewer for 3D multimedia. The Active Animation viewer is an ActiveX control and can be used inside client-side VBScript in Microsoft Internet Explorer 3.0. Web pages that use Active Animation can include interactive 2D and 3D animation, accompanied by synchronized sounds. These effects can also be triggered by events from VBScript in IE 3.0 and from other scripting languages, such as JavaScript.

Active Animation synchronizes all media interaction without developers needing to write low-level code. It supports the operation and media types, such as 3D geometry, images, sound, montages, 2D and 3D points, vectors, 2D and 3D transforms, colors, numbers, text, strings, characters, and so on.

The following is a list of the operations and media types supported by Active Animation:

- Sound: Supports importing, mixing, and rendering 3D models of sound waves.
- Images: Supports infinite resolutions, 2D transformation, overlaying, and rendering images from 3D models.
- 3D geometry: Supports texture mapping of animated images combined with control of color and opacity, aggregation, and transformations.
- Advanced 2D and 3D coordinate systems and transformations: Supports many advanced manipulations of vector/vector, point/vector, and scalar/vector. Also supports construction and destruction of rectangular or polar/spherical coordinates. Translate, scale, rotate, shear, inversion, identity, composition, and matrix-based constructions.
- Montages: Supports multi-layered cel animation and 2D images.

---

note

The word *cel* is synonymous with a frame of animation.

- Text: Supports formatted text, its colors and its font families, including optional bold and italics.
- Colors: Construction and destruction in RGB and HSL colors.

ActiveMovie is based on the Microsoft ActiveMovie Streaming Format (.ASF), a new data-independent format for storing and transmitting multimedia content across the Internet. Because .ASF files can be streamed, you can begin playback of these files immediately. ActiveMovie is an ActiveX control and can be used inside client-side VBScript or JavaScript.

.ASF is an open and extendable data-independent format. With this format, you can combine and store different data objects, such as audio objects, video objects, URLs, and HTML pages, into a single synchronized multimedia stream. This encapsulation feature enables popular media types and formats, such as MPEG, .avi, .wav, and Apple QuickTime, to be synchronized and stored efficiently on a variety of servers.

.ASF data is also network-independent and can be transmitted over different protocols and networks, including TCP/IP, UDP, RTP, IPX/SPX, and ATM.

.ASF also provides efficient packaging for different network transports, and supports multiple-bit rates, error correction, and other multimedia-content storage and transmissions.

You can efficiently play back .ASF content by using ActiveMovie, Microsoft's next-generation, cross-platform video technology for the desktop.

Why Use ActiveX?

With ActiveX, you can make the most of Internet resources with less effort. ActiveX controls and scripting give you the infrastructure needed to add language- and tool-independent extensions to Web pages. Using ActiveX controls lets developers take advantage of existing OLE development tools and the investment they have already made in OLE. ActiveX scripting allows you to drop any scripting engine into IE 3.0, enabling developers to add behavior to Web pages in whatever scripting language they prefer.

ActiveX has also greatly improved extending the HTTP and FTP protocols. The ActiveX IBindXXX interfaces encapsulate a new protocol that supports the concept of binding to a URL dynamically from within your application. An application binds to a URL moniker, which then communicates through the appropriate protocol to activate the OLE object. This abstraction allows newly developed protocols to integrate into your existing objects, independent of your object design or expressed functionality.

Using the Internet Extensions for the Win32 API (WinINet) makes it easy for developers to add Internet access to their applications. WinINet abstracts the TCP/IP protocol-specific details and gives developers a simplified programming interface to access the Internet instead of worrying about the WinSocket details. This API includes HTTP, FTP, and Gopher access.

As with most systems, server efficiency and resource use become a concern when designing multi-user server applications for the Internet. The Internet Information Server offers a high-performance, secure, and extendible framework. An ISAPI Internet Server Application (ISA) is a dynamic link library that loads into the same address space as the HTTP Server component. In contrast, CGI creates a separate process for every work request. Each new process in the CGI model requires more server resources. The advantage of developing an ISA rather than a CGI is high-level performance that requires considerably fewer resources, which frees up resources that can then be used by the server.

ISAPI filters can be used to enhance the Microsoft Internet Information Server with custom features, such as enhanced logging of HTTP requests, custom encryption, aliases for URLs, compression schemes, or new authentication methods. The filter applications sit between the client network connection to the HTTP server.

IIS has a few built-in ISAPI DLLS. One of them is `Httpodbc.dll`, which is called the Internet Database Connector. The Internet Database Connector allows ODBC database access through an HTTP request. Developers can use this feature to create Web pages with information from the database so that they can retrieve, insert, update, and delete information in the database based on user input and perform any other SQL commands.

ActiveMovie provides next-generation, cross-platform video; the ActiveMovie Stream Format solves several important synchronization issues in multimedia-content storage and transmission.

Active Animation gives you a powerful foundation for Internet interactive, animated, and multimedia-based content, targeting domains such as advertising, entertainment, online shopping, and technical illustration.

Microsoft is building an infrastructure around the client/server model that enables secure transactions, billing, and user authentication. IE 2.0 and 3.0 support the secure socket layer (SSL) versions 2.0 and 3.0 and personal communications technology (PCT) version 1.0 . Most importantly, ActiveX is built on Win32 and OLE, which enables developers to build on their existing investments. ActiveX is the doorway to a whole new world of Internet applications.

ActiveX Program Development

The most fundamental model that you should understand before embarking on ActiveX development is the COM (Component Object Model). This model is the same model as discussed in the OLE COM specification.

COM is the "Object Model" for ActiveX and OLE. Microsoft also provides the OLE COM Wizard and ActiveX Template Library (ATL) so that developers can develop lightweight, fast COM objects. ATL offers a template to write OLE automation servers, OLE controls, and the very basic dual interface or any arbitrary COM objects. ATL also provides a custom AppWizard (called OLE COM AppWizard in VC 4.x project workspace), which can be used with Visual C++ 4.1 or later to create a COM object skeleton.

Microsoft Visual C++ 4.1 Development Studio integrates different AppWizards and Control Wizards to simplify the development process. Along with Visual C++ 4.x, Microsoft offers version 4.x of the Microsoft Foundation Classes. In Microsoft Visual C++ 4.2, there is new support for ActiveX programming, such as

- WinINet
- Active document
- Asynchronous moniker
- URL moniker
- Control for Internet

Besides the tools, wizards, frameworks, and foundation classes, Microsoft also provides a set of specifications to implement certain ActiveX controls. For instance, it provides the OLE controls for the Internet, Document objects, ActiveX scripting interface, Hyperlink interface, and Asynchronous Moniker specification.

ActiveX controls can be easily manipulated by any scripting languages in IE 3.0. The scripting languages include JavaScript, the client-side VBScript, or any other third-party scripting language that implements the ActiveX scripting interface. ActiveX controls, particularly OLE automation servers, can also be used with the server-side VBScript.

Microsoft also provides J++ to develop Java applets and Java applications. Java applets can be used as ActiveX controls.

Besides these ActiveX client-side scripts, Microsoft also provides a system on top of the IIS 2.0 to use the server-side VBScript. ActiveX controls, particularly OLE automation servers, can be referenced in the server-side VBScript.

A variety of tools can be used to develop server-side components, such as Perl and C for CGI programming.

To facilitate developing ISAPI applications, Microsoft Visual C++ 4.x provides the ISAPI Extension Wizard and some foundation classes for ISAPI. Along with this, Microsoft also provides the ISAPI specification.

The ActiveMovie add-on toolkit includes tools to develop applications that handle streamed media. This toolkit allows software developers to integrate real-time audio and video content in virtually any type of application.

Active Animation and ActiveMovie controls can be manipulated through client-side VBScript. A developer can glue the controls' functions together without the need for complex stream synchronization methods.

Summary

ActiveX is a technology that has the potential to change the way information is accessed and used on the Internet. Powerful abstractions based on OLE have been developed that enable fast, scaleable integration of your objects within the Internet. Microsoft is making a major effort to make the Internet everything it can possibly be. By using ActiveX, developers can make the best use of their system resources while providing instant, dynamic content and functionality in their Internet applications. How information is presented greatly affects how interesting and usable people find it.

2

OLE Components

by Vincent W. Mayfield

Is ActiveX just Microsoft's new, trendy name for OLE? To a large extent, that is the case. ActiveX is a set of technologies that extend OLE to facilitate the development and implementation of applications for the Internet. OLE, and now ActiveX, is a set of technologies that standardize the interface between different programming objects. OLE was specifically designed for desktop applications, and ActiveX has been designed for Internet-based applications. COM is the underlying technology for both ActiveX and OLE.

OLE, COM, and ActiveX— Definitions and History

Users have long been seeking an effective way to allow unrelated applications to share information. Programmers have also been trying to find a means by which they can eliminate much of the redundancy inherent in software development. They are frustrated by the fact that they have to retrace so many steps when creating new software applications, and frustrated by the difficulties involved in updating or modifying even a small part of a large application. Traditionally, there have been numerous obstacles in the software industry, first in sharing code between applications, and then in sharing components of applications. It's a cliche to talk about reinventing the wheel, but that's what software developers have had to do, in large part, with every new application they have created. OLE, COM, and ActiveX are Microsoft's attempts at a solution to these problems.

The Historical Development of OLE

DOS programs, such as word processors, allowed the user to copy or cut text and then paste it elsewhere within a document. This feature worked only within a single application. The clipboard idea was extended with DDE (dynamic data exchange), a technology that was present in the earliest versions of Microsoft Windows. DDE used a means of transferring data between applications using a clipboard metaphor. Many programs, particularly older ones, still use DDE. DDE was somewhat limited in how it could handle different types of data between applications.

OLE 1.0 was an integral part of the Windows 3.0 release in 1991. At that time, OLE's only significance was reflected in its acronym, Object Linking and Embedding. OLE 1.0 was a replacement for the less flexible and powerful DDE. In this incarnation, OLE 1.0 was mainly concerned with compound documents. When preparing a presentation or report, for example, users often want to include text, graphics, spreadsheets, and other media all within the same unit. OLE 1.0 allowed the user to create a document containing various media. You could prepare a Microsoft Word document and insert bitmap files, CorelDRAW! charts, Excel spreadsheets, or other document objects into the document.

With OLE 1.0, when you clicked on one of these embedded objects, the application for that object would open, and you could edit the object in a separate window. Microsoft Word was the most common container application, but it was not the only one. You could use Excel as the container application, for example, and insert a graphic or other media into the Excel document. Embedding was not necessary, either, because you could simply create a link to the object instead of actually including it within the document itself.

If you placed a linked or an embedded object inside an application, that application became the OLE client. The OLE server was the application that the object called to manipulate the object. For example, if you placed a CorelDRAW! chart inside an MS Word document, CorelDRAW! would be the OLE server, and MS Word would be the OLE client. Without ever leaving MS Word (or whatever OLE client you happened to be using), you could have all the capabilities of any other OLE 1.0 application. Being able to create compound documents is a feature that most users can appreciate, and having software packages that can work together to do that is important.

OLE 2.0 extended the capabilities of OLE 1.0 in respect to compound documents, and it also added many other features as well. Unlike OLE 1.0, OLE 2.0 allows in-place activation of document objects. When you click on an OLE 1.0 object within a compound document, a separate program that corresponds to that object opens to allow you to edit it. With OLE 2.0, the object actually can be edited from within the original container. You can easily switch from editing the native data for the application to editing the data for the embedded object. In Figure 2.1, a MIDI file has been inserted into an ordinary MS Word document. The Microsoft toolbars are in place, and you can continue to manipulate text as usual. When you activate the object, the toolbars within the application are replaced by the toolbars necessary to edit the sound clip, as you can see in Figure 2.2. When you are finished editing the sound clip, you just click again, and the document again has its MS Word toolbars as in Figure 2.1. You can do in-place activation with an Excel spreadsheet, a movie clip, or any other media for which the relevant application is an OLE server. Microsoft has set specific guidelines for the user interfaces that OLE applications are to have in order to make them as uniform as possible across applications.

As mentioned, there is much more to OLE 2.0 than those features, such as compound documents, which are visible to the user. After OLE 1.0, the general problem of software components being unable to "talk" to each other remained. Microsoft realized (as did other software developers) that being able to create software components that could work together, whether within the context of a compound document or otherwise, would be very helpful to both users and developers. OLE 2.0 focuses on creating a modular software design model. Without OLE 2.0, a software component created by one software designer probably cannot communicate with a software component created by another designer, unless the developers have specifically decided to work together. With OLE 2.0, Microsoft created a standard means by which software components, no matter by whom they were designed, would be able to work with other software components.

Figure 2.1.
A MIDI file not activated within an MS Word document.

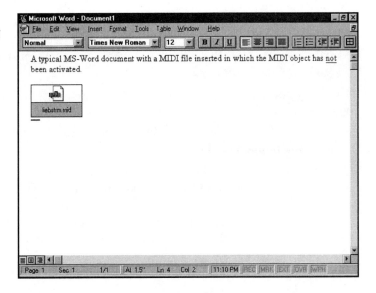

Figure 2.2.
In-place activation of a
MIDI file within an MS
Word document.

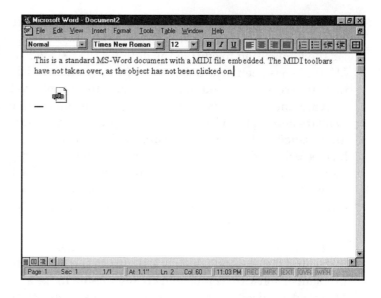

With OLE 2.0, an OLE server does not have to be a complete application. It might just be a DLL (dynamic link library) file or set of DLL files. OLE 2.0 improves the way compound documents work, and it also adds many other capabilities that the user does not see. With OLE, an application consists of various components. These components can each be modified separately, and other components can plug in to the application. OLE components are required to be backward-compatible. The upgrades do not require a recompile of the application. Old versions and new versions of components within an OLE application will be able to work together.

OLE was originally limited to Windows. It has, however, been ported to the Macintosh operating system, and work is underway to port it to UNIX, VMS, and MVS. Many observers fear that OLE is just another way for Microsoft to gain further control over the software market, but Microsoft has promised that OLE is to be an open standard.

Many applications (or DLL files) can be either OLE servers or OLE containers (clients), depending on the context. For example, you can embed a Web browser document inside an MS Word document, and you can also embed an MS Word document inside a Web browser.

OLE does not require the user to be editing, or otherwise manipulating, objects directly (as in a compound document). One example of OLE in action is Netscape's plug-in model. The Netscape browser is an OLE container, and the plug-ins, such as Shockwave, RealAudio, or any one of a host of other possibilities, are OLE servers. You can activate the Shockwave file from inside the Netscape browser, as shown in Figure 2.3. In this example, the Netscape toolbars themselves do not change, because the object is entirely self-contained, and the object does not require those toolbars.

Figure 2.3.

Netscape as an OLE container, and Shockwave as an OLE server.

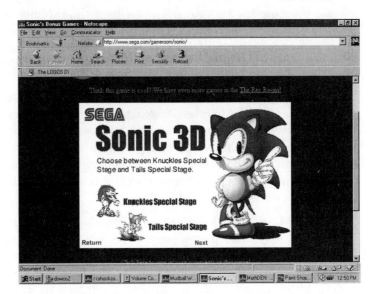

Microsoft has decided not to release a new version of OLE. OLE is an extensible architecture, meaning that new features can be added as needed. For example, OLE controls were not introduced for some time after OLE 2.0 was introduced. OLE is usually not used with a version number anymore, unless you are talking about the original OLE 1.0.

With OLE, you can program in whatever language you want and incorporate the COM interfaces between the components. There's no doubt that an object-oriented programming language such as Visual C++ or Smalltalk is somewhat of a better "fit" for the OLE model, but you can use other languages as well.

OLE encompasses various technologies, with the most significant being COM. Sometimes COM and OLE are used interchangeably, because COM is the basis of OLE.

COM (Component Object Model)

COM is a standard developed so that software components can interact with each other. Despite the fact that a boundless array of software packages seems to be available, these programs have many things in common. Nearly all programs, for example, have the user input some data, process it in some fashion, and then output a result. Software design is hindered by the fact that so many of the same steps must be repeated "from scratch" every time a new application is created.

To alleviate redundancy, at least to some extent, computer programmers have used precompiled subroutines for a long time. Many programs have various operations in common, and the programmer need not reinvent the code every time the same problem arises. With DOS, you could use a library, and every application that relied on the library would carry a copy of the code within it. With Windows, the DLL was developed. The DLL files are not linked to the application until the application is run, and many applications can share the same DLL file. No standard DLL file interface exists, however. Furthermore, updating a DLL file might work for some applications, but not for other applications that also used the original DLL file. You can purchase a code library and use it in your application, but that's not the same as being able to use different COM objects. You can upgrade an application with a new DLL, but there are no interface standards for DLLs without COM.

With COM, you have a defined set of interfaces, and COM objects use these in a standard way. The programmer does not have to understand the complex workings of each COM object. The data and processing details are kept away from the surface. COM objects also can be accessed only through these specifically defined interfaces. COM establishes a common means of interaction between different sorts of software, including applications, libraries, and more.

note

What is an object? It's difficult to pin down a precise, yet generic, definition. An object is a discrete "thing," such as a document, icon, a file, or an application. An object contains a set of data, also called attributes, and a group of methods. These methods are implemented as functions or procedures, and a client of the object uses these methods to perform different tasks. The methods are grouped together to form an *interface*. A typical application is composed of various interacting objects. You can move an object from one application to another while still retaining the native format of that object.

COM facilitates the replacement, modification, customization, and reuse of software components. The way COM has been designed, you can replace an old component of an application with a new component of an application, without having to recompile the application. The application will automatically detect the new version. You can mix and match software components without having to worry about the inner workings of the components. COM takes care of those details.

You can create a specific COM component specially suited to the needs of each user or group of users. You can also reuse the COM objects in other applications. You do not have to rely on the source code, and you do not have to recompile the objects. COM components do not have to be manufactured by the same developer, nor do developers have to work together for their products to work together.

COM objects share many similarities with C++ objects. For example, both COM and C++ objects support encapsulation, polymorphism, and inheritance.

Encapsulation means that an object's data can be accessed only through its methods (also called functions). Encapsulation prevents inadvertent access to data and helps preserve data quality.

Polymorphism assists in the standardization process. A client can treat different objects in the same way, but each object responds correctly.

COM objects and C++ objects support the concept of *inheritance* differently. When you create an object based on an existing object, the newer object can inherit the features of the older object. This method saves considerable effort in redefining every object individually. However, the type of inheritance differs.

COM objects support *interface inheritance*, meaning that the child object must provide its own code when a client of the child object calls for one of the methods that the child object has inherited. A COM object does not rely on its parent's code.

C++ objects support interface inheritance. They also, however, support *implementation inheritance*. With implementation inheritance, the client of the child object actually executes the code of the parent object when the methods of the child object are called.

Particularly for COM objects, interface inheritance is "safer" than implementation inheritance, because implementation inheritance could expose the data of the parent object, breaking its encapsulation and making it possible for the data to be altered inadvertently.

Besides COM, some of the other significant OLE technologies are uniform data transfer, in-place activation, automation, structured storage, and OLE controls.

The Historical Development of ActiveX

ActiveX can be seen as a general term for the whole concept of component object-oriented programming technologies such as OLE and COM as extended to the Internet. With ActiveX, it's not always clear which features are the same as for OLE, which features have been left out, and which features have been added. In general, though, OLE is designed for desktop applications, and ActiveX, for the Web.

Microsoft's stated purpose for ActiveX is to "activate the Internet." As stated in Microsoft's ActiveX FAQ, the ActiveX infrastructure is significantly "slimmed down" in relation to OLE in order to facilitate the use of ActiveX on the Internet, where bandwidth is at a premium and file sizes must be minimized.

Although the situation is changing, the Internet largely has static content. The Web consists mostly of HTML pages that are not dynamically generated. ActiveX is one means by which developers can add interactive content to the Web. Netscape plug-ins, CGI (Common Gateway Interface) programs, and Java are other ways of making the Web dynamic. These alternatives are not necessarily opposed to or in competition with ActiveX; all of these could be used together. To take an example, Java, as an object-oriented programming language, is in some ways ideally suited for use with ActiveX.

Microsoft's vision is of a desktop where you can transfer and share information among applications on different machines on different networks. The Internet itself will become just another set of directories. Internet Explorer 4.0, which was due to be released in beta in March 1997, will be integrated into the desktop. When you need a certain type of program, the Microsoft scenario would have you just download the appropriate ActiveX control on the spot (the matter of payment for these controls is a separate issue, not discussed here). Many Windows applications are well-known for "code bloat," because they have an extraordinary number of features that greatly increase their size. ActiveX applications, because they will be downloaded when and if they are specifically needed, can be small and tightly focused.

Visual C++ naturally tends to be associated with OLE, COM, and ActiveX. All of these use the object-oriented programming paradigm, and the Microsoft Foundation Class Library 2.0 wraps the OLE API (application programming interface) in a C++ class library. Encapsulation and polymorphism are used by both Visual C++ and OLE. Some developers see this programming model as being too closely allied with C++, because DCOM requires passing memory pointers between applications, and many programming languages do not support memory pointers.

The Object Management Group (OMG) has put together an alternative to OLE, COM, and ActiveX, called CORBA (Common Object Request Broker Architecture). OMG has criticized ActiveX as lacking an "overall architecture" and of being continually redefined and retargeted. The latter criticism is true, because ActiveX, OLE, and COM are continually evolving. With the incredible pace of developments in the computer industry, however, one cannot blame Microsoft for refining its programming models frequently.

Everything done with OLE and ActiveX could conceivably be done another way. CORBA is an alternative object-oriented software model, one that its proponents claim is far more appropriate to the World Wide Web than ActiveX, and one that does not suffer either the handicap or the benefit of being associated with Microsoft.

DCOM (Distributed Component Object Model)

ActiveX also extends COM itself—with DCOM (Distributed Component Object Model). The term *DCOM* simply means that the various COM components do not have to be physically located on the same machine. DCOM was formerly known as Network OLE. With the current browser-server paradigm in place for most Web servers, there is a clear distinction between the user's machine and the Web server, and the processing of each is clearly delineated. DCOM allows for a more efficient model, because processing can be done wherever it is more convenient. With DCOM, software components and objects can interact no matter which machine they are located on.

ActiveX components can be custom-tailored to individual situations and user setups. A user can have a desktop application that is OLE-enabled, and then can download ActiveX components to customize it and add specific features as they become available.

ActiveX Technologies

In addition to being an extension of OLE to the Internet, ActiveX includes various other features. These include URL monikers, windowless objects, OLE hyperlinks, and features such as asynchronous monikers and progressive downloading to make it possible to begin to show a file (such as a video or sound clip) before it's finished downloading. Because ActiveX controls can be manufactured by anyone and downloaded automatically, special safeguards are in place that don't exist for OLE. ActiveX is still evolving; it was introduced only recently, in early 1996.

Some of the more important technologies that are part of both ActiveX and OLE include these:

- OLE (ActiveX) controls
- In-place activation
- Uniform data transfer
- Automation
- Structured storage

These particular technologies are discussed in greater detail later in this chapter.

ActiveX also includes additional technologies not specifically related to OLE, although these rely on the same general principles. You can find information about these technologies on the Microsoft ActiveX Web site at http://

`www.microsoft.com/activex/` or elsewhere in this book. Some of these technologies are described briefly here:

Active Server: Most of the discussion has concerned the effect of ActiveX controls on the user's machine. ActiveX server extensions, however, allow you to attain the same functionality as CGI.

ActiveX scripting: Just as you can use Visual Basic for Applications to create a customized application involving different applications in the Office 97 suite (to give one example), you can use scripting languages such as JavaScript and VBScript to integrate various ActiveX controls within a Web site.

Code signing: ActiveX is often seen as a dangerous security threat, because the controls are not well-controlled as to how they can interact with the user's machine. In theory, an ActiveX control can wipe out a hard drive. Clever programmers have created an ActiveX control that can shut down the user's machine, as well as an ActiveX control that can run the program Quicken and perform transactions. ActiveX controls can easily harbor Trojan horses. To help alleviate these kinds of problems, Microsoft has introduced a code-signing system so that code can be traced to a particular author. Many Web users find this system imperfect, and it's still quite possible for a programmer to make a somewhat harmful ActiveX control inadvertently. Most users feel safe as long as they use only ActiveX controls provided by major vendors.

HTML Extensions: The <OBJECT> tag allows you to embed ActiveX controls within your HTML pages. The World Wide Web Consortium, the Web's standard-setting body, will include support for the <OBJECT> tag in an upcoming HTML specification.

ActiveMovie: ActiveMovie is an ActiveX control that acts as a programming interface to handle multimedia streams.

Conferencing: This conferencing technology allows users from all over the world to have real-time video and multimedia connections. You can use an ActiveX conferencing control with a product such as Microsoft NetMeeting, at `http://www.microsoft.com/netmeeting`.

OLE Controls, COM Objects, and ActiveX Controls

What is the precise distinction between OLE controls and ActiveX controls? The issue is somewhat confused, as Microsoft itself states in a Knowledge Base article at `http://www.microsoft.com/kb/articles/q159/6/21.htm`. Generally speaking, there is no reason to use the term *OLE control* anymore, and Microsoft advises against it. OLE still has the connotations of its original acronym, Object Linking and Embedding, and the new term ActiveX is a way to get around that. An OCX is not an ActiveX control, but it is a file that can hold one or more ActiveX controls. Microsoft Foundation Class controls are ActiveX controls. ActiveX controls can be created in many programming languages, including C++, Java, Visual Basic, and others. In practice, most controls probably are written in C++ or Visual Basic.

OLE controls have a different specification than ActiveX controls. The rules have been relaxed for ActiveX controls. ActiveX controls, generally speaking, have a more specific function than a typical OLE control would have. With ActiveX controls, you can just download another control (assuming that such a control exists) if your current control doesn't satisfy the purpose. OLE controls are a concept suited to traditional software production, in which you want to have as many features as possible. Because ActiveX controls usually must be downloaded over the Internet, objects the size of a typical OLE control would not be welcomed by most users. ActiveX controls do not require the programmer to implement the large number of interfaces that are required with OLE controls. The OLE specification requires that a certain number of interfaces be implemented for an OLE control, even if these interfaces are completely unrelated to the purpose or function of the application.

A COM object is required to support the IUnknown interface. An ActiveX control is required to be self-registering. In practice, the two terms mean almost the same thing, because an ActiveX control will by definition support the IUnknown interface. The IUnknown interface contains the methods QueryInterface, Release, and AddRef. Every interface in a COM object inherits the methods from IUnknown. Each COM object implements a vtable, which is an array of pointers to each method in the interfaces.

OLE controls that were created before ActiveX was invented are likely already ActiveX controls, or they might just need a little adjustment to make them self-registering. If you have created OLE controls in the past, you can likely use or adapt them for your ActiveX work.

ActiveX documents are not the same as ActiveX controls, although you can activate ActiveX controls within an ActiveX document. In contrast to ActiveX documents, ActiveX controls support communication to and from the control to the client application, a technology called Connectable Objects. Typically, most of the ActiveX controls released so far extend the capabilities of Microsoft Internet Explorer and make it possible for Internet Explorer and the control to "talk" to each other. ActiveX controls can be activated within the client, as you can see if you download a control while using Internet Explorer 3.0 or later.

Drag-and-drop, which is discussed later in the section titled "OLE and Uniform Data Transfer," can be enabled in an ActiveX control if the programmer chooses to include that functionality. Property pages for both ActiveX controls and OLE controls expose their methods and properties to the user, making it possible for these controls to be programmable with automation. ActiveX controls are automation servers, and they can be programmed with an automation controller. Scripting languages such as JavaScript and VBScript are used for automation of ActiveX controls. ActiveX controls use persistent storage to save the settings for the next time the control is initialized.

Some ActiveX controls are oriented to the user, and some are oriented to other programmers. For example, at the Microsoft ActiveX Control gallery at `http://www.microsoft.com/activex/gallery/`, you can download an ActiveX control that allows you to play chess. You can also download a control that can perform long-integer arithmetic for the purposes of programming.

ActiveX and Storage

How does ActiveX handle storage of data? Its storage model is based on the COM structured storage service. ActiveX has to work with various file systems and data storage systems, and structured storage is a means of standardization.

Persistent storage just refers to the fact that certain data must be stored for later usage, normally on the user's hard drive. Asynchronous storage is used when you have a large file to download, and a slow or unreliable link (such as over the Internet), and you want to begin to use or display the data before waiting for the entire file to be downloaded to the user's machine.

Structured Storage

DOS looked at storage in terms of file systems, with a file handle with a data pointer to point to the currently read position in the file. With ActiveX and OLE, however, more than one COM object might have to access a single file. Also, with COM objects, you cannot know the internal details of how those objects are handling data. In addition, different platforms have different file storage systems. ActiveX allows you to work with these different systems together by using structured storage; it uses two ways of looking at a data—storage and streams.

Structured storage can be visualized as being similar to the Win95 Explorer, as shown in Figure 2.4. It involves a hierarchical system of folders and subfolders, with files inside. Structured storage extends this to the data inside each of the files. The Win95 Explorer folders are similar to storage objects. Win95 files are similar to stream objects. The stream object can hold data of any type. Each stream object has a data pointer to which you can assign rights, but the stream object does not attempt to subdivide the data any further. Each storage object and each stream object is itself a COM object.

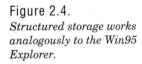

Figure 2.4.
*Structured storage works
analogously to the Win95
Explorer.*

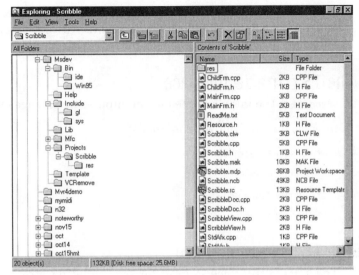

You can manipulate storage and stream objects with the interfaces detailed in the
following sections.

The `IPersistStorage` Interface

`IPersistStorage` is the interface used for persistent storage. With persistent
storage, you can save settings, such as a particular color, font, or some other user-
defined preference, for the next time an object is used. You can also save data that
the control needs for the next time it is initialized. These are the methods for the
`IPersistStorage` interface:

- `InitNew`
- `Load`
- `Save`
- `SaveCompleted`
- `HandsOffStorage`

`InitNew` is called when the object is first initialized. The object's client can pass a
pointer to the storage object that the client should use.

`Load` causes the object to load the persistent data.

`Save` causes the object to save its persistent data. You cannot, however, write to
the storage itself with `Save`.

`SaveCompleted` causes the object to write to its storage.

HandsOffStorage causes an object to release any storage objects that it is holding and to be unable to complete any operation until a SaveCompleted method is invoked and completed.

The IStorage Interface

IStorage is the interface used for manipulating storage objects.

IStorage has the following methods:

- CreateStream
- OpenStream
- CreateStorage
- OpenStorage

The IStream Interface

The IStream interface is used for manipulating streams. It has a number of different methods, including the following ones:

- Read
- Write
- Seek
- SetSize
- CopyTo
- Commit
- Revert
- LockRegion
- UnlockRegion
- Stat
- Clone

Asynchronous Storage

Asynchronous storage can be used for streaming applications. If you are downloading a large video or sound file over the Internet, you don't have to wait until the entire file downloads before you can see or hear the content. With asynchronous storage, the user downloads a series of nested objects.

In a typical application, the file would be available on the local drive, so there would be no need to start playing the file before it was completely loaded into memory. Synchronous storage would therefore be appropriate. You use ActiveX hyperlinks and ActiveX monikers to achieve this effect.

Using Monikers to Reference and Link Objects (ActiveX and OLE)

Just as directories and files are not satisfactory for ActiveX, and you need the more sophisticated concept of structured storage, monikers extend the concept of filenames. A moniker can be more specific than a filename. You can access particular pieces of data, files, or other objects.

The five standard classes of monikers are file, item, generic composite, anti, and pointer:

> *File monikers* store the filename persistently.
>
> *Item monikers* refer to a particular piece of data
>
> consist of a character string.
>
> A *composite moniker* is a container that stores monikers. For example, you might have several item monikers and a file moniker together to refer to some specific data. The composite moniker would hold all of these moniker objects.
>
> An *anti-moniker* deletes the last in a chain of monikers.
>
> *Pointer monikers* point to other monikers and are not persistent.

Monikers are used to link data objects within an OLE document. Every moniker requires the IMoniker interface. IMoniker calls the BindToObject function to bind the moniker to the object. IMoniker calls the BindToStorage function to bind the moniker to storage.

A moniker object uniquely defines each object. The IMoniker interface is derived from the IPersistStream interface.

URL Monikers

URL monikers extend the functionality of monikers to any objects, such as files or pieces of data, that are available on a network or on the World Wide Web. With OLE, you can create hyperlinks between documents as easily (when you understand how) as you can create hyperlinks between different HTML documents. ActiveX extends this hyperlink capability to all documents, whether or not these documents are on the Internet.

OLE and ActiveX Documents

OLE documents can be extended to the Web to become ActiveX documents. With ActiveX, the objects in a compound document do not have to be on the local machine. ActiveX hyperlinks between ActiveX documents and other objects are a natural extension to traditional HTML hyperlinks.

All ActiveX containers, whether or not they support in-place editing, are required to implement the IOleClientSite and IAdviseSink interfaces. IAdviseSink gives notification when data has changed.

In-Place Activation

In-place activation looks simple from the user's point of view. To the user, it looks as if a single object is being edited. As usual, of course, a lot is happening under the surface. Actually, several objects are running in different processes.

The embedded object must negotiate with the container as to which application will own the menu bar.

For in-place editing, you require the IOleInPlaceSite, IOleInPlaceActive-Frame, and IOleInPlaceUIObject interfaces. Other interfaces are optional.

ActiveX and Automation

With Automation, formerly known as OLE Automation, you can automate particular tasks. For example, you could devise a small program or macro that could download specific data from the Internet, enter it into Excel, and then produce an MS Word report with an Excel spreadsheet embedded in it.

Using OLE Automation to create special programs and integrate various OLE applications is not the same as actually programming the OLE objects, of course.

To support Automation, you need an Automation controller. Visual Basic for Applications is the most prevalent example of such a controller, although the controller can be any suitable scripting language or application. The controller typically uses the IDispatch interface, which exposes all the available services to the Automation component (such as an ActiveX control).

The Automation controller acts on Automation components. As defined by Microsoft, an Automation component (also called an Automation object) is "an instance of a class defined within an application that is exposed for access by other applications or programming tools by Automation interfaces."

OLE and Uniform Data Transfer

Uniform data transfer is another COM service extended to ActiveX. You can transfer data in several ways, including by using the clipboard, by employing drag-and-drop, and by linking and embedding. The IDataObject interface is used by all COM data objects. Not all data transfer is visible to the user as it is, for example, when the user is copying and pasting between applications, because much of the data transfer takes place at the level of device drivers or at the operating-system level.

The Clipboard

The clipboard metaphor for cutting or copying data and then pasting it into another application or another location within the application is very familiar to most computer users. When the clipboard is used, data is copied or cut into a data object. The `OleSetClipboard` function places the `IDataObject` pointer to the specified object onto the clipboard. The `OleGetClipboard` function retrieves the data object from the clipboard.

Drag-and-Drop

OLE drag-and-drop allows the user to drag objects out of and drop objects into different applications. You can see this capability with the Explorer interface, as you drag files and directories to different locations. Microsoft Exchange, the e-mail client included with Windows 95, includes OLE drag-and-drop capability. Figure 2.5 shows how a graphic created in a paint program can be pasted into the text of a Microsoft Exchange e-mail message. Of course, the recipient would also need to have an e-mail client with OLE capability in order to be able to interpret the message. Otherwise, the reader is likely to receive what would appear to be unintelligible attachments.

Figure 2.5.
Dragging and dropping a graphic into e-mail.

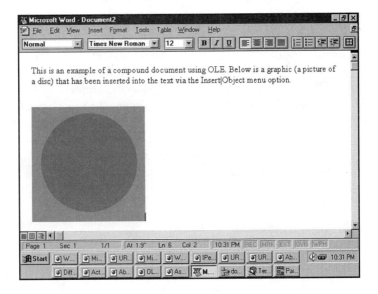

The source application from which the data is to be dragged implements the IDataObject interface, which is the COM standard for data transfer. The source application also must implement the IDropSource interface. The target application into which the data is to be dropped must implement the IDropTarget interface. Of course, many OLE applications have been programmed so that they can work as either a source or a target.

Linking and Embedding

With OLE, the linked object will be on the same machine as the document. ActiveX means, though, that a link need not be to a file on the same machine. In either case, a moniker references the linked object. If you embed the object inside the compound document, the entire file will be increased in size. With a simple link, the extra size of the file will be negligible. With a linked file, different users can access that file for multiple purposes. The container uses the IOLELink interface to manipulate linked objects.

The OLE/COM Object Viewer

To find out which COM classes are installed on your system, you can download the OLE/COM Object Viewer from http://www.microsoft.com/oledev/olecom/oleview.htm. This program is also included in the ActiveX SDK. You can configure COM classes, look at their Windows registry entries, enable or disable DCOM, and find the interfaces and methods used by ActiveX controls, as well as perform other operations. OLE2View32.exe, a similar utility included with Microsoft Visual C++, is installed in the \MSDEV\BIN\ directory.

Each OLE server and container adds information to the Windows registry. ActiveX controls, by definition, have to be self-registering, and you can find considerable information about each control on your machine with these viewers. Figure 2.6 shows the Type Library information for a typical ActiveX control, IEChart, as seen with the OLE/COM Object Viewer. Figure 2.7 shows the Internal OLE Objects in the left screen, the registry information for the selected control in the upper-right screen, and the beginning of a listing of all the interfaces for all the COM objects on my machine. Neither of these figures comes close to capturing the capabilities of these very powerful viewers. Be sure to try them out for yourself.

Figure 2.6.
The OLE/COM Object Viewer.

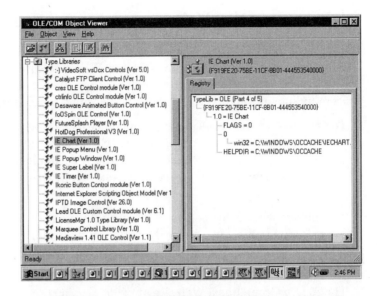

Figure 2.7.
The OLE2View32 viewer.

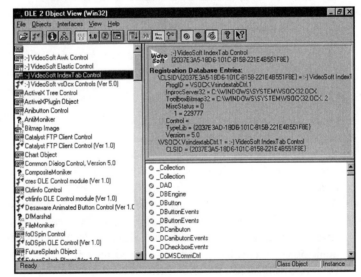

OLE and ActiveX Resources on the Web

Because OLE and ActiveX are developing so rapidly, the best place to find the latest information about them is on the Web. The sites listed in the following paragraphs are a start. When downloading ActiveX controls, particularly those from unknown sources, remember basic security procedures.

To find out more about OLE development, check `http://www.microsoft.com/oledev/`. Two particularly useful articles about OLE are located at `http://www.microsoft.com/oledev/olecom/ddjole.htm` ("OLE Integration Technologies: A Technical Overview") and `http://www.microsoft.com/oledev/olecom/aboutole.htm` ("What OLE Is Really About").

To find out what Microsoft is doing with ActiveX, the URL to check is `http://www.microsoft.com/activeplatform/default.asp`. To perform a search on a particular interface, function, or technology, or any other aspect of ActiveX, the Microsoft search engine at `http://www.microsoft.com/sitebuilder/nav-fi.htm` is very helpful.

The Active Group has a Web site at `http://www.activex.org/`. As described on the site, the Active Group is a "consortium of software and systems vendors promotion and widespread adoption of ActiveX technologies."

C I Net has an ActiveX Web site at `http://www.activex.com/`.

Summary

OLE, COM, and ActiveX are all Microsoft technologies for extending the object-oriented programming model to software design itself. OLE was first developed as a way to support compound documents, meaning documents that could support more than one data format without difficulty. OLE was later extended to include an entire system for creating modular software components that can freely exchange information and that can readily be reused in other applications. The second version of OLE, called OLE 2.0, was released in 1993, before the Internet was as hyped as it is today. OLE 2.0 was almost entirely aimed at desktop applications. ActiveX, introduced in early 1996, extends OLE to the Internet. It was Microsoft's natural response to the inescapable reality that the Internet was becoming increasingly important to businesses and consumers.

COM is the underlying technology for both OLE and ActiveX. COM components, COM objects, OLE components, and OLE objects are essentially synonymous terms for objects programmed to support the Component Object Model. ActiveX documents and ActiveX controls share many similarities with their OLE counterparts.

3

Creating COM Objects

by Weiying Chen

The Component Object Model (COM) is an open architecture for cross-platform development of client/server applications. It is the cornerstone for ActiveX technology and OLE 2.0.

This chapter presents the fundamental concept of COM, such as COM client/server architecture, COM server, and COM client. A set of fundamental COM interfaces is also examined in detail to describe their roles in creating COM objects.

To illustrate the fundamental blocks and the concept of the COM architecture, several examples are built step-by-step to demonstrate how to create various COM servers and corresponding COM client applications. All the sample source code is written in Microsoft VC++ 4.1.

Microsoft Active Template Library (ATL) simplifies the procedure of creating COM servers by providing commonly used templates. At the end of this chapter, an example demonstrates ATL creating COM objects.

COM Client/Server Architecture

COM is the cornerstone for ActiveX technology and OLE 2.0, as shown in Figure 3.1.

Figure 3.1.
COM, ActiveX, and OLE 2.0.

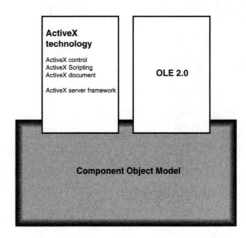

All ActiveX controls are COM objects. COM objects refer to any object that implements the IUnknown interface.

ActiveX scripting provides a set of OLE interfaces for a scripting engine and a scripting engine host. All these interfaces inherit from IUnknown.

An ActiveX document provides a set of Document objects and Document object container interfaces, which inherit from IUnknown interfaces.

ActiveX server-side scripting uses OLE technology. OLE 2.0 is built on COM, which provides a client/server architecture. The COM client uses the COM server via the COM library, as Figure 3.2 illustrates.

Figure 3.2.
COM client/server model.

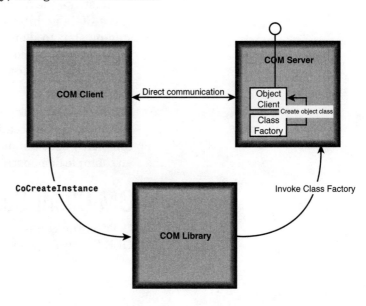

COM Server

A COM server is a component that implements one or more COM Class objects. A COM Class object is a COM object that is creatable via a COM Class Factory object. A COM Class object has a CLSID associated with it. A COM object is anything that implements the IUnknown interface. It is different from an object in object-oriented programming. In object-oriented programming, an object called the OO object is an entity that has state, behavior, and identity. The OO object's state is represented by the value of the attributes in the object. But a COM object's state is implied by the interface; the state is not explicitly stated because there are no public attributes exposed in the interface. The interface is just a set of functions without any attributes.

The OO object's behavior is a sequence of messages sent to the object, which is a sequence of methods called on this object, but for a COM object, the object's behavior is defined as the interface it supports.

The OO object's identity is a way to look at the object, whereas for a COM object, the identity is defined by moving between interfaces exposed by the COM object, which is done by invoking the IUnknown::QueryInterface interface.

Each COM object provides functionality via exposing interfaces. An interface is a group of related functions and provides some specific service. For example, the COM server shown in Figure 3.3 exposes two interfaces: One is IPrint, and the other is IHelp. The IPrint interface provides the print service, whereas IHelp supports the help service. Each interface groups its own functionality.

Figure 3.3.
CPrint *COM server.*

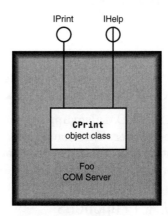

In order to uniquely identify the class object provided by the COM server, a class identifier (CLSID) is used; to identify the interface, an interface identifier (IID) is used.

A COM server is usually a DLL or EXE file. A DLL-based COM server is called an in-process (in-proc for short) server because it loads into the same address space as the client. The client can make direct calls to the object, which is faster and more efficient. But the crash of the DLL can destroy the client's address space.

An EXE-based COM server is called an out-process (out-proc for short) server, because it runs in its own separate process space.

An EXE-based COM server isolates itself from the address space of the caller, which makes it more reliable. If the server crashes, it will not destroy the address space of the client. But because it is in a separate process, all interface calls must be marshaled across processes (data gets copied), which affects the performance.

Note: Now part of Java, the COM server could be a Java class.

COM Client

A COM client (client for short) is an application that uses a COM server. A COM client asks the COM server to instantiate objects in exactly the same manner regardless of the COM server types. This is done by invoking the COM function CoCreateInstance. After the COM client retrieves the first pointer to the COM object, it cannot determine from the interface whether the COM server being used is an in-proc or out-proc server.

A COM client is an executable (EXE) application as compared with a COM server, which can be DLL-based.

COM Library

The COM library provides an implementation of the Application Programming Interface (API). The specification also defines a set of interfaces that will be used by different COM objects.

The component in COM also supports the communication establishment between the client and server. This component provides location transparency for the client. In other words, the client does not need to know where the server locates; all these locations are taken care of by the COM library.

COM Library API Functions

COM library API functions provide the functionality to the COM applications. COM applications are any applications that use COM. The following gives examples of API functions:

- CoInitialize: Initializes the COM library. The COM library must be initialized before calling its functions. This API should be called when the COM application starts.

- CoUninitialize: Uninitializes the COM library. This will free all the maintained COM resources and close all RPC connections. This API should be called when the COM application exits.

- CoCreateInstance: Creates an instance of the object class. This API is a helper function. A helper function encapsulates other functions and interface methods defined in the COM specification. CoCreateInstance wraps the following sequence calls: COM API CoGetClassObject, IClassFactory method CreateInstance, and IClassFactory method Release.

COM Fundamental Interfaces

COM predefines a set of interfaces to be used by client/server applications. Among these, the IUnknown and IClassFactory interfaces are the most fundamental ones. The IUnknown interface is required for any COM object. The QueryInterface method in the IUnknown interface allows the client to access the object's identity and move between interfaces.

A Class Factory object is required for every object identified by a given CLSID. A Class Factory object implements the IClassFactory interface.

IUnknown Interface

IUnknown is the interface from which all other interfaces inherit. In other words, every interface except IUnknown inherits from IUnknown. Listing 3.1 illustrates the IUnknown interface definition.

Listing 3.1. IUnknown interface.

```
interface IUnknown
{
    HRESULT QueryInterface([in] REFIID riid, [out] void **ppv);
    ULONG AddRef();
    ULONG Release();
}
```

The COM object must implement this interface. The COM client will invoke the methods in the interface implemented by the COM object.

QueryInterface Method

QueryInterface provides the mechanism by which a client, having obtained one interface pointer on a particular object, can request additional pointers to other interfaces on the same object. The COM object exposes itself via a set of interfaces.

There are two parameters for QueryInterface. riid is the IID of the interface requested. ppv is a return value. It is an indirect pointer to the interface. If the interface requested does not exist, ppv must be set to NULL and an E_NOINTERFACE error code should be this method's return value.

Listing 3.2 demonstrates an implementation of the QueryInterface method for the CLowerStr class.

> ## note
>
> The code listings in this chapter are from the example created in this chapter.

Listing 3.2. Example of the `QueryInterface` implementation.

```
STDMETHODIMP CLowerStr::QueryInterface(REFIID iid, void **ppv)
{
    HRESULT hr;

    *ppv = NULL;
    if((iid == IID_IUnknown) ¦¦ (iid == IID_ILowerStr) )
    {
        *ppv = (ILowerStr *)this;
        //increase reference count
        AddRef();
        hr = S_OK;
    }
    else
    {
        //if interface does not exist, *ppv set to be NULL, and E_NOINTERFACE
_returns.
        *ppv = NULL;
        hr = E_NOINTERFACE;
    }
    return hr;

}
```

Here, CLowerStr is an implementation of the ILowerStr interface. The ILowerStr interface inherits from IUnknown. CLowerStr can be called a COM object because it implements the IUnknown interface.

AddRef Method

The AddRef method provides the technique for an object to keep track of the reference count. The reference count should be incremented whenever an interface pointer is queried.

Listing 3.3 shows an implementation of the AddRef method.

Listing 3.3. `AddRef` method implementation.

```
STDMETHODIMP_(ULONG) CLowerStr::AddRef()
{
    m_dwRef++;
    return m_dwRef;
}
```

`m_dwRef` is a reference count defined in the object `CLowerStr`. It is defined as a DWORD.

`Release` Method

The `Release` method decrements the reference count. If the reference count is zero, the object should be destroyed since the object is no longer needed. The client application needs to invoke this method whenever the interface is not accessed.

Listing 3.4 demonstrates an implementation of the `Release` method.

Listing 3.4. `Release` method implementation.

```
STDMETHODIMP_(ULONG) CLowerStr::Release()
{
    m_dwRef—;
    if(m_dwRef == 0)
        delete this;
    return m_dwRef;
}
```

`IClassFactory` Interface

The `IClassFactory` is the interface from which Class Factory objects inherit. In other words, Class Factory implements the `IClassFactory` interface. The Class Factory object is required in COM to create an instance of the object. This is a rule. For example, when the client application uses that object, that object has to be created via its class factory.

Look at Figure 3.4; the COM server has a class factory, which creates an instance of the object.

Figure 3.4.
Relationship between Class Factory object and object.

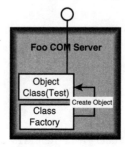

The IClassFactory interface has two fundamental methods, as shown in Listing 3.5.

Listing 3.5. IClassFactory interface.

```
interface IClassFactory : IUnknown
{
    STDMETHODIMP CreateInstance(IUnknown *punkOuter, REFIID riid, void **ppv);
    STDMETHODIMP LockServer(BOOL fLock);
}
```

The CreateInstance method creates an instance of the object class. It has to be implemented by the Class Factory object to instantiate the object. This method will be used inside the CoCreateInstance function call. CoCreateInstance will first return a pointer to the IClassFactory and then invoke IClassFactory's CreateInstance method to create an object's instance and will then return an indirect pointer to the object's requested interface. This method only needs to be implemented but never needs to be invoked by the application itself.

punkOuter indicates whether the object is being created as part of the aggregate. If there is no aggregation in the COM server, NULL should be provided; otherwise, a pointer to the controlling IUnknown of the aggregate should be provided.

riid is the IID of the interface queried by the client. If the punkOuter is NULL, the IID of the initializing interface should be provided. Otherwise, riid must be IUnknown.

ppv is a pointer to the pointer of the requested interface. If the object does not support the interface specified in riid, ppv should be set as NULL, and E_NOINTERFACE should be returned as the method's return value.

LockServer locks the server in memory. The class factory will be revoked when the lock count is decremented to zero. LockServer (TRUE) will increment the lock count and ensure that the class factory will not be revoked.

Listing 3.6 illustrates an example of the implementation of CreateInstance.

Listing 3.6. Sample CreateInstance method implementation.

```
STDMETHODIMP CLowerStrClassFactory::CreateInstance (IUnknown *pUnkOuter,REFIID
_iid,void **ppv)
{
    HRESULT hr;
    CLowerStr *pObj;

    *ppv = NULL;

    pObj = new CLowerStr;

    if (pObj)
    {
        hr=pObj->QueryInterface(iid,ppv);
```

```
            pObj->Release();
    }
    else
    {
        hr = E_OUTOFMEMORY;
        *ppv = NULL;
    }

    return hr;
}
```

CreateInstance first instantiates the CLowerStr object and then queries whether the iid interface exists in the CLowerStr object. If so, ppv will return an indirect pointer to the interface, and the CLowerStr object will be released.

Listing 3.7 illustrates how to implement the LockServer method.

Listing 3.7. Sample LockServer method implementation.

```
long g_cLock = -1;
STDMETHODIMP CLowerStrClassFactory::LockServer(BOOL fLock)
{
    if (fLock)
        g_cLock++;
    else
        g_cLock—;

    return S_OK;
}
```

The LockServer first checks fLock to see whether it is true; if yes, the g_cLock will be increased; otherwise, the g_clock will be decreased. This LockServer method will be invoked by the client application.

In the following section, a set of examples will be demonstrated to further illustrate the concept. First, an in-proc server will be created and used. Then this in-proc server will be built as an out-proc server and used. After that, ATL will be used to create this in-proc server.

Create and Use an In-Proc Server

The server (lst31.dll) is illustrated in Figure 3.5.

There is one interface, ILowerStr, exposed by the CLowerStr object. There is only one method called Lower in this interface.

```
virtual STDMETHODIMP Lower(char *lpInput, char**lpOutput) = 0;
```

This method accepts input, converts the input string to lowercase, and then returns the input string to the caller.

Figure 3.5.
lst31.dll *COM server.*

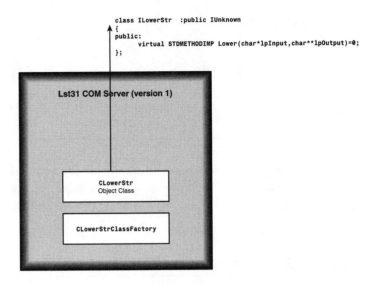

```
class ILowerStr  :public IUnknown
{
public:
          virtual STDMETHODIMP Lower(char*lpInput,char**lpOutput)=0;
};
```

Lst31 COM Server (version 1)

CLowerStr
Object Class

CLowerStrClassFactory

Specifically, lpInput in the Lower method indicates the input string.

lpOutput indicates the returned string that converts the strInput to uppercase.

Create lst31.dll COM Server

The following steps demonstrate how to implement this in-proc server:

1. Generate two GUIDs in DEFINE_GUID format—one for IID, the other for CLSID—by using guidgen.exe. Replace the <<name>> in the code generated by guidgen.exe with the IID of the interface and the CLSID of the object class.

   The CLSID and IID are universal, unique IDs (UUIDs). CLSID stands for class identifier, whereas IID is for interface identifier. The use of this unique ID precludes the possibility of a naming collision among COM objects and interfaces.

   COM clients use these unique identifiers at runtime to locate the object and its interfaces. The COM library uses these IDs to locate the COM server module path in the registry.

   The UUID can be obtained through the uuidcreate RPC function. There are tools that use this function directly or indirectly to generate the UUID, such as guidgen.exe and uuidgen.exe.

   guidgen.exe is a window-based application, and uuidgen.exe is a console-based application. They both are contained in Microsoft Visual C++. uuidgen.exe generates only a UUID in a registry format, whereas guidgen.exe generates four formats, as shown in Figure 3.6.

Figure 3.6.
GUID formats provided
by guidgen.exe.

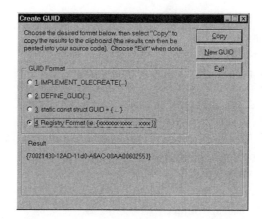

Format 2: DEFINE_GUID(...) is used to identify a CLSID or IID. For example, a CLSID is defined in

```
DEFINE_GUID(CLSID_CLowerStr, 0x4f126d90, 0x1319, 0x11d0, 0xa6,
_0xac, 0x0, 0xaa, 0x0, 0x60, 0x25, 0x53);
```

Format 4: Registry Format is used to build a registry entry for the COM server.

```
REGEDIT

; CUpperStr Server Registration

HKEY_CLASSES_ROOT\CLSID\{4F126D90-1319-11d0-A6AC-00AA00602553} =
_CLowerStr Object
HKEY_CLASSES_ROOT\CLSID\{4F126D90-1319-11d0-A6AC-00AA00602553}
_\InprocServer32 = d:\areview\ch3\lst31\debug\lst31.dll
```

Format 1: IMPLEMENT_OLECREATE(...) and Format 3: static const struct GUID={...} are not used as often as Formats 1 and 4.

By convention, symbolic constants are used to identify a specific CLSID or IID. They are in the form of CLSID_<class name> or IID_<interface name>.

---

note

I've used d: for my drive letter, but you should substitute the letter of the hard drive to which you installed the code.

For example, Listing 3.8 demonstrates how to use these formats.

Listing 3.8. CLSID and IID.

```
// {4F126D90-1319-11d0-A6AC-00AA00602553}
DEFINE_GUID(CLSID_CLowerStr, 0x4f126d90, 0x1319, 0x11d0, 0xa6, 0xac, 0x0, 0xaa,

 // {4F126D91-1319-11d0-A6AC-00AA00602553}
DEFINE_GUID(IID_ILowerStr, 0x4f126d91, 0x1319, 0x11d0, 0xa6, 0xac, 0x0, 0xaa,
0x0, _0x60, 0x25, 0x53);
```

For the interfaces defined in the COM, such as IUnknown, the IIDs are predefined because every interface needs to have an IID associated with it.

Listing 3.9 demonstrates the IID_ILowerStr and CLSID_CLowerStr for the CLowerStr object.

Listing 3.9. IID_ILowerStr and CLSID_CLowerStr.

```
// {4F126D90-1319-11d0-A6AC-00AA00602553}
DEFINE_GUID(CLSID_CLowerStr, 0x4f126d90, 0x1319, 0x11d0, 0xa6, 0xac, 0x0, 0xaa,
_0x0, 0x60, 0x25, 0x53);
// {4F126D91-1319-11d0-A6AC-00AA00602553}
DEFINE_GUID(IID_ILowerStr, 0x4f126d91, 0x1319, 0x11d0, 0xa6, 0xac, 0x0, 0xaa,
0x0, _0x60, 0x25, 0x53);
```

2. Define the interface ILowerStr.

    Listing 3.10 demonstrates the ILowerStr interface definition. Every interface in a COM object requires inheritance from IUnknown to provide the interface navigation and reference-counting capability.

Listing 3.10. ILowerStr interface definition.

```
class ILowerStr    : public IUnknown
{
public:
    virtual STDMETHODIMP  Lower(char *lpInput, char**lpOutput) = 0;
};
```

3. Listing 3.11 demonstrates the ILowerStr interface implementation.

Listing 3.11. ILowerStr interface implementation.

```
class CLowerStr : public ILowerStr
{
public:
    STDMETHODIMP QueryInterface(REFIID iid, LPVOID *ppv);
    STDMETHODIMP_(ULONG) AddRef();
    STDMETHODIMP_(ULONG) Release();
```

```
        STDMETHODIMP Lower(char *lpString, char**lpOutput);

        CLowerStr();
        ~CLowerStr();

private:
        DWORD m_dwRef;
};
STDMETHODIMP CLowerStr::QueryInterface(REFIID iid, void **ppv)
{
        HRESULT hr;

        *ppv = NULL;

        if((iid == IID_IUnknown) ¦¦ (iid == IID_ILowerStr) )
        {
                *ppv = (ILowerStr *)this;
                AddRef();
                hr = S_OK;
        }
        else
        {
                *ppv = NULL;
                hr = E_NOINTERFACE;
        }

        return hr;

}

STDMETHODIMP_(ULONG) CLowerStr::AddRef()
{
        m_dwRef++;
        return m_dwRef;
}

STDMETHODIMP_(ULONG) CLowerStr::Release()
{
        m_dwRef—;
        if(m_dwRef == 0)
                delete this;
        return m_dwRef;
}

STDMETHODIMP  CLowerStr::Lower(char *lpInput, char **pOutput)
{
        int i;

        *pOutput = new char[strlen(lpInput) + 1];

        for (i=0; i< strlen(lpInput); i++)
        {
                if(isupper(*(lpInput+i)))
                        *(*pOutput+i) = _tolower(*(lpInput + i));
                else
                        *(*pOutput+i) = *(lpInput + i);
        }
```

continues

Listing 3.11. continued

```
    *(*pOutput+i) = '\0';

    return S_OK;

}


CLowerStr::CLowerStr()
{
    m_dwRef = 1;
}
CLowerStr::~CLowerStr()
{
}
```

CLowerStr is the implementation of the ILowerStr interface. In the
CLowerStr::QueryInterface(...) method, AddRef() is invoked whenever an
interface is successfully queried.

AddRef() and Release() are the most standard implementations.

Method Lower(...) accepts the input and converts the input string to
lowercase.

In the CLowerStr constructor, m_dwRef is initialized to 1 because this object
is successfully instantiated by the client application.

4. Implement the IClassFactory interface.

Listing 3.12 demonstrates implementation of the Class Factory object for
the CLowerStr object. This Class Factory object implements two methods
(CreateInstance and LockServer) defined in the IClassFactory interface, and
three methods (QueryInterface, AddRef, and Release) defined in the IUnknown
interface, because IClassFactory inherits from the IUnknown interface.

Listing 3.12. Class Factory implementation.

```
class CLowerStrClassFactory:public IClassFactory
{
  protected:
    DWORD m_dwRef;

  public:
    CLowerStrClassFactory(void);
    ~CLowerStrClassFactory(void);

//IUnknown
    STDMETHODIMP QueryInterface (REFIID iid ,void **ppv);
    STDMETHODIMP_ (ULONG) AddRef(void);
    STDMETHODIMP_ (ULONG) Release(void);
```

```
   STDMETHODIMP CreateInstance(IUnknown *punkOuter,REFIID
   _iid,void **ppv);
   STDMETHODIMP LockServer(BOOL);
};
 CLowerStrClassFactory::CLowerStrClassFactory()
{
    m_dwRef=1;
}

CLowerStrClassFactory::~CLowerStrClassFactory()
{
}

STDMETHODIMP CLowerStrClassFactory::QueryInterface (REFIID
  _iid,void **ppv)

  HRESULT hr;
  *ppv = NULL;

  if (IID_IUnknown== iid ¦¦ IID_IClassFactory== iid)
  {
      *ppv=this;
      AddRef();
      hr = S_OK;
  }
  else
  {
      *ppv = NULL;
      hr = E_NOINTERFACE;
  }

  return hr;
}
STDMETHODIMP_(ULONG) CLowerStrClassFactory::AddRef(void)
{
    return m_dwRef++;
}
STDMETHODIMP_(ULONG) CLowerStrClassFactory::Release(void)
{
    m_dwRef—;

    if(m_dwRef == 0)
        delete this;

    return m_dwRef;
}
STDMETHODIMP CLowerStrClassFactory::CreateInstance (IUnknown
  _*pUnkOuter,REFIID
  _iid,void **ppv)

  HRESULT hr;
  CLowerStr *pObj;

  *ppv = NULL;

  pObj = new CLowerStr;
```

continues

Listing 3.12. continued

```
    if (pObj)
    {
        hr=pObj->QueryInterface(iid,ppv);
        pObj->Release();
    }
    else
    {
        hr = E_OUTOFMEMORY;
        *ppv = NULL;
    }

    return hr;
}

STDMETHODIMP CLowerStrClassFactory::LockServer(BOOL fLock)
{
    if (fLock)
        g_cLock++;
    else
        g_cLock—;

    return S_OK;
}
```

The implementation of AddRef and Release is the same as in CLowerStr in Listing 3.11. QueryInterface is almost the same except the interface exposed by CLowerStr is different from CLowerStrClassFactory. CLowerStr inherits from two interfaces, IUnknown and ILowerStr, whereas CLowerStrClassFactory inherits from IUnknown and IClassFactory.

5. Define and implement export functions from the lst31 COM server.

Because lst31.dll is an in-proc server, functions need to be exported in order to be accessed by the client application. For every in-proc server, the DllGetClassObject function needs to be exported so that the COM library can access this function to create an instance of the COM object.

Listing 3.13 demonstrates the module-definition (DEF) file provided for the lst31 COM server.

Listing 3.13. lst31 COM server.

\source\vol3\
chap-03\lst31

```
EXPORTS
    DllGetClassObject   @1
DllCanUnloadNow     @2
```

Exporting DllGetClassObject is mandatory for every in-proc server. It is the function invoked by the COM library to create an instance of the COM object.

Listing 3.14 demonstrates the implementation of the `DllGetClassObject` function.

Listing 3.14. `lst31.dll`'s `DllGetClassObject`'s implementation.

\source\vol3\
chap-03\lst31

```
long g_cLock = -1;
long g_cObj = 0;

STDAPI DllGetClassObject (REFCLSID rclsid,REFIID riid,void **ppv)
{
    HRESULT hr;
    CLowerStrClassFactory *pObj;

    if (CLSID_CLowerStr!= rclsid)
        return ResultFromScode(E_FAIL);

    pObj = new CLowerStrClassFactory();

    if (!pObj)
        return ResultFromScode (E_OUTOFMEMORY);

    hr= pObj->QueryInterface(riid,ppv);

    if (FAILED(hr))
        delete pObj;
    return hr;
}
STDAPI DllCanUnloadNow (void)
{
  SCODE sc;

  sc=(0L==g_cObj && 0L==g_cLock)? S_OK : S_FALSE;
  return ResultFromScode (sc);
}
```

`DllGetClassObject` returns the interface to `IClassFactory`. This function has three parameters: `rclsid` is the input parameter that refers to the CLSID of the Class object. `iid` is the input parameter that is the interface ID which the caller uses to communicate with the Class object. In most cases, it is `IID_IClassFactory`. `ppv` is the return value; `ppv` is an indirect pointer to the `IClassFactory` interface of the class factory object.

6. Build `lst31.dll`.

7. Register the `lst31` COM server by providing the REG file.

   Before a COM server can be used, the proper information—such as the CLSID and the full path of the DLL—has to be stored in the registry under the `HKEY_CLASSES_ROOT\CLSID`. This is required for every COM server because the registry information will be accessed by the COM library to access the COM server location so that the COM library can access exported functions such as `DllGetClassObject` from the COM server.

Listing 3.15 demonstrates the 1st31.REG file for the Lst31 COM server. Run regedit /s 1st31.reg to register 1st31.dll.

Listing 3.15. 1st31 COM server REG file.

```
REGEDIT

; CUpperStr Server Registration

HKEY_CLASSES_ROOT\CLSID\{4F126D90-1319-11d0-A6AC-00AA00602553}
_ = CLowerStr Object
HKEY_CLASSES_ROOT\CLSID\{4F126D90-1319-11d0-A6AC-00AA00602553}
_\InprocServer32 = d:\areview\ch3\1st31\debug\1st31.dll
```

For every COM server, all the information has to be stored under the string representation of the CLSID, which is an immediate subkey of the HKEY_CLASSES_ROOT\CLSID.

The string representation of the CLSID is in the CLSID's registry format, denoted as {CLSID}. The value associated with the {CLSID} is the description of the COM object. The InProcServer32 subkey is defined by OLE to indicate the full path to the 32-bit, in-proc server. There are other subkeys, such as Control and LocalServer32, that are defined by OLE to serve their different purposes.

The Control subkey with no value indicates that the COM server is an OLE control. The value associated with the LocalServer32 subkey indicates the full path to the local server.

For more information on this, please refer to Chapter 7 in the *Windows NT Registry Guide* by Addison-Wesley.

For the complete project, see the 1st31 directory on the CD-ROM.

Use 1st31.dll COM Server

The following example will demonstrate how to use the COM server just created (1st31.dll) in a console application. This console application is called 1st31use.exe.

note
The COM server is a binary reusable component. It can be used in any application, such as Visual C++ or Visual Basic.

The following steps illustrate how to use 1st31.dll.

1. Initialize the COM library by calling `CoInitialize(NULL)`. `OleInitialize` can be called instead of `CoInitialize`, because `OleInitialize` initializes the OLE library, which is a superset of the COM library.

2. Create an instance of `CLowerStr` by invoking

   ```
   CoCreateInstance(CLSID_CLowerStr 0, CLSCTX_INPROC_SERVER, IID_
   _ILowerStr, (void**)&pLoweStr)
   ```

   `CLSID_CLowerStr` specifies the `CLSID` of the `CLowerStr` object.

   `0` indicates that the object is not created as part of an aggregate.

   `CLSCTX_INPROC_SERVER` is one type of `CLSCTX`. It indicates that `lst31.dll` is an in-proc server. It will run in the same address space as the `lst31use.exe`. Listing 3.16 enumerates `CLSCTX`.

Listing 3.16. CLSCTX enumeration.

```
typedef enum tagCLSCTX
{
    CLSCTX_INPROC_SERVER   = 1,
    CLSCTX_INPROC_HANDLER  = 2,
    CLSCTX_LOCAL_SERVER    = 4
   CLSCTX_REMOTE_SERVER = 16
} CLSCTX;
```

`CLSCTX_INPROC_HANDLER` indicates that the COM server is an in-process handler.

`CLSCTX_LOCAL_SERVER` indicates that the COM server runs on the same machine as the client but in a different process.

`CLSCTX_REMOTE_SERVER` indicates that the COM server runs on a different machine from the client.

`IID_ILowerStr` refers to the interface to communicate with `lst31` COM server.

COM also predefines

```
#define CLSCTX_SERVER (CLSCTX_INPROC_SERVER¦ CLSCTX_LOCAL_
_SERVER¦ CLSCTX_REMOTE_SERVER)

#define CLSCTX_ALL (CLSCTX_INPROC_HANDLER ¦ CLSCTX_SERVER)
```

`pLowerStr` points to the location of the `IID_ILowerStr` interface pointer.

3. Check the returned value from `CoCreateInstance` in step 2.

   For a robust system, I strongly suggest checking the returned value.

4. Invoke the `Lower` method.

   ```
   char *lpOutput;
   pILowerStr->Lower("hEllo World", &lpOutput);
   printf("the output is %s\n", lpOutput);
   ```

5. Release the `ILowerStr` interface.

   ```
   pLowerStr->Release();
   ```

   The `pLowerStr` object needs to be released because it is no longer needed.

6. Invoke `CoUninitialize()` to uninitialize the COM library so that all COM resources and RPC connections can be released.

---

note

`OleUninitialize` can be invoked to uninitialize the OLE library, because the OLE library is a superset of the COM library.

```
CoUnInitialize();
```

Listing 3.17 demonstrates the complete program for the `lst31use` application.

Listing 3.17. `lst31use` program.

`\source\vol3\`
`chap-03\`
`lst31use`

```c
#include <objbase.h>
#include <initguid.h>
#include <stdio.h>

class ILowerStr    : public IUnknown
{
public:
    virtual STDMETHODIMP Lower(char *lpInput, char**lpOutput) = 0;
};
const CLSID CLSID_CLowerStr =
{0x4f126d90, 0x1319, 0x11d0, {0xa6, 0xac, 0x0, 0xaa, 0x0, 0x60, 0x25, 0x53}};

const CLSID IID_ILowerStr =
{0x4f126d91, 0x1319, 0x11d0, {0xa6, 0xac, 0x0, 0xaa, 0x0, 0x60, 0x25, 0x53}};

void main()
{

    HRESULT hr;
     ILowerStr    *pILowerStr;


    hr = CoInitialize(NULL);

    if(FAILED(hr))
    {
        printf("CoInitialize failed[0x%x]\n", hr);
        exit(1);
    }

    //Create an instance of the COM object
    hr = CoCreateInstance(CLSID_CLowerStr, NULL, CLSCTX_INPROC_SERVER,
        IID_ILowerStr,(void**) &pILowerStr);

    if(FAILED(hr))
```

```
    {
        printf("CoCreateInstance failed[0x%x]\n", hr);
        if(hr == REGDB_E_CLASSNOTREG)
            printf("please register the class\n");
        exit(1);
    }

    char *lpOutput;

    pILowerStr->Lower("hEllo World", &lpOutput);
    printf("the output is %s\n", lpOutput);

    pILowerStr->Release();
    CoUninitialize();
}
```

Before `lst31.dll` can be invoked, the interface `ILowerStr` needs to be included; so does the CLSID and IID declared by the COM server.

This complete project is under the `lst31use` directory contained on the CD-ROM.

Create lst31 COM Server (New Version)

Assuming some new requirements are coming up for the `lst31.dll` COM server, a new version needs to be released. In many circumstances, the client application that uses the DLL needs to be recompiled if the library is statically linked. But the COM client using the old version of `lst31.dll` can use the new version of `lst31.dll` without any changes to the source code and compilation.

Figure 3.7 illustrates the functionality provided by the new version of `lst31.dll`.

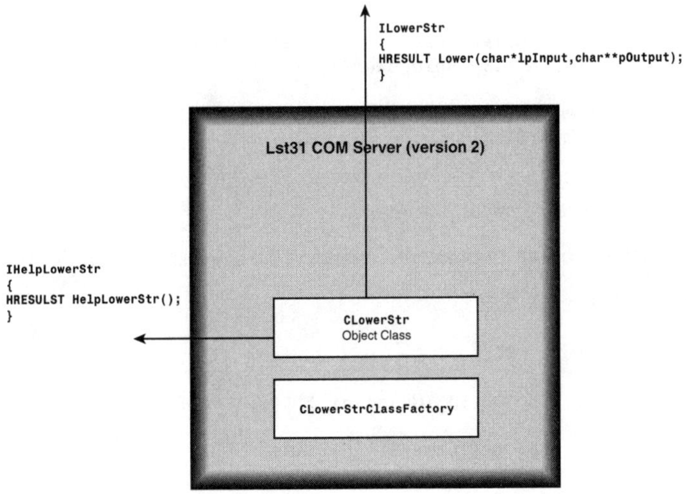

Figure 3.7.
New version of `lst31.dll`.

There are two interfaces exposed by the lst31.dll. ILowerStr is the old interface, and IHelpLowerStr is the new interface. This new interface includes one method, HelpLower(), which provides the help information. Here, for simplicity, S_OK will be returned.

The following steps demonstrate how to create the new lst31.dll COM server:

1. Generate a new IID for the new interface IHelpLowerStr.

```
// {9EC1CA01-133F-11d0-A6AD-00AA00602553}
DEFINE_GUID(IID_IHelpLowerStr, 0x9ec1ca01, 0x133f, 0x11d0, 0xa6,
_0xad, 0x0, 0xaa, 0x0, 0x60, 0x25, 0x53);
```

2. Define the new interface IHelpLowerStr.

```
class IHelpLowerStr: public IUnknown
{
public:
    virtual STDMETHODIMP HelpLower() = 0;
};
```

3. Implement IHelpLowerStr by modifying the CLowerStr class, as shown in Listing 3.18.

Listing 3.18. New CLowerStr class.

```
class IHelpLowerStr : public IUnknown
{
public:
    virtual STDMETHODIMP HelpLower()=0;
};
class CLowerStr : public ILowerStr , public IHelpLowerStr
{
public:
    STDMETHODIMP QueryInterface(REFIID iid, LPVOID *ppv);
    STDMETHODIMP_(ULONG) AddRef();
    STDMETHODIMP_(ULONG) Release();

    STDMETHODIMP Lower(char *lpString, char**lpOutput);
    STDMETHODIMP HelpLower();

    CLowerStr();
    ~CLowerStr();

private:
    DWORD m_dwRef;
};
STDMETHODIMP CLowerStr::QueryInterface(REFIID iid, void **ppv)
{
    HRESULT hr;

    *ppv = NULL;

    if((iid == IID_IUnknown) || (iid == IID_ILowerStr) )
    {
        *ppv = (ILowerStr *)this;
        AddRef();
        hr = S_OK;
```

```
    }
    else if(iid == IID_IHelpLowerStr)
    {
        *ppv = (IHelpLowerStr *) this;
        AddRef();
        hr = S_OK;
    }
    else
    {
        *ppv = NULL;
        hr = E_NOINTERFACE;
    }

    return hr;

}
STDMETHODIMP CLowerStr::HelpLower()
{
    return S_OK;
}
```

Because a new interface (IHelpLowerStr) is exposed by the CLowerStr object, QueryInterface needs to check the IHelpLowerStr interface, too.

4. IUnknown rebuilds the lst311 project.

5. Create the registry setting.

Following is the code for the lst311.reg file.

```
REGEDIT
; CUpperStr Server Registration
HKEY_CLASSES_ROOT\CLSID\{4F126D90-1319-11d0-A6AC-00AA00602553} = CLowerStr
Object
HKEY_CLASSES_ROOT\CLSID\{4F126D90-1319-11d0-A6AC-00AA00602553}
_\InprocServer32 = d:\areview\ch3\lst311\debug\lst311.dll
```

Run lst31use.exe. It still works! But the value associated with the InprocServer32 has been changed; it is now d:\areview\ch3\lst311\debug\lst311.dll. The reason is that from the client perspective, no one really cares what DLL name is associated with the COM server. The client side is interested only in the CLSID exposed by the COM server. It is the COM library's role to locate the COM server and instantiate the COM object. The library also returns the interface pointer requested by the client application.

Create and Use an Out-Proc Server

To illustrate how to create an out-proc server, changes will be made to lst31.dll so that it is an out-proc server.The out-proc server runs in a separate address space from the client application; all interface calls must be marshaled across processes (data gets copied). It is more reliable than the in-proc server because the corruption of the out-proc server will not influence the process space of the caller application, whereas the in-proc server will destroy the caller's process space. The local out-proc server should be created when an application supports automation. A remote out-proc server should be used to take advantage of resources on another machine.

The following steps illustrate how to create the 1st32 out-proc server:

1. Create the custom interface by using Interface Definition Language (IDL).

   Listing 3.19 demonstrates the lower.idl file for the ILowerStr interface. Because all interface calls must be marshaled for the out-proc server, the ILowerStr interface must be marshaled.

Listing 3.19. `lower.idl` for the `ILowerStr` interface.

```
[
        object,
        uuid(4F126D91-1319-11d0-A6AC-00AA00602553),
        pointer_default(unique)
]
    interface ILowerStr: IUnknown
    {
        import "oaidl.idl";
        HRESULT Lower([in,string] LPSTR inString, [out, string] LPSTR
*outString);
}
```

An IDL file specifies the contract between the client and server using IDL.

The IDL file consists of two parts, the interface header and the interface body.

Table 3.1 illustrates the attributes for IDL. For more information on the IDL, please refer to the Microsoft RPC document.

Table 3.1. IDL attributes.

Keyword	Meaning
object	COM interface object.
uuida	Universal unique identifier associated with a particular interface.
usage	uuid(80FA6EE2-0120-11d0-A6A0-00AA00602553).
dual	Dual interface, which inherits from IDispatch and IUnknowndual.

Keyword	*Meaning*
`import`	Imports the IDL file of the base interface import `oaidl.idl`.
`out`	Output parameter `[out, retval]BSTR *pBSTR`.
`in`	Input parameter.
`in, out`	Data is sent to the object initialized and will be changed before sending it back.
`retval`	Designates the parameter that receives the return value.
`helpstring`	Sets the help string `helpstring("test only")`.
`pointer_default`	Specifies the default pointer attribute.
`unique pointer`	Attribute that designates a pointer as a full pointer ref attribute and identifies a reference pointer.

2. Create a makefile for `lower.idl`.

Listing 3.20 demonstrates the makefile for compiling `lower.idl`.

Listing 3.20. Makefile for `lower.idl`. (Change CPU to MIPS or ALPHA for compiling on those platforms.)

```
CPU=i386
TARGETOS=BOTH

!include <win32.mak>

all:  lower.dll

.cxx.obj:
    $(cc) $(cflags) $(cvarsmt) $<

.c.obj:
    $(cc)  $(cflags) $(cvarsmt) $<

#the files that make up the dll
lower_i.obj : lower_i.c

lower_p.obj : lower_p.c lower.h

dlldata.obj : dlldata.c
    $(cc)  $(cflags) $(cvarsmt) -DREGISTER_PROXY_DLL dlldata.c


# run midl to produce the header files and the proxy file
lower.h lower_p.c lower_i.c dlldata.c: lower.idl
                midl /ms_ext /c_ext lower.idl

lower.dll: lower_p.obj lower_i.obj dlldata.obj lower.def
    $(link)             \
    -dll                \
```

continues

Listing 3.20. continued

```
-entry:_DllMainCRTStartup$(DLLENTRY) \
-DEF:lower.def     \
-out:lower.dll     \
lower_p.obj lower_i.obj  dlldata.obj rpcrt4.lib $(olelibs)

# Clean up everything
cleanall: clean
        @-del *.dll 2>nul

# Clean up everything but the .EXEs
clean:
        @-del *.obj 2>nul
        @-del dlldata.c 2>nul
        @-del *.h 2>nul
        @-del lower_?.* 2>nul
        @-del *.exp 2>nul
        @-del *.lib 2>nul
        @-del *.ilk 2>nul
        @-del *.pdb 2>nul
        @-del *.res 2>nul
```

midl in Listing 3.20 stands for Microsoft IDL compiler. It takes the lower.idl file and generates the following files:

- lower_p.c contains proxy/stub code.
- lower_i.c contains the actual definition of IIDs and CLSIDs.
- lower.h contains the definition for the interface.
- dlldata.c is regenerated by the MIDL compiler on every IDL file.

The midl switch /m_ext will support Microsoft extensions to DCE IDL. These extensions include interface definition for OLE objects, multiple interfaces, enumeration cpp_quote (quoted_string), wide character types (wchar_t), and so on.

Let's say that if the IDL file includes

```
typedef enum
{
A=1,
B,
C
} BAD_ENUM;
```

The /m_ext switch needs to be turned on.

The /c_ext switch enables the use of C-language extensions in the IDL file. For instance, if // is used to comment the code, the /c_ext switch needs to be on.

3. Lower.Def

```
LIBRARY        LOWER

DESCRIPTION    'Proxy/Stub DLL for ILowerStr interfaces'

EXPORTS
        DllGetClassObject          PRIVATE
        DllCanUnloadNow            PRIVATE
        DllRegisterServer          PRIVATE
        DllUnregisterServer        PRIVATE
```

4. Build proxystub.dll.

5. Register the custom interface.

   Run the command: regsvr32 lower.dll.

   The ILowerStr interface information will be written to the system registry under HKEY_CLASSES_ROOT\Interface.

   For the complete lower.dll project, please refer to lst32\proxy.

6. Create a main entry point for lst32.exe.

   Listing 3.21 demonstrates a main program for lst32.exe.

Listing 3.21. lst32.exe main program.

\source\vol3\
chap-03\lst32

```c
HRESULT RegisterClassFactory()
{
    HRESULT hr;
    CLowerStrClassFactory *pClassFactory;

    pClassFactory = new CLowerStrClassFactory;

    if (pClassFactory != 0)
    {
        hr = CoRegisterClassObject(CLSID_CLowerStr,
                                   (IUnknown *) pClassFactory,
                                   CLSCTX_LOCAL_SERVER,
                                   REGCLS_SINGLEUSE,
                                   &g_dwRegister);
        pClassFactory->Release();
        hr = S_OK;
    }
    else
    {
        hr = E_OUTOFMEMORY;
    }

    return hr;
}
```

CoRegisterClassObject is the function that needs to be called on startup. It registers OLE so that other applications can connect to this class object. There are five parameters in the function. In particular, REGCLS_SINGLEUSE indicates the types of connection to the Class object. If an application has connected to the Class object via CoGetClassObject, no other application can connect to it.

There are two other connection types: REGCLS_MULTIPLEUSE and REGCLS_MULTI_SEPARATE. REGCLS_MULTIPLEUSE indicates that multiple applications can connect to the Class object via CoGetClassObject, whereas REGCLS_MULTI_SEPARATE indicates that the application has separate control over each copy of the Class object context.

g_dwRegister is a returned value, identifying the class object registered. It will be used in the CoRevokeClassObject function call.

```
HRESULT RevokeClassFactory()
{
    HRESULT hr;

    hr = CoRevokeClassObject(g_dwRegister);

    return hr;
}
```

The CoRevokeClassObject function indicates that the Class object, previously registered with OLE via the CoRegisterClassObject function, is no longer available for use.

```
void main(int argc, char *argv[])
{
    HRESULT hr = S_OK;
    int i;
    BOOL bRegisterServer = FALSE;
    BOOL bUnregisterServer = FALSE;
    MSG msg;
    for (i = 1; i < argc; i++)
    {
        if (_stricmp( argv[i], "/REGSERVER" ) == 0) {
            bRegisterServer = TRUE;
        }
        else if (_stricmp( argv[i], "/UNREGSERVER" ) == 0) {
            bUnregisterServer = TRUE;
        }
    }
    if(bRegisterServer)
    {
        RegisterLocalServer(CLSID_CLowerStr);
        return;
    }

    if(bUnregisterServer)
    {
        UnregisterLocalServer(CLSID_CLowerStr);
        return;
    }
```

```
    hr = CoInitialize(NULL);

    if (FAILED(hr)) {
        printf("CoInitialize failed [0x%x].\n", hr);
        return;
    }

    hr = RegisterClassFactory();
    if (SUCCEEDED(hr))
    {
        printf("Waiting for client to connect...\n");

        while (GetMessage(&msg, NULL, 0, 0))
        {
            TranslateMessage(&msg);
            DispatchMessage(&msg);
        }

        RevokeClassFactory();
    }
    else
    {
        printf("Failed to register class factory [0x%x].\n", hr);
    }

    CoUninitialize();

    return;
}


HRESULT RegisterLocalServer(REFCLSID rclsid)
{
    HRESULT hr;
    LONG lError;
    HKEY hKeyCLSID;
    HKEY hKeyClassID;
    HKEY hKey;                  // current key
    DWORD dwDisposition;
    char szServer[MAX_PATH];
    char szClassID[39];
    ULONG ulLength;

    ulLength = GetModuleFileNameA(0, szServer, sizeof(szServer));

    if (ulLength == 0)
    {
        hr = HRESULT_FROM_WIN32(GetLastError());
        return hr;
    }

    //create the CLSID key
    lError = RegCreateKeyExA(
            HKEY_CLASSES_ROOT,
            "CLSID",
            0,
            "REG_SZ",
            REG_OPTION_NON_VOLATILE,
```

```
                            KEY_ALL_ACCESS,
                            0,
                            &hKeyCLSID,
                            &dwDisposition);

        if (!lError) {
            //convert the class ID to a registry key name.
            sprintf(szClassID,
                "{%08lX-%04X-%04X-%02X%02X-%02X%02X%02X%02X%02X%02X}",
                rclsid.Data1, rclsid.Data2, rclsid.Data3,
                rclsid.Data4[0], rclsid.Data4[1],
                rclsid.Data4[2], rclsid.Data4[3],
                rclsid.Data4[4], rclsid.Data4[5],
                rclsid.Data4[6], rclsid.Data4[7]);

            //create key for the server class
            lError = RegCreateKeyExA(hKeyCLSID,
                            szClassID,
                            0,
                            "REG_SZ",
                            REG_OPTION_NON_VOLATILE,
                            KEY_ALL_ACCESS,
                            0,
                            &hKeyClassID,
                            &dwDisposition);

            if (!lError) {
                //create LocalServer32 key.
                lError = RegCreateKeyExA(hKeyClassID,
                            "LocalServer32",
                            0,
                            "REG_SZ",
                            REG_OPTION_NON_VOLATILE,
                            KEY_ALL_ACCESS,
                            0,
                            &hKey,
                            &dwDisposition);

                if (!lError) {
                    //Set the server name.
                    lError = RegSetValueExA(hKey,
                                    "",
                                    0,
                                    REG_SZ,
                                    (const unsigned char
*)szServer,
                                    strlen(szServer) + 1);

                    RegFlushKey(hKey);
                    RegCloseKey(hKey);
                }
                RegCloseKey(hKeyClassID);
            }
            RegCloseKey(hKeyCLSID);
        }

        if (!lError)
            hr = S_OK;
```

```
    else
        hr = HRESULT_FROM_WIN32(lError);

    return hr;
}


HRESULT UnregisterLocalServer(REFCLSID rclsid)
{
    HRESULT hr;
    HKEY hKeyCLSID;
    HKEY hKeyClassID;
    long lError;
    char szClassID[39];

    //open the CLSID key
    lError = RegOpenKeyExA(
                HKEY_CLASSES_ROOT,
                "CLSID",
                0,
                KEY_ALL_ACCESS,
                &hKeyCLSID);

    if (!lError) {
        //convert the class ID to a registry key name.
        sprintf(szClassID,
                "{%081X-%04X-%04X-%02X%02X-%02X%02X%02X%02X%02X%02X}",
                rclsid.Data1, rclsid.Data2, rclsid.Data3,
                rclsid.Data4[0], rclsid.Data4[1],
                rclsid.Data4[2], rclsid.Data4[3],
                rclsid.Data4[4], rclsid.Data4[5],
                rclsid.Data4[6], rclsid.Data4[7]);

        //open registry key for class ID string
        lError = RegOpenKeyExA(
                hKeyCLSID,
                szClassID,
                0,
                KEY_ALL_ACCESS,
                &hKeyClassID);

        if (!lError) {
            //delete LocalServer32 key.
            lError = RegDeleteKeyA(hKeyClassID, "LocalServer32");
            RegCloseKey(hKeyClassID);
        }

        lError = RegDeleteKeyA(hKeyCLSID, szClassID);
        RegCloseKey(hKeyCLSID);
    }

    if (!lError)
        hr = S_OK;
    else
        hr = HRESULT_FROM_WIN32(lError);

    return hr;
}
```

1st32.exe provides the self-registration features. Self-registration means that the COM server can register itself. An in-proc server registers by providing two entry points to the in-proc server. They are

```
HRESULT DllRegisterServer(void)
HRESULT DllUnRegisterServer(void);
```

The DllRegisterServer entry point adds or updates registry information for all the classes implemented by the in-proc server. The DllUnRegisterServer entry point removes all the information for the in-proc server from the registry.

For an out-proc server, there is no way to publish well-known entry points. The self-registration for the out-proc server is supported by using special command-line flags. The command-line flags are the /regserver and /unregister arguments.

The /regserver argument should add the registry information for all classes implemented by the out-proc server and then exit. The /unregister argument should do all the necessary uninstallation and then exit.

1st32.exe supports the /regserver and /unregserver arguments.

7. Register 1st32.exe by running 1st32 /regserver.

    The 1st32.exe out-proc server needs to be registered before being used. Without proper information in the registry, the out-proc server will not be seen by any other COM applications or the COM library.

    Because 1st32.exe supports self-registration, 1st32.exe can be registered by invoking 1st32 /regserver.

Use 1st32.exe COM Server

A COM client will be created to use this out-proc (1st32.exe) COM server. Listing 3.22 demonstrates how to use 1st32.exe.

Listing 3.22. 1st32use.exe program.

\source\vol3\
chap-03\
1st32use

```c
#include <windows.h>
#include <stdio.h>
#include <olectl.h>
#include <initguid.h>
#include <olectlid.h>

// the class ID of the server exe
// {4F126D90-1319-11d0-A6AC-00AA00602553}
const CLSID CLSID_CLowerStr =
{0x4f126d90, 0x1319, 0x11d0, {0xa6, 0xac, 0x0, 0xaa, 0x0, 0x60, 0x25, 0x53}};

 // {4F126D91-1319-11d0-A6AC-00AA00602553}
const CLSID IID_ILowerStr =
```

```
{0x4f126d91, 0x1319, 0x11d0, {0xa6, 0xac, 0x0, 0xaa, 0x0, 0x60, 0x25, 0x53}};

class ILowerStr: public IUnknown
{
public:
    virtual STDMETHODIMP Lower(char* lpInput, char **lpOutput)=0;
};

void __cdecl main(int argc, char *argv[])
{
    ILowerStr *pILowerStr = NULL;
    HRESULT hr;

    hr = CoInitialize(NULL);
    if (FAILED(hr))
    {
        printf("CoInitialize failed [0x%x]\n", hr);
        exit(1);
    }

    hr = CoCreateInstance(CLSID_CLowerStr, 0, CLSCTX_LOCAL_SERVER,
        IID_ILowerStr,(void**)&pILowerStr);

    if (FAILED(hr))
    {
        printf("CoCreateInstance failed [0x%x]\n", hr);
        if (hr == REGDB_E_CLASSNOTREG)
        {
            printf("Run lst32.exe /REGSERVER to install server program.\n");
        }
        exit(1);
    }

    char *lpOutput;

    pILowerStr->Lower("HELLO", &lpOutput);

    printf("this is it %s\n", lpOutput);

    pILowerStr->Release();
    CoUninitialize();
}
```

From Listing 3.22, no changes need to be made from lst31use.cpp to lst32use.cpp except in the CoCreateInstance activation call. The execution context changes from CLSCTX_INPROC_SERVER to CLSCTX_LOCAL_SERVER.

Create and Use an In-Proc COM Server by Using ATL

Active Template Library is an OLE COM AppWizard that provides the framework for building COM servers.

From the previous section, a lot of implementation, such as `IUnknown` and `IClassFactory`, can be reused as needed. ATL encapsulates these implementations in a template class so that the COM server functionality can be concentrated.

Create `lst33.dll` COM Server

`lst33.dll` will be created to illustrate the ATL. `lst33.dll` provides the same functionality as `lst31.dll` Version 1.

The following steps demonstrate how to create `lst33.dll` by using ATL.

1. Choose File | New and select Project Workspace.
2. In the New Project Workspace dialog box, select OLE COM AppWizard. Enter `lst33` in the name text box. Click the Create button. The dialog box in Figure 3.8 will be displayed.

Figure 3.8.
OLE COM AppWizard—Step 1 of 2.

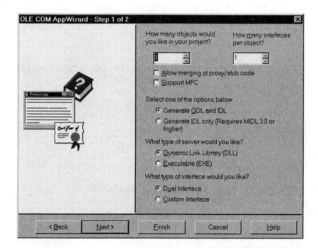

3. In the dialog box shown in Figure 3.8, select the Generate IDL only option. Note: This option can be chosen only when MIDL Version 3.0 or higher is available.
4. Select the Custom Interface option. Note: Custom interface refers to the fact that all the interfaces are inherited from `IUnknown`.
5. Click the Finish button.

The OLE COM AppWizard will generate the new skeleton project with the following files:

- `StdAfx.cpp`: Source file that includes just the standard include file.

- StdAfx.h: Include file for standard system include files.
- lst33.cpp: The DLL initialization code, the same role as in example 1.
- lst33.def: As described before, an in-proc server needs to expose DllGetClassObject so that COM can use this exported function. DllRegisterServer should be exported to support the self-registration function. The wizard will generate all these exported functions in lst33.def, which is equivalent to lst31.def.
- resource.h: Include file generated by Microsoft Developer Studio, used by lst33.rc.
- lst33.rc: Resource script generated by Microsoft Developer Studio.
- lst33obj.h: Object class definition.
- lst33obj.cpp: Object class implementation.
- lst33.mak: COM server project.
- lst33ps.def: A custom interface needs to be registered in order to export the proper functions as described in lower.def. This wizard generates all these automatically.
- ps.mak: proxystub makefile to compile proxystub.dll for the custom interface, the same as created in lower.mak.
- lst33.idl: IDL source file.

This also conforms to the DCOM design, because all of the custom interface has been marshaled.

It will not be difficult to spot where the changes need to be made.

1. One interface in this method, lst33.idl, will be changed to add the (Upper) method.

   The changes in the skeleton code created by the ATL are in bold font.

```
interface ILst33 : IUnknown
    {
        import "oaidl.idl";
        HRESULT Upper([in,string] LPSTR inputString, [out, string]
        ➥LPSTR _*pOutputString);
        };
[2] Implement this method for ILst33 interface, exposed by the lst33
        object _class by adding the definition in the lst33obj.h
        class CLst33Object :
    public ILst33,
    public CComObjectBase<&CLSID_Lst33>
{
public:
    CLst33Object() {}
BEGIN_COM_MAP(CLst33Object)
    COM_INTERFACE_ENTRY(ILst33)
END_COM_MAP()
```

```
// Use DECLARE_NOT_AGGREGATABLE(CLst33Object) if you don't want your
object
// to support aggregation
DECLARE_AGGREGATABLE(CLst33Object)

// ILst33
public:

    STDMETHOD(Lower)( LPSTR bstrInput, LPSTR *pbstrOutput);
};
```

2. The method STDMETHOD(Lower) is added in the object definition.

3. Implement the method in the ILst33 interface by adding the following code in lst33obj.cpp:

```
STDMETHODIMP CLst33Object::Lower(LPSTR lpInput, LPSTR* pOutput)
{
    int i;

    *pOutput = new char[strlen(lpInput) + 1];

    for (i=0; i< strlen(lpInput); i++)
    {
        *(*pOutput+i) = *(lpInput + i)-'A'+'a';
    }

    *(*pOutput+i) = '\0';

    return S_OK;
}
```

The implementation of the (Lower) method is the same as implemented in lst31.dll and lst32.dll.

After the custom interface has been implemented, the following steps need to be followed to create this COM server.

Run the command midl lst33.idl. This requires MIDL 3.0 or higher. Otherwise, the following error will be generated:

```
Microsoft (R) MIDL Compiler Version 2.00.0102

Copyright (c) Microsoft Corp 1991 -1995. All rights reserved.
Processing .\lst33.idl
.\lst33.idl(8) : error MIDL2141 : use of this attribute
➡needs /ms_ext :[object]
.\lst33.idl(10) : error MIDL2017 : syntax error :expecting an idl
➡attribute near "helpstring"
.\lst33.idl(10) : error MIDL2018 : cannot recover from earlier
➡syntax errors; aborting compilation
```

In order to avoid this error, MIDL 3.0 must be available. It is contained in the Win32 SDK.

After lst33.idl is compiled successfully, the following files will be generated:

```
lst33.tlb: type library
lst33_p.c: proxy code
```

```
dlldata.c:
lst33_i.c
```

Build the COM server project (lst33.mak).

The COM server lst33.dll will be generated.

Before this COM server can be used, it needs to be registered first by running regsvr32 lst33.dll. These steps also can be followed to register the server after compile:

- Choose Build | Setting.
- Select the Custom Build tab in the Project Settings dialog box displayed in Figure 3.9.

Figure 3.9.
Project Settings—
Custom Build.

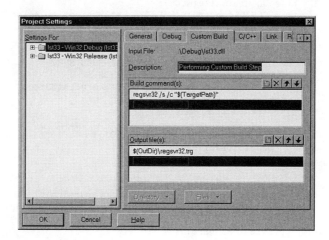

4. In the Build command(s) list box, enter

```
regsvr32 /s /c "$(TargetPath)"
echo regsvr32 exec. time > $(OutDir)\regsvr32.trg
```

5. In the Output file(s) list box, enter

```
$(OutDir)\regsvr32.trg
```

The Microsoft Developer Studio will perform the following custom build step

```
egSvr32: DllRegisterServer in .\Debug\lst33.dll
```

after successfully compiling lst33.dll.

This will cause lst33.dll to register every time the project is built. To avoid this, the custom build option can be deleted.

Use lst33 COM Server

A console application will be created to use the lst33.dll COM server shown in Listing 3.23.

Listing 3.23. `lst33Use.exe` program.

```
#include <objbase.h>
#include <initguid.h>
#include <stdio.h>
// These equivalent definitions will be from lst33_i.c
#include "..\lst33\lst33.h"

void main()
{

    HRESULT hr;
     ILst33   * m_pILst33; // interface pointer
    CLSID     clsid;

    hr = CoInitialize(NULL);
    hr = CLSIDFromProgID(L"LST33.Lst33Object.1",&clsid);

    hr = CoCreateInstance(clsid,
                          NULL,
                          CLSCTX_INPROC_SERVER,
                          IID_ILst33,
                          (LPVOID*)&m_pILst33);

    if(FAILED(hr))
    {
        printf("can not create Lst33");
        CoUninitialize();
        return;
    }
    char *lpLowerString;
    m_pILst33->Lower("HELLO", & &lpLowerString);
    printf("the return string is %s\n", lpLowerString);

    m_pILst33->Release();
    CoUninitialize();
}
```

Here, `CLSIDFromProgID` is used to retrieve the CLSID of the Class object by providing the `ProgId` for this COM server.

A Word About DCOM

The Distributed Component Object Model (also known as DCOM and previously known as Distributed OLE) extends the power of OLE objects from running only on a local machine to running in any way on a network. Using DCOM, an OLE client on one machine can run an OLE server on another machine, and the client and server can exchange information, typically with few to no changes in the source code for the client or the server application. In order to explain how to create a object using DCOM, a quick review of creating an object using COM is in order.

To create an object without using DCOM, an application will typically call CoCreateInstance to create a new instance of the requested object. Internally, CoCreateInstance is effectively equivalent to the following code (although the real implementation checks result codes and takes appropriate actions):

```
CoGetClassObject(rclsid, grfContext, NULL, IID_IClassFactory, (void **)&ppx);
ppx->CreateInstance(pUnkOuter, iid, (void **)&ppv);
ppx->Release();
```

Notice that the third parameter of CoGetClassObject is NULL. When we move to the DCOM world, we will see that this parameter is no longer NULL, but contains the location where the object should be created.

Creating an object using DCOM is similar to creating an object using COM, except instead of calling CoCreateInstance, the application would call a new API, CoCreateInstanceEx. The parameters to CoCreateInstanceEx are as follows:

```
CoCreateInstanceEx(REFCLSID rclsid,
                   IUnknown *pUnkOuter,
                   DWORD *dwClsCtx,
                   COSERVERINFO *pServerInfo,
                   ULONG cmq,
                   MULTI_QI rgmqResults);
```

where

> rclsid is the CLSID of the object to be created.
>
> pUnkOuter is the pointer to the IUnknown interface of the outer object if the new object is to be aggregated. dwClsCtx is a pointer to a DWORD that tells OLE how to create the object.
>
> pServerInfo is a pointer to a structure that tells OLE where to create the object cmq that contains the number of interfaces your application needs from the object.
>
> rgmqResults contains an array of interfaces returned from the object.

The main difference between CoCreateInstance and CoCreateInstanceEx is that CoCreateInstanceEx adds three parameters: pServerInfo, cmq, and rgmqResults. When an application calls CoCreateInstanceEx, the pServerInfo parameter can be NULL, in which case the requested object will be created on a machine indicated in the registry or on the local machine—or pServerInfo can point to a COSERVERINFO structure. COSERVERINFO is a structure that contains two elements, the size of the structure and the server where the object should be created. For example,

```
COSERVERINFO csiObject;
csiObject.dwSize = sizeof(COSERVERINFO);
csiObject.pszName = "MyObjSvr";
```

The name of the server can be either a UNC format name (such as \\MyObjSvr) or a DNS format name (such as MyObjSvr.com or 127.2.1). Because the server for the object could be anywhere in the world, it would not be efficient to continually ask the object for various interfaces; it may be more efficient to request multiple interfaces in a single call. CoCreateInstanceEx addresses the efficiency problem by adding two parameters: cmq and rgmqResults. The value in cmq contains the number of interfaces you are requesting from the object; rgmqResults contains a list of the requested interfaces and if found also contains pointers to the requested interfaces.

> ## note
>
> To work with Distributed OLE, you need Windows NT 4.0 and the Win32 SDK, which supports Windows NT 4.0. At the time of writing this book, the date for the include files that support Windows NT 4.0 was 5/96, whereas the non–Windows NT 4.0 include files were dated 7/95. Also, if objbase.h contains the definition for CoCreateInstanceEx, the include files support Distributed OLE.
>
> Windows 95 currently does not support Distributed OLE, although support is expected in a future release.

Summary

From the previous example, it is not difficult to see that COM supports

- Versioning: Provides an interface without the COM client's concern.
- Network independence: An out-of-process COM server can run locally as the client application or remotely. A COM server can be DLL-based or EXE-based without the COM application, doing extra work except informing the COM library about the execution context of the Class object.
- Language independence: A COM server can be used in C++ applications and any other applications such as Visual Basic. For a basic COM object that supports only the IUnknown interface, there is a lot of work to be done so that Visual Basic can use the COM server. For examples of how to use basic COM objects in Visual Basic, please refer to "MFC/COM Objects 6: Using COM Objects from Visual Basic" in MSDN.

In order for a Visual Basic application to use a COM server easily, the IDispatch interface is defined in COM.

4

Creating OLE Automation Servers

by Weiying Chen

An OLE automation server exposes automation objects that have methods and properties as their external interfaces. The methods and properties exposed by the automation objects can be directly accessed by the automation controllers such as Visual Basic or by invoking methods defined in the IDispatch interface.

In this chapter, an automation server will be created through the implementation of the IDispatch interface to illustrate the fundamental OLE automation concept. This automation server will be used in both C++ and Visual Basic.

Then, this automation server will be created through the use of MFC AppWizard (exe), Control Wizard, and the Active Template Library (ATL).

At the end of the chapter, this automation server will be used in Internet Explorer 3.0 and the HTTP Web Server.

Create and Use an Automation Server: lst41.exe

lst41.exe is an automation server implemented without using any wizards or code generation tools. This automation server exposes one method called GetMachineName. GetMachineName has no input parameter. The return value is the name of the computer where the application runs.

To expose the objects, the IDispatch interface must be implemented. There are two ways to implement the IDispatch interface. One way is to implement four methods in the IDispatch interface. The other way used in lst41.exe is to expose the objects through OLE automation by using the CreateStdDispatch method. CreateStdDispatch creates a standard implementation of the IDispatch interface through a single function call.

The following steps illustrate how to create lst41.exe.

1. Define the interface using the Object Definition Language (ODL).

   Listing 4.1 highlights lst41.odl.

Listing 4.1. lst41.odl.

\source\vol3\
chap-04\lst41

```
[
    uuid(9FBBEDE2-1B40-11d0-88E0-00AA004A7C7B),
    helpstring("Lst41 Type Library"),
    lcid(0x0409),
    version(1.0)
]
library Lst41
{
    importlib("stdole32.tlb");

    [
     odl,
     uuid(9FBBEDE3-1B40-11d0-88E0-00AA004A7C7B),
    ]
    interface ILst41: IUnknown
    {
        BSTR GetMachineName(void);
    }

    [
     uuid(9FBBEDE4-1B40-11d0-88E0-00AA004A7C7B),
    ]
    dispinterface DLst41
    {
      interface ILst41;
    }

    [
      uuid(9FBBEDE5-1B40-11d0-88E0-00AA004A7C7B),
      helpstring("Lst41")
    ]
```

```
coclass CLst41
{
  dispinterface DLst41;
  interface ILst41;
}
};
```

In Listing 4.1, the `uuid` attribute specifies the UUID of the item.

The `helpstring` attribute sets the help string associated with `library`, `interface`, and so on. This information can be retrieved via the `GetDocumentation` function in the `ITypeLib` and `ITypeInfo` interfaces to retrieve the documentation string.

The `lcid` attribute indicates that the parameter is a locale ID that provides locale information for the international string comparisons and localized member names.

The `version` attribute specifies a version number. Here, the version number is 1.0.

The `odl` attribute indicates that this interface is an ODL interface.

The `library` statement defines a type library.

The `importlib` directive indicates that `stdole32.tlb` will be accessible from `lst41.tlb`.

The `interface` statement defines an interface that contains the automation server's function, `GetMachineName`.

The `dispinterface` statement defines a set of properties and methods that can be called by `IDispatch::Invoke`. Besides listing a single interface (interface `Ilst41`) in Listing 4.1, a `dispinterface` can also be defined by listing the set of methods and properties—for example,

```
interface ILst41: IUnknown
{
    BSTR GetMachineName(void);
}

[
 uuid(9FBBEDE4-1B40-11d0-88E0-00AA004A7C7B),
]
dispinterface DLst41
{
  interface ILst41;
}
```

can be described as

```
dispinterface DLst41
{
    BSTR GetMachineName(void);
}
```

The `coclass` statement defines the class ID for class name `CLst41` and the interfaces supported by `CLst41`.

2. Create the `lst41.tlb` type library.

The type library is used by the automation clients to access the methods and properties exposed by the automation server.

`lst41.tlb` can be generated by executing the following command:

```
mktyplib -h ilst41.h lst41.odl
```

`mktyplib` is a type library creation tool. It processes `lst41.odl` scripts and produces the `ilst41.h` header file and a type library; `lst41.tlb`. `lst41.tlb` can be read by the `ITypeInfo` or `ITypeLib` interfaces.

The `ilst41.h` header file is shown in Listing 4.2.

\source\vol3\
chap-04\lst41

Listing 4.2. C++ header file: `ilst41.h`.

```
/* This header file machine-generated by mktyplib.exe */
/* Interface to type library: Lst41 */

#ifndef _Lst41_H_
#define _Lst41_H_

DEFINE_GUID(LIBID_Lst41,0x9FBBEDE2L,0x1B40,0x11D0,0x88,0xE0,0x00,
0xAA,0x00,0x4A,0x7C,0x7B);
#ifndef BEGIN_INTERFACE
#define BEGIN_INTERFACE
#endif

DEFINE_GUID(IID_ILst41,0x9FBBEDE3L,0x1B40,0x11D0,0x88,0xE0,0x00,
0xAA,0x00,0x4A,0x7C,0x7B);

/* Definition of interface: ILst41 */
#undef INTERFACE
#define INTERFACE ILst41

DECLARE_INTERFACE_(ILst41, IUnknown)
{
BEGIN_INTERFACE
#ifndef NO_BASEINTERFACE_FUNCS

    /* IUnknown methods */
    STDMETHOD(QueryInterface)(THIS_ REFIID riid, LPVOID FAR* ppvObj) PURE;
    STDMETHOD_(ULONG, AddRef)(THIS) PURE;
    STDMETHOD_(ULONG, Release)(THIS) PURE;
#endif

    /* ILst41 methods */
    STDMETHOD_(BSTR, GetMachineName)(THIS) PURE;
};

DEFINE_GUID(DIID_DLst41,0x9FBBEDE4L,0x1B40,0x11D0,0x88,0xE0,0x00,
0xAA,0x00,0x4A,0x7C,0x7B);

/* Definition of dispatch interface: DLst41 */
```

```
#undef INTERFACE
#define INTERFACE DLst41

DECLARE_INTERFACE_(DLst41, IDispatch)
{
BEGIN_INTERFACE
#ifndef NO_BASEINTERFACE_FUNCS

    /* IUnknown methods */
    STDMETHOD(QueryInterface)(THIS_ REFIID riid, LPVOID FAR* ppvObj) PURE;
    STDMETHOD_(ULONG, AddRef)(THIS) PURE;
    STDMETHOD_(ULONG, Release)(THIS) PURE;

    /* IDispatch methods */
    STDMETHOD(GetTypeInfoCount)(THIS_ UINT FAR* pctinfo) PURE;

    STDMETHOD(GetTypeInfo)(
      THIS_
      UINT itinfo,
      LCID lcid,
      ITypeInfo FAR* FAR* pptinfo) PURE;

    STDMETHOD(GetIDsOfNames)(
      THIS_
      REFIID riid,
      OLECHAR FAR* FAR* rgszNames,
      UINT cNames,
      LCID lcid,
      DISPID FAR* rgdispid) PURE;

    STDMETHOD(Invoke)(
      THIS_
      DISPID dispidMember,
      REFIID riid,
      LCID lcid,
      WORD wFlags,
      DISPPARAMS FAR* pdispparams,
      VARIANT FAR* pvarResult,
      EXCEPINFO FAR* pexcepinfo,
      UINT FAR* puArgErr) PURE;
#endif

/* Capable of dispatching all the methods of interface ILst41 */
};

DEFINE_GUID(CLSID_CLst41,0x9FBBEDE5L,0x1B40,0x11D0,0x88,0xE0,0x00,
0xAA,0x00,0x4A,0x7C,0x7B);

#ifdef __cplusplus
class CLst41;
#endif

#endif
From Listing 4.2,
dispinterface DLst41
    {
      interface ILst41;
    }
```

From Listing 4.2,

```
dispinterface DLst41
    {
        interface ILst41;
    }
```

has been expanded into seven methods, three IUnknown methods and four IDispatch methods, which include GetTypeInfoCount, GetTypeInfo, GetIDsOfNames, and Invoke.

Method GetTypeInfoCount retrieves the number of type-information interfaces provided by an object. If the object provides the type information, pctinfo will be 1; otherwise, it will be 0.

The GetTypeInfo method retrieves a type-information object. This object can be used to get the type information for an interface.

The GetIDsOfNames method retrieves a DISPID corresponding to the methods and arguments provided.

The Invoke method accesses the properties and methods, given their DISPID.

3. Implement the ILst41 interface. (See Listings 4.3 and 4.4.)

Listing 4.3. `ILst41` implementation (`Clst41I` and `CLst41` class definition).

\source\vol3\
chap-04\lst41

```
#include <objbase.h>
#include "clsid.h"
#include "ilst41.h"

class CLst41;

class CLst41I : public ILst41
{
  public:

STDMETHOD(QueryInterface)(THIS_ REFIID riid, LPVOID* ppvObj);
    STDMETHOD_(ULONG, AddRef)(THIS);
    STDMETHOD_(ULONG, Release)(THIS);

    STDMETHOD_(BSTR, GetMachineName)(THIS);

    CLst41*    m_pLst41;
};

class CLst41 : public IUnknown
{

 public:
    CLst41();
    ~CLst41();
    static CLst41* Create();

    STDMETHOD(QueryInterface)(REFIID riid, void ** ppv);
    STDMETHOD_(ULONG, AddRef)(void);
    STDMETHOD_(ULONG, Release)(void);
```

```
    private:
        ULONG m_refs;                    // Reference count.
        IUnknown* m_disp_interface;      // Pointer to the standard dispatch object.
        CLst41I* m_prog_interface;  //programmable interface.
    };
```

Listing 4.4. ILst41c.cpp.

\source\vol3\
chap-04\
lst41use

```
Clst41I and CLst41 class implementation
#include <objbase.h>
#include "resource.h"
#include "lst41c.h"

BSTR CreateBSTR(char *lpString)
{

    BSTR bsz;
    UINT cch;

    cch = strlen(lpString);


    bsz = SysAllocStringLen(NULL , cch);
    if(bsz == NULL)
        return NULL;

    if(cch > 0)
        MultiByteToWideChar(CP_ACP, 0, lpString, cch, bsz, cch);

    bsz[cch] = NULL;
    return bsz;
}
STDMETHODIMP_(BSTR)
CLst41I::GetMachineName()
{
    BSTR b;

    ULONG ulLen;

    char *lpName;
    lpName = new char[MAX_PATH];
    ulLen = MAX_PATH;

    GetComputerName(lpName, &ulLen);
    b = CreateBSTR(lpName);

    return b;
}

//standard IUunknown methods implementation

STDMETHODIMP CLst41I::QueryInterface(REFIID riid, void** ppv)
{
    return m_pLst41->QueryInterface(riid, ppv);
}
```

continues

Listing 4.4. continued

```
STDMETHODIMP_(ULONG) CLst41I::AddRef()
{
    return m_pLst41->AddRef();
}

STDMETHODIMP_(ULONG) CLst41I::Release()
{
    return m_pLst41->Release();
}

IUnknown FAR*
CreateDispatchInterface(IUnknown* punkController,  void * pProgInterface)
{
    HRESULT hresult;
    ITypeLib* ptlib;
    ITypeInfo* ptinfo;
    IUnknown* punkStdDisp;

    hresult = LoadRegTypeLib(LIBID_Lst41, 1, 0, 0x0409, &ptlib);
    if (hresult != S_OK)
    {
        if((hresult = LoadTypeLib(L"lst41.tlb", &ptlib)) != S_OK)
            return NULL;
    }

    hresult = ptlib->GetTypeInfoOfGuid(IID_ILst41, &ptinfo);
    if (hresult != S_OK)
        return NULL;
    ptlib->Release();


    hresult = CreateStdDispatch(punkController,pProgInterface,
                                ptinfo, &punkStdDisp);
    if (hresult != S_OK)
        return NULL;

    ptinfo->Release();

    return punkStdDisp;
}
CLst41::CLst41()
{
    m_refs = 1;
    m_disp_interface = NULL;
    m_prog_interface = new CLst41I;
    m_prog_interface->m_pLst41 = this;
}

CLst41::~CLst41()
{
    delete m_prog_interface;
}

CLst41 * CLst41::Create()
{
    CLst41* pLst41;
    IUnknown* punkStdDisp;
```

```
    pLst41 = new CLst41();
    if(pLst41 == NULL)
      return NULL;

    punkStdDisp = CreateDispatchInterface((IUnknown *) pLst41,
                        pLst41->m_prog_interface);
    if (punkStdDisp == NULL) {
      pLst41->Release();
      return NULL;
    }

    pLst41->m_disp_interface = punkStdDisp;
    return pLst41;
}

STDMETHODIMP CLst41::QueryInterface(REFIID riid, void ** ppv)
{
    if (riid == IID_IUnknown)
        *ppv = this;
    else if (riid == IID_IDispatch || riid == DIID_DLst41)
        return m_disp_interface->QueryInterface(IID_IDispatch, ppv);
    else if (riid == IID_ILst41)
        *ppv = &m_prog_interface;
    else
    {
        *ppv = NULL;
        return ResultFromScode(E_NOINTERFACE);
    }

    AddRef();
    return S_OK;
}
STDMETHODIMP_(ULONG) CLst41::AddRef()
{
    return ++m_refs;
}

STDMETHODIMP_(ULONG) CLst41::Release()
{
    if(--m_refs == 0)
    {
        if(m_disp_interface != NULL)
            m_disp_interface->Release();
        PostQuitMessage(0);
        delete this;
        return 0;
    }

    return m_refs;
}
```

Function CreateBSTR will convert an ASCII string to a wide character (Unicode) string. In particular, function MultiByteToWideChar will convert an ASCII string pointed to by lpString to a wide character string pointed to by bsz. CP_ACP specifies the code page to be used by the conversion. It stands for ANSI code page. Other code pages include CP_MACCP, which indicates a Macintosh code page, and `CP_OEMCP`, which indicates an OEM code page.

Function `CreateDispatchInterface` will first use registry information to load the type library by invoking the `LoadRegTypeLib` function. There are four parameters. `LIBID_Lst41` is the library ID being loaded. `1` is the type library (`lst41.tlb`)'s major version number. `0` is `lst41.tlb`'s minor version number. `0x0409` is U.S. English, which is the library's national language code. `ptlib` is an indirect pointer to the `ITypeLib` interface.

If the type library information cannot be loaded from the registry, the `LoadTypeLib` function will be called. `LoadTypeLib` loads and registers the type library stored in `lst41.tlb`.

`GetTypeInfoOfGuid` will retrieve `IID_ILst41` type description, and return `ptinfo`, which is an indirect pointer to `ITypeInfo`.

After successfully invoking `GetTypeInfoOfGuid`, the `CreateStdDispatch` function will be invoked. This function creates a standard implementation of the `IDispatch` interface through one single function call. There are four parameters in this function. `punkController` is a pointer to the `ILst41` `IUnknown` implementation. `pProgInterface` is a pointer to the object to expose. `ptinfo` is a pointer to the `ILst41` type information that describes the exposed object. `punkStdDisp` is an indirect pointer to the `ILst41` `IDispatch` interface implementation.

`QueryInterface` will check the interface identifier `riid`. If `riid` is equal to `IID_IUnknown`, this value will be assigned to `*ppv` because `CLst41` is the controlling `IUnknown`. If `riid` is equal to `IID_IDispatch` or `DIID_DLst41` or `IID_ILst41`, `*ppv` will be the standard dispatch interface. Otherwise, `*ppv` will be `NULL` and the error code `E_NOINTERFACE` will be returned.

The `PostQuitMessage` function will indicate to the system that the thread will be terminated by posting a `WM_QUIT` message to the thread's message queue. When the thread receives `WM_QUIT` from the message queue, it will terminate the message loop and return control to the window.

4. Implement the class object for `CLst41`.

   Listing 4.5 demonstrates the `CLst41` class factory implementation.

Listing 4.5. The `CLst41` class factory.

`\source\vol3\`
`chap-04\lst41`

```
class CLst41CF : public IClassFactory
{
  public:
    CLst41CF();
    static IClassFactory* Create();

    STDMETHOD(QueryInterface)(REFIID riid, void ** ppv);
    STDMETHOD_(ULONG, AddRef)(void);
    STDMETHOD_(ULONG, Release)(void);
```

```
        STDMETHOD(CreateInstance)(      IUnknown* punkOuter,
                    REFIID riid,
                    void** ppv);
        STDMETHOD(LockServer)(BOOL fLock);

    private:
        ULONG m_refs;
};

CLst41CF::CLst41CF()
{
    m_refs = 1;
}

IClassFactory* CLst41CF::Create()
{
    return new  CLst41CF();
}

STDMETHODIMP CLst41CF::QueryInterface(REFIID riid, void** ppv)
{
    if(riid == IID_IUnknown ¦¦ riid == IID_IClassFactory)
    {
        AddRef();
        *ppv = this;
        return S_OK;
    }

    *ppv = NULL;
    return ResultFromScode(E_NOINTERFACE);
}

STDMETHODIMP_(ULONG) CLst41CF::AddRef()
{
    return ++m_refs;
}

STDMETHODIMP_(ULONG) CLst41CF::Release()
{
    if(—m_refs == 0)
    {
        delete this;
        return 0;
    }

    return m_refs;
}

STDMETHODIMP CLst41CF::CreateInstance(IUnknown* punkOuter,REFIID riid,
                                      void** ppv)
{
    extern CLst41 * g_pLst41;

    return g_pLst41->QueryInterface(riid, ppv);
}
```

continues

Listing 4.5. continued

```
STDMETHODIMP CLst41CF::LockServer(BOOL fLock)
{
    return S_OK;
}
```

5. Create the main entry.

   An automation server can be one of two types. One is DLL based and can be driven only by automation clients. The other is EXE based and can run as a stand-alone.

   Lst41.exe is an EXE-based automation server. To create an EXE-based automation server, you must provide a main entry. Listing 4.6 demonstrates how to implement the main entry.

Listing 4.6. Main entry for Lst41.exe.

\source\vol3\
chap-04\lst41

```
#include <objbase.h>
#include "lst41c.h"
#include <stdio.h>

CLst41 FAR* g_pLst41 = NULL;

void  main()
{
    MSG msg;
    DWORD g_dwLst41CF = 0;
    HRESULT hr;

    IClassFactory FAR* pcf;

    if((hr = OleInitialize(NULL)) != S_OK)
    {
        printf("OleInitialize Failed [0x%x]\n", hr);
        return;
    }

    if((g_pLst41 = CLst41::Create()) == NULL)
        return;

    pcf = CLst41CF::Create();
    if (pcf == NULL)
        goto Clean;

    hr = CoRegisterClassObject(CLSID_CLst41,
                                pcf,
                                CLSCTX_LOCAL_SERVER,
                                REGCLS_MULTIPLEUSE,
                                &g_dwLst41CF);

    if (hr != NOERROR)
        goto Clean;

    pcf->Release();
```

```
    while(GetMessage(&msg, NULL, NULL, NULL))
    {
        TranslateMessage(&msg);
        DispatchMessage(&msg);
    }
Clean:
    if(g_dwLst41CF != 0)
        CoRevokeClassObject(g_dwLst41CF);

    if (g_pLst41 != NULL)
        g_pLst41->Release();

    OleUninitialize();
}
```

In Listing 4.6, first `OleInitialize` is invoked to initialize the OLE library. This function must be called before calling any OLE functions. Then `CLst41::Create` is invoked to create a single global instance of `CLst41`. `CLst41CF::Create` is called to create an instance of the class factory for `CLst41`. Register the class factory by invoking `CoRegisterClassObject`. Then the message loop is provided. When the `WM_QUIT` message is received, the message loop will be terminated. `CoRevokeClassFactory` will be called to inform OLE that the object is no longer available if the class factory was successfully created earlier. Finally, `OleUninitialize` will be called to uninitialize the OLE library and release all the resources.

6. Create the registration entry.

    `lst41.exe` has to be registered before being used. Listing 4.7 shows the registration file for `lst41.exe`. Remember to change the paths to your own directories.

Listing 4.7. The `lst41.reg` file.

\source\vol3\
chap-04\lst41

```
REGEDIT

HKEY_CLASSES_ROOT\Lst41.Application.1 = Lst41 Automation Server
HKEY_CLASSES_ROOT\Lst41.Application.1\Clsid =
{9FBBEDE5-1B40-11d0-88E0-00AA004A7C7B}

HKEY_CLASSES_ROOT\CLSID\{9FBBEDE5-1B40-11d0-88E0-00AA004A7C7B} =
 IDispatch Lst41
HKEY_CLASSES_ROOT\CLSID\{9FBBEDE5-1B40-11d0-88E0-00AA004A7C7B}\ProgID =
Lst41.Application.1
HKEY_CLASSES_ROOT\CLSID\{9FBBEDE5-1B40-11d0-88E0-00AA004A7C7B}\
VersionIndependentProgID = Lst41.Application
HKEY_CLASSES_ROOT\CLSID\{9FBBEDE5-1B40-11d0-88E0-00AA004A7C7B}\
LocalServer32 =c:\ch4\lst41\debug\lst41.exe /Automation

; registration info Lst41 TypeLib
```

continues

Listing 4.7. continued

```
HKEY_CLASSES_ROOT\TypeLib\{9FBBEDE2-1B40-11d0-88E0-00AA004A7C7B}
HKEY_CLASSES_ROOT\TypeLib\{9FBBEDE2-1B40-11d0-88E0-00AA004A7C7B}\
1.0 = Lst41 Type Library
HKEY_CLASSES_ROOT\TypeLib\{9FBBEDE2-1B40-11d0-88E0-00AA004A7C7B}\
1.0\HELPDIR =
;Localized language is US english
HKEY_CLASSES_ROOT\TypeLib\{9FBBEDE2-1B40-11d0-88E0-00AA004A7C7B}\
1.0\409\win32 = c:\ch4\lst41\lst41.tlb

HKEY_CLASSES_ROOT\Interface\{9FBBEDE4-1B40-11d0-88E0-00AA004A7C7B} = DLst41
HKEY_CLASSES_ROOT\Interface\{9FBBEDE4-1B40-11d0-88E0-00AA004A7C7B}\
ProxyStubClsid = {00020420-0000-0000-C000-000000000046}
HKEY_CLASSES_ROOT\Interface\{9FBBEDE4-1B40-11d0-88E0-00AA004A7C7B}\
NumMethod = 7
HKEY_CLASSES_ROOT\Interface\{9FBBEDE4-1B40-11d0-88E0-00AA004A7C7B}\
BaseInterface = {00020400-0000-0000-C000-000000000046}
```

In Listing 4.7, `Lst41.Application.1` is the `ProgID`, which is required for any automation objects. It is used by an automation controller to reference an automation server. The `LocalServer32` subkey specifies the full path to the 32-bit automation server `lst41.exe`.

Use `lst41` in a C++ Application: `lst41use.exe`

`lst41use.exe` is a C++ application that uses `lst41.exe`. It uses `IDispatch` to access exposed objects.

Listing 4.8 demonstrates how to use `IDispatch` to access the methods exposed by `lst41.exe`.

Listing 4.8. `lst41use.cpp`.

```cpp
#include <objbase.h>
#include <initguid.h>
#include <stdio.h>

DEFINE_GUID(CLSID_CLst41,0x9FBBEDE5L,0x1B40,0x11D0,0x88,0xE0,
0x00,0xAA,0x00,0x4A,0x7C,0x7B);

LPSTR BstrToSz(LPCOLESTR pszW)
{
    ULONG cbAnsi, cCharacters;
    DWORD dwError;
    LPSTR lpString;

    if(pszW == NULL)
        return NULL;

    cCharacters = wcslen(pszW) + 1;

    cbAnsi = cCharacters * 2;
```

```
    lpString = (LPSTR) CoTaskMemAlloc(cbAnsi);

    if(NULL == lpString)
        return NULL;

    if(WideCharToMultiByte(CP_ACP, 0, pszW, cCharacters, lpString,
                           cbAnsi, NULL, NULL) == 0)
    {
        dwError = GetLastError();
        CoTaskMemFree(lpString);
        lpString = NULL;
    }

    return lpString;
}
```

Function BstrToSz converts a wide character (Unicode) string to an ASCII string. CoTaskMemAlloc allocates a memory block using the default allocator. It behaves the same way as IMalloc::Alloc. The application should always check the return value from this function. Function WideCharToMultiByte maps a wide character string pointed to by pszW to an ASCII string pointed to by lpString.

```
void main()
{
    HRESULT hr;
    IDispatch *pIDispatch;
    DISPPARAMS dispparms = {NULL, NULL, 0,0};
    DISPID dispidGetMachineName;
    OLECHAR *pGetMachineName = L"GetMachineName";
    IUnknown *pIUnknown;
    VARIANT varResult;

    hr = OleInitialize(NULL);

    hr = CoCreateInstance(CLSID_CLst41, 0, CLSCTX_SERVER, IID_IUnknown,
                          (void**)&pIUnknown);

    if(FAILED(hr))
        printf("the error is %x\n", hr);

    pIUnknown->QueryInterface(IID_IDispatch, (void**)&pIDispatch);
    pIUnknown->Release();

    pIDispatch->GetIDsOfNames(IID_NULL,
                              &pGetMachineName,
                              1, LOCALE_SYSTEM_DEFAULT, &dispidGetMachineName);
    pIDispatch->Invoke(dispidGetMachineName, IID_NULL, LOCALE_SYSTEM_DEFAULT,
                       DISPATCH_METHOD, &dispparms,
                       &varResult, NULL, NULL);

    printf("the striing is %s\n", BstrToSz(varResult.bstrVal));

    pIDispatch->Release();
    CoUninitialize();
}
```

Function `CoCreateInstance` creates a `CLst41` object. Because `lst41.exe` is a local server, execution context `CLSCTX_SERVER` is used. `CLSCTX_SERVER` is defined as

```
#define CLSCTX_SERVER (CLSCTX_INPROC_SERVER| CLSCTX_LOCAL_SERVER|
➥CLSCTX_REMOTE_SERVER)
```

`GetIDsOfNames` retrieves the `DISPID` and will be stored in `dispidGetMachineName`. There are four other parameters in `GetIDsOfNames`. `IID_NULL` must be `NULL`; it is reserved for future use. `pGetMachineName` points to the method name. `1` indicates there is only one name to be mapped. `LOCALE_SYSTEM_DEFAULT` indicates the locale context in which to interpret the name.

`Invoke` accesses the `GetMachineName` method by providing its `DISPID`. `varResult` is used to hold the return value from the `GetMachineName` method.

Use `lst41` in a Visual Basic Application

With Visual Basic, using `lst41.exe` is straightforward. Listing 4.9 demonstrates how to use `lst41.exe`.

\source\vol3\
chap-04\lst41

Listing 4.9. `lst41.exe` used in Visual Basic.

```
Dim x As Object
Dim strMachineName As String

Set x = CreateObject("lst41.application.1")
strMachineName = x.getmachinename
MsgBox strMachineName
```

In Listing 4.8, variable `x` is declared as an object and assigned the return of the `CreateObject` call. The parameter in the `CreateObject` call is the `ProgID` of `lst41.exe`.

After the automation server (`lst41.exe`) is instantiated, the method `GetMachineName` can be invoked; the return value is assigned to `strMachineName`.

To try the example, place a CommandButton control on a form, and type Listing 4.8 into the command button's click procedure. Run the example and click the Command1 button. A dialog box with the computer name on which the application is running will be displayed.

Create `lst41` by Using the MFC ClassWizard (exe): `lst42.exe`

There are two MFC ClassWizard options provided by the New Project Workspace, as shown in Figure 4.1.

Figure 4.1.
New Project Workspace.

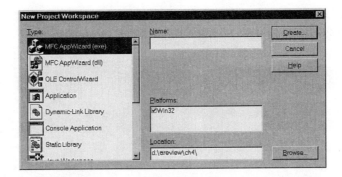

MFC AppWizard is designed to configure the skeleton of a new C++ application using the MFC.

MFC AppWizard (exe) is designed to create an MFC extension EXE, whereas MFC AppWizard (dll) is designed to create an MFC extension DLL. The following steps illustrate how to create lst42.exe

1. Choose File | New. In the New dialog box, select the file type Project Workspace.
2. In the New Project Workspace dialog box, choose the MFC AppWizard (exe) in the Type box. Type lst42 in the Name edit box and click the Create button shown in Figure 4.2.

Figure 4.2.
New Project Workspace dialog box.

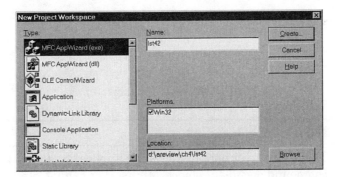

3. Choose the Single document option shown in Figure 4.3.
4. Choose the Mini-server option and the OLE automation option, as shown in Figure 4.4.

Figure 4.3.
MFC AppWizard—Step 1.

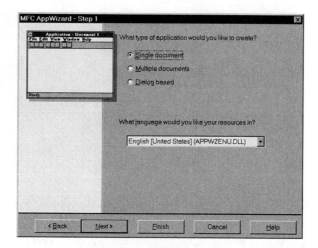

Figure 4.4.
MFC AppWizard—Step 3 of 6.

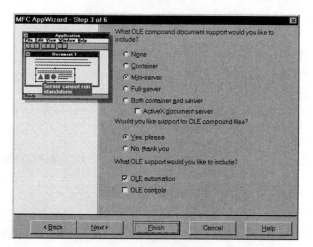

note

The Mini-server option allows the application to create and manage the compound document object. Mini-server cannot run as a stand-alone, and only supports embedded objects, whereas Full-server can run as a stand-alone and supports both linked and embedded objects.

The OLE automation option allows the application to be accessed by the automation clients, such as Visual Basic, Access, and Excel.

5. Click the Finish button. The files listed in Figure 4.5 will be generated by the MFC AppWizard (exe). Click the OK button to generate all the files.

Figure 4.5.
New Project Information.

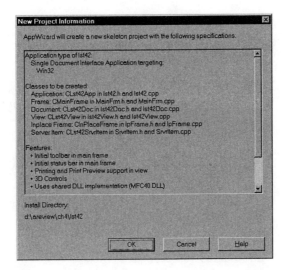

Among the files listed in Figure 4.5, the following classes and source files are specific to OLE:

SrvrItem.h, SrvrItem.cpp: This is the class that connects CLst42Doc to the OLE system. It also optionally provides links to the document.

IpFrame.h, IpFrame.cpp: This class is derived from COleIPFrameWnd and controls all frame features during in-place activation.

lst42.reg: This is a REG file. This file can be used to manually register the application.

lst42.odl: This is the ODL file, which is read by MkTypLib to create a type library (.TLB). A type library is used by automation clients to retrieve information about the server's properties and its data types, methods, and its return value and parameters. Listing 4.10 shows the lst42.odl file.

Listing 4.10. lst42.odl.

\source\vol3\
chap-04\lst42

```
// lst42.odl : type library source for lst42.exe

// This file will be processed by the Make Type Library (mktyplib) tool to
// produce the type library (lst42.tlb).

[ uuid(06B70DA1-1818-11D0-A6AD-00AA00602553), version(1.0) ]
library Lst42
{
    importlib("stdole32.tlb");

    // Primary dispatch interface for CLst42Doc
```

continues

Listing 4.10. continued

```
[ uuid(06B70DA2-1818-11D0-A6AD-00AA00602553) ]
dispinterface ILst42
{
    properties:
        // NOTE - ClassWizard will maintain property information here.
        //     Use extreme caution when editing this section.
        //{{AFX_ODL_PROP(CLst42Doc)
        //}}AFX_ODL_PROP

    methods:
        // NOTE - ClassWizard will maintain method information here.
        //     Use extreme caution when editing this section.
        //{{AFX_ODL_METHOD(CLst42Doc)
        [id(1)] BSTR GetMachineName();
        //}}AFX_ODL_METHOD
};

//  Class information for CLst42Doc

[ uuid(06B70DA0-1818-11D0-A6AD-00AA00602553) ]
coclass Document
{
    [default] dispinterface ILst42;
};

//{{AFX_APPEND_ODL}}
};
```

ODL consists of attributes, statements, and directives.

```
[ uuid(06B70DA1-1818-11D0-A6AD-00AA00602553), version(1.0) ]
```

is the attribute, which associates information with the library. The uuid is for the type library. All applications that expose type information must register the information to the system registry so that it is available to type browsers or any automation clients.

The definition on the library Lst42 is enclosed between { and }. In the definition, import indicates that lst42.tlb imports the standard OLE library stdole32.tlb. dispinterface defines a set of methods and properties that can be invoked by IDispatch::Invoke. The coclass named document indicates that the supported interface ILst42 is in this component object (lst42.exe). A GUID must be given on a coclass. This GUID is the same as the CLSID registered in the system.

6. From the View menu, choose the ClassWizard command, select the OLE Automation tab, and choose CLst42Doc in the Class name dropdown list box shown in Figure 4.6.

Figure 4.6.
MFC ClassWizard—OLE
Automation.

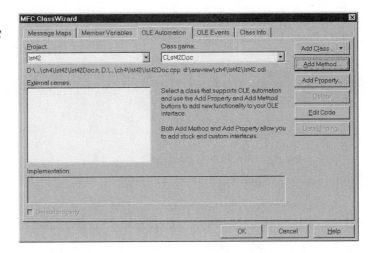

7. Click the Add Method button in Figure 4.6. Type `GetMachineName` in the External name dropdown combo box, select `BSTR` in the Return type dropdown list box, and click the OK button in the Add Method dialog box displayed in Figure 4.7.

Figure 4.7.
Add Method dialog box.

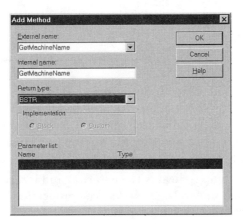

---

note

External name is used by the automation clients to invoke the exposed method, whereas Internal name is the member function that implements the exposed method.

---

8. Modify the class `lst42Doc.cpp`. Add the code shown in Listing 4.11.

Listing 4.11. Method implementation.

\source\vol3\
chap-04\lst42

```
BSTR CLst42Doc::GetMachineName()
{
    CString strResult;
    ULONG ulLen;

    char *lpName;

    lpName = new char[MAX_PATH];
    ulLen = MAX_PATH;

    GetComputerName(lpName, &ulLen );
    strResult = lpName;
    delete [] lpName;

    return strResult.AllocSysString();
}
```

Lst42.exe only has one exposed method, GetMachineName. Listing 4.12 demonstrates the dispatch map generated by the MFC AppWizard (exe).

Listing 4.12. Dispatch map for lst42.exe.

\source\vol3\
chap-04\lst42

```
BEGIN_DISPATCH_MAP(CLst42Doc, COleServerDoc)
    //{{AFX_DISPATCH_MAP(CLst42Doc)
    DISP_FUNCTION(CLst42Doc, "GetMachineName", GetMachineName,
    VT_BSTR, VTS_NONE)
    //}}AFX_DISPATCH_MAP
END_DISPATCH_MAP()
```

Listing 4.12 is abridged from lst42Doc.cpp to emphasize the essential parts. The DISP_FUNCTION macro is used in the dispatch map to define an exposed method. The dispatch map is a mechanism provided by MFC to dispatch the request made by the automation clients, such as calling the methods and accessing the properties.

The dispatch map indicates the external and internal names of the properties and methods, as well as the properties' data types and methods' arguments and return types.

In Listing 4.12, CLst42Doc is the name of the class. COleServerDoc is the base class. The DISP_FUNCTION macro is used to define an automation method. GetMachineName is the external name used by the automation clients, GetMachineName is the internal name, VT_BSTR is the return type, and VTS_NONE is the method's parameter list. In this case, there is no input parameter.

Besides the DISP_FUNCTION macro defined in the dispatch map, other macros are provided as shown in the following list.

- `DISP_DEFVALUE` defines a property as the default value for an object.
- `DISP_PROPERTY` defines an automation property.
- `DISP_PROPERTY_EX` defines an automation property and names the `get` and `set` functions.
- `DISP_PROPERTY_NOTIFY` defines an automation property with notification.
- `DISP_PROPERTY_PARAM` defines an automation property and names the `get` and `set` functions and an index parameter.
- `DECLARE_DISPATCH_MAP` is used in the class declaration to indicate that a dispatch map will be used.

  For example:

  ```
  class CLst42Doc : public COleServerDoc

  ...
      // Generated OLE dispatch map functions
      //{{AFX_DISPATCH(CLst42Doc)
      afx_msg BSTR GetMachineName();
      //}}AFX_DISPATCH
      DECLARE_DISPATCH_MAP()
      DECLARE_INTERFACE_MAP()
  }
  ```

  is used in `lst42Doc.h` to indicate that a dispatch map will be used in the `CLst42Doc` class.

- `BEGIN_DISPATCH_MAP` is used in the class implementation to indicate the start of the dispatch map definition, as shown in Listing 4.12.
- `END_DISPATCH_MAP` is used in the class implementation to indicate the end of the dispatch map definition, as shown in Listing 4.12.

9. Build the project to generate `lst42.exe`.

   Before `lst42.exe` can be used by the automation clients or any other information, `lst42.exe` must be registered with the system. This can be done by running one of the following commands:

   - `regedit /s lst42.reg`
   - `lst42.exe /regserver`

---

tip

The automation server generated by the MFC AppWizard (exe) provides self-registration features. In other words, `lst42.exe` accepts the program argument `/regserver` to register itself to the system registry.

After `lst42.exe` is registered with the system, it can be used by automation clients, such as Visual Basic, Access, and Excel. `lst42.exe` can be accessed by using the `IDispatch` interface in the C++ application.

The following example demonstrates how `lst42.exe` can be used in Visual Basic 4.0.

With Visual Basic, using `lst42.exe` is straightforward. Listing 4.13 demonstrates how to use `lst42.exe` inside Visual Basic.

Listing 4.13. `lst42.exe` used in Visual Basic.

\source\vol3\
chap-04\lst42

```
Dim x As Object
Dim strMachineName As String

Set x = CreateObject("lst42.document")
strMachineName = x.getmachinename
MsgBox strMachineName
```

In Listing 4.13, variable `x` is declared as an object and assigned the return of the `CreateObject` call. The parameter in the `CreateObject` call is the `ProgID` of `lst42.exe`. For any application generated by the MFC AppWizard with OLE automation enabled, the `ProgID` is always the name for the new project workspace plus the `.document`.

After the automation server (`lst42.exe`) is instantiated, the method `GetMachineName` can be invoked and the return value is assigned to `strMachineName`.

To try the example, place a CommandButton control on a form and type Listing 4.13 into the command button's click procedure. Run the example and click the Command1 button. A dialog box with the name of the computer the application is running on will be displayed.

Create `lst41` by Using the ControlWizard: `lst43.ocx`

Besides using MFC AppWizard (exe) to create the automation server, ControlWizard can be used. The `IsInvokeAllowed()` method is required to be overridden to support the automation.

The following steps demonstrate how to implement an automation server supporting the same functionality as `lst41.exe`.

1. Choose File | New. In the New dialog box, select the file type Project Workspace.

2. In the New Project Workspace dialog box, choose the OLE
   ControlWizard. Type lst43 in the Name edit box and click the Create
   button shown in Figure 4.8.

Figure 4.8.
New Project
Workspace—OLE
ControlWizard.

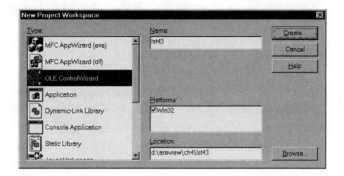

3. Click the Finish button. Files shown in Figure 4.9 will be generated.
   Click the OK button in the dialog box displayed in Figure 4.9.

Figure 4.9.
Files generated by the
OLE ControlWizard.

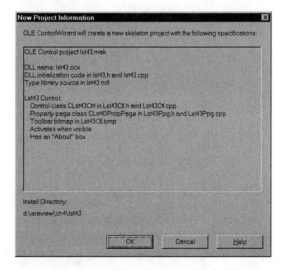

Among the files shown in Figure 4.9, the following files are specifically
related to the ControlWizard:

lst43.odl: Containing the ODL script.

lst43Ctl.h, lst43Ctl.cpp: All the methods, properties, and events will
be placed in this class.

lst43Ppg.h, lst43Ppg.cpp: Default property page class.

lst43Ctl.bmp: Containing a bitmap displayed in the container's toolbox, such as Visual Basic's toolbox.

4. Choose View | ClassWizard. Select the OLE Automation tab shown in Figure 4.10, click the Add Method button, enter GetMachineName, and choose BSTR as the return type in the Add Method dialog box displayed in Figure 4.11.

Figure 4.10.
OLE Automation tab in MFC ClassWizard.

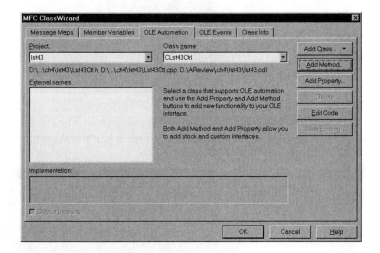

Figure 4.11.
Add Method in the OLE Automation tab.

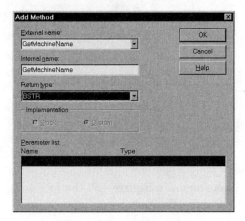

5. Implement the GetMachineName method by modifying lst43Ctl.cpp.

```
BSTR CLst43Ctrl::GetMachineName()
{
    CString strResult;
    ULONG ulLen;
```

```
    char *lpName;

    lpName = new char[MAX_PATH];
    ulLen = MAX_PATH;

    GetComputerName(lpName, &ulLen );
    strResult = lpName;
    delete [] lpName;

    return strResult.AllocSysString();
}
```

6. Override `IsInvokeAllowed`.

   Add the following declaration in class `CLst43Ctrl` in `lst43Ctl.h`.

   ```
   private:
       BOOL IsInvokeAllowed(DISPID dispid);
   ```

   Add the `IsInvokeAllowed` implementation in `lst43Ctl.cpp`.

   ```
   BOOL CLst43Ctrl::IsInvokeAllowed(DISPID dispid)
   {
       return TRUE;
   }
   ```

7. Build the application to generate `lst43.ocx`.

   `lst43.ocx` can be used in Visual Basic the same way as `lst42.exe`. Instead
   of Listing 4.13, code in Listing 4.14 should be entered.

Listing 4.14. `lst43.ocx` used in Visual Basic.

\source\vol3\
chap-04\lst43

```
Dim x As Object
Dim strMachineName As String

Set x = CreateObject("lst43.lst43ctrl.1")
strMachineName = x.getmachinename
MsgBox strMachineName
```

`lst43.ocx` supports self registration. To register `lst43.ocx`, run `regsvr32 lst43.ocx`;
to unregister `lst43.ocx`, run `regsvr32 /u lst43.ocx`.

In Listing 4.14, `ProgID` for `lst43.ocx` is `lst43.lst43ctrl.1`. The default `ProgID`
generated by the OLE ControlWizard is always the name for the new project
workspace plus `.lst43ctrl.1`.

There is one method exposed by `lst43.ocx`. Listing 4.15 is the dispatch map
generated by the ClassWizard.

Listing 4.15. Dispatch map for `lst43.ocx`.

\source\vol3\
chap-04\lst43

```
BEGIN_DISPATCH_MAP(CLst43Ctrl, COleControl)
    //{{AFX_DISPATCH_MAP(CLst43Ctrl)
    DISP_FUNCTION(CLst43Ctrl, "GetMachineName", GetMachineName,
```

continues

Listing 4.15. continued

```
      VT_BSTR, VTS_NONE)
      //}}AFX_DISPATCH_MAP
      DISP_FUNCTION_ID(CLst43Ctrl, "AboutBox", DISPID_ABOUTBOX, AboutBox,
      VT_EMPTY, VTS_NONE)
END_DISPATCH_MAP()
```

In Listing 4.15, `DISP_FUNCTION` is exactly the same as in Listing 4.13, except the class name is `CLst43Ctrl` instead of `CLst42Doc`.

Create `lst41` by Using the Active Template Library: `lst44.dll`

ATL provides an OLE COM AppWizard to create COM objects. It supports COM objects with a custom interface, `IDispatch`, `IConnectionPoint`, and so on. ATL is designed to create COM objects.

The following example illustrates how to use ATL to create an automation server supporting the same functionality as `lst41.exe`.

1. Choose File | New. In the New dialog box, select "Project Workspace" in the type box.
2. In the New Project Workspace dialog box, choose the ATL COM AppWizard. Type `lst44` in the Name edit box and click the Create button shown in Figure 4.12.

Figure 4.12.
ATL COM AppWizard.

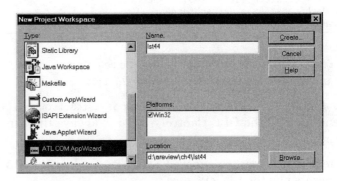

3. Use the default option displayed in Figure 4.13.

Figure 4.13.
ATL COM AppWizard—
Step 1 of 2.

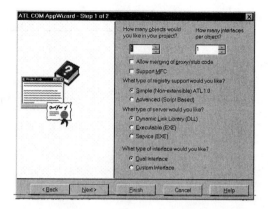

---

note

The Dual Interface option indicates that the interface supports
`IDispatch` and `Unknown`.

The Custom Interface option indicates that the interface only supports
`IUnknown`.

---

4. Implement the `GetMachineName` method.

   Add the following code to interface the `ILst44` definition in `lst44.idl`.

   ```
   interface ILst44 : IDispatch
   {
       import "oaidl.idl";

       HRESULT GetMachineName([out,retval] BSTR *retval);
   }
   ```

   Add the following code to `CLst44Object.h` in `lst44obj.h`.

   ```
   public:
       STDMETHOD(GetMachineName)(BSTR *retval);
   ```

   Add the `GetMachineName` implementation in `lst44obj.cpp`, shown in Listing 4.16.

Listing 4.16. Addition to `lst44obj.cpp`.

`\source\vol3\`
`chap-04\lst44`

```
BSTR CreateBSTR(LPCSTR lpa)
{
    BSTR bsz;
    UINT cch;

    cch = strlen(lpa);
```

continues

Listing 4.16. continued

```
        bsz = SysAllocStringLen(NULL, cch);
        if (bsz == NULL)
            return NULL;

        if (cch > 0)
            MultiByteToWideChar(CP_ACP, 0, lpa, cch, bsz, cch);

        bsz[cch] = NULL;
        return bsz;
}

STDMETHODIMP CLst44Object::GetMachineName(BSTR* retval)
{
    ULONG ulLen;

    char *lpName;

    lpName = new char[MAX_PATH];
    ulLen = MAX_PATH;

    GetComputerName(lpName, &ulLen);

    if(ulLen == 0)
        *retval = NULL;
    else
        *retval = CreateBSTR(lpName);

    return S_OK;

}
```

In Listing 4.16, function CreateBSTR accepts an ASCII string and converts it into a Unicode string. Unicode stands for a 16-bit character set that can encode all known character sets and is used as a worldwide character encoding standard.

5. Before building the project, use the midl lst44.idl command to generate a source file for a custom OLE interface.

6. Build the project to generate lst44.dll.

lst44.dll can be used in Visual Basic the same way as lst42.exe. Instead of inputting Listing 4.11, the code in Listing 4.17 should be entered.

\source\vol3\
chap-04\lst44

Listing 4.17. lst44.dll used in Visual Basic.

```
Dim x As Object
Dim strMachineName As String

Set x = CreateObject("lst44.lst44object.1")
strMachineName = x.getmachinename
MsgBox strMachineName
```

Before running the preceding code, 1st44.d11 needs to be registered by running regsvr32 1st44.d11.

In Listing 4.16, ProgID for 1st44.d11 is 1st44.1st44object.1. The default ProgID generated by OLE COM AppWizard is the name of the project workspace plus .1st44object.1.

The default ProgID can be modified by replacing the code in bold font as shown in the following; this code is contained in 1st44.cpp.

```
BEGIN_OBJECT_MAP(ObjectMap)
    OBJECT_ENTRY(CLSID_Lst44, CLst44Object, "LST44.Lst44Object.1",
    "LST44.Lst44Object.1", IDS_LST44_DESC, THREADFLAGS_BOTH)
END_OBJECT_MAP()
```

Reusable components such as automation servers not only can be used in the automation clients such as Visual Basic, Access, and Excel, but also in the applications that access the automation servers via IDispatch. Microsoft Internet Explorer (IE) 3.0 also supports the use of automation servers.

The automation server inside IE 3.0 requires an <OBJECT> tag to be used to include the object.

Listing 4.18 demonstrates how to use 1st44.d11 inside an HTML page and displayed in the IE 3.0 browser.

Listing 4.18. `1st44.d11` used in IE 3.0.

```
<HTML>
<HEAD>
<OBJECT  classid="clsid:C566CC25-182E-11D0-A6AD-00AA00602553"
    id= MachineName
</OBJECT>


<SCRIPT language="VBScript">
    msgbox MachineName.getmachinename
</SCRIPT>
</HEAD>
</HTML>
```

\source\vol3\
chap-04\lst44

In Listing 4.18, "clsid:..." is the string representation of the clsid, denoted as {clsid}, for 1st44.d11. The following steps illustrate how to get the {clsid} for 1st44.d11.

1. Run regedt32.
2. Go to HKEY_CLASSES_ROOT and then find the 1st44.1st44object.1 subkey in HKEY_CLASSES_ROOT.
3. Get the value of the clsid subkey under 1st44.1st44object.1, shown in Figure 4.14.

Figure 4.14.
ProgID *and* {CLSID}
registry key for
lst44.dll.

4. Double-click the data, and a string editor dialog box will be displayed, as shown in Figure 4.15.

Figure 4.15.
String editor for data.

5. Paste the value in the string editor to the HTML page.

When IE 3.0 browses this page, a message box will pop up, showing the computer name.

The automation server can be used not only on the browser's side, but also on the Web server side.

To use the automation server on the Web server side, Internet Personalization System (IPS) needs to be installed on top of the Internet Information Server (IIS). IPS provides the environment to support the usage of automation servers. It also provides the intrinsic controls listed as follows:

- The Request component is composed of three items within a collection: ServerVariables, QueryString, and Body. The collection can be accessed via

  `<% Request.[ServerVariables¦QueryString¦Body]("variable name") %>`

  The collection name is optional; if it is not provided, the server will search the collection in the following order:

  ServerVariables, QueryString, Body

- The ServerVariables collection supports all HTTP headers by prefixing them with HTTP_ and the variables, including AUTH_TYPE, CONTENT_LENGTH, CONTENT_TYPE, GATEWAY_INTERFACE, PATH_INFO, PATH_TRANSLATED, QUERY_STRING, REMOTE_ADDR, REMOTE_HOST, REMOTE_IDENT, REMOTE_USER, REQUEST_METHOD, SCRIPT_NAME, SERVER_NAME, SERVER_PORT, SERVER_PROTOCOL, and SERVER_SOFTWARE.

  The HTTP headers can be found at http://www.w3.org.

- The QueryString collection provides access to all parameters in the Get method.

- The `Body` collection provides access to all parameters in the `Post` method.
- The Response component exposes methods or properties including `Add(header-value, header-name)`, `AppendToLog(string)`, `Clear`, `Expires`, `Redirect(url)`, `SetCookie(name, value[expires, [domain,[path,[secure,]]]])`, and `Status`.
- The Server component exposes three methods: `HTMLEncode(string)`, `Include(filename)`, and `MapPath(virtual path)`.

Listing 4.19 demonstrates how to use `lst44.dll` on the Web server side so that the user can get the Web server machine name.

Listing 4.19. Use `lst44.dll` on the Web server (`getmachinename.asp` file).

\source\vol3\
chap-04\lst44

```
<% x = server.createobject("lst44.lst44object.1") %>
<% = x.getmachinename %>
machinename.html file
<HTML>
<BODY>
<A HREF="/scripts/machinename.asp"> Get the Server Machine Name</A>
</BODY>
</HTML>
```

In Listing 4.19, `.asp` stands for active server page, which is a designated script file. The extension `.asp` will cause the Web server to invoke the IPS script interpreter. `<% ... %>` indicates that scripting language expressions are to be interpreted. `<% = %>` indicates that the value of the expression will be put into the HTML stream and returned to the client.

In Listing 4.19, `getmachinename.asp` should be placed under the `scripts` directory, and `machinename.html` placed under the `wwwroot` directory. When the `machinename.html` page is launched and the link "Get the Server Machine Name" is clicked, the Web server machine name will be displayed in the browser.

Summary

An OLE automation server is a COM server with the support of the `IDispatch` interface. Applications can use `IDispatch` to access exposed objects in automation servers. A lot of tools can be used to develop the automation servers by using MFC AppWizard, ControlWizard, and Active Template Library. The automation server is a reusable component, which can be used in the automation controller, IE 3.0, and Web server.

5

OLE Controls

by Vincent W. Mayfield

This chapter covers OLE controls. OLE controls, also called OLE Control Extensions, are commonly referred to as OCXs for their file extension, and also as ActiveX controls, which are OLE controls extended for use in Internet applications. A developer can create ActiveX controls for use in Internet applications, and those controls can also be utilized in non-Internet applications. ActiveX controls are a superset of OLE controls. Therefore, throughout this chapter, the terms OLE control, OCX, and ActiveX control are used somewhat interchangeably. (See Figure 5.1.)

If a control is an OLE control, it is not necessarily an ActiveX control. Conversely, though, if a control is an ActiveX control it is also an OLE control. There are some distinct things that make a control an ActiveX control. Not to overtrivialize things, but for all intents and purposes, OLE controls and ActiveX controls are the same except for a few differences. I don't want you to feel that ActiveX controls are some entirely new thing as the marketing types would have us believe. This chapter highlights those differences. Take a look at the origins of the OLE control.

Figure 5.1.
OLE controls, OCXs, and
ActiveX controls are
terms that refer to
similar entities.

A Short History

The term *control*, or *custom control*, has been around since Windows 3.0, when it was first defined. In fact, a custom control was nothing more than a dynamic link library that exported a defined set of functions. Unlike a DLL, a custom control can manipulate properties and handle the firing of events in response to user or programmatic input.

The Visual Basic development environment had caught on in the development community. Custom controls were necessary because developers found they needed better ways to express the user interface of their applications, and many times there was simply no way to perform a complex operation in Visual Basic. Unfortunately (or fortunately, depending on your perspective), these C DLLs had no way of allowing Visual Basic to query the control for information on the properties and methods supported by the control. This made custom controls difficult to use in the Visual Basic development environment.

In 1991, Microsoft unveiled the VBX. The VBX stood for Visual Basic Extension. The idea was that these little reusable software components could be embedded in their containers. To everyone's surprise, VBXs took off like wildfire. Companies cropped up all over the place, developing these little reusable software components. VBXs were able to provide a wide range of functionality, from a simple text label to a complex multimedia or communications control. VBXs were written in C and C++ and provided a wide variety of capabilities that did not exist in a Visual Basic application otherwise. VBXs became extremely popular.

Because VBXs had become popular, demand for them grew within the developer market. Soon developers wanted them for 32-bit applications and even on non-Intel platforms such as the DEC Alpha, RISC, Power PC, and the MIPS. Developers wanted to extend VBXs by using Visual Basic for Applications to connect VBXs with applications such as Access, PowerPoint, Excel, Project, and Word.

Unfortunately, VBXs are severely restricted. They are built on a 16-bit architecture that is not designed as an open interface. They were designed primarily to accommodate the Visual Basic environment. This made VBXs almost impossible to port to a 32-bit environment.

In 1993, OLE 2.0 was released. With the release of OLE 2.0, Microsoft extended the OLE architecture to include OLE controls. OLE controls, unlike their predecessors, the VBX and the custom control, are founded on a binary standard, the Component Object Model. In addition, OLE controls support both 16- and 32-bit architecture.

---

note

Kraig Brockschmidt wrote what is sometimes considered the Bible for OLE programmers. The book is *Inside OLE*, published by Microsoft Press. The original title of the book was *Inside OLE 2.0*, but as you discovered in Chapter 2, "OLE Components," OLE is an ostensibly virtual standard building on each layer. Therefore, in the second edition, the 2.0 was dropped. *Inside OLE* thoroughly explores the OLE standard from the API level. Every OLE programmer should read *Inside OLE*.

Instead of creating an extended architecture for VBXs, Microsoft decided to develop the OCX to offer the benefits of a component architecture to a wider variety of development environments and development tools. (See Figure 5.2.) The Component Object Model and OLE are open architectures, giving them a wider variety of input from the industry. Like their predecessor the VBX, OLE controls are also known by their file extension; OCXs (OLE Control Extension), likewise, have taken the market by storm.

From 1993 to 1995, OLE controls flourished. Many independent software vendors (ISVs) converted their VBXs to OLE controls, and in some cases they maintained three versions: VBX, 16-bit OCX, and 32-bit OCX. The makers of Visual C++ and MFC created the OLE control Developer's Kit, and even incorporated it into Visual C++ 2.0 and 1.5, further adding to the success of OLE custom controls.

Between 1995 and 1996, the Internet took the world like a blitzkrieg, causing Internet mania. Everyone had to become Web-enabled. Companies found themselves making Web sites because they saw the Internet as the great advertisement media for the year 2000 and beyond. Unfortunately, in previous years the Internet had been a relatively static environment. This is due in part to the Internet's roots with the big-iron diehards who grew up with the IBM mainframes, the VAXs, and the UNIX boxes. However, PCs have become household devices for the common person. Users have become accustomed to graphical interaction with their machines, thanks to the Macintosh, Microsoft Windows, and X Window/Motif. Thanks to Sun and their invention of the Java programming language and the Java applet, the Internet is no longer a static environment. Web pages exploded to life with multimedia, sound, and dynamic interaction.

Figure 5.2.
The progression of development of the OLE and ActiveX controls.

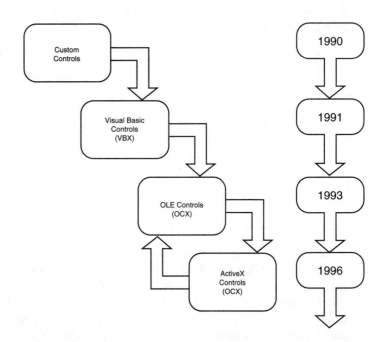

Microsoft, realizing the potential and the hype surrounding the Internet Explosion, decided they needed to get with the program and take a role of leadership in this emerging environment. Microsoft boldly announced they were going to "activate" the Internet in 1996 with ActiveX technologies (a little late, but better late than never). Thus, from these ActiveX technologies, the ActiveX controls were born. ActiveX controls were nothing really new, just an extension of their mother, the OLE control. ActiveX controls are simply OLE controls, intelligently implemented and enhanced to be utilized across the Internet.

What Is an OLE Custom Control?

Now that you know a little of the history behind an OLE control, this section explores just what an OLE control is. An OLE control is an embeddable Component Object Model object that is implemented as an in-process server dynamic link library (DLL). It supports in-place activation as an inside-out object.

> **note**
>
> The title of the book *OLE Controls—Inside Out*, by Adam Denning, Microsoft Press, is a play on words because OLE controls are activated from the inside out. This book is also an excellent reference.

As an OLE In-Proc object, an OLE control is loaded into the address space of its container. As you are probably aware, every WIN32 process has a 4GB address space.

> **note**
>
> A WIN32 process is a running instance of an application loaded into memory.

The lower 2GB is where the application is loaded, and the upper 2GB is where the system is loaded. An OLE control is loaded in the lower 2GB with the application. Therefore, they share the same resources with the application—hence the term in-process.

An OLE control is also a server. Why is it a server? Well, it provides two-way communication between the "container application" and the control. It can also respond to user-initiated events such as mouse movements, keyboard input, and programmatic scripting input—and it can pass that input to the container application for action.

OLE controls are also in-place activated. This means that they can be placed in the active state by the user or the container and edited or manipulated. This is a functionality OLE controls inherit from OLE documents. Like a dynamic link library, the OLE control is a library of functions. In fact, an OLE control might be considered a "super DLL." More than just a "super DLL," an OLE control is a detached object that can fire and respond to events, process messages, has unique properties, and possesses multi-threaded capabilities. OLE controls are also known as OCXs because of their file extension, but they are actually DLLs. OCXs can contain several controls. Unlike DLLs, OCXs respond to user input and support two-way communication or notification between themselves and their containers.

An OLE control can have its own data set and act as an OLE Automation component because you can manipulate its properties and methods. OLE controls can be both 16- and 32-bit as well as Unicode. OLE controls, like OLE Automation objects, can have properties set at both compile time and runtime; OLE controls also have methods that can perform certain operations. The difference between OLE controls and OLE Automation objects is that they are self-contained objects. They provide two-way communication between the control and the container. In addition, OLE controls do not have to have a user interface. As such, they can provide hidden services such as a timer, communications, or mail.

OLE controls cannot stand alone; they must be embedded in an OLE container. OLE controls provide prepackaged components of functionality that are reusable and customizable. OLE controls are at the top of the OLE architecture. Thus, they are built on several OLE technologies. In addition, OLE controls can be used in a wide variety of development tools, such as Delphi, Visual C++, Borland C++, Gupta, Visual Basic, Oracle Developer 2000, and PowerBuilder. OLE controls can also be used in a variety of non-programming environments, such as Microsoft Word, Microsoft Excel, Lotus, HTML, and Internet Explorer. OLE controls are a very powerful reusable component.

OLE Control Architecture

The beauty of OLE controls is that they are programmable and reusable. They expose themselves to the outside world and can be utilized in a variety of programming and non-programming environments. An OLE control is like an OLE Compound Document, but it is extended by using OLE Automation through IDispatch to support properties and methods. What makes OLE controls unique are events. OLE controls have three sets of attributes that are exposed to the outside world:

- Properties
- Methods
- Events

Properties

Properties are named attributes or OLE characteristics of an OLE control. These properties can be set or queried. Some examples of properties are color, font, and number.

Usually, OLE controls provide access to their properties through property sheets. Property sheets are separate OLE Automation entities. This feature is not limited to design/compile time but also can be displayed at runtime to allow the user to manipulate the control's properties, events, or methods. A property sheet is a user interface component that is a tabbed dialog. OLE Automation provides the mechanism by which controls communicate with their property sheets.

OLE controls have what are called stock properties. These are properties common to all OLE controls. If you are using the Base Control Framework provided in the ActiveX SDK or the ActiveX Template Library, you will have to implement the stock properties and their pages yourself. However, if you are using Microsoft Foundation Classes, you can take advantage of these stock properties because they are already built in. These are General (see Figure 5.3), Fonts (see Figure 5.4), Colors (see Figure 5.5), and Pictures stock properties (see Figure 5.6).

Figure 5.3.
A property sheet with the General stock properties.

Figure 5.4.
A property sheet with the Fonts stock properties.

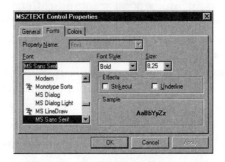

Figure 5.5.
A property sheet with the Colors stock properties.

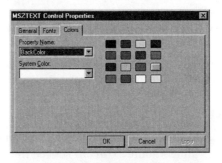

Figure 5.6.
A property sheet with the various Pictures stock properties.

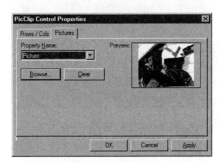

OLE controls also have persistent properties. These properties are stored in the container and set at design or compile time. Controls also have the ability to save persistent information about their properties at runtime, and thus, in effect, can save their state. This means that the controls can also load their persistent properties at initial load time.

Events

Events are notifications triggered by the control in response to some external action on the control. Usually this is some input by the user, such as a mouse click or keyboard input. That event is then communicated to the control's container by the controls. This is done through a communications mechanism known as Lightweight Remote Procedure Call (LRPC). LRPC is the scaled-down brother of the Remote Procedure Call (RPC).

An RPC is an interprocess communications mechanism used to provide two-way communications between applications. This can be on the same computer or between computers across a network. RPC is the mechanism that Network OLE, also known as Distributed COM (DCOM), uses to exchange objects across process and computer boundaries. RPC is much more than just a communications method. It allows a function in a process on one computer to evoke a function in a process on another computer. These can even be computers across an enterprise-wide network or the Internet.

Lightweight Remote Procedure Call, unlike its big brother RPC, is only for communications between processes, or within processes on a single computer. LRPCs are the mechanism by which an OLE control dispatches, through the `IDispatch` interface, through control notifications to the container, and the reverse, from the container to the control. This communication is based on posting messages or events to window handles to transfer data between processes. It is also known as marshaling.

Methods

Methods are functions performed by the control to access the control's functionality. This allows some external source the capability to manipulate the appearance, behavior, or properties of the control. These are actions such as `GetColor`, `SetColor`, `CutToClipBoard`, and `PasteFromClipboard`. Methods are inherited from OLE automation. A method is the interface in which an application or a programmer can set or receive values from an OLE control.

Methods are a lot like member functions in C++. They provide accessor functions that grant access to an OLE control's properties and data. An OLE control's properties are like a C++ class's member variables. Methods are both stock and custom, as are properties. Stock methods provide access to stock properties, such as color, font, and picture. Likewise, custom methods provide access to custom properties. With methods, you can change a control's appearance or initialize it with a value. Using Visual Basic or Visual C++, you can program a link between it and another application or control.

OLE Control Interfaces

Like all other COM objects, OLE controls are manipulated through interfaces. In the original OLE control and OLE container specification, OLE controls were required to support certain interfaces, whether they needed or utilized them or not. This left some controls bloated with code and overhead that they did not need.

Currently, the only interface a control is required to implement is IUnknown. This is mentioned so that you realize that a new standard has been published. In December of 1995, Microsoft published the OLE Controls and OLE Container Guidelines Version 2.0. This was an extension of Version 1.1. With the advent of ActiveX controls, the standard was changed to the 1996 standard for ActiveX controls and ActiveX containers and is again an extension to the previous standard. The next section discusses the specifics of an ActiveX control.

An OLE control exposes interfaces. Likewise, a container exposes interfaces to the OLE control. OLE controls and OLE containers link through interfaces. (See Figure 5.7.)

Figure 5.7.
OLE controls and their
containers communicate
through interfaces using
LRPCs.

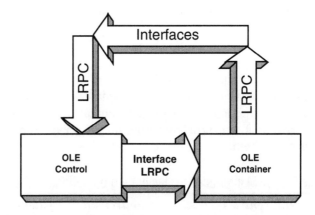

There are approximately 26 interfaces for OLE controls and their containers. The next section on ActiveX controls discusses the new interfaces. This is not considered an all-inclusive list; there are a few other interfaces that are used, but these represent the main interfaces.

In Table 5.1, notice that each object supports IUnknown. This is now the only interface required to be supported by an OLE control. However, if you implemented only IUnknown, you would have a control that did pretty much nothing. The idea is to implement only the interfaces needed to support the control. In Figure 5.8, you can see how an OLE control's interfaces relate to the container interfaces. In addition, when you write the code for your control, you must be cognizant of the interfaces the control supports, as you must also be cognizant that all OLE containers do not support all interfaces. In order to be compatible with as many containers as possible, you must check for the support of your interfaces by the container and degrade your control's functionality gracefully, in the event an interface is not supported. This can be likened to error checking, except that you still want your control to function, but with degraded capability or through an alternative interface.

Figure 5.8.
How the OLE control interfaces relate to the OLE container interfaces.

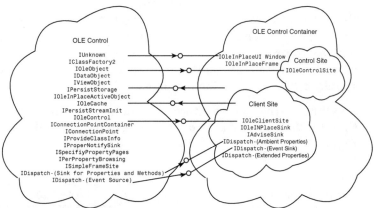

The most important interfaces are IOleControl and IDispatch. IDispatch is the mechanism through which OLE controls communicate. IOleControl encapsulates the basic functionality of an OLE control. Table 5.1 shows the COM interfaces an OLE control or an OLE container may support in order to facilitate the operations between them.

Table 5.1. COM interfaces for facilitating operations between controls and containers.

OLE control	Control site	Client site	Container
IClassFactory2	IOleControlSite	IOleClientSite	IOleInPlaceUIWindow
IOleObject	IUnknown	IOleInPlaceSite	IOleInPlaceFrame
IDataObject		IAdviseSink	IUnknown
IViewObject		IDispatch	

OLE control	Control site	Client site	Container
IPersistStorage		IUnknown	
IOleInPlaceActiveObject			
IOleCache			
IPersistStreamInit			
IOleControl			
IConnect tContainer			
IConnectionPoint			
IProvideClassInfo			
IProperNotifySink			
ISpecifyPropertyPages			
IPerPropertyBrowsing			
ISimpleFrameSite			
IDispatch			
IUnknown			

The important thing to remember is that the interfaces and control supports define that control. However, you should implement only the interfaces your control needs in order to function. This idea will become more apparent in the following section, "ActiveX Controls."

ActiveX Controls

An ActiveX control is a superset of an OLE control that has been extended for the Internet environment. This does not mean that ActiveX controls can be utilized only in the Internet environment; quite the contrary, they can be utilized in any container that can support their interfaces. ActiveX controls must still be embedded in a container application. When an end user encounters a page with an ActiveX control, that control is downloaded to the client machine if it is not already there and used. This is, of course, provided that the user's browser supports ActiveX controls. The two most prevalent browsers that support ActiveX controls are Microsoft Internet Explorer and Netscape Navigator, with the help of the NCompass plug-in.

The major difference between the OLE control and the "superset" ActiveX control is that the standard is different. In the new standard an ActiveX control must support at least the IUnknown interface and be self-registering. It is a simple COM object. The control must have more interfaces than just IUnknown, or it would have no functionality. The idea is that the control should support only the interfaces it needs, so it can be as lightweight as possible. In contrast, in the previous standard, an OLE control was required to support a whole armada of COM interfaces, whether the control needed them or not. This made some controls bloated with code that was not utilized or needed. In the world of Internet development, this code bloat is unacceptable.

Supporting IUnknown

The minimum interface for an ActiveX control to support is IUnknown. As already discussed, IUnknown is an interface that supports three methods; QueryInterface, AddRef, and Release.

All COM interfaces are inherited either directly or indirectly from IUnknown; hence, all other interfaces have these three functions also. With a pointer to IUnknown, a client can get a pointer to other interfaces the object supports through QueryInterface. In short, an object can use QueryInterface to find out the capabilities of another object. If the object supports the interface, it returns a pointer to the interface. Listing 5.1 demonstrates the use of the pointer to a control's IUnknown interface to QueryInterface to find out the class information using MFC.

Listing 5.1. The use of the pointer to a control's **IUnknown** interface and then utilizing **QueryInterface** to get the class information.

```
 1:   // Function to get a pointer to a control's IUnknown and use
 2:   // QueryInterface to see if it supports the interface.
 3:   int MyClass::DoControlWork()
 4:   {
 5:       LPUNKNOWN lpUnknown;
 6:       LPPPROVIDECLASSINFO lpClassInfo;
 7:
 8:    lpUnknown = GetControlUnknown();
 9:
10:       if(lpUnknown == NULL)
11:       {
12:           // return my error code to let me know IUnknown was NULL
13:           return ERROR_CODE_IUNKNOWN_NULL;
14:       }
15:       else
16:       {
17:           if(SUCCEEDED(lpUnknown->QueryInterface(IID_IProvideClassInfo,
18:                                                   (void**) &lpClassInfo)))
19:           {
20:               // QueryInterface Returned a Succeeded so this
21:               // Interface is Supported
22:               // {
23:               //          Perform some function with lpClassInfo such as
24:               // getting the class info and examining the class attributes
25:               // {
26:
```

```
27:                    lpClassInfo->Release();
28:            }
29:            else
30:            {
31:                    // Control Does Not Support Interface
32:                    return ERROR_INTERFACE_NOT_SUPPORTED;
33:            }
34:        }
35:        return SUCCESSFUL;
36:    }
```

In addition, the object can manage its own lifetime through the AddRef and Release functions. If an object obtains a pointer to an object, AddRef is called, incrementing the object's reference count. Once an object no longer needs the pointer to the interface, Release is called, decrementing the object's reference count. Once the reference count reaches zero, an object can safely destroy itself.

Although IUnknown must be implemented, you should also take a look at the other interfaces that an ActiveX control might want to implement. Table 5.2 shows the potential COM interfaces that an ActiveX control may want to support.

In addition, the control might want to implement its own custom interfaces. By implementing only the interfaces it needs, the ActiveX control can be as lean as possible. The previous OLE control standard required that in order to be compliant with the standard, the control had to implement certain interfaces. With ActiveX controls, this is no longer the case; you are only required to implement IUnknown.

Table 5.2. The potential COM interfaces for an ActiveX control.

Interface	Purpose
IOleObject	Principal mechanism by which a control communicates with its container.
IOleInPlaceObject	Means by which activation and deactivation of an object is managed.
IOleInPlaceActiveObject	Provides communication between an in-place active object and the outermost windows of the container.
IOleControl	Allows support for keyboard mnemonics, properties, and events.
IDataObject	Allows for the transfer of data and the communication of changes in the data.
IViewObject	Allows the object to display itself.

continues

Table 5.2. continued

Interface	Purpose
IViewObject2	An extension of the IViewObject interface. It allows you to find the size of the object in a given view.
IDispatch	An interface that can call virtually any other COM interface. It is used in OLE Automation to evoke late binding to properties and methods of COM objects.
IConnectionPointContainer	Supports connection points for connectable objects.
IProvideClassInfo	Encapsulates a single method by which to get all of the information about an object's co-class entry in its type library.
IProvideClassInfo2	An extension to the IProvideClassInfo interface to provide quick access to an object's IID for its event set.
ISpecifyPropertyPages	An interface that denotes an object as supporting property pages.
IPerPropertyBrowsing	Supports methods to get access to the information in the property pages supported by an object.
IPersistStream	Provides methods for loading and storing simple streams.
IPersistStreamInit	Designed as a replacement for IPersistStream. Adds an initialization method InitNew.
IPersistMemory	Allows the method to access a fixed-sized memory block for an IPersistStream object.
IPersistStorage	Supports the manipulation of storage objects to include loading, saving, and exchanging.
IPersistMoniker	An interface to expose to asynchronous objects the ability to manipulate the way they bind data to the object.
IPersistPropertyBag	Allows the storage of persistent properties.
IOleCache	An interface to control access to the cache inside an object.
IOleCache2	An interface that allows the selective update of an object's cache.

Interface	Purpose
IExternalConnection	An interface that allows the tracking of external locking on an embedded object.
IRunnableObject	An interface that enables a container to control its executable objects.

Be Self-Registering

In order for an ActiveX control, or any other COM object, to be utilized, it must be registered in the System Registry. The System Registry is a database of configuration information divided into a hierarchical tree. This tree consists of three levels of information: Hives, Keys, and Values. The System Registry is a centralized place where you can go to find out information about an object. (See Figure 5.9.)

Figure 5.9.
The Windows 95 System Registry as seen through the regedit *program.*

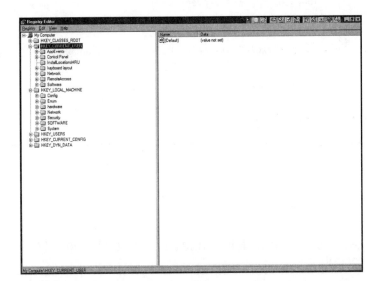

note

The System Registry in Windows 95 can be viewed through a program called regedit.exe. This program can be found in the \WINDOWS directory of Windows 95 and the \WINNT\SYSTEM32 directory in Windows NT 4.0. If you are using Windows NT 3.51, the System Registry can be viewed with a program called regedit32.exe, which is found in the same directory as specified for Windows NT 4.0 above.

If the control is not registered in the Registry, it is unknown, and therefore unusable, by the system.

Thus, it is a requirement for ActiveX controls to be self-registering. This means an ActiveX control must implement and export the functions DllRegisterServer and DllUnregisterServer. In addition, it is a requirement for ActiveX controls to register all of the standard Registry entries for Automation servers and embeddable objects. Listing 5.2 demonstrates the use of DllRegisterServer to support self-registration of the control using MFC. This code is generated for you by Visual C++'s ControlWizard.

Listing 5.2. Using the `DllRegisterServer` to support self-registration of the control.

```
1:  //////////////////////////////////////////////////////////////////////
2:  // DllRegisterServer - Adds entries to the system registry
3:
4:  STDAPI DllRegisterServer(void)
5:  {
6:      AFX_MANAGE_STATE(_afxModuleAddrThis);
7:
8:      if (!AfxOleRegisterTypeLib(AfxGetInstanceHandle(), _tlid))
9:          return ResultFromScode(SELFREG_E_TYPELIB);
10:
11:     if (!COleObjectFactoryEx::UpdateRegistryAll(TRUE))
12:         return ResultFromScode(SELFREG_E_CLASS);
13:
14:     return NOERROR;
15: }
```

Listing 5.3 demonstrates the use of DllUnregisterServer to support self-unregistration of a control using MFC. This code is generated for you by Visual C++'s ControlWizard.

Listing 5.3. Using `DllUnregisterServer` to support self-unregistration of a control.

```
1:  //////////////////////////////////////////////////////////////////////
2:  // DllUnregisterServer - Removes entries from the system registry
3:
4:  STDAPI DllUnregisterServer(void)
5:  {
6:      AFX_MANAGE_STATE(_afxModuleAddrThis);
7:
8:      if (!AfxOleUnregisterTypeLib(_tlid))
9:          return ResultFromScode(SELFREG_E_TYPELIB);
10:
11:     if (!COleObjectFactoryEx::UpdateRegistryAll(FALSE))
12:         return ResultFromScode(SELFREG_E_CLASS);
13:
14:     return NOERROR;
16: }
```

Listings 5.2 and 5.3 show how you support registration and unregistration, and Listing 5.4 shows how you register your control and its capabilities. Notice in line 15 of Listing 5.4 the variable dwMyControlOleMisc. It contains the status bits of your control. This is very important because it contains the capabilities of your control. These capabilities can be looked up in the System Registry to find out what capabilities your control contains, without instantiating the object.

Listing 5.4. How to register your control and your controls capabilities in MFC.

```
 1:  ////////////////////////////////////////////////////////////////////
 2:  // CMyCtrl::CMyCtrlFactory::UpdateRegistry -
 3:  // Adds or removes system registry entries for CMyCtrl
 4:  BOOL CMyCtrl::CMyCtrlFactory::UpdateRegistry(BOOL bRegister)
 5:  {
 6:       if (bRegister)
 7:            return AfxOleRegisterControlClass(
 8:               AfxGetInstanceHandle(),
 9:               m_clsid,           // Records the Object's CLSID
10:               m_lpszProgID,      // Records a Unique Program ID for MyControl
11:               IDS_MYCONTROL,     // Records a Human Readable Name of MyControl
12:               IDB_MYCONTROL,     // Recordes the Bitmap to Represent MyControl
13:               TRUE,              // Records that MyControl can be insertable
14:                                  // in a Container's Insert Object Dialog
15:               dwMyControlOleMisc, // Records the Status bits of MyControl
16:               tlid,              // Records the Unique ID of the MyControls
17:                                  // Control Class
18:               wVerMajor,         // Records the Major Version of MyControl
19:               wVerMinor);        // Recorde the Minor Version of MyControl
20:       else
21:            return AfxOleUnregisterClass(m_clsid, m_lpszProgID);
22:  }
```

The possible status bits that can be set for a control are shown in Table 5.3. These bits identify the capabilities of the control. Take a moment to become familiar with them.

Table 5.3. The OLE miscellaneous status bits symbolic constants and what they mean to controls and objects.

Symbolic constant	Meaning
OLEMISC_RECOMPOSEONRESIZE	Identifies an object that upon re-sizing by the container will rescale its presentation data.
OLEMISC_ONLYICONIC	Identifies an object that exists only in the iconic state.

continues

Table 5.3. continued

Symbolic constant	Meaning
OLEMISC_INSERTNOTREPLACE	Identifies an object that initializes itself from the currently selected container data.
OLEMISC_STATIC	Identifies an object that is static and contains no native data, only presentation data.
OLEMISC_CANTLINKINSIDE	Identifies items such as OLE 1.0 objects, static objects, and links. None of these objects can be a linked source that when bound runs to another object.
OLEMISC_CANLINKBYOLE1	Identifies an object that can be linked by the containers that conform to OLE 1.0 specification.
OLEMISC_ISLINKOBJECT	Identifies an object that is a linked object. This is important only for OLE 1.0 objects.
OLEMISC_INSIDEOUT	Identifies an object that can be in-place activated without the need for toolbars or menus.
OLEMISC_ACTIVATEWHENVISIBLE	Identifies an object that can only be activated in the visible state. The OLEMISC_INSIDEOUT flag must also be set.
OLEMISC_RENDERINGISDEVICEINDEPENDENT	This flag specifies that the object's presentation data will remain the same regardless of the target container.
OLEMISC_INVISIBLEATRUNTIME	Identifies controls that are invisible at runtime, such as Internet Explorer's Timer control or Internet Explorer's Preloader control.
OLEMISC_ALWAYSRUN	Tells a control that a control should be set in the running state even when not visible.

Symbolic constant	Meaning
OLEMISC_ACTSLIKEBUTTON	Identifies controls that can act like buttons.
OLEMISC_ACTSLIKELABEL	Identifies controls that can change the label provided by the container.
OLEMISC_NOUIACTIVATE	Identifies whether a control supports user-interface activation.
OLEMISC_ALIGNABLE	Specifies that a control may be aligned with other controls for containers that support control alignment.
OLEMISC_SIMPLEFRAME	Specifies that the control supports the ISimpleFrameSite interface.
OLEMISC_SETCLIENTSITEFIRST	In the new OLE container specification, this flag identifies controls that support the SetClientSide function being called after the control is created but before it is displayed.
OLEMISC_IMEMODE	In the double-byte, character-set versions of Windows, specifies that the control supports the Input Method Editor Mode, for internationalized controls.

These miscellaneous status bits are especially important when used in conjunction with component categories as an accurate picture of what a control can or cannot do. This picture of what the control can do can be obtained from the System Registry.

Component Categories

Previously, in order to be registered on the system, an OLE control was registered through entries in the Registry with the Control keyword. To your benefit, controls can be utilized for multiple purposes. Therefore, a way was needed to identify a control's functionality, as opposed to just listing the interfaces it supports. This is where component categories come in.

Component categories are a way of describing what a control does. They provide a better method for containers to find out what a control does without creating it and having to query for its methods using an IUnknown pointer and QueryInterface. Creating a control object involves a lot of overhead. A container would not want to create a control if the container itself does not support the functionality the control requires.

Component categories are not specific to ActiveX but are an extension of the OLE architecture. Each component category has its own GUID (globally unique identifier) and a human-readable name stored in a well-known place in the System Registry. When a control registers itself, it does so using its component category ID. In addition, it also registers the component categories it supports and the component categories it requires its container to support.

For backward compatibility, the control should also register itself with the Control keyword for containers that do not support the new component categories. The control should also register the key ToolBoxBitmap32. This key identifies the module name and resource ID for a 16×15 bitmap. ToolBoxBitmap32 provides a bitmap to use for the face of a toolbar or toolbox button in the container application. If a control can be inserted in a compound document, it should also register the Insertable key.

Component categories can be mixed and matched, depending on their type. Microsoft maintains a list of component categories. Any categories that are new should be submitted to Microsoft for inclusion in the list. This promotes interoperability. The following component categories have been identified:

- Simple Frame Site Containment
- Simple Data Binding
- Advanced Data Binding
- Visual Basic Private Interfaces
- Internet-Aware Controls
- Windowless Controls

Simple Frame Site Containment

A Simple Frame Site container control is a control that contains other controls, for example a 3D group box that contains a group of check boxes. The GUID for this component category is

```
CATID - {157083E0-2368-11cf-87B9-00AA006C8166} CATID_SimpleFrameControl.
```

In order to support a Simple Frame Site container, the OLE container application must implement the ISimpleFrameSite interface, and the control must have its status bit set to OLEMISC_SIMPLEFRAME.

Simple Data Binding

A control or container that supports simple data binding also supports the IPropertyNotifySink interface. Data binding is how controls affiliate their persistent properties and how containers exchange property changes from their user interface to the control's persistent properties. This allows the persistent storage of their properties and at runtime binds the data to the control synchronizing property changes between the control and the container. The GUID for this component category is

```
CATID - {157083E1-2368-11cf-87B9-00AA006C8166} CATID_PropertyNotifyControl.
```

> **note**
>
> Although a control that supports simple data binding is meant to provide binding to a datasource, such binding should not be required for the functionality of the control. Even though a lot of the functionality the control has is lost, that control should degrade gracefully and still be able to function, although potentially limited, independent of any data binding.

Advanced Data Binding

Advanced data binding is similar to simple data binding except that it supports more advanced binding techniques, such as asynchronous binding and Visual Basic data binding. The GUID for this component category is

```
CATID - {157083E2-2368-11cf-87B9-00AA006C8166} CATID_VBDataBound.
```

Visual Basic Private Interfaces

These component categories are for components that specifically support the Visual Basic environment. Controls or containers might want to support alternative methods in case a container encounters a control, or a control encounters a container that does not support the Visual Basic private interfaces. The GUID for this component category is

```
CATID - {02496840-3AC4-11cf-87B9-00AA006C8166} CATID_VBFormat,
```

if the container implements the IBVFormat interface for data formatting to specifically integrate with Visual Basic or

```
CATID - {02496841-3AC4-11cf-87B9-00AA006C8166} CATID_VBGetControl
```

if the container implements IVBGetControl so that controls can enumerate other controls on a Visual Basic form.

Internet-Aware Controls

Internet-aware controls implement one or more persistent interfaces to support operation across the Internet. All these categories provide persistent storage operations. The following are GUIDs for components that fall into this category:

- CATID - {0de86a50-2baa-11cf-a229-00aa003d7352} CATID_RequiresDataPathHost
- CATID - {0de86a51-2baa-11cf-a229-00aa003d7352} CATID_PersistsToMoniker
- CATID - {0de86a52-2baa-11cf-a229-00aa003d7352} CATID_PersistsToStorage
- CATID - {0de86a53-2baa-11cf-a229-00aa003d7352} CATID_PersistsToStreamInit
- CATID - {0de86a54-2baa-11cf-a229-00aa003d7352} CATID_PersistsToStream
- CATID - {0de86a55-2baa-11cf-a229-00aa003d7352} CATID_PersistsToMemory
- CATID - {0de86a56-2baa-11cf-a229-00aa003d7352} CATID_PersistsToFile
- CATID - {0de86a57-2baa-11cf-a229-00aa003d7352} CATID_PersistsToPropertyBag

The RequiresDataPathHost category means that the object requires the container to support the IBindHost interface because the object requires the capability of saving data to one or more paths.

All of the rest of the categories listed above are mutually exclusive. They are used when an object supports only a single persistence method. If a container does not support a persistence method that a control supports, the container should not allow itself to create controls of that type.

Windowless Controls

Windowless controls are controls that do not implement their own windows and rely on the use of their container's window to draw themselves. These types of controls are non-rectangular controls such as arrow buttons, gauges, and other items modeled after real-world objects. In addition, this includes transparent controls. The GUID for this component category is

```
CATID - {1D06B600-3AE3-11cf-87B9-00AA006C8166} CATID_WindowlessObject
```

Component Categories and Interoperability

Components that do not support a category should degrade gracefully. In a case in which a control or container is unable to support an interface, the control should either clearly document that a particular interface is required for the proper operation of the component or at runtime notify the user of the component's degraded capability.

By using self-registration, components can be self-contained, which is necessary for Internet operations. By using `DllRegisterServer` and `DllUnregisterServer` and the component categories API functions to register itself and the component categories it supports, a control can further its interoperability in a variety of environments.

Code Signing

In the Internet environment, users must download components to their local machines and utilize them. This creates an extreme hazard to the local machine by allowing the implementation of this foreign code.

This is where a new security measure called code signing comes in. Browsers typically warn users that they are downloading a potentially unsafe object; however, it does not physically check the code for authenticity to ensure the object has not been tampered with nor does the browser verify the object's source.

Microsoft has implemented Authenticode, which embodies the Crypto API. This allows developers to digitally sign their code so that it can be checked and verified at runtime. This function is built into the browser and displays a certificate of authenticity (see Figure 5.10) if the control is verified.

Figure 5.10.
The certificate the user is shown at runtime after the code has been authenticated.

Currently, the code signing specification and the certification process are being reviewed by the World Wide Web Consortium (W3C) and the current specifications are subject to change. Internet Explorer and all Microsoft controls naturally support code signing and Authenticode, but as of yet Netscape does not. Netscape has gone to W3C with a proposal to extend its own "digital certificate" standard. In the spirit of cooperation, Netscape eventually will support the code signing specification, or at a minimum Microsoft will embrace both standards.

Code signing works with DLLs, EXEs, CABs, and OCXs. When a developer creates these items, they receive a digital certificate from an independent certification authority. It then runs a one-way hash on the code and produces a digest that has a fixed length. Next, the developer encrypts the digest using a private key. This combination of an encrypted digest coupled with the developer's certificate and credentials is a signature block unique for the item and the developer. This signature block is embedded into the executable program.

Here's the way code signing works on the client machine. When a user downloads a control, for example, from the Internet, the browser application such as Internet Explorer or Netscape Navigator calls a Win32 API function called WinVerifyTrust.

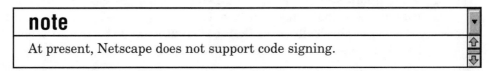

note

At present, Netscape does not support code signing.

WinVerifyTrust then reads the signature block. With the signature block, the WinVerifyTrust can authenticate the certificate and decrypts the digest using the developer's public key. Using the public key, the function then rehashes the code with the hash function stored in the signature block and creates a second digest. This digest is then compared with the original. If they do not match, this indicates tampering and the user is warned (see Figure 5.11). On the contrary, if the digest had matched, instead of the warning in Figure 5.11, the user would have gotten the certificate of authenticity shown in Figure 5.10.

Figure 5.11.

The warning the user is shown at runtime to tell the user of a potential danger because the code cannot be authenticated.

Despite code signing, the user is in control and may choose to heed or ignore the warning. If the hashes check out, then a certificate is displayed by the browser.

The code signing mechanism provides some security for end users and developers alike. It is a deterrent to malicious tampering with executable code for the intent of information warfare such as viruses, and it is also a deterrent for those who might pirate the code developed by others. Please be aware again that this is a proposed standard and has not yet been officially accepted, although there is nothing I can see at this time that can compete with it. It is safe to say that no matter what, Microsoft will continue to support it and, in addition, continue to refine it. The bottom line is that you will need to continue to monitor the standard.

Performance Considerations

ActiveX controls are designed to work across the Internet. As such, they are Internet-aware. Unfortunately, the Internet is low-bandwidth and highly subject to server latency. This means that ActiveX controls must be lean and mean or, to put it more plainly, highly optimized. Because ActiveX controls implement only the interfaces they need, they are already partially optimized. ActiveX controls are optimized to perform specific tasks. However, there are several things you can do to help optimize your controls:

- Optimize control drawing.
- Don't always activate when visible.
- Provide flicker-free activation.
- Provide windowless activation.
- Optimize persistence and initialization.
- Use windowless controls.
- Use a device context that is unclipped.
- While the control is inactive, provide mouse interaction.

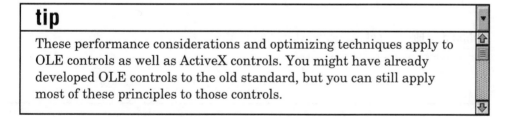

tip

These performance considerations and optimizing techniques apply to OLE controls as well as ActiveX controls. You might have already developed OLE controls to the old standard, but you can still apply most of these principles to those controls.

Optimize Control Drawing

When you draw items, you have to select items such as pens, brushes, and fonts into the device context to render an object on the screen. Selecting these into the device context requires time and is a waste of resources when the container has multiple controls that are selecting and deselecting the same resources every time they paint. The container can support optimized drawing. This means that the container handles the restoration of the original objects after all the items have been drawn. IViewObject::Draw supports optimized drawing by using the DVASPECTINFOFLAG flags set in the DVASPECTINFO structure. You must use this to determine whether your container supports optimized drawing when implementing API functions. MFC encapsulates this check for you in the COleControl::IsOptimizedDraw function. You can then optimize how you draw your code by storing your GDI objects as member variables instead of local variables. This prevents them from being destroyed when the drawing function finishes. Then, if the container supports optimized drawing, you do not need to select the objects back because the container has taken care of this for you.

Don't Always Activate When Visible

If your control has a window, it might not need to be activated when visible. Creating a window is a control's single biggest operation and therefore should not be done until it is absolutely necessary. Therefore, if there is no reason for your control to be activated when visible, you should turn off the OLEMISC_ACTIVATEWHENVISIBLE miscellaneous status bit.

Provide Flicker-Free Activation

When your control has a window, it must sometimes transition from the active to the inactive state. There is a visual flicker that occurs when the control redraws from the active to the inactive state. Flicker can be eliminated by two methods: drawing off-screen and copying to the screen in one big chunk, and drawing front to back. The IViewObjectEx API function provides the necessary functions to use either method or a combination of both. With MFC, the implementation is much simpler. (See Listing 5.5.)

Listing 5.5. How to set the windowless flag in MFC.

```
1:   DWORD CMyControl::GetControlFlags()
2:   {
3:       return COleControl::GetControlFlags() | noFlickerActivate;
4:   }
```

Optimize Persistence and Initialization

Optimizing persistence and initialization means basically one thing: Keep your code as lean as possible. Because of the cheapness of hard drive space and memory, some programmers have gotten lazy in the creation of this code and allowed it to become bloated and slow. With Internet applications, this is a death sentence. Most people access the Internet with 14.4 modems. A megabyte of data takes almost nine minutes on a 14.4 modem. Users will get impatient if they have to wait long periods of time. What can you do? You can do several things.

First of all, make sure you do not leave any non-utilized blocks of code or variables. You should also take any debugging or testing blocks out of your code. For example, you have written your code so a message box displays when you reach a certain segment of code. Take it out! It only adds to your code size. However, if you delimit your debugging blocks of code using the preprocessor `#ifdef _DEBUG` and `#endif`, you will not have to worry about the code being included in the release builds, because the debugging blocks of code will be left out of the compile.

Second, today's compilers have optimizing options on them. In the past, these optimizing compilers were not very efficient and sometimes introduced bugs in an application that had already been tested. But compilers have gotten much better. Use them! Let the compiler do some of the work for you. You might have to tweak and play with the optimizations to find the best combination of options.

---

warning

Make sure you perform your compiler optimizations before you send your code to testing. However, any time you touch the code, it should go back through testing. Therefore, if you should have to tweak the compiler optimizations after it has been through testing, make sure you send it back through testing! This can help prevent discovering a bug after release.

You should also turn off the incremental linking option on your compiler when you do a release build. Incremental linking can add serious bloat to your code.

---

note

For an excellent article on keeping your code small, see "Removing Fatty Deposits from Your Applications Using This 32-bit Liposuction Tool," by Matt Pietrek in *Microsoft Systems Journal*, October 1996, Vol. 11, No. 10. Matt Pietrek has many useful suggestions and even provides a nice tool to assist you.

The last thing you should take into account is utilizing asynchronous operations to perform initialization and persistence operations. Asynchronous downloading gives the user the illusion that things are occurring faster than they are. In addition, you might want to give the user other visual cues that progress is being made, such as a progress indicator or a message box. However, you will have to weigh the performance issues associated with their addition.

Use Windowless Controls

You should consider making your control a windowless control if appropriate. Creating a window is a control's single biggest operation, taking almost two-thirds of its creation time. This is a lot of unnecessary overhead for the control. Most of the time, a control does not need a window and can utilize its container's window and allow the container to take on the overhead of maintaining that window. This will allow you to model your controls after real-world objects, such as gauges, knobs, and other non-rectangular items.

By using the API function `IOleInPlaceSiteEx::OnInPlaceActivateEx` and setting the `ACTIVATE_WINDOWLESS` flag, your control is in the windowless mode. With MFC, you can do the following:

```
DWORD CMyControl::GetControlFlags()
{
    return COleControl::GetControlFlags() | windowlessActivate;
}
```

In addition, there is a whole series of API functions that allow you to manipulate windowless controls. MFC has encapsulated many of these functions for you also. The books online in Visual C++ have a complete reference for these functions. In addition, the Win 32 API references have the API level functions.

Use a Device Context that Is Unclipped

If you have a window and you are sure your control does not draw outside of that window, you can disable the clipping in your drawing of the control. This can yield a small performance gain by not clipping the device context. With MFC, you can do the following to remove the `clipPaintDC` flag:

```
DWORD CMyControl::GetControlFlags()
{
    return COleControl::GetControlFlags() & ~clipPaintDC;
}
```

> **note**
>
> The `clipPaintDC` flag has no effect if you have set your control as windowless.

With the API functions in the ActiveX SDK, you can implement the IViewObject, IViewObject2, and IViewObjectEx interfaces to optimize your drawing code so you do not clip the device context.

While Control Is Inactive, Provide Mouse Interaction

You can set your control to inactive, because it does not always need to be activated when visible. You might still want your control to process mouse messages such as WM_MOUSEMOVE and WM_SETCURSOR. You will need to implement the IPointerInactive interface to allow you to process the mouse messages. If you are using MFC, you need to implement only the following function, because the framework handles the rest for you.

```
DWORD CMyControl::GetControlFlags()
{
    return COleControl::GetControlFlages() ¦ pointerInactivate;
}
```

However, you will need to override the OLEMISC_ACTIVATEWHENVISIBLE miscellaneous status bit with OLEMISC_IGNOREACTIVATEWHENVISIBLE. This is because the OLEMISC_ACTIVATEWHENVISIBLE forces the control to always be activated when visible. You have to do this to prevent the flag from taking effect for containers that do not support the IPointerInactive interface.

Reinventing the Wheel

In today's software development environment, software engineers are not only designers and programmers, but increasingly, are taking on the role of component integrators. End users demand that their software be developed quickly, be rich in features, and integrate with the rest of the software they use. With the advent of OLE, CORBA, and OpenDoc, you now have hundreds of thousands of reusable components and objects to choose from. There is an abundance of dynamic link libraries, controls, automation components, and document objects at your fingertips. OLE controls especially provide an off-the-shelf self-contained reusable package of functionality, created by someone else. OLE controls provide functionality of all types, such as multimedia, communications, user interface components, report writing, and computational. (See Figure 5.12.)

This is functionality that you do not have to create. The major key to component integration is to be able to integrate all of the components with a custom application so that they work in single harmonious union, as if they were native to the application.

Figure 5.12.
*One of the numerous
OLE/ActiveX controls
available.*

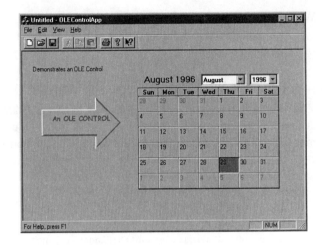

However, before you embark on creating this application, you should take care not to "reinvent the wheel." OLE/ActiveX controls, the Component Object Model, and the object-oriented paradigm present a unique opportunity for you to truly have code reuse. In order to achieve this nirvana of code reuse, you should evaluate what components are already out there. Likewise, before you decide to write your own OLE controls, you should take a look at what is already out there and see if you can utilize what is already available, as opposed to reinventing the wheel.

When you choose to utilize off-the-shelf components, there are a few things you should consider. How long has the manufacturer been in business? does the company supply the source code with the component? (The source code would come in handy if the manufacturer went out of business or had a bug in its component that it was not going to fix.) What are the licensing fees and distribution costs? Is the company Web-enabled? What kind of support and money-back guarantee does the manufacturer provide? What tools will the component be supported in?

Resolving these questions can save you a lot of heartache later. Integration of these off-the-shelf components is sometimes tricky. Make sure you thoroughly research the components you choose.

Internet Explorer Stock Controls

So that you do not go out and reinvent the wheel, it is important to note that there are several controls that come as stock items with Internet Explorer. You can utilize these controls in your Web pages and in your application development efforts. These controls provide a variety of functionality. The following ActiveX controls come with Internet Explorer.

- Animated button control
- Chart control
- Gradient control
- Label control
- Marquee control
- Menu control
- Popup menu control
- Popup window control
- Preloader control
- Stock ticker control
- Timer control
- View tracker control

> **note**
>
> A demo of the functionality of each of these controls is available on the Microsoft World Wide Web site at the following Internet URL: http://www.microsoft.com/activex/gallery/default.htm. In addition, a number of other third-party vendors have their controls demonstrated at the same Microsoft WWW site.

Animated Button

The Animated Button ActiveX control displays frame sequences of an AVI file using the Microsoft Windows Animation common control, based on the state of the button.

Chart

The Chart ActiveX control allows you to display a variety of charts, such as bar charts, pie charts, and graphs.

Gradient

The Gradient ActiveX control allows you to display a gradient of one palettized color to another, gradually fading the pixels from one color to another.

Label

The Label ActiveX control allows you to display text at various angles, sizes, and colors. It will even allow you to display text around a user-defined curve.

Marquee

The Marquee ActiveX control allows you to have scrolling, bouncing, or sliding text and URLs within a window, much like the old cinema marquees.

Menu

The Menu ActiveX control allows you to embed menu button or pull-down menu functionality in your Web page.

Popup Menu

The Popup Menu ActiveX control allows you to embed a popup menu in your Web page. This control sends a Click event when the user selects a menu item.

Popup Window

The Popup Window control enables you to display a specified HTML document in a popup window. In addition, this control can be used to provide tooltips or preview links.

Preloader

The Preloader ActiveX control holds the position of a URL and stores it in cache. Once it is activated, it downloads asynchronously in the background the item pointed to by the URL. This control is not visible at runtime.

Stock Ticker

The Stock Ticker ActiveX control acts just like a stock ticker and displays data across the screen at a set speed. It utilizes text files or XRT files that are downloaded asynchronously at specified intervals.

Timer

The Timer ActiveX control fires an event periodically at a set time interval. The timer control is invisible at runtime.

View Tracker

The View Tracker ActiveX control fires OnShow and OnHide events, based on whether the control is in or out of the viewable area of the screen.

As you can see, there are several controls provided in Internet Explorer that have a lot of useful capability built into them. Be aware of what is already out there, and it might save you development time when every minute counts.

Displaying a Control in a Web Page

In order to "activate the Internet" with ActiveX controls, as the Microsoft marketing folks are fond of saying, you need a way of embedding those ActiveX controls in an HTML file.

The World Wide Web Consortium (W3C) controls the HTML standard. The current HTML standard is Version 3.2. Like most standards, it is continually updated and modified as technology progresses. As the standard progresses, the controlling agency tries to ensure backward compatibility. This is so that any HTML browser that does not yet support the newest standard will degrade gracefully and allow the HTML to be viewed.

> **note**
>
> The current World Wide Web Consortium (W3C) HTML standard is available at the following URL: http://www.w3.org/pub/WWW/.

The <OBJECT> HTML tag is used to allow the insertion of dynamic content, such as ActiveX controls in the Web page. The tag is just a way of identifying such dynamic elements. It is up to the browser to parse the HTML tags and perform the appropriate action based on the meaning of the tag. In Listing 5.6, you can see the HTML syntax for the <OBJECT> tag. This syntax comes directly from the World Wide Web Consortium (W3C) controls HTML standard Version 3.2.

Listing 5.6. The HTML syntax for the <OBJECT> tag.

```
 1:  <OBJECT
 2:      ALIGN= alignment type
 3:      BORDER= number
 4:      CLASSID= universal resource locator
 5:      CODEBASE= universal resource locator
 6:      CODETYPE= codetype
 7:      DATA= universal resource locator
 8:      DECLARE
 9:      HEIGHT= number
10:      HSPACE= value
11:      NAME= universal resource locator
12:      SHAPES
13:      STANDBY= message
14:      TYPE= type
15:      USEMAP= universal resource locator
16:      VSPACE= number
17:      WIDTH= number
18:  </OBJECT>
```

By utilizing the <OBJECT> tag, you can insert an object such as an image, document, applet, or control into the HTML document.

Table 5.4 shows the acceptable range of values to be utilized by the parameters of the <OBJECT> tag.

Table 5.4. The values for the parameters of the <OBJECT> tag.

Parameter	Values
ALIGN= alignment type	Sets the alignment for the object. The alignment type is one of the following values: BASELINE, LEFT, MIDDLE, CENTER, RIGHT, TEXTMIDDLE, TEXTTOP, and TEXTBOTTOM.
BORDER= number	Specifies the width of the border if the object is defined to be a hyperlink.
CLASSID= universal resource locator	Identifies the object implementation. The syntax of the universal resource locator depends on the object type. For example, for registered ActiveX controls, the syntax is CLSID:class-identifier.
CODEBASE= universal resource locator	Identifies the codebase for the object. The syntax of the universal resource locator depends on the object.
CODETYPE= codetype	Specifies the Internet media type for code.
DATA= universal resource locator	Identifies data for the object. The syntax of the universal resource locator depends on the object.
DECLARE	Declares the object without instantiating it. Use this when creating cross-references to the object later in the document or when using the object as a parameter in another object.
HEIGHT= number	Specifies the height for the object.
HSPACE= number	Specifies the horizontal gutter. This is the extra empty space between the object and any text or images to the left or right of the object.
NAME= universal resource locator	Sets the name of the object when submitted as part of a form.
SHAPES	Specifies that the object has shaped hyperlinks.

Parameter	Values
STANDBY= message	Sets a message to be displayed while an object is loaded.
TYPE= type	Specifies the Internet media type for data.
USEMAP= universal resource locator	Specifies the image map to use with the object.
VSPACE= number	Specifies a vertical gutter. This is the extra white space between the object and any text or images above or below the object.
WIDTH= number	Specifies the width for the object.

In Listing 5.7, you can see HTML document source code with an embedded ActiveX object in it. In addition, notice the <PARAM NAME= value> tag. This tag was utilized to set any properties your ActiveX control might have.

Listing 5.7. The HTML page with an embedded <OBJECT> tag showing an ActiveX ActiveMovie control embedded in the page.

```
 1:  <HTML>
 2:  <HEAD>
 3:  <TITLE>AN EMMBEDDED ActiveX Control</TITLE>
 4:  </HEAD>
 5:  <BODY>
 6:
 7:  <p align=center><font size=6><em><strong><u>An EMMBEDDED ActiveX Control
     </u></strong></em></font></p>
 8:  <OBJECT
 9:  ID="ActiveMovie1"
10:  WIDTH=347
11:  HEIGHT=324
12:  ALIGN=center
13:  CLASSID="CLSID:05589FA1-C356-11CE-BF01-00AA0055595A"
14:  CODEBASE="http://www.microsoft.com/ie/download/activex/amovie.ocx#
     Version=4,70,0,1086"
15:     <PARAM NAME="_ExtentX" VALUE="9155">
16:     <PARAM NAME="_ExtentY" VALUE="8573">
17:     <PARAM NAME="MovieWindowSize" VALUE="2">
18:     <PARAM NAME="MovieWindowWidth" VALUE="342">
19:     <PARAM NAME="MovieWindowHeight" VALUE="243">
20:     <PARAM NAME="FileName" VALUE="E:\vinman\duds.avi">
21:     <PARAM NAME="Auto Start" VALUE="TRUE">
22:  </OBJECT>
23:
24:  </BODY>
25:  </HTML>
```

When a browser such as Internet Explorer encounters this page, it begins to parse the HTML source code. When it finds the `<OBJECT>` in line 8, it realizes it has encountered a dynamic object. The browser then takes lines 10–12, the WIDTH, HEIGHT, and ALIGN attributes, which in this case are 347, 324, and CENTER, respectively, and sets up a placeholder for the object on the rendered page. It then takes the `ID="ActiveMovie1"` in line 9 and the `CLASSID="CLSID:05589FA1-C356-11CE-BF01-00AA0055595A"` in line 13 and checks to see whether this control has been registered before in the Registry. If the control object has never been registered, it uses the CODEBASE attribute to locate the OCX on the server machine and proceeds to download the object into the `\Windows\Ocache` directory. The browser then registers the `AMOVIE.OCX` by calling the function `DllRegisterServer` to register the control on the local machine. Now, with the control properly registered, the browser can get the CLSID for the object from the Registry. In order to utilize the control, it passes the CSLID to `CoCreateInstance` to create the object, and this returns the pointer to the control's `IUnknown`. It can utilize this pointer and the property information in lines 15–22 to actually render the object on the page. Figure 5.13 shows the HTML document displayed in Internet Explorer.

Figure 5.13.
The HTML document as it appears in Internet Explorer with the ActiveX ActiveMovie control embedded in it.

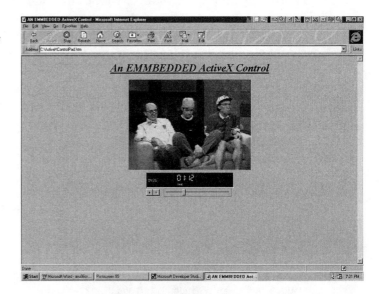

Now you can see that embedding controls to enhance a Web page with dynamic content is fairly easy. It is important that you, as an ActiveX control designer, understand how they are rendered.

ActiveX Control Pad

The ActiveX Control Pad provides a method of generating the HTML code that was discussed earlier to embed ActiveX and other dynamic objects into HTML source. (See Figure 5.14.) This is a free tool provided by Microsoft to aid in the production of Internet-enabled applications.

Figure 5.14.
The ActiveX Control Pad with the ActiveMovie control properties being edited.

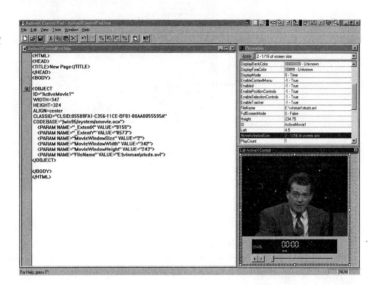

> **note**
>
> The ActiveX Control Pad can be downloaded from Microsoft at the following Internet URL: http://www.microsoft.com/workshop/author/cpad.

This tool can be used to quickly embed your control in a page so you can test its functionality. The ActiveX Control Pad can be a great time-saver, freeing you from having to remember how to write HTML source code. It will even allow you to test your ability to utilize VBScript (see Figure 5.15) to do OLE Automation with your code.

In addition, the ActiveX Control Pad comes with a suite of ActiveX controls for you to utilize in the development of your Web pages and your OLE-enabled applications. Some of these controls are the same ones that come with Internet Explorer; however, there are a few new ones to add to your bag of OLE controls.

Figure 5.15.
*The ActiveX Script
Wizard to help you create
scripts to further
"activate" your controls.*

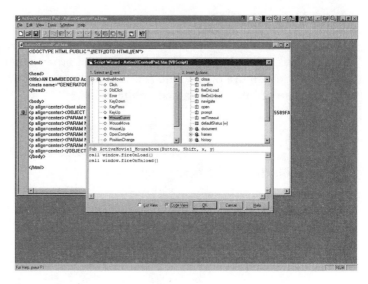

OLE Controls in Development Tools

One last place to look for OLE controls is in your development tools. Visual C++, Borland C++, Visual Basic, Delphi, PowerBuilder, Access, and almost all other mainstream Windows or Internet development suites come with OLE controls. Become familiar with the development tools you use and take advantage of the components provided for you. This will make your job much easier and make your users much happier.

Methods of Creating OLE (ActiveX) Controls

This section examines the ways to write ActiveX controls. Each method is discussed, and you will create a sample OLE control. Presently, there are three ways of creating ActiveX controls:

- Visual C++ and Microsoft Foundation Classes (MFC)
- ActiveX Template Library (ATL)
- ActiveX Development Kit (BaseCtl Framework)

Every major PC C++ compiler manufacturer now supports MFC, so it should be possible to create an ActiveX control with another vendor's product; however, for the purposes of this chapter, you will do this example utilizing Visual C++ 4.2a or greater. In addition, you should be able to use any C++/C compiler to use the ActiveX Development Kit and the ActiveX Template Library.

The traditionally used programming language for creating OLE controls is C++ and C; however, Microsoft has promised a compiled version of Visual Basic, called

Visual Basic 5.0, that will be able to create OLE controls. It has been rumored that Microsoft is also creating a converter that will convert ActiveX controls into Java applets. Those of you who are Borland Delphi PASCAL programmers can now create ActiveX controls with a third-party add-on from Apiary, Inc., called OCX Expert. This Delphi add-on takes VCLs created in Delphi and converts them to 32-bit ActiveX controls.

note

Information on OCX Expert can be obtained from Apiary, Incorporated, at the following Internet URL: http://www.apiary.com/.

Visual Basic is a very popular language/development tool because it is very easy to learn and utilize. It has even been called a quasi-4GL. Many times it is chosen for development endeavors for these reasons. However, C++ provides much more power and flexibility in the development of applications as a whole, but most importantly, in the development of user interface elements such as OLE controls.

Developers are often almost fanatical about their development tools. As a software engineer, you should be concerned with the right tool to fit the job. I highly recommend Visual C++ and Microsoft Foundation Classes. Programming in C++ is now much easier with class libraries such as MFC and Integrated Development Environments such as Visual C++. Some even consider it a 4GL, but theoreticians might argue that point. Nevertheless, it is a very powerful tool, one you should consider using. There are also a number of powerful C++ development tools such as Borland C++, Symantec C++, and IBM Visual Age. There is a veritable plethora of tools for you to choose from. In addition, Borland Delphi is a powerful tool with which you can develop Windows applications using object-oriented Pascal, but its principal strength is its integrated development environment. If you are unfamiliar with some of these tools, you might want to get an evaluation copy of them and try them. This will better aid you in picking the right tool for the job.

This book covers OCXs created with C++. The authors want to make you aware that there are many new emerging technologies and products associated with ActiveX controls.

The next sections examine three ways of creating ActiveX controls. These sections assume that you have a working knowledge of C++ and a Windows class library such as Microsoft Foundation Classes (MFC) or Borland's Object Windows Library (OWL). They make no attempt to teach you C++ or MFC. Although these sections are for intermediate to advanced programmers, if you are new to or curious about C++, MFC, or Visual C++, some information is highlighted to aid you.

Take a look now at an example of an OLE control created with Visual C++ and MFC.

The Visual C++ and MFC Way

Visual C++ and MFC comes in three flavors: 16-bit, Win32s/32-bit, and 32-bit. Visual C++ 1.52c and MFC 2.53 are for 16-bit developers and Visual C++ 4.2 and MFC 4.2 are for 32-bit developers. For those of you who still desire the Win32s development platform for the development of 32-bit applications to run under 16-bit Windows, there are Visual C++ 4.1 and MFC 4.1. The newer versions of Visual C++ will no longer support Win32s. This section concentrates on the 32-bit environment and does not cover Win32s or 16-bit development. Building 16-bit OLE controls is possible with Visual C++ 1.52c, but 16-bit development is rapidly being left behind. In addition, the statement about 16-bit development being left behind can be said of the Win32s world as well.

Obtaining the ActiveX SDK

First, you need to get the ActiveX Software Development Kit. An updated version of the ActiveX SDK was released at the same time Internet Explorer 3.0 was released. The new ActiveX SDK was updated to include the new technology and features of Internet Explorer 3.0.

---

note

The most current ActiveX SDK is available from Microsoft, at no charge, at the following Internet URL: `http://www.microsoft.com/intdev/sdk/`.

---

caution

The ActiveX SDK is intended only to run on Windows 95 and Windows NT 4.0 (release) machines running the release version of Internet Explorer 3.0.

The ActiveX SDK file obtained from the Microsoft Web site is a self-extracting archive. In addition, if you subscribe to Level II or higher of the Microsoft Developers Network Library, the most recent ActiveX SDK should be included in future releases of MSDN.

tip

If you do not already subscribe to the Microsoft Developers Network library (MSDN), the authors highly recommend that you do so. It is an invaluable source of technical information for developers of software and hardware for the Windows family of operating systems. You can obtain information about MSDN by calling Microsoft at 1-800-759-5474 or at the Microsoft Web site at the following Internet URL: http://www.microsoft.com/msdn/.

The Microsoft Developers Network is a subscription for four levels of information and products. It contains, depending on what level you subscribe to, all the Software Development Kits, all the Knowledge Bases, documentation for all of Microsoft's developer products, how-to articles, samples, bug lists, and workarounds, as well as all the operating systems, specifications, Device Driver Kits, and the latest breaking developer news. It is issued in CD-ROM format (see Figure 5.16) and is released and updated quarterly. The Level II subscription alone comes with over 35 CD-ROMs, packed full of development information that is updated quarterly. The MSDN library CD-ROM directly integrates with the Visual C++ IDE.

Figure 5.16.
The Microsoft Developers Network library CD-ROM.

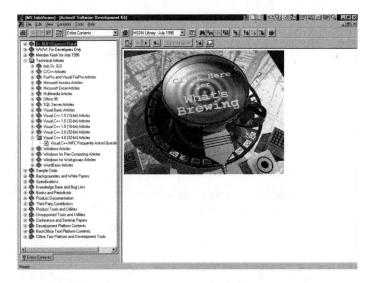

Using the Right Version of Visual C++ and MFC

Visual C++ comes as a yearly subscription, or you can purchase the single release professional version. The professional version is Version 4.0. With the subscription, you get the updates throughout the year. Right now that is Version 4.2. You can get Version 4.2 only through the subscription. You can still create OLE controls with Version 4.0, but to get the enhancements to create ActiveX controls, you must have Version 4.2. In addition, Microsoft recently released Visual C++ Enterprise edition 4.2. The Enterprise edition of Visual C++ includes additional database tools such as an SQL debugger and visual database views. The Enterprise edition 4.2 or greater can be utilized to develop ActiveX controls.

As previously mentioned, a version of the ActiveX SDK was released in September 1996. The Visual C++ development team at Microsoft has also released a patch for Visual C++ Version 4.2 and MFC Version 4.2 to enable developers to utilize the new features to create ActiveX applications. This patch will be included in the next subscription release of Visual C++ and MFC Version 4.3. The patch is called Visual C++ Patch Version 4.2b. You will need to download this patch and incorporate it with Visual C++ Version 4.2 in order to create ActiveX controls.

---

warning

The Visual C++ 4.2b release is for use only on Visual C++ and MFC Version 4.2. Do not apply this patch to any other version of Visual C++, or your software and operating system may not operate properly.

---

note

The Visual C++ 4.2b release patch is available from Microsoft at the following Internet URL: `http://www.microsoft.com/visualc/v42/v42tech/v42b/vc42b.htm`.

The patch is a self-extracting archive. Once you get the patch and extract it, make sure you follow the directions in the `readme` file. (If you are reading this and Visual C++ and MFC 4.3 have been released and you have them loaded, then you need not apply the patch.)

Using Visual C++ and MFC for ActiveX and OLE Controls

Previously, OLE controls had to have certain interfaces implemented, whether they needed them or not. This means that controls were larger than necessary.

This is fine if you are utilizing them on a local machine, but with ActiveX controls that need to be downloaded and installed across the low-bandwidth, high-latency Internet, any excess baggage reduces efficiency in achieving this end. In order to get Webmasters to utilize your controls to activate their Web pages, your ActiveX controls need to be lean, mean, efficient downloading machines.

Visual C++ comes with a ControlWizard to help you create controls. It provides one of the fastest ways to create a control. In fact, if you are a newcomer to creating controls, it is the best way to learn. Why? Because it creates a framework for you. You can be up and running very quickly. However, there are a few drawbacks you need to be aware of.

In order to utilize a control created with Visual C++ and based on MFC, the MFC dynamic link library (DLL) must reside on the client machine. This file is about 1.2MB and must be downloaded to the client machine. However, this must occur only the first time, if the MFC DLL does not reside on the client machine already. So you will take a small performance hit the first time your control is used. Furthermore, it should also be noted that MFC-based controls tend to be fatter than the controls created by the other two methods.

You will need to weigh the options carefully, considering performance, programmer skill, timetable, and environment. This is not to say that MFC-based controls are not suitable for use in the ActiveX environment, but simply to make you aware of the factors associated with choosing this method. If you are building controls for an intranet, which is high bandwidth and has potentially low latency, the size of the control and the associated DLL is not a major factor. Speed of development, reduced complexity, and rich features may be more important. In fact, a basic OCX created with the OLE ControlWizard is only 23KB. 23KB, even on the sluggish Internet, is not extremely large, especially in comparison to some of the large graphic files and AVI files embedded in Web pages. The name of the game is optimization and asynchronous downloading.

Help is on the way. The Visual C++/MFC team at Microsoft realizes that performance is very important in the Internet environment. They are feverishly working to make ActiveX controls created with Visual C++ and MFC leaner and meaner, as well as working the download of the MFC DLL issue. Visual C++ and MFC might be the best ways to create controls, but you will have to weigh each situation accordingly.

MFC Encapsulation of ActiveX and OLE Controls

MFC encapsulates the OLE control functionality in a class called `COleControl` (see Figure 5.17). `COleControl` is derived from `CWnd` and in turn from `CCmdTarget` and `CObject`.

Figure 5.17.
The class hierarchy for
COleControl.

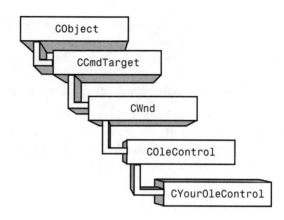

COleControl is the base class from which you derive to create any OLE control you want. What's nice is that your control inherits all the functionality of the base class COleControl. (See Table 5.5.) You can then customize the control to the capabilities you want to include in it. As you know, an OLE control is nothing more than a COM object. With MFC, the complexities of dealing with the COM interfaces are abstracted into an easy-to-use class. In addition, MFC provides a framework for your control so you can worry about the details of what you want your control to do instead of recreating functionality that all controls must contain in order to work.

Table 5.5. The member functions of COleControl that are encapsulated by the Microsoft Foundation Classes.

Function	Function
COleControl	ControlInfoChanged
RecreateControlWindow	GetClientSite
InitializeIIDs	GetExtendedControl
EnableSimpleFrame	LockInPlaceActive
SetInitialSize	TransformCoords
PreModalDialog	IsModified
PostModalDialog	SetModifiedFlag
ExchangeExtent	ExchangeStockProps
GetClientRect	OnGetPredefinedValue
ExchangeVersion	IsConvertingVBX
SetModifiedFlag	WillAmbientsBeValidDuringLoad
DoSuperclassPaint	InvalidateControl

Function	*Function*
IsOptimizedDraw	SelectFontObject
SelectStockFont	OnMapPropertyToPage
TranslateColor	GetNotSupported
SetNotPermitted	SetNotSupported
ThrowError	GetReadyState
AmbientBackColor	InternalSetReadyState
AmbientDisplayName	Load
AmbientForeColor	DisplayError
AmbientFont	DoPropExchange
AmbientLocaleID	GetClassID
AmbientScaleUnits	GetMessageString
AmbientShowGrabHandles	IsSubclassedControl
AmbientShowHatching	OnClick
AmbientTextAlign	OnDoVerb
AmbientUIDead	OnDraw
AmbientUserMode	OnDrawMetafile
GetAmbientProperty	OnEdit
FireClick	OnEnumVerbs
FireDblClick	OnEventAdvise
FireError	OnKeyDownEvent
FireEvent	OnKeyPressEvent
FireKeyDown	OnKeyUpEvent
FireKeyPress	OnProperties
FireKeyUp	OnResetState
FireMouseDown	OnAppearanceChanged
FireMouseMove	OnBackColorChanged
FireMouseUp	OnBorderStyleChanged
FireReadyStateChange	OnEnabledChanged
DoClick	OnFontChanged
Refresh	OnForeColorChanged
GetAppearance	OnTextChanged
SetAppearance	OnAmbientPropertyChange

continues

Table 5.5. continued

Function	Function
GetBackColor	OnFreezeEvents
SetBackColor	OnGetControlInfo
GetBorderStyle	OnMnemonic
SetBorderStyle	OnRenderData
GetEnabled	OnRenderFileData
SetEnabled	OnRenderGlobalData
GetForeColor	OnSetClientSite
SetForeColor	OnSetData
GetFont	OnSetExtent
GetFontTextMetrics	OnSetObjectRects
GetStockTextMetrics	OnGetColorSet
InternalGetFont	SetFont
SelectStockFont	GetHwnd
GetText	InternalGetText
SetText	OnGetInPlaceMenu
GetControlSize	OnHideToolBars
SetControlSize	OnShowToolBars
GetRectInContainer	OnGetDisplayString
SetRectInContainer	OnGetPredefinedStrings
BoundPropertyChanged	BoundPropertyRequestEdit

You are probably wondering why all of these member functions are listed here for you. The purpose is to emphasize the amount of work already done for you by the Microsoft Foundation Classes. In the COleControl class, there are 128 member functions; when you derive your control from COleControl, your control inherits the capability of using those predefined functions.

In addition, MFC itself provides a whole range of capability already created for you when you utilize it. It also includes a functionality to do messaging and automated data exchange.

With MFC Version 4.2, Microsoft added some new classes to MFC to facilitate the creation of ActiveX controls. These new classes add to MFC's impressive range of functionality. These five new classes are listed in Table 5.6.

Table 5.6. The new classes added to Microsoft Foundation Classes Version 4.2 to support ActiveX controls.

Function	Definition
CMonikerFile	When this class is instantiated as an object, it encapsulates a stream of data named by an IMoniker interface object. It allows you to have access and manipulate that data stream pointed to by an IMoniker object.
CAsyncMonikerFile	Works much the same as a CMonikerFile, except it allows asynchronous access to the IStream object pointed to by the IMoniker object.
CDataPathProperty	This class encapsulates the implementation of OLE control properties so they can be implemented asynchronously.
COleCmdUI	This class encapsulates the process by which MFC updates the user interface.
COleSafeArray	This class encapsulates the function of an array of arbitrary type and size.

In addition to the new classes in MFC, Microsoft also enhanced COleControl to simplify the creation of ActiveX controls. These functions add to the already impressive array of capabilities encapsulated in COleControl. Table 5.7 lists the 31 new member functions added to COleControl.

Table 5.7. The member functions of COleControl that have been added to support ActiveX controls.

Function	Function
ClientToParent	GetWindowlessDropTarget
GetCapture	ClipCaretRect
GetControlFlags	GetClientOffset
GetDC	GetClientRect
InvalidateRgn	GetFocus
GetActivationPolicy	OnGetNaturalExtent
OnGetViewExtent	ReleaseCapture
OnInactiveMouseMove	ResetVersion
OnQueryHitRect	SerializeStockProps
SetFocus	OnGetViewRect

continues

Table 5.7. continued

Function	Function
OnGetViewStatus	OnInactiveSetCursor
OnQueryHitPoint	OnWindowlessMessage
ReleaseDC	ParentToClient
ResetStockProps	ScrollWindow
SerializeVersion	SerializeExtent
SetCapture	

The OLE ControlWizard

The beauty of Visual C++ and MFC is that they perform the mundane task of creating the framework for your control, leaving you the task of making your control perform the functionality you want it to create. At the center of this is the AppWizard, which houses the OLE ControlWizard. Visual C++ Version 4.2 with the 4.2b patch has augmented the OLE ControlWizard to specifically support ActiveX controls. In this section, you examine each feature of the ControlWizard and create your first ActiveX MFC control.

First you will need to launch Visual C++. Once you have Visual C++ up and running, select File from the menu and then New from the popup menu. You will then see the New dialog box, as shown in Figure 5.18.

Figure 5.18.
*The New dialog box in
Visual C++.*

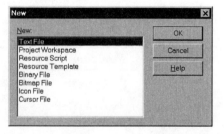

Select Project Workspace. This yields the New Project Workspace dialog box. (See Figure 5.19.) At the New Project dialog box, select the OLE ControlWizard from the list box on the left, and give your control a title and a location. In this case, call it Simple Control and accept the default location.

Figure 5.19.
*The New Project
Information dialog box
in Visual C++.*

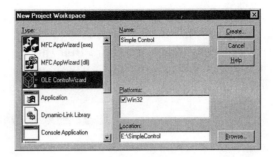

You are now looking at the first page of the OLE ControlWizard. (See Figure 5.20.) Here the OLE ControlWizard asks you a series of questions as to what you would like in your control:

- How many controls do you want in the project?
- Do you want a runtime license for your controls?
- Do you want the wizard to document your controls with source file comments?
- Do you want a help file generated for your control?

Figure 5.20.
*Step 1 of the OLE
ControlWizard in
Visual C++.*

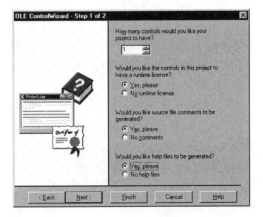

In this case, you are going to create only one control, so select one control for this project. As you have already learned earlier in this chapter, one OCX can contain several controls.

Next, select the choice for the ControlWizard to include licensing support for this control. In addition, ask the ControlWizard to document the code it is going to write for you in the control framework with comments.

Lastly, ask the ControlWizard to generate a basic help file, so you can provide online help for the Webmasters and programmers who will be utilizing this control. It is extremely important that this control be well documented. Then select the Next button and go to page 2 of the OLE ControlWizard. (See Figure 5.21.)

Figure 5.21.
Step 2 of the OLE ControlWizard in Visual C++.

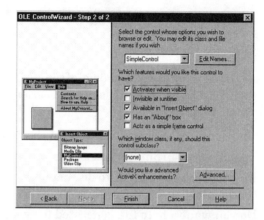

Step 2 of the OLE ControlWizard presents you with more options for this OLE control:

- Editing the names of the classes for your control.
- What features do you want in your control?

    Activates when visible?

    Invisible at runtime?

    Available in Insert Dialog dialog box?

    Has an About box?

    Acts as a simple frame control?

- Would you like the wizard to create your control as a subclass to an existing control?
- Would you like advanced ActiveX Enhancements for your control?

The OLE ControlWizard enables you to control the naming of each of the controls in your project (refer to Figure 5.21) to include the class names, source file names, and property sheet names. If you press the Edit Names button (see Figure 5.21) you will get the Edit Names dialog box, as shown in Figure 5.22. It does provide a default naming convention, and in this case, you will accept the defaults provided by the ControlWizard.

Figure 5.22.
The Edit Names dialog box in Step 2 of the OLE ControlWizard in Visual C++.

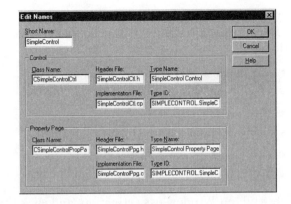

Next are questions regarding what features you want in this control. You need to keep in mind the previously discussed section on optimizations. Does the control need to be active when visible, or is it invisible at runtime like a timer control or a communications control? This control will need to be active and visible. You want this control to be available in the Insert Object dialog, so you will choose this option. No doubt you are proud of the controls you create, so you can include an About dialog box to post your name or your company's name. Lastly, do you want this control to be a simple frame control that supports the ISimpleFrameSite interface? This is so the control can act as a frame for other controls. For this example's purposes, you will not choose this option.

You now need to look at and select the advanced options that support ActiveX Enhancements. Click the Advanced button and go to the Advanced ActiveX Controls Features dialog box, as depicted in Figure 5.23.

Figure 5.23.
The Advanced ActiveX Features dialog box of Step 2 of the OLE ControlWizard in Visual C++.

From the Advanced ActiveX Controls Features dialog box, you can choose one of six options. Keep in mind the information you have covered previously on these options.

- Windowless activation
- Unclipped device context
- Flicker-free activation
- Mouse-pointer notification when inactive
- Optimized drawing code
- Loads properties asynchronously

Choose all but Windowless activation, and click the OK button. Then select the Finish button. Here you will get a summary of the features the OLE ControlWizard will create for you in the New Project Information dialog box (see Figure 5.24).

Figure 5.24.
The New Project
Information dialog of the
OLE ControlWizard in
Visual C++.

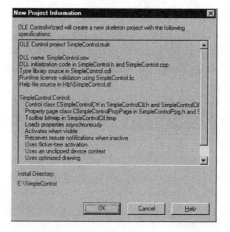

When you click the OK button of the New Project Information dialog box, the OLE ControlWizard will create a basic control for you and implement all the features you selected in it. This control need only be compiled to be up and running. The OLE ControlWizard even added an ellipse in this control's drawing code so it will have something to display. You now have the framework to start customizing this control. The nice thing is that most of that functionality is already encapsulated in MFC. To assist you in this endeavor, Visual C++ provides you the Class Wizard. The sky is the limit on what types of creations are possible now that you have the framework built for you.

The ActiveX Template Library (ATL) Way

Because MFC-based controls come with the overhead of the MFC runtime dynamic link libraries, the Visual C++ development team created the ActiveX Template Library. The ActiveX Template Library is a set of template-based C++ classes to create small, fast COM objects. These classes eliminate the need for any external DLLs or any C runtime library code.

In fact, the ATL will produce an in-process server less than 5KB. Compared to the 22KB control plus the 1.4MB MFC DLL, that is a significant decrease in size. However, this reduction in size comes with an increased complexity and an increase in the work required to create an ActiveX control. The ATL provides all the COM connections for you and a Visual C++ wizard called the ATL COM AppWizard to guide you in setting up the framework for your control.

The ATL not only allows you to build controls, but also has support to help you build the following COM objects:

- In-process servers
- Local servers
- Service servers
- Remote servers that use the Distributed Component Object Model or Remote Automation
- COM thread models including Single threading, Apartment-model threading, and Free threading
- Aggregatable servers
- Various interface types including custom COM interfaces, dual interfaces, and IDispatch interfaces
- Enumerations
- Connection points
- OLE error mechanisms

Because the ActiveX Template Library provides C++ templates, you have a lot of flexibility to customize a COM object, which in this case is an OLE control. As such, you utilize the classes by instantiating an instance of the provided class from the template and use it as the basis for your class. This differs from the traditional method of deriving your control's classes from the classes in MFC. This is the distinction between a class library and a template library.

The code in the ATL is highly optimized for the task of creating light, fast COM objects. It still has a lot of the flexibility of the MFC way, and like the MFC way of creating the controls it precludes your having to write a lot of low-level COM code. It requires a thorough understanding of OLE, COM, and their interfaces.

How to Obtain the ATL

In order to use the ActiveX Template Library, you will first have to download it.

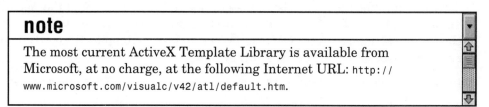

note

The most current ActiveX Template Library is available from Microsoft, at no charge, at the following Internet URL: `http://www.microsoft.com/visualc/v42/atl/default.htm`.

The ActiveX Template Library file is a self-extracting archive. In addition, it may also be obtained in future releases of Visual C++. If you subscribe to Level II or higher of the Microsoft Developers Network Library, the ActiveX Template Library should be included in the future releases of MSDN. The location and availability are subject to change by Microsoft.

You will also need Visual C++ Version 4.1 or higher and the ActiveX SDK. See the previous section's instructions for obtaining the ActiveX SDK and the required Visual C++ components. You must also be running Windows NT 4.0 or higher (non-beta), or Windows 95.

Installing the ATL

The ActiveX Template Library comes in three files: `atlinst.exe`, `docsinst.exe`, and `sampleinst.exe`. The `atlinst.exe` file contains the ActiveX Template Library. The `docsinst.exe` contains the documentation for the ATL, including setup instructions and a very good white paper. Lastly, the `sampleinst.exe` file contains some sample applications to guide you in your creation of applications with the ATL.

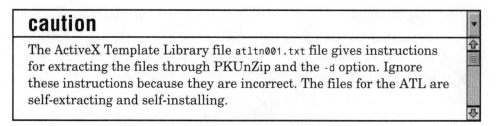

caution

The ActiveX Template Library file `atltn001.txt` file gives instructions for extracting the files through PKUnZip and the `-d` option. Ignore these instructions because they are incorrect. The files for the ATL are self-extracting and self-installing.

The ATL COM AppWizard

One of the nice features the developers of the ActiveX Template Library included is a Visual C++ wizard to perform some of the more mundane tasks of creating a framework for a COM object, such as a control. This leaves you the task of making your control perform the functionality you want it to have, as opposed to recreating abilities all ActiveX controls need. The ATL COM AppWizard is the mechanism to create that framework. It will get you up and running quickly, though not as quickly as OLE ControlWizard and MFC.

You will first need to launch Visual C++. Once you have Visual C++ up and running, select File from the menu and then New from the popup menu. You will then see the New dialog box.

Select Project Workspace. This yields the Project dialog box. At the New Project dialog box, you need to select the ATL COM AppWizard from the list box on the left, and you need to give your control a title and a location. In this case, call it ATL Simple Control and accept the default location. Then press the Create button.

You are now looking at the first page of the ATL COM AppWizard (see Figure 5.25). Here the ATL COM AppWizard asks you a series of questions about what kind of COM object you want to create.

Figure 5.25.
Step 1 of the ATL
COM AppWizard in
Visual C++.

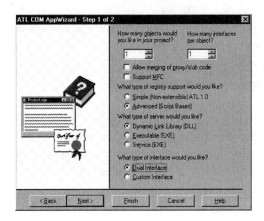

- How many objects do you want in the project?
- How many interfaces per object?
- Do you want to allow the merging of proxy/stub code?
- Do you want support for MFC?
- What type of Registry support would you like? Simple? Advanced?
- What kind of server would you like? DLL? EXE? Service?
- What type of interface would you like? Dual? Custom?

At the top of the wizard is a spin button with an edit control to enter the number of COM objects you want in your project. Don't worry; you can add more later if you are unsure. However, you will have to do this by hand. You know in this case you are creating the framework for one control, so choose one.

Right next to the number of objects spin button is the interfaces per object spin button. This enables you to generate up to three interfaces for each object. Note that you cannot have a different number of interfaces on different objects. If you want this, you will have to implement it by hand.

When marshaling interfaces are required, you will need to select the Allow merging of proxy/stub code checkbox. This option places the proxy and stub code generated by the MIDL Compiler in the same DLL as the server. Even though the wizard does some of the work for you, note that in order to merge the proxy/stub code into the DLL, the wizard adds the file dlldatax.c to your project. Make sure that precompiled headers are turned off for this file, and add _MERGE_PROXYSTUB to the defines for the project.

Why the Support MFC checkbox was included is unclear. The main purpose of using the ATL is to get away from the overhead of MFC. You could have just used the OLE ControlWizard with MFC and saved yourself a lot of time and effort in the first place. However, if for some reason you want to utilize the MFC Class Library, check this option. It will give you access to the MFC Class Library functions.

The ATL COM AppWizard asks you the type of Registry support you want for your control. There are two options: Simple (Non-extensible) ATL 1.0 and Advanced (Script Based). The Simple option provides the control with basic self-registration abilities. On the other hand, the Advanced option uses a scripting language. This special scripting language enables you to utilize replaceable parameters during control self-registration.

You now need to select the type of server you want the ATL COM Wizard to create. Your options are: an in-process server (DLL), Local (EXE), or a Service (EXE). When creating a service, you are required to use script-based registration. In addition, when creating a service or executable, you are unable either to use MFC or allow merging of proxy/stub code.

The last choice on the ATL COM AppWizard is the type of interfaces to create. The ATL COM AppWizard can create either custom interfaces, derived from IUnknown, or it can create dual interfaces derived from IDispatch.

You then select the next button and go to page 2 of the ATL COM AppWizard.

Step 2 of the ATL COM AppWizard presents you with a single option for this ActiveX control. It enables you to edit the class and the COM names of this control.

Once you are satisfied with the names of your classes and your COM objects, click the OK button. Then click the Finish button on page 2 of the ATL COM AppWizard. The ATL COM AppWizard will then show the New Project Information dialog box. This dialog box shows the selections you have made in creating your COM object.

When you click the OK button of the New Project Information dialog box, the ATL COM AppWizard will create a basic COM object for you and implement all the features you selected in it. This control need only be compiled to be up and running. You now have the framework to start customizing this control.

The ActiveX Development Kit (BaseCtl Framework) Way

The ActiveX Software Development Kit provides a third way to produce ActiveX controls. This is by far the most difficult way to create a control. It is provided by Microsoft as a "bare bones" method of creating a control. This is not for the faint of heart and requires extensive knowledge of OLE, COM, and the OLE control interfaces. Only minimal functionality is provided in the code base. You will have to hand code all your messaging, which is at best a daunting task. The only reason to use this method is to try to create the lightest and fastest control possible; however, the time and complexity of creating a control with this method may not be worth the performance gains. This method is not recommended unless you absolutely have to use it. The ActiveX Template Library and Microsoft Foundation Class methods are much easier to implement and much more flexible. Creating and testing a control is no easy task; there are a lot of factors involved. Tools are not talent, but why not use the tools available to make your job easier? As the ATL and MFC methods of creating a control improve, the BaseCtl Framework method in the ActiveX SDK will die away. Some die-hard, low-level C programmers or assembly language programmers may want to dive into this low-level approach head first, but make sure you are prepared. It would take an entire chapter to even begin addressing this method of creating a control. The next section covers how to get the framework and set it up, but it is up to you to examine the samples that come with the SDK and explore the mess that awaits you in using this method. The authors highly discourage you from using this method.

Getting the BaseCtl Framework

To get the BaseCtl Framework, first you will need to get the ActiveX Software Development Kit. An updated version of the ActiveX SDK was released at the same time as Internet Explorer 3.0. The new ActiveX SDK was updated to include the new technology and features of Internet Explorer 3.0.

---

note ▼
⇧
The most current ActiveX SDK is available from Microsoft, at no
charge, at the following Internet URL: `http://www.microsoft.com/intdev/`
`sdk/`.
⇩

In addition, you need to obtain the Win32 Software Development Kit. The
ActiveX SDK requires the August 1996 or later version of the Win32 SDK. The
Win32 SDK is available in the Microsoft Developers Network Library Subscrip-
tion Level II. The required Win32 SDK components come with Visual C++.
In addition, you will need to have Visual C++ 4.2b or greater to use the Win32
SDK.

---

note ▼
⇧
The most current Win32 SDK is available from Microsoft through an
MSDN Library Professional Subscription Level II. Microsoft Sales can
be reached at 1-800-426-9400.
⇩

Once you have the Win32 SDK, you will need to follow the instructions included
with it. Pay particular attention to the environment variable that must be set.
Included in the Win32 SDK is a `SETENV.BAT` batch file that will set these Win32 SDK
environment variables for you.

If you have Visual C++, your Win32 environment is already set for you.

Setting Up the BaseCtl Framework

The BaseCtl Framework comes on the ActiveX SDK. Once the ActiveX SDK
is installed, the BaseCtl Framework is in the following location
`C:\INetSdk\Samples\BaseCtl\Framewrk` (assuming that you installed it on your
`c:` drive. You will have to compile the BaseCtl Framework libraries before you can
either create a control or compile any of the samples that come with the ActiveX
SDK.

To compile the BaseCtl Framework using the Win32 SDK or another compiler,
follow the instructions in the ActiveX SDK. To compile them from the Visual C++
Integrated Development Environment (IDE), follow these instructions:

1. Click the Options_ menu item in the Tools popup menu.
2. Click the Directories tab in the Options dialog box.
3. Add the full path to the installed components.
   `INetSDK\Include` to the `includes` directories.

INetSDK\Lib to the library directories.

INetSDK\Bin to the executable files directories.

4. These paths must be moved to the top of the search paths.

5. Create a project file and make files.

    a. Click the New menu item on the File popup menu.

    b. From the New dialog box, select Project Workspace and click OK.

    c. Type the name of the project in the New Project Workspace dialog box.

    d. Select what type of application you are building. If you are building an ActiveX control, choose Dynamic Link Library. If you are going to build the BaseCtrl Framework libraries, choose Static Library.

    e. Type the path to the sample or library. You can use the Browse button if you are unsure.

    f. Click the Create button.

    g. Click the Files into Project_ menu item on the Insert popup menu.

    h. Select all the *.CPP, *.C, *.DEF, and *.RC files in the directory including any ODL files, and click the Add button.

    i. Click the Settings_ menu item on the Build popup menu.

    j. Select the Link tab.

    k. Add the libraries needed to compile the application.

    l. If the sample you are building does not use MFC, you will need to turn off MFC support in the Project Settings dialog box.

6. You can now build the project in Visual C++.

Once you have compiled the debug and release versions of the BaseCtrl Framework, you can start creating your control. You might want to use one of the sample controls as a template, but if you were going to do that, you might want to use just MFC or the ATL.

Summary

This chapter discussed the ActiveX control, which is a superset of the OLE control. OLE controls are nothing more than COM objects. ActiveX controls are a leaner and meaner implementation of the OLE control to facilitate its use on the Internet. ActiveX/OLE controls enable you to use prepackaged components of functionality to aid you in creating useful applications.

Creating OLE Control Containers

by Thomas L. Fredell

Before OLE Custom controls, or OCXs/ActiveX controls, the major software component container was Visual Basic. Visual Basic used a proprietary means of communicating with its components, which were called VBXs, or Visual Basic Custom controls. Using a VBX in a C or C++ application basically meant emulating the specific control containment functionality of Visual Basic.

With the advent of the generic standard of OLE Custom controls, there are no restrictions on the type of applications that can act as control containers. The minimum requirements for a functional control container are

- It can provide COM-style interfaces to a control.
- It supports the minimum set of control container interfaces expected by an embedded control.
- It implements the minimum number of required functions in the aforementioned interfaces.

The complexity of control containers ranges from full development environments such as Visual Basic 4, which allow controls to be integrated into the environment through the toolbar and implement design-mode and run-mode versions, to very simple control containers such as dialog boxes, implemented using the Microsoft Foundation Classes. This chapter discusses the characteristics of control containers and the implementation of containers using the Microsoft Foundation Classes.

A Primer on Control/Container Interaction

Control and container interaction is based on the same foundation as the interaction of standard OLE document objects and their containers. Several of the interfaces required for control containers, such as `IOleInPlaceSite` and `IOleInPlaceUIWindow`, are used for interaction between OLE compound document objects and their containers. The standard interfaces are supplemented by several required interfaces designed specifically for control and container interaction, such as `IOleClientSite` and `IOleControlSite`. All required interfaces are listed later in this chapter, with detailed information about the purpose of the interface methods. There are also several optional container interfaces; containers may elect to implement or use them if they require the interface functionality.

One of the most important interfaces required for control/container interaction is `IDispatch`, the OLE automation dispatch interface. The control exposes an `IDispatch` interface that its container uses to access the control's properties and methods. The container also exposes an `IDispatch` interface to the control that allows the control to pass events to its container.

Each control embedded in a container is allocated a control site by the container. The container lays out the contained control, manages keyboard interaction, enables the properties of controls to be saved in some persistent format, handles events generated by controls, and exposes ambient properties to controls. Ambient properties allow OLE controls to retrieve information about the control site provided by their container.

Some containers wrap their controls with extended controls. Extended controls allow containers to maintain additional properties and events for controls without changing the mechanism through which they interact with the controls.

The next few sections describe in more detail the issues involved with creating controls, communicating with them, and wrapping them with extended controls.

Creating an OLE Control Instance

The control container can create a control by retrieving the control's `IClassFactory` interface through the standard OLE function `CoGetClassObject()`. The container can then use the `ClassFactory::CreateInstance()` function to create an instance of the OLE control. `ClassFactory::CreateInstance()` might return the error

CLASS_E_NOTLICENSED if the control requires the container to specify control-licensing information before it can be created.

The ClassFactory2 interface handles control licensing; it extends the ClassFactory interface with the GetLicInfo(), RequestLicKey(), and CreateInstanceLic() functions.

HRESULT ClassFactory2::GetLicInfo(LICINFO* pLicInfo);

GetLicInfo() enables the container to retrieve information regarding the licensing capabilities of the control. The function fills a LICINFO structure whose members describe the control's licensing information on the current machine:

```
typedef struct tagLICINFO
    {
    ULONG cbLicInfo;
    BOOL fRuntimeKeyAvail;
    BOOL fLicVerified;
    } LICINFO;
```

The LICINFO.cbLicInfo structure member simply specifies the size (in bytes) of the LICINFO structure. The LICINFO.fRuntimeKeyAvail member indicates whether or not the control can be instantiated on an unlicensed machine; if it is TRUE, the control can be created using a key obtained from ClassFactory2::RequestLicKey(). The LICINFO.fLicVerified structure indicates whether or not a full machine license for the control exists.

HRESULT ClassFactory2::RequestLicKey(DWORD dwReserved, BSTR* pbstrKey);

RequestLicKey() allows a control container to create a runtime instance of a control on a machine that doesn't have a full license for the control (see the preceding example). If RequestLicKey() succeeds, the control's ClassFactory2 implementation will fill the pbstrKey with a string allocated using SysAllocString(). The container can pass the key to CreateInstanceLic(); the container is responsible for freeing the key using SysFreeString() after it is finished with it.

HRESULT ClassFactory2::CreateInstanceLic(IUnknown*
    pUnkOuter, IUnknown* pUnkReserved, REFIID riid,
    BSTR bstrKey, void** ppvObject);

CreateInstanceLic() uses the key obtained from the control through RequestLicKey() to create an instance of the control (see the preceding example). The pUnkOuter argument is a pointer to the controlling unknown for the control if the control is being aggregated; a control container that uses extended controls would pass its IUnknown implementation as an argument. pUnkReserved is a currently unused argument; it must be specified as NULL. The riid argument is the type of interface pointer requested by the container; a container may use the IID_IOleObject to retrieve the control's implementation of the IOleObject interface. The bstrKey is the key obtained using the ClassFactory2::RequestLicKey() function. Finally, the ppvObject is a pointer to the interface returned by the control.

Control/Container Communication Using `IDispatch`

The primary communication link between a container and a control is through the OLE automation `IDispatch` interface. `IDispatch`, the foundation of OLE automation, provides a generic means through which function calls may be passed to an object. For OLE controls, a control-provided `IDispatch` allows a container to access control properties and methods. Likewise, a container-provided `IDispatch` enables controls to access container ambient properties and alert the container of events.

> **note**
>
> Communication between a control and container is pretty complex. The next few sections describe some details of the communication, but I should forewarn you that the Microsoft Foundation Classes basically handle all of the details for you.

Fundamentals of `IDispatch`

The primary `IDispatch` method used for control/container communication is `Invoke()`. The prototype for `Invoke()` is

```
HRESULT IDispatch::Invoke(DISPID dispidMember,
    REFIID riid, LCID lcid, unsigned short wFlags,
    DISPPARAMS FAR* pdispparams, VARIANT FAR* pvarResult,
    EXECPINFO FAR* pexcepinfo, unsigned int FAR* puArgErr);
```

Callers of `IDispatch::Invoke()` use a dispatch ID, or `DISPID`, to identify the OLE automation member that they want to access. The value of `wFlags` indicates whether a property or method is the target of `Invoke()`. Parameters to the property or method are passed to `Invoke()` as an array of variants, and the return value from the call is used to fill the `pvarResult` parameter.

Using `IDispatch` to Access Control Properties and Methods

Controls may contain a large number of properties and methods. As you know from the previous chapter, the capabilities of the control are defined in the control's type information, or type library. Control containers get access to the properties and methods using a control's `IDispatch` interface.

To get or set a property value or to call a control method, you use the control's `IDispatch::Invoke()` implementation. You specify a property or method using its dispatch ID; you can determine the dispatch IDs statically by using a tool like the OLE viewer to examine the control's type library; or you can use the control's type information at runtime.

Later in the chapter, the examples use a control called, appropriately enough, SimpleControl. SimpleControl really doesn't do anything interesting; it exposes two properties, no methods, and two events. One of the properties is a SimpleName property with a DISPID of 2. SimpleName is a string; setting the value of SimpleName causes the control to fire an OnSimpleNameChange event. The following code can be used to change the SimpleName property:

```
VARIANT varArg;          // New property value
DISPPARAMS dispparams;   // Structure containing property parameter
DISPID dispidNamed;      // DISPID of named argument (just one here)
EXCEPINFO excepinfo;     // Contains exception information, should one occur
HRESULT hres;            // Result of property set
UINT uiArgErr;           // Index to erroneous parameter

// Setup new property value parameter
VariantInit(&varArg);
V_VT(&varArg) = VT_BSTR;
V_BSTR(&varArg) = SysAllocString(L"A new name");

// ...setup parameter information...
memset(&dispparams, 0, sizeof dispparams);
dispparams.rgvarg = &varArg;
dispparams.cArgs = 1;
dispidNamed = DISPID_PROPERTYPUT;
dispparams.rgdispidNamedArgs = &dispidNamed;
dispparams.cNamedArgs = 1;

// ...and initialize EXECPINFO structure
memset(&excepinfo, 0, sizeof EXCEPINFO);

// Call Invoke to set the property; assumes pDispatch is the
// interface pointer for SimpleControl's IDispatch
hres = pDispatch->Invoke(2, IID_NULL, 0, DISPATCH_PROPERTYPUT, &dispparams,
    NULL, &excepinfo, &uiArgErr);
if (FAILED(hres))
{
    // Handle error
}
else
{
    // Call was successful
}

VariantClear(&varArg);
```

The level of effort illustrated in the code snippet is representative of what's necessary to manipulate control properties or methods. You will probably notice that most of the work in manipulating a control's properties or methods is in setting up the parameters. The preceding example is a simple one; if you're dealing with named arguments for method calls, it can get more complex. For more information, you can check out the documentation for the IDispatch interface in the Win32 SDK help.

Using `IDispatch` to Get Control Events

Controls notify their containers of events using their pointer to the container's `IDispatch` interface. Before a control can do so, the container must connect its `IDispatch` to the control as an outgoing interface. To connect its `IDispatch`, the container must find the control's connection point for the interface.

Connection points are maintained by controls that fire events. The interface to the set of control points, or more precisely `IConnectionPoint` objects, is through the control's implementation of `IConnectionPointContainer`. The `IConnectionPointContainer` interface allows the container to enumerate the control's outgoing interfaces, or to find a specific outgoing interface using an interface ID, or `IID`. For events, the container needs the `IID` of the control's `IDispatch` interface with the `default` and `source` attributes. You can get the `IID` statically using the aforementioned OLE Viewer tool, or you can find it at runtime using the control's type information interfaces. Once the container has acquired the correct `IConnectionPoint` interface, it can attach its event `IDispatch` using the `IConnectionPoint::Advise()` method.

When a control fires an event, it passes the parameters through the standard `IDispatch` array mechanism. The control uses the `DISPID` in the call to `IDispatch::Invoke()` to indicate which event occurred.

Container Ambient Properties

Ambient properties are control-container properties analogous to control properties. A container maintains ambient properties for all of its controls; typically, the container will expose the same values to all controls within a given frame. The OLE standards define a set of ambient properties with associated IDs that should be implemented by a container. The container also has means through which it can indicate to controls that the ambient properties have changed.

The implementation of control-container properties is very similar to the implementation of control properties; container ambient properties are provided by an `IDispatch` interface that can be retrieved from the `IOleControlSite` interface that hosts the control. Controls get ambient property values in the same manner that containers get control properties; the container returns the value of the property in the return value from the `IDispatch` call.

The following list contains the standard ambient properties that may be provided by an OLE control container:

> BackColor
> Type: `OLE_COLOR`
> Description: This specifies the color for the control's interior.

DisplayName
Type: VT_BSTR
Description: The control can use this property to retrieve a container-specified name that it should display in error messages.

Font
Type: OLE_FONT
Description: This specifies the standard font that the control should use. The control can interpret this property in whatever fashion it chooses.

ForeColor
Type: OLE_COLOR
Description: This specifies the color for text and graphics in a control.

LocaleID
Type: VT_I4
Description: This property specifies the locale identifier for the container's UI.

MessageReflect
Type: VT_BOOL
Description: The MessageReflect property indicates whether or not the container reflects Windows messages back to the control.

ScaleUnits
Type: VT_BSTR
Description: The container specifies the name of its coordinate units using this property.

TextAlign
Type: VT_I2
Description: The container uses this property to specify the text alignment in the control. Valid values for the property, with their meaning, are 0—general alignment, numbers to the right and text to the left; 1—left-justify text; 2—center-justify text; 3—right-justify text; and 4—full-justify text.

UserMode
Type: VT_BOOL
Description: This indicates the current user-interaction mode. If it is FALSE, the user-interaction mode is Design Mode; otherwise, the user-interaction mode is viewing or interacting.

UIDead
Type: VT_BOOL
Description: The control can use this to determine whether or not the container is allowing user input. A situation in which it is very useful for a control to disallow control interaction is during a container's "Debug" mode (assuming, of course, that the container has such a mode).

ShowGrabHandles

Type: VT_BOOL

Description: The container uses ShowGrabHandles to indicate to controls whether or not they should display grab handles when they are UI active.

ShowHatching

Type: VT_BOOL

Description: This property allows the container to indicate the desired hatching feedback for UI-active controls.

DisplayAsDefaultButton

Type: VT_BOOL

Description: Button-like controls use this property to determine whether they should display themselves using a visual default button indication (such as a thick border).

SupportsMnemonics

Type: VT_BOOL

Description: Containers indicate support for control mnemonics using this property.

AutoClip

Type: VT_BOOL

Description: This property indicates whether or not the container will perform automatic clipping for the control.

Some ambient properties, such as UserMode, may apply to all the controls within a control container. Other ambient properties, such as BackColor, may depend on the window to which the control is connected.

Extended Controls

Extended controls may be implemented by control containers to provide a wrapper for contained controls. Extended controls allow containers to associate any additional information or events they may need to maintain controls. Wrapping a control with an extended control simply involves performing standard COM aggregation. When a container creates a control instance, it passes in a controlling unknown that implements IDispatch for extended properties and events. If a request for a control property is received by the extended control, it passes the request through to the control's interface implementation.

The advantage of wrapping controls with extended controls is that the container can treat its properties and events, and the control's properties and events, without specialized code. Visual Basic is one of the best examples of a container that implements extended controls due to the seamless integration with its user interface.

Visual Basic and Extended Controls

Visual Basic uses extended controls. Each control embedded in a Visual Basic form has extended properties that store information such as a control's top and left coordinates within a form.

Visual Basic does an excellent job of integrating extended properties and events with standard control properties and events. Earlier in this chapter, you were introduced to the SimpleControl OLE control. SimpleControl has only two properties, SimpleName and SimpleName2, and two events, Click and OnSimpleNameChange. However, after you've added a SimpleControl to a VB form, a whole bunch of properties appear for the SimpleControl object. Figure 6.1 illustrates the properties box for the SimpleControl object in Visual Basic. Notice that SimpleControl's properties are integrated with the other Visual Basic extended properties. From the user's perspective, there is no difference between the properties maintained by the control and the properties maintained by Visual Basic.

Figure 6.1.
*The Visual Basic
Property Editor.*

Visual Basic also has a tool called the Object Browser. The Object Browser displays the methods and properties exposed by either a Visual Basic control or a referenced type. A user can add referenced types to Visual Basic using type libraries and Visual Basic's Tools | References_ menu option. Figure 6.2 illustrates the display from the Object Browser when SimpleControl is added as a control to a Visual Basic project.

Figure 6.2.
*The Object Browser's
view of* SimpleControl
as a control.

If `SimpleControl` is added to a Visual Basic project as a reference instead of a control, only the properties and methods that are part of `SimpleControl` are visible in the Object Browser. Figure 6.3 shows the Object Browser when `SimpleControl` is loaded as a reference.

Figure 6.3.
The Object Browser's view of `SimpleControl` *as a reference.*

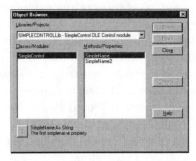

As indicated previously, Visual Basic also adds events to its controls. `SimpleControl` has only `Click` and `OnSimpleNameChange` events; Figure 6.4 illustrates `SimpleControl`'s events and the events added by Visual Basic.

Figure 6.4.
Visual Basic's Code Editor listing `SimpleControl`'s *events.*

Unlike ambient property guidelines, there is no standard for the set of extended properties or events implemented by a control container. Visual Basic provides a good model for extended property integration; it includes properties that handle generic issues such as storing control layout information (top, left, and so on), and it integrates those properties seamlessly with its user interface.

Required Container Interfaces

There are a substantial number of OLE interfaces that must be implemented by an OLE control container. The following sections describe the interfaces and the expected behavior of the container upon receiving a method call on the interface.

Some of the methods are indicated as optional methods; the optional methods are not essential for the functioning of controls in a control container. Containers can return E_NOTIMPL or S_OK as appropriate for the optional methods.

OleClientSite

Controls use IOleClientSite to obtain information about their container, including information that can be used to interact with other controls in the container.

```
HRESULT IOleClientSite::GetContainer(LPOLECONTAINER FAR* ppContainer);
```

The control uses this method to acquire a pointer to the container's IOleContainer interface. A control may use the IOleContainer interface to navigate to other controls contained within the control's container.

```
HRESULT IOleClientSite::ShowObject();
```

The control uses this method to ask its container to show itself; this ensures that the control and container are visible.

```
HRESULT IOleClientSite::OnShowWindow(BOOL fShow);
```

The control calls this to notify its container when its window is about to become visible or invisible:

```
HRESULT IOleClientSite::SaveObject();(optional)
```

This method is typically used to save the object that is connected to a client site. The embedded object uses SaveObject() to request its container to save it to persistent storage; the object will probably call this method during the call to its IOleObject::Close() method.

```
HRESULT IOleClientSite::GetMoniker(DWORD dwAssign, DWORD dwWhichMoniker,
_IMoniker **ppmk);(optional)
```

GetMoniker() is used by an embedded object to request a moniker, which is used to support OLE linking, from its container.

```
HRESULT IOleClientSite::RequestNewObjectLayout();(optional)
```

A loaded but inactive control uses RequestNewObjectLayout() to ask its container to allocate more or less space to display the control. In the implementation of RequestNewObjectLayout(), the container can query the control for the desired size by calling the control's GetExtent() method.

IAdviseSink

Control containers need to implement IAdviseSink only if they want to receive notifications of changes to controls that support IDataObject or IViewObject. Containers may also choose to implement this if they support insertion of controls as standard embedded OLE objects.

```
void IAdviseSink::OnDataChange(FORMATETC* pFormatetc, STGMEDIUM* pStgmed);
```

If a control supports IDataObject, it can notify its container of data changes through this method.

```
void IAdviseSink::OnViewChange(DWORD dwAspect, LONG lindex);
```

If a control supports IViewObject, it can call this container method to indicate that the view of the control has changed.

```
void IAdviseSink::OnRename(IMoniker *pmk);
```

This container member will be called when a control's moniker changes—if the control supports linking.

```
void IAdviseSink::OnSave();
```

The control uses OnSave() to notify its container that it has been saved.

```
void IAdviseSink::OnClose();
```

Controls use OnClose() to indicate a transition from running to loaded state.

OleInPlaceSite

This interface is used to manage interaction between a control container and a control's client site. The client site is the display site for the control; consequently, the interface is derived from the IOleWindow interface. IOleInPlaceSite provides methods that may be used to manage the activation and deactivation of a control, retrieve information about the position in the parent window where the control should place its in-place activation window, manage scrolling of the control, the control's undo state, and control borders.

```
HRESULT IOleWindow::GetWindow(HWND* phwind);
```

The control uses this to retrieve the handle to its in-place window.

```
HRESULT IOleWindow::ContextSensitiveHelp(BOOL fEnterMode);
```

A control can notify its container of a request for context-sensitive help by calling this container method.

```
HRESULT IOleInPlaceSite::CanInPlaceActivate();
```

This is used by the control to determine whether or not the container will allow it to be active in place.

```
HRESULT IOleInPlaceSite::OnInPlaceActivate();
```

The control calls this to notify its container that it is in the process of becoming in-place active.

```
HRESULT IOleInPlaceSite::OnUIActivate();
```

The control uses this method to notify its container that it is about to be activated in place. In response and if appropriate, the container should remove whatever user interface is part of its own activation. If a different control is being deactivated as this control becomes active, the container should notify the other control of its state change using its UIDeactivate() method.

```
HRESULT IOleInPlaceSite::GetWindowContext(IOleInPlaceFrame** ppFrame,
_IOleInPlaceUIWindow** ppDoc,LPRECT lprcPosRect, LPRECT lprcClipRect,
_LPOLEINPLACEFRAMEINFO lpFrameInfo);
```

A control calls this on activation to retrieve pointers to the IOleInPlaceFrame and IOleInPlaceUIWindow interfaces provided by its container, the position and clipping rectangles for the control, and an OLEINPLACEFRAMEINFO structure listing accelerators supported by a container during an in-place session.

```
HRESULT IOleInPlaceSite::Scroll(SIZE scrollExtent);
```

This is called by a control to request its container to scroll. After the container has finished scrolling, it should check whether the control's visible rectangle has been affected. If it has been affected, the container should call the control's SetObjectRects() on the IOleInPlaceObject interface to give the control a new clipping rectangle.

```
HRESULT IOleInPlaceSite::OnUIDeactivate(BOOL fUndoable);
```

The control uses this to notify its container that it is deactivating its user interface components; correspondingly, the container should reinstall its user interface. The fUndoable flag indicates whether or not the control can undo changes that occurred; to undo the changes, the container can call the control's OleInPlaceObject::ReactivateAndUndo() method.

```
HRESULT IOleInPlaceSite::OnInPlaceDeactivate();
```

Controls call the container's OnInPlaceDeactivate() method to indicate that they are fully deactivated. After a control has called this method, it is no longer possible for the container to undo changes.

```
HRESULT IOleInPlaceSite::DiscardUndoState();
```

This method is used by the control to indicate to its container that there is no longer any undo state; therefore, the container should not call the control's `OleInPlaceObject::ReactivateAndUndo()` method.

```
HRESULT IOleInPlaceSite::DeactivateAndUndo();
```

The control calls this if the user invokes undo immediately after activating it. In response, the container should call the control's `IOleInPlaceObject::UIDeactivate()` method to activate itself, remove the control's UI, and undo changes to the control's state.

```
HRESULT IOleInPlaceSite::OnPosRectChange(LPCRECT lprcPosRect);
```

This is called by a control to indicate a size change; the container should call the control's `IOleInPlaceObject::SetObjectRects()` to inform the control of the new size and position of the in-place window and new clipping rectangle.

IOleControlSite

Control containers implement this interface to communicate with embedded controls. The following methods are part of the `IOleControlSite` interface.

```
HRESULT IOleControlSite::OnControlInfoChanged(void);
```

The control calls this method to indicate to the container that the control's control information has changed. The control information is stored within the CONTROLINFO structure; the container can retrieve the updated information from the control using the `GetControlInfo` method on the control's `IOleControl` interface. The CONTROLINFO structure contains control keyboard accelerators and keyboard behavior flags.

```
HRESULT IOleControlSite::LockInPlaceActivate(BOOL fLock);
```

The control calls this to determine whether or not it should remain in-place active even if some type of deactivation event occurs.

```
HRESULT IOleControlSite::GetExtendedControl(IDispatch** ppDisp);
```

This is called by the control to obtain the IDispatch pointer to the extended control implemented by the container. Extended controls are used by the control container to maintain additional properties for a control, such as its X and Y location within the control container. Control containers such as Visual Basic use extended controls to implement standard control properties such as top, left, height, and width.

```
HRESULT IOleControlSite::TransformCoords(POINTL* pptlHimetric,
_POINTF* pptfContainer, DWORD dwFlags);
```

The control uses this to convert OLE standard HIMETRIC units in a POINTL structure to the units preferred by the container in a POINTF structure. This method may also be used to do the reverse—that is, convert coordinates from control into standard HIMETRIC units.

```
HRESULT IOleControlSite::TranslateAccelerator(LPMSG pMsg, DWORD grfModifiers);
```

UI-active controls use this method to defer keystroke processing to their container. After a control becomes UI active, the container transfers keystrokes to the control using the TranslateAccelerator() method on the control's IOleInPlaceActiveObject interface.

```
HRESULT IOleControlSite::OnFocus(BOOL fGotFocus);
```

This is called by the control to indicate to the container whether it has gained or lost input focus; the container can manage Default and Cancel button states accordingly.

```
HRESULT IOleControlSite::ShowPropertyFrame();
```

The control uses this method to request that the container display a property page frame for the control. The container can take the opportunity to create a property frame that includes pages for extended control properties; this ensures that both extended and standard control properties are maintained within a single, consistent user interface.

IOleInPlaceFrame

Controls that have associated frame-level tools, such as toolbars or menu items, use this container interface to manage container user-interface changes on control activation. Containers can choose to implement optional methods based on their user-interface characteristics. For example, if a container has toolbars, it may choose to implement the toolbar-oriented negotiation functions such as GetBorder() and RequestBorderSpace().

```
HRESULT IOleWindow::GetWindow(HWND* phwind);
```

The control uses this to retrieve the handle to its in-place window.

```
HRESULT IOleWindow::ContextSensitiveHelp(BOOL fEnterMode);(optional)
```

A control can notify its container of a request for context-sensitive help by calling this container method.

```
HRESULT IOleInPlaceUIWindow::GetBorder(LPRECT lprcBorder);(optional)
```

Controls can use this container method to retrieve the outer rectangle, relative to the frame window, where the control can install its toolbar(s).

```
HRESULT IOleInPlaceUIWindow::RequestBorderSpace(LPCBORDERWIDTHS
_pborderwidths);(optional)
```

A control calls RequestBorderSpace() with a rectangle indicating the desired space for a toolbar before attempting to install its toolbar UI. If the container accepts the request by returning S_OK, the control can call SetBorderSpace() to ask the container to allocate the requested space.

```
HRESULT IOleInPlaceUIWindow::SetBorderSpace(LPCBORDERWIDTHS
_pborderwidths);(optional)
```

The container's SetBorderSpace() method is called when the control requests the allocation of space for the control's toolbar.

```
HRESULT IOleInPlaceUIWindow::SetActiveObject(IOleInPlaceActiveObject*pActiveObject,
_LPCOLESTR pszObjName);
```

Controls call SetActiveObject() to establish a communication link to the container's frame window.

```
HRESULT IOleInPlaceFrame::InsertMenus(HMENU hmenuShared,
_LPOLEMENUGROUPWIDTHS lpMenuWidths);(optional)
```

This method is called by controls to build up a composite menu containing the container and control's menu items.

```
HRESULT IOleInPlaceFrame::SetMenu(HMENU hmenuShared, HOLEMENU holemenu,
_HWND hwndActiveObject);(optional)
```

SetMenu() is called by controls to request that the container install a composite menu built up by previous calls to InsertMenus().

```
HRESULT IOleInPlaceFrame::RemoveMenus(HMENU hmenuShared);(optional)
```

The control calls this method to allow the container to remove its menu elements from the composite menu.

```
HRESULT IOleInPlaceFrame::SetStatusText(LPCOLESTR pszStatusText);(optional)
```

A control can call SetStatusText() to request that the container display status text from the control in the container's status line.

```
HRESULT IOleInPlaceFrame::EnableModeless(BOOL fEnable);(optional)
```

The control can call EnableModeless(FALSE) to ask its container to disable any modeless dialog boxes that it may be displaying. After the container has done so, the control may display its own modal dialog. When it is finished, the control should call EnableModeless(TRUE) to re-enable the container's modeless dialogs.

```
HRESULT IOleInPlaceFrame::TranslateAccelerator(LPMSG lpmsg, WORD wID);
```

This method is used to translate keystrokes intended for a container's frame window when a control is active in place.

IOleContainer

Controls can use a container's implementation of IOleContainer to retrieve information about other controls in the container or to perform object-linking functions.

```
RESULT IOleContainer::ParseDisplayName(IBindCtx* pbc, LPOLESTR pszDisplayName,
_UNLONG* pchEaten, IMoniker** ppmkOut);(optional)
```

Controls that support linking use this to ask their container to parse a display name and create a moniker. Containers need to implement this method only if they support links to controls or other embedded objects.

```
HRESULT IOleContainer::LockContainer(BOOL fLock);(optional)
```

If a control and its container support linking, the control will call LockContainer(TRUE) to keep the container running until all link clients have been updated. After the clients have been updated, the control should call LockContainer(FALSE) to remove external locks on the container and allow the container to terminate.

```
HRESULT IOleContainer::EnumObjects(DWORD grfFlags, IEnumUnknown** ppenum);
```

A control can use this method to enumerate all the controls and objects in its container. It's important to note that the enumerator may not actually return all visible controls in the container because some of them may be standard Windows controls.

Optional Container Interfaces

There are a number of container interfaces that are not required but that may be implemented or supported by containers that require their functionality. The following sections describe the interfaces and the expected behavior of the control or container upon receiving a method call on the interface.

SimpleFrameSite

Containers can choose to implement support for the ISimpleFrameSite interface if they want to support controls that contain other controls. An example of a control that might make use of this interface is a group box that handles certain interaction characteristics of its contained controls. The purpose of this class is to allow controls to filter messages to controls that they contain while allowing them to defer messages for processing by the root control container.

```
HRESULT ISimpleFrameSite::PreMessageFilter(HWND hwnd,
    UINT msg, WPARAM wParam, LPARAM lParam,
    LRESULT* plResult, DWORD* pdwCookie);
```

This method gives a control the opportunity to process a message that is received by a contained control's window before the contained control does any processing.

```
HRESULT ISimpleFrameSite::PostMessageFilter(HWND hwnd,
    UINT msg, WPARAM wParam, LPARAM lParam,
    LRESULT* plResult, DWORD* pdwCookie);
```

A control can use this method to defer message processing to the control's container after the control and its contained control have had an opportunity to process the message.

PropertyNotifySink

Containers implement the IPropertyNotifySink interface if they want to receive notifications about control property changes. This is useful, for example, if a container maintains its own property-editing user interface. Because this is an outgoing interface, the container must connect this to the control using the connection-point mechanism.

```
HRESULT IPropertyNotifySink::OnChanged(DISPID dispid);
```

The control uses this method to notify the container that the property with the dispatch ID dispid has changed.

```
HRESULT IPropertyNotifySink::OnRequestEdit(DISPID dispid);
```

The control uses OnRequestEdit() to notify its container that one of its properties is going to change. The container can respond with S_OK or S_FALSE. The result S_OK allows the control to proceed with the change; S_FALSE indicates that the container won't allow the control to make the change.

ClassFactory2

Support for IClassFactory2, described earlier in this chapter in the section titled "Creating an OLE Control Instance," allows a control container to support runtime licensing. It is implemented by the control, not the control container. If the control implements it, the container may use it as an alternative to IClassFactory to instantiate a control.

Creating an MFC-Based Dialog Box Control Container

The AppWizard, Microsoft Foundation Classes, and the ClassWizard, all of which are integrated pieces of the Microsoft Developer's Studio, make it trivial to create a dialog box that is a very functional OLE control container.

To create a dialog-based control container, perform the following steps from the Microsoft Developer's Studio:

1. Create a new project named DlgContainer using the MFC AppWizard. The application type should be executable.
2. On the first wizard page, select Dialog Base and click Next.
3. On the second wizard page, select the OLE Controls option.
4. Click Finish and OK to allow the AppWizard to create your project.
5. Go to the Resources tab in the project workspace, expand the list of dialog resources by double-clicking the Dialog folder, and double-click to edit the dialog resource with the IDD_DLGCONTAINER_DIALOG identifier.
6. Select Insert, Component from the menu bar. The Component Gallery dialog box will appear. Click the OLE Controls tab. Figure 6.5 shows the Component Gallery dialog.

Figure 6.5.
The Component Gallery dialog.

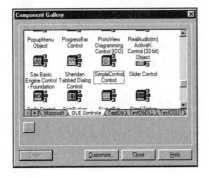

7. Select a control to insert into the project. I've selected the SimpleControl, indicated with a red "thumbs-up" bitmap, that was generated using the MFC OLE Control classes. Click the Insert button to add the OLE control to your project.
8. After you have clicked the Insert button, a dialog box will appear that asks you to confirm the name of the control wrapper class that will automatically be generated. Figure 6.6 illustrates the Confirm Classes dialog. Select OK to accept the CSimpleControl class name. The Component Gallery will generate a C++ header and source files for the CSimpleControl class. Select Close to return to the resource editor.

Figure 6.6.
*The Confirm Classes
dialog.*

> **note**
>
> The SimpleControl that is being used here has only simple BSTR-based
> properties; if a control had been inserted that supports fonts or pic-
> tures, two additional classes would have been created—CFont and
> CPicture.

9. On the Resource Editor toolbar, you will notice an additional item, a red
   thumbs-up that is identical to the control bitmap in the Component
   Gallery. Select the thumbs-up and draw a SimpleControl on the dialog box.

10. Select the new control on the dialog box, and right-click or press
    Alt+Enter to display the control properties. Figure 6.7 illustrates the
    Resource Editor display after showing the properties. The first page
    includes properties from the Developer's Studio, the second and third
    pages are directly provided by the SimpleControl, and the last page
    contains all of the control properties presented by the Developer's Studio
    in list format.

Figure 6.7.
*The Resource Editor
with* SimpleControl's
properties.

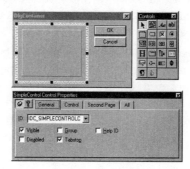

11. Save the modified dialog resource (File | Save from the menu); then
    press Control+W to display the Control Wizard.

12. Go the Member Variables tab in the Control Wizard, select the
CDlgContainerDlg class, and then select the IDC_SIMPLECONTROLCTRL1 control
ID. Click the Add Variable button; a dialog box will appear prompting for
the name of the variable. Enter m_simpctrl for the variable name; the
variable category should already be control and the variable type should
be CSimpleControl.

That's all it takes to create an MFC project that includes a dialog box that contains
an OLE control! It's truly remarkable considering the amount of effort that would
be needed to support the same functionality if you implemented the equivalent
dialog from scratch.

The Developer's Studio is doing some pretty interesting things here. First, to
create the OLE Control page in the Component Gallery, it's scanning the registry
to find controls, extracting their toolbar bitmaps, and finally adding them to what
looks like a ListView control for user selection.

Second, the Developer's Studio is generating a C++ class that wraps the OLE
control. Each of the properties of the control is exposed through Get/Set class
methods; likewise, the OLE control methods are exposed as class methods. Later
in this chapter, you'll learn about some of the magic behind the implementation
of the MFC classes that enables them to take standard C++ function calls and
convert them to IDispatch calls that OLE controls understand.

Third, event information from the control is scanned and included in the
ClassWizard Message Maps tab. Figure 6.8 shows the ClassWizard with message
maps for SimpleControl.

Figure 6.8.
The ClassWizard with
SimpleControl
messages.

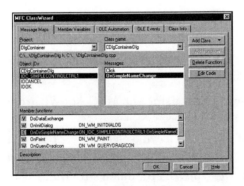

To handle the OnSimpleNameChange event fired by the SimpleControl included in the
aforementioned example, all you need to do is select the IDC_SIMPLECONTROL1 object
ID and the OnSimpleNameChange message, and then click the Add Function button.
The ClassWizard integrates window-message handling and control-event handling into the same easy-to-use user interface. That's very impressive when you

consider that the method of retrieving standard window-type events is completely different from that of retrieving Event Sink–based OLE control messages.

Having read the descriptions of the interfaces required for OLE control containers and the information about the interaction between control and container, you should be very impressed with the Microsoft Developer's Studio and MFC! The Developer's Studio integrates OLE controls directly into the development environment and alleviates literally all of the work required to implement a control container.

Creating a Non-Dialog, Resource-Based MFC SDI Control Container

Creating a non-dialog, resource-based MFC SDI control container is somewhat more complex than creating a dialog-resource–based control container. MFC includes several types of `CView`-derived classes. Some of them, such as `CFormView`, use dialog resources to lay out controls. Others, like the base `CView` class, don't use dialog resources for layout. Adding controls to `CView` classes is more complex than adding controls to resource-based views because it requires that you create the control explicitly in code and it doesn't automatically integrate control events into the ClassWizard.

Luckily, creating the control in code is pretty simple. Unfortunately, handling control events involves significantly more manual code editing. The explanations will cover control events after discussing the basic details of creating an SDI control container.

Create the SDI Container Application

To create an SDI control container, perform the following steps from the Microsoft Developer's Studio:

1. Create a new project using the MFC AppWizard for executables; name the project `SDIContainer`.

2. In Step 1 of the AppWizard, select Single document for the type of application. Click Next twice to go to Step 3 of the AppWizard.

3. In Step 3 of the AppWizard, make sure that the check box next to OLE controls is checked. Click Finish to generate the application.

4. Select Insert | Component from the Main Menu. The Component Gallery dialog box will launch. Select the `SimpleControl` control from the OLE Controls tab and then click Insert. Click Confirm in the class confirmation dialog, then click Close in the Component Gallery.

After completing these steps, you will notice that the ClassView tab of the project browser contains a new class—CSimpleControl. The Developer's Studio created this class in the same manner that the CSimpleControl class was created in the previous dialog box control-container example.

Now the manual code editing begins; open SDIContainerView.h in the code editor and make the changes shown in bold in the following code snippet:

```
Excerpt from SDIContainerView.h -
// SDIContainerView.h : interface of the CSDIContainerView class
//
/////////////////////////////////////////////////////////////////

#include "SimpleControl.h"

class CSDIContainerView : public CView
{
...
protected:
    // m_simpctrl is the member that will be used to
    // manipulate the OLE control
    CSimpleControl m_simpctrl;
// Generated message map functions
protected:
    //{{AFX_MSG(CSDIContainerView)
        // NOTE - the ClassWizard will add and remove member functions here.
        //      DO NOT EDIT what you see in these blocks of generated code !
    //}}AFX_MSG
    DECLARE_MESSAGE_MAP()
    DECLARE_EVENTSINK_MAP()
};
...
```

The basic change is adding the SimpleControl.h header file to the view implementation header file, as well as a new member, m_simpctrl, to access and create an instance of the SimpleControl OLE control. You may not recognize the addition of the DECLARE_EVENTSINK_MAP() macro. That macro sets up the event sink for the view object; if you go back to the previous dialog box control container example, you'll notice that this was added without any intervention on your behalf.

Next, use the ClassWizard to create the CSDIContainerView::OnCreate function to handle the WM_CREATE message for the View class. In the body of CSDIContainerView:: OnCreate, add code to create the SimpleControl OLE control instance. The required changes are marked in bold in the following code snippet:

```
Excerpt from SDIContainerView.cpp -

/////////////////////////////////////////////////////////////////
// CSDIContainerView message handlers

int CSDIContainerView::OnCreate(LPCREATESTRUCT lpCreateStruct)
{
    if (CView::OnCreate(lpCreateStruct) == -1)
        return -1;
```

```
    // TODO: Add your specialized creation code here
    m_simpctrl.Create(NULL, WS_VISIBLE, CRect(10, 10, 100, 100),
        this, ID_SIMPLECTRL);

    return 0;
}
```

The call to CSimpleControl::Create() initializes the OLE control and attaches it to the CView object (or specifically, in this case, the CSDIContainerView object that is derived from CView). One of the parameters to the call, ID_SIMPLECTRL, hasn't been defined yet. ID_SIMPLECTRL is an arbitrary identifier that will be associated with the SimpleControl instance; the identifier will be used when you make additions to the CSDIContainerView's Event Sink map. You're also missing the implementation of the Event Sink map, which you previously declared in the header using DECLARE_EVENTSINK_MAP(). To add the identifier and Event Sink map, make the following (bold) additions to SDIContainerView.cpp:

Excerpt from SDIContainerView.cpp -

```
// SDIContainerView.cpp : implementation of the CSDIContainerView class
//

#include "stdafx.h"
#include "SDIContainer.h"

#include "SDIContainerDoc.h"
#include "SDIContainerView.h"

#ifdef _DEBUG
#define new DEBUG_NEW
#undef THIS_FILE
static char THIS_FILE[] = __FILE__;
#endif

#define ID_SIMPLECTRL    0

/////////////////////////////////////////////////////////////////////////////
// CSDIContainerView

IMPLEMENT_DYNCREATE(CSDIContainerView, CView)

BEGIN_MESSAGE_MAP(CSDIContainerView, CView)
...
END_MESSAGE_MAP()

BEGIN_EVENTSINK_MAP(CSDIContainerView, CView)
END_EVENTSINK_MAP()
```

Now you have a functional SDI OLE control container application that contains a single OLE control. Properties and methods of the control can be accessed using the member functions of the CSimpleControl class; the only major piece of functionality that's missing is the capability of getting events from the control. You've already established the foundation for the event dispatch by including the necessary macro declarations in the CSDIContainer header and implementation files.

Add Event Handling

The SimpleControl OLE control exposes only two events: Click and OnSimpleNameChange. In the previous dialog box control-container example, events from the SimpleControl control object were listed directly in the ClassWizard. Unfortunately, such is not the case with SDI or MDI MFC applications; you must add the code manually. As previously indicated, you've already added the necessary Event Sink macros. Now you need to add entries to the Event Sink map that correspond to the events you want to capture.

Events are added to the Event Sink using the ON_EVENT() macro. The details of the ON_EVENT() macro are described later in this chapter; for now, the explanation covers only what is necessary to handle the OnSimpleNameChange event.

To use the ON_EVENT() macro, you need to know the DISPID or member ID of the event that you want to capture, and the types of parameters passed to the event. You can get that information using the OLE Object View utility (OLE2VW23.EXE), which can be launched from the Tools menu in the Developer's Studio. To get the parameters and ID of the event, open the type information for the SimpleControl control by using the Object | View File | View Type | Library_ menu option and selecting SimpleControl.ocx from the File | Open dialog box. Figure 6.9 illustrates the information from Object View.

Figure 6.9.
SimpleControl *type information in Object View.*

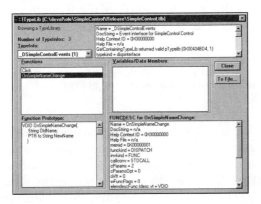

The following is the function prototype reported by the Object Viewer for the OnSimpleNameChange event:

```
VOID OnSimpleNameChange(
    String OldName,
    PTR to String NewName
    )
```

Translated into a C++ prototype, with the function attribute required for MFC message handlers, that is

```
afx_msg void OnSimpleNameChange(LPCTSTR OldName, BSTR FAR* NewName);
```

The DISPID for the event is 1; it's listed in the Object Viewer as memid = 0x00000001.

Go ahead and add a member function that handles the event to the CSDIContainerView class. You'll call the member function OnSimpleNameChange() in accordance with the aforementioned prototype. The changes to the SDIContainerView.h and SDIContainerView.cpp are listed in bold as follows:

```
Excerpt from SDIContainerView.h -

...

    DECLARE_MESSAGE_MAP()
    DECLARE_EVENTSINK_MAP()
    afx_msg void OnSimpleNameChange(LPCTSTR OldName, BSTR FAR* NewName);
};
...


Excerpt from SDIContainerView.cpp -

...
afx_msg void CSDIContainerView::OnSimpleNameChange(LPCTSTR OldName,
    BSTR FAR* NewName)
{
    AfxMessageBox("CSDIContainerView::OnSimpleNameChange");
}
...
```

Now you can add the ON_EVENT() entry to the Event Sink map. Add the following changes, marked in bold, to SDIContainerView.cpp:

```
...
BEGIN_EVENTSINK_MAP(CSDIContainerView, CView)
    ON_EVENT(CSDIContainerView, ID_SIMPLECTRL, 1, \
        OnSimpleNameChange, VTS_BSTR VTS_PBSTR)
END_EVENTSINK_MAP()
...
```

The arguments to the ON_EVENT() macro are pretty straightforward: the name of the class that gets the event; the ID of the control that generates the event (this was the ID that was used to create the control in CSDIContainerView::OnCreate()); the dispatch ID of the event; the name of the CSDIContainerView member function that is called when the event occurs; and the arguments to the event function encoded as strings. The reason why they are encoded as strings will be discussed later in the chapter.

Now test your newly implemented Event Sink. To do so, you need to write some code that causes the OLE control to fire the OnSimpleNameChange event. Go to the resource tab on the project workspace and edit the main menu, IDR_MAINFRAME. Add a separator after Paste on the Edit menu, and then add a menu item called Change SimpleName, with C as the hot key. Change the ID of the option to IDM_CHANGE_SIMPLENAME (you can do this in the Menu Item Properties dialog). Next, add a message handler to CSDIContainerView using the ClassWizard; the default name for the menu message handler (assuming that you correctly chose the Object ID IDM_CHANGE_SIMPLENAME and the COMMAND message) will be OnSimpleNameChange. Change it so it is OnMenuSimpleNameChange—then click the Edit Code button.

Make sure that your implementation of the message handler for IDM_CHANGE_ SIMPLENAME is as follows:

```
void CSDIContainerView::OnMenuChangeSimpleName()
{
    m_simpctrl.SetSimpleName("ANewName");
}
```

Setting the SimpleName property of the SimpleControl instance causes the OnSimpleNameChange() event to fire; MFC ensures that the CSDIContainerView:: OnSimpleNameChange() function is called to handle it.

Details of MFC Control Container Implementation

The Microsoft Foundation Classes do some very interesting things to ease the use of controls in a control container. As previously indicated, the Microsoft Developer's Studio contains integrated tools that automatically generate classes to wrap the complexity of the control/container interface. Two of the most interesting and enlightening examples of MFC's control/container code are evident in the MFC implementation of property Get/Set and the implementation of event handling.

MFC Implementation of Property Get/Set

The Microsoft Foundation Classes use a unique and intricate, but easy-to-use, mechanism to implement property Get/Set methods for controls embedded in a container. The foundation (no pun intended!) of the mechanism is the COleDispatchDriver class. COleDispatchDriver contains a public function named InvokeHelperV that is used to translate standard C++ style function calls into Dispatch type calls.

There are some interesting problems that MFC tackles here; the arguments to the property Get/Set method are on the stack, which is the convention for C++ function calls. The parameters are also standard C/C++ data types, such as longs. Furthermore, the fact that exposed C++ member functions can be called as standard C++ member functions is remarkable if you consider that the target for the function call is an OLE control, which uses OLE automation as the means for property and method calls.

C++ format function calls are, of course, not what the IDispatch::Invoke() function expects. The convention for calls using IDispatch::Invoke involves passing parameters as variants in a parameter array to a function called using a DISPID.

To demonstrate the MFC answer to the thorny problem of mapping C++ style calls to IDispatch::Invoke() calls, I created a dialog-based MFC application using the AppWizard. I then added a grid control to the main dialog using the component browser; after saving the modified dialog resource, I used ClassWizard to create a member variable to wrap the grid in the main dialog class. In the process of creating the member variable, the ClassWizard scanned the OLE type information from the control, and generated gridctrl.cpp and gridctrl.h files.

The gridctrl.h Header File

The gridctrl.h header file contains the definition for a CGridCtrl class, derived from CWnd, that implements the properties and methods exposed by the control as C++ class member functions. An excerpt of the class definition from gridctrl.h follows:

```
...
class CGridCtrl : public CWnd
{
protected:
    DECLARE_DYNCREATE(CGridCtrl)
public:
    CLSID const& GetClsid()
    {
        static CLSID const clsid = { 0xa8c3b720, 0xb5a, 0x101b,
            { 0xb2, 0x2e, 0x0, 0xaa, 0x0, 0x37, 0xb2, 0xfc } };
        return clsid;
    }
...
// Attributes
public:
...
    short GetRows();
    void SetRows(short);
    short GetCols();
    void SetCols(short);
...
// Operations
public:
    void AboutBox();
    long GetRowHeight(short Index);
    void SetRowHeight(short Index, long nNewValue);
    long GetColWidth(short Index);
    void SetColWidth(short Index, long nNewValue);
...
};
```

The class contains the CLSID of the wrapped control and a function to access the CLSID, as well as function declarations that correspond to properties and methods exposed by the control.

The GetRows and SetRows functions provide functionality that would be provided inside a container such as Visual Basic using the standard assignment operator. In Visual Basic, ctrl.Rows = 10 would therefore correspond to the C++ function call ctrl.SetRows(10).

The interesting part of this equation—the implementation of the property Get/Set functions—is in the automatically generated gridctrl.cpp file.

The gridctrl.cpp Implementation File

The following excerpt from the gridctrl.cpp file illustrates the implementation of some of the aforementioned property Get/Set methods and general method calls:

```
// CGridCtrl
...
/////////////////////////////////////////////////////////////////////////////
// CGridCtrl properties
...
short CGridCtrl::GetRows()
{
    short result;
    GetProperty(0x8, VT_I2, (void*)&result);
    return result;
}

void CGridCtrl::SetRows(short propVal)
{
    SetProperty(0x8, VT_I2, propVal);
}

short CGridCtrl::GetCols()
{
    short result;
    GetProperty(0x9, VT_I2, (void*)&result);
    return result;
}

void CGridCtrl::SetCols(short propVal)
{
    SetProperty(0x9, VT_I2, propVal);
}
...
/////////////////////////////////////////////////////////////////////////////
// CGridCtrl operations
...
long CGridCtrl::GetRowHeight(short Index)
{
    long result;
    static BYTE parms[] =
        VTS_I2;
    InvokeHelper(0x1f, DISPATCH_PROPERTYGET, VT_I4, (void*)&result, parms,
        Index);
    return result;
}

void CGridCtrl::SetRowHeight(short Index, long nNewValue)
```

```
{
    static BYTE parms[] =
        VTS_I2 VTS_I4;
    InvokeHelper(0x1f, DISPATCH_PROPERTYPUT, VT_EMPTY, NULL, parms,
        Index, nNewValue);
}

long CGridCtrl::GetColWidth(short Index)
{
    long result;
    static BYTE parms[] =
        VTS_I2;
    InvokeHelper(0x20, DISPATCH_PROPERTYGET, VT_I4, (void*)&result, parms,
        Index);
    return result;
}

void CGridCtrl::SetColWidth(short Index, long nNewValue)
{
    static BYTE parms[] =
        VTS_I2 VTS_I4;
    InvokeHelper(0x20, DISPATCH_PROPERTYPUT, VT_EMPTY, NULL, parms,
        Index, nNewValue);
}
...
```

The manifest constants in the parms[] arrays are expanded to strings during precompilation. The output from the precompiler for CGridCtrl::GetRowHeight follows:

```
long CGridCtrl::GetRowHeight(short Index)
{
    long result;
    static BYTE parms[] =
        "\x02";
    InvokeHelper(0x1f, 0x2, VT_I4, (void*)&result, parms,
        Index);
    return result;
}
```

The precompiled output is interesting because it makes the definition of the parms[] array somewhat more clear. It's also interesting because it shows how the mapping from the C++ function name to the DISPID required by IDispatch::Invoke occurs; the ClassWizard fills the first parameter to InvokeHelper with the DISPID, in this case the constant 0x1f, of the corresponding GetRowHeight IDispatch-exposed method.

From the definition of the Get/SetRowHeight functions, it's clear that MFC is using the InvokeHelper function to somehow translate the C++ function calls to IDispatch::Invoke() calls.

The `InvokeHelper` Function

The CGridCtrl's reference to the InvokeHelper() function is a reference to the CWnd::InvokeHelper() function. In turn, CWnd::InvokeHelper() is little more than a wrapper for the COleControlSite::InvokeHelper() function, which is pretty trivial; it sets up a variable argument list and forwards the function call to the COleControlSite::InvokeHelperV() function. Unsurprisingly, the COleControlSite::InvokeHelperV() call still isn't the end of the road; MFC aficionados will attest to the fact that the path of execution through MFC code can be very complex. COleControlSite::InvokeHelperV() ensures that an IDispatch interface pointer has been retrieved for the control object, wraps the pointer using an instance of COleDispatchDriver, and then, finally, calls COleDispatchDriver::InvokeHelperV() to actually make the IDispatch call.

The implementation of the COleDispatchDriver::InvokeHelperV() is very interesting. Each element of the variable argument list, prepared by InvokeHelper(), is converted to a variant and inserted in an instance of the DISPPARAMS structure, which is expected by the standard IDispatch::Invoke() method. During the iteration through the variable argument list, the aforementioned parms[] array is used to set the correct type of the variant and to calculate the correct amount to increment the list pointer using the va_arg() macro.

After the parameter conversion is complete, IDispatch::Invoke() is called using the IDispatch control interface pointer maintained by the COleDispatchDriver class. When Invoke() returns, MFC deallocates temporary memory used for the DISPARAMS structure, checks the return code for the Invoke() call, and, if an error occurred during the call, throws a COleDispatchException containing all the available information from the OLE exception structure.

It should be obvious at this point that the amount of work that MFC shields the casual control container from is just amazing! If MFC weren't used to implement the container, each property call would need to be implemented using the standard IDispatch mechanism, which is tedious at best, from C++.

The MFC Implementation of Control Event Handling

Speaking from the perspective of the Microsoft Foundation Classes, control-event handling is more or less the opposite of using a control's properties and methods. To use a control's properties and methods, MFC does the work to translate a C++ function call into a call to IDispatch::Invoke(). When handling events, MFC has to take a IDispatch::Invoke() call from a control connected to a container's IDispatch event sink, and convert it into a call to a container's C++ member function.

The Framework for Event Handlers

Event handlers are declared within a CCmdTarget-derived class using the DECLARE_EVENTSINK_MAP() macro. DECLARE_EVENTSINK_MAP() establishes the existence of a table that contains information that MFC requires to dispatch events. It must be supplemented by BEGIN_EVENTSINK_MAP(), ON_EVENT(), and END_EVENTSINK_MAP() macros in the class implementation file.

Earlier, you saw an example where I added the code necessary to instantiate an OLE control in a non-resource–based MFC view class. After adding code to create the control, I added event handling to handle the SimpleControl's OnSimpleNameChange event. Recall the following code snippet:

```
BEGIN_EVENTSINK_MAP(CSDIContainerView, CView)
    ON_EVENT(CSDIContainerView, ID_SIMPLECTRL, 1, \
        OnSimpleNameChange, VTS_BSTR VTS_PBSTR)
END_EVENTSINK_MAP()
```

ON_EVENT() is the macro that establishes an entry in a table of event handlers. When dispatching events, MFC will scan this table to find a function that matches an incoming event. The definition of ON_EVENT(), from AfxDisp.h, follows:

```
#define ON_EVENT(theClass, id, dispid, pfnHandler, vtsParams) \
    { _T(""), dispid, vtsParams, VT_BOOL, \
        (AFX_PMSG)(void (theClass::*)(void))pfnHandler, (AFX_PMSG)0, 0, \
        afxDispCustom, id, (UINT)-1 }, \
```

It contains all the information necessary for MFC to map an IDispatch::Invoke() call to a C++ class function call. As with the aforementioned InvokeHelper() function, used for property Get/Set calls, the event parameters are encoded as a string within ON_EVENT() macro use.

MFC Event "Forwarding"

When MFC receives an event from a contained control, MFC attempts to find an entry in the aforementioned Event Sink map. If MFC finds an entry that matches the event dispatch ID, it checks the parameters in the string parameter signature recorded with the entry. After doing so, it performs an intricate conversion of a DISPPARAM array from an array to arguments on the stack, suitable to be passed to a C++ member function.

The MFC "event forwarding" mechanism is one of the most useful elements of the class library; like the MFC property implementation, it shelters the container implementer from the details of managing parameters from IDispatch by converting calls to standard C++ function invocations.

Future Directions with OLE Control Containers

Microsoft's ActiveX Internet strategy plays heavily on existing technology such as COM, OLE, or ActiveX controls. As you learned from the previous chapter, OLE controls require a large number of interfaces to be implemented. Lots of implementation generally means large controls, and large controls are a problem when users have low bandwidth modem connections. Part of the goal of ActiveX is to simplify the requirements for controls; as the requirements change, it's quite conceivable that the requirements for control containers will also change.

I have no doubt that Microsoft will continually update the Microsoft Foundation Classes to reflect the changing standards for OLE or ActiveX controls. When implementing a control container in the future, it's a safe bet to say that you will probably want to use the Microsoft Foundation Classes, unless you have specific requirements that aren't met by MFC.

Summary

This chapter has presented some of the issues involved with the creation of OLE control containers. OLE controls use literally all of the various OLE technologies; consequently, they are very complex to implement. As you can tell from the number of required interfaces for OLE control containers, it is also very complex to implement a control container.

The Microsoft Foundation Classes radically decrease the amount of code necessary to generate a control container. As a matter of fact, implementing a dialog-resource–based control container is trivial! And as the developer, you have to worry about the logic, not the infrastructure, when you use MFC for control containers.

ActiveX and MFC

by Daniel N. Leeks

The Microsoft Foundation Classes library, or MFC for short, is a collection of classes that provide an application framework from which a programmer is able to build a Windows application. In addition to providing a framework for the application, the MFC library also provides sets of classes that are useful for manipulating or altering a program's data or other various entities such as windows, status bars, menus, strings, common controls, and ActiveX controls.

History of ActiveX Control Support in MFC

Support for ActiveX controls in MFC, previously named OLE controls, can be traced back to version 2.5 of the library. This version of MFC introduced OLE classes that allowed programmers to write OLE containers, database applications, and OLE objects that could be used by these applications. This simplified the creation of OLE objects somewhat by reducing the amount of code that programmers typically had to write to utilize OLE 1.0. Next came version 3.0 of MFC, which added 32-bit OLE and ODBC support, property sheets, and property pages (covered in the next chapter). Also, of particular note, were C++ templates, containers, and multithreading classes. It wasn't until MFC 4.0 that the capability to create OLE control containers was added.

As mentioned earlier, ActiveX controls were previously OLE controls that were commonly referred to as OCX controls, for OLE control extension. An OLE control is an OLE Automation in-process server packaged within a DLL that simply has an .OCX extension. OLE controls support the same features as standard automation servers and also implement the same IDispatch interface. OLE controls are now called ActiveX controls. ActiveX controls differ in several ways from older OLE controls. These differences are detailed in the OLE Controls 96 specification, which is available at http://www.microsoft.com/developers/.

Wrapping the OLE/COM Interface

MFC is an excellent library for developing ActiveX controls because it simplifies the creation and maintenance of the controls while providing easy access to the powerful features of OLE/COM. Classes available in MFC provide a means to support OLE Automation within a control. OLE Automation allows controls to expose their container-writeable properties and a set of callable methods. Also, there is robust support for the creation, manipulation, and altering of control events, methods, and properties. The definition of the classes that provide this support and wrap the OLE/COM interfaces for controls is defined in AFXCTL.H.

The main focus of this chapter is to examine these classes and provide a guide to the functionality that they contain. The two classes that will be inspected are the COleControlModule and COleControl classes. Because of the size of COleControl class, the descriptions will be as concise as possible. Rest assured, however, that an ample amount of useful information will be presented.

The COleControlModule Class

The COleControlModule class is a CWinApp-derived class—the base class from which all OLE control module objects are derived. The main function of this class is to provide member functions for initializing a control module. Because of its function, which is detailed below, only one object derived from COleControlModule can be contained in an OLE control module object that uses the MFC. Figure 7.1 shows the COleControlModule classes' position in the MFC library hierarchy.

Figure 7.1.
The position of
COleControlModule *in*
the MFC class hierarchy.

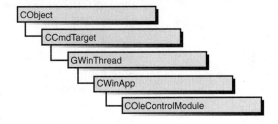

As you might have guessed from looking at Figure 7.1, a COleControlModule object provides the main thread for the OLE control. This is because it is derived from CWinApp, which ordinarily provides the main process thread for controls and applications that rely on the MFC.

The COleControlModule Class Structure

Two overridden methods are the only differences between COleControlModule and CWinApp. The class definition, which can be found in AFXCTL.H, looks like this:

```
////////////////////////////////////////////////////////////////////////
// COleControlModule - base class for .OCX module
//   This object is statically linked into the control.
class COleControlModule : public CWinApp
{
    DECLARE_DYNAMIC(COleControlModule)
public:
    virtual BOOL InitInstance();
    virtual int ExitInstance();
};
```

This class declaration is short and illustrates that an OCX control is not much more than a DLL with an .OCX extension and several OLE capabilities provided by the MFC classes. (Actually, it is more complicated than that, but by using MFC, we have made it much simpler.) The declarations of the methods InitInstance() and ExitInstance(), which are overridden from CWinApp, handle the necessary task of initializing and deinitializing an OLE, or ActiveX, control. These methods are implemented in the MFC source file CTLMODUL.CPP. They are short but also quite powerful. InitInstance() is implemented as

```
////////////////////////////////////////////////////////////////////////
// COleControlModule::InitInstance
BOOL COleControlModule::InitInstance()
{
    // wire up resources from OLE DLL
    AfxOleInitModule();
    COleObjectFactory::RegisterAll();
    return TRUE;
}
```

As you can see, the implementation is succinct but accomplishes the initialization of an OLE or ActiveX control module. The COleObjedctFactory::RegisterAll() method registers all of the object factories of the module with the operating system. AfxOleInitModule() is a global MFC function located in the source file DLLOLE.CPP. The function uses the class CDynaLinkLibrary to load the library so that its resources are available for the module to use.

```
////////////////////////////////////////////////////////////////////////
// Special initialization entry point for controls
void AFXAPI AfxOleInitModule()
{
```

```
      ASSERT(AfxGetModuleState() != AfxGetAppModuleState());
      CDynLinkLibrary* pDLL = new CDynLinkLibrary(extensionDLL, TRUE);
      ASSERT(pDLL != NULL);
      pDLL->m_factoryList.m_pHead = NULL;
}
```

The implementation of ExitInstance is equally as short as InitInstance. It is shown here:

```
///////////////////////////////////////////////////////////////////////////
// COleControlModule::ExitInstance
int COleControlModule::ExitInstance()
{
      COleObjectFactory::RevokeAll();
      return CWinApp::ExitInstance();
}
```

The method COleObjectFactory::RevokeAll() is called to revoke the OLE system registrations of all of the object factories within the module.

The COleControl Class

The COleControl class is the powerful base class of OLE controls that are developed using the MFC library. The COleControl class is a CWnd-derived class. This allows the COleControl class to provide all of the functionality of the CWnd class through inheritance while providing functionality that is specific to OLE controls, such as methods to read ambient properties, and methods to fire events and to interact with a control's container and its control site. Figure 7.2 shows the position of COleControl in the MFC library.

Figure 7.2.
The position of
COleControl *in the MFC*
class hierarchy.

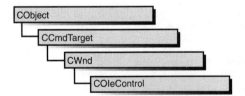

If you have ever taken the time to browse AFXCTL.H, you might have been overwhelmed by the sheer number of methods that the COleControl class offers for creating truly powerful OLE controls in the MFC. The next several pages give an overview, without the in-depth analysis, of the methods contained within the COleControl class. These methods fall into the following categories:

- Construction/destruction
- Initialization
- Control modification
- Persistence

- Update/paint
- Dispatch exceptions
- Ambient property
- Event-firing
- Stock methods/properties
- OLE control sizing
- OLE data binding
- Simple frame
- OLE control site
- Modal dialog
- Overridable
- Change notification
- OLE interface notification
- In-place activation
- Property browsing
- Windowless operations
- Asynchronous control
- `IviewObject` interface notification overridables
- Inactive pointer-handling functions

Construction/Destruction Methods

The construction/destruction methods in `COleControl` are used to create and destroy an OLE control object. The three methods supported in `COleControl` are detailed in the following subsections.

void COleControl::COleControl()

This is the constructor for the `COleControl` class. It creates a `COleControl` object. Normally, this function is not called directly. Instead the control is typically created by its class factory.

Parameters: none.

void COleControl::~COleControl()

This is the destructor for the `COleControl` class. It destroys its `COleControl` object.

Parameters: none.

void COleControl::RecreateControlWindow()

This function's purpose is to destroy and then re-create the control's window. If you change the window style bits for the control, you will need to call this method for the changes to take effect.

Parameters: none.

Initialization Methods

The initialization methods that are members of COleControl provide the functionality to inform the base class of the interface IDs that the control will be using. Also, the initialization methods set up the control's initial size. These methods are detailed in the following subsections.

void COleControl::InitializeIIDs(const IID* piidPrimary, const IID* piidEvents)

This method needs to be called in the control's constructor to inform the base class of the interface IDs your control will be using.

Parameters:

piidPrimary: A pointer to the interface ID of the control's primary dispatch interface.

piidEvents: A pointer to the interface ID of the control's event interface.

void COleControl::SetInitialSize(int cx, int cy)

Call this function in your constructor to set the initial size of your control. The initial size is measured in device units, or pixels. It is recommended that this call be made in your control's constructor.

Parameters:

cx: An integer that is the initial width of the OLE control in pixels.

cy: An integer that is the initial height of the OLE control in pixels.

Control Modification Methods

COleControl's control modification functions are used to determine whether the control has been modified. They are also used to set the modification state of a control. Below are the functions that make up this category.

BOOL COleControl::IsModified( );

This function should be called to determine whether the control's state has been modified. When a property changes value, the state of a control is modified.

Parameters: none.

Return Value

The return value is nonzero if the control's state has been modified since it was last saved. Otherwise, 0 is returned.

void COleControl::SetModifiedFlag(BOOL *bModified* = TRUE);

You should call this function whenever a change occurs that would affect your control's persistent state. For example, if the values of the persistent properties have been saved, call this function with bModified equal to FALSE.

Parameters:

bModified: A Boolean that is the new value for the control's modified flag. A bModified value of TRUE indicates that the control's state has been modified. FALSE denotes that the control's state has just been saved.

Persistence

This set of member functions provided by the COleControl class provides a way to save and load the a control's properties to persistent storage. Some of these functions, such as ExchangeStockProperties and ExchangeExtent, are used by the default version of DoPropExchange to read and write properties to persistent storage. Other functions, such as IsConvertingVBX and WillAmbientsBeValidDuringLoad, are used to handle special cases of loading and saving the control's properties. The property persistence member functions are detailed in the following subsections.

BOOL COleControl::ExchangeExtent (CPropExchange* *pPX*);

This function, normally called by the default implementation of COleControl::DoPropExchange, is called to initialize or serialize the state of the control's extent. The control's extent are its dimensions in HIMETRIC units.

Parameters:

pPX: This is a pointer to a CPropExchange object. This object is supplied by the framework to define the context of the property exchange and its direction.

Return Value

If the function succeeded, the return value is nonzero; otherwise the return value is 0.

void COleControl::ExchangeStockProps (CPropExchange* *pPX*);

This function, normally called by the default implementation of COleControl::DoPropExchange, is called to initialize or serialize the state of the control's stock properties.

Parameters:

pPX: This is a pointer to a CPropExchange object. This object is supplied by the framework to define the context of the property exchange and its direction.

BOOL COleControl::ExchangeVersion (CPropExchange* *pPX*, DWORD *dwVersionDefault*, BOOL *bConvert* = TRUE);

This function is called to initialize or serialize the state of a control's version information. This function will usually be the first function called by a control's override of COleControl::DoPropExchange. When saving, this function writes the version number of the persistent data. When loading the control's persistent data, this function reads the version number of the persistent data and sets the version attribute of the CPropExchange object provided by the framework.

Parameters:

pPX: This is a pointer to a CPropExchange object. This object is supplied by the framework to define the context of the property exchange and its direction.

dwVersionDefault: A DWORD that is the current version number of the control.

bConvert: A Boolean that indicates whether the control's persistent data should be converted to the latest format when saved or maintained in the same format that was loaded. TRUE updates the persistent data to the latest format when saved; FALSE maintains the persistent data in the same format that was loaded.

Return Value

If the function succeeded, the return value is nonzero; otherwise the return value is 0.

BOOL COleControl::IsConvertingVBX( );

This function should be called when converting a form that uses VBX controls to one that uses OLE controls. The reason for calling this function is that special loading code for the OLE controls might be required. For example, suppose that your VBX control saved proprietary binary data and your OLE control now saves its binary data in a completely different format. If you wanted your OLE control to be backward-compatible, you could provide the capability to load either set of data by using a call to IsConvertingVBX to determine whether the VBX control or the OLE control was being loaded.

In your control's DoPropExchange function, you would check for this condition by making a function call to IsConvertingVBX. If the function call returned TRUE, loading code specific to the conversion would be executed. If the control is not being converted, the normal loading code would be executed. This functionality applies only to controls being converted from VBX counterparts.

Parameters: none.

Return Value

If the control is being converted, the return value is nonzero; otherwise, the return value is 0.

BOOL COleControl::WillAmbientsBeValidDuringLoad ( );

This function is called to determine whether your control should use the values of the ambient properties and the default values when the control is loaded from its persistent state.

Your control will not have access to its ambient properties during the initial call to the override of COleControl::DoPropExchange. This will be the case if the container does not honor the OLEMISC_SETCLIENTSITEFIRST status bit.

Parameters: none.

Return Value

Nonzero is returned if the ambient properties will be valid; otherwise, ambient properties will not be valid.

Update/Paint Methods

The CoLeControL class provides a set of functions to aid the control developer in updating and painting the control. These member functions provide the functionality to select stock and custom fonts into the control's device context. There are also functions to invalidate the control and to redraw a control that subclasses a Windows control. The CoLeControL class methods for updating and painting a control are listed in the following subsections.

void COleControl::DoSuperclassPaint(CDC* *pDC*, const CRect& *rcBounds*);

You should call this function to properly handle painting a nonactive OLE control that subclasses a Windows control. This function should be called in the OnDraw function of your control.

Parameters:

pDC: This parameter is a pointer to the device context of the control container.

rcBounds: This parameter is a pointer to the area in which the control is to be drawn.

void COleControl::InvalidateControl (LPCRECT *lpRect* = NULL);

This function should be called to force the control to redraw itself. This function should be used instead of CWnd::InvalidateRect or ::InvalidateRect.

Parameters:

lpRect: This parameter is a pointer to the rectangular region of the control to be invalidated. If lpRect points to a NULL value, the entire control will be redrawn. If lpRect is not NULL, it contains a rectangular portion of the control's rectangle that is to be invalidated. When the control has no window or is not currently active, the parameter is ignored. Then the client site's IAdviseSink::OnViewChange member function is callled.

CFont* COleControl::SelectFontObject(CDC* pDC, CFontHolder& fontHolder);

This function is called to select a font object into a device context.

Parameters:

pDC: This parameter is a pointer to a device context object.

fontHolder: This parameter is a reference to the CFontHolder object, which represents the font to be selected.

Return Value

This function returns a pointer to the previously selected CFont object. The caller should reselect the previously selected font by passing it as a parameter to CDC:SelectObject when all of the drawing operations that use fontHolder have been completed.

CFont* COleControl::SelectStockFont(CDC* pDC);

This function is called to select the stock font property into a device context.

Parameters:

pDC: This parameter is a pointer to the device context into which the font will be selected.

Return Value

This function returns a pointer to the previously selected CFont object. The caller should reselect the previously selected font by passing it as a parameter to CDC:SelectObject when all of the drawing operations have been completed.

COLORREF TranslateColor(OLE_COLOR clrColor, HPALETTE hpal = NULL);

This function is called to convert a color value from the OLE_COLOR data type to the COLORREF data type. Use this function to translate the stock ForeColor and BackColor properties to the COLORREF types used by the CDC member functions.

Parameters:

clrColor: This parameter is an OLE_COLOR data type. For more information on the OLE_COLOR data type, see "Standard Color Type", in Appendix A of *Programming with MFC; Programming with MFC* is available on the Visual C++ version 4.0 and higher CD-ROM.

hpal: This parameter is a handle to an optional palette that can be NULL.

Return Value

The return value is a 32-bit RGB (red, green, blue) color value. This value defines the solid color which closest matches the clrColor value that the device can represent.

Dispatch Exceptions

The dispatch exception methods provide the functionality to handle errors within the control. Exceptions can be thrown for operations not permitted in the control, such as the setting of read-only properties. The methods and their descriptions are listed in the following subsections.

void COleControl::GetNotSupported( );

This function should be called in place of the Get function for any property that does not support the retrieval of the property by the control's user. An example is a property that is write-only.

Parameters: none.

void COleControl::SetNotPermitted( );

This function should be called when BoundPropertyRequestEdit fails. This function throws an exception of the type COleDispScodeException to indicate that the attempted set operation was not permitted.

Parameters: none.

void COleControl::SetNotSupported( );

This function should be called in place of the Set function for any property that does not support the modification of the property by the control's user. An example is a property that is read-only.

void COleControl::ThrowError(SCODE sc, UINT nDescriptionID, UINT nHelpID = -1);

You should call this function only from within a Get or Set function for an OLE property or an implementation of an OLE automation method. This function signals the occurrence of an error in your control. To signal errors that occur at other times in your control, you should fire the stock Error event.

Parameters:

sc: This parameter is the status code value to be reported. If you would like to see a complete list of possible codes, see the article "OLE Controls: Advanced Topics" in *Programming with MFC. Programming with MFC* is available on the Visual C++ 4.0 and higher CD-ROM.

nDescriptionID: This parameter is the string resource ID of the exception to be reported.

nHelpID: This parameter is the help ID of the topic to be reported on.

pszDescription: This parameter is a string that contains an explanation of the exception to be reported.

Ambient Property Methods

The following group of member functions of COleControl allows you to set and examine the values of the common ambient properties. Each of the functions examines the control site for the property and returns the value provided by the container if it is supported. If the container doesn't support the ambient property requested, an appropriate default value is returned.

There is a member function, GetAmbientProperty, that can be utilized to get the values of all of the ambient properties. This function is also useful to retrieving container-specific ambient properties. The one major difference this function has with the other ambient property methods is that it does not return a default value. This is because it can't know in advance which ambient property you will ask for.

> **note**
>
> The control's container is not required to support any of the ambient properties.

OLE_COLOR COleControl::AmbientBackColor( );

This container defines the ambient BackColor property and provides it to all controls.

Parameters: none.

Return Value

This function returns the value of the container's ambient BackColor property if it exists as an OLE_COLOR data type.

If the ambient property is not supported, this function returns the system-defined Windows background color.

CString COleControl::AmbientDisplayName( );

This function should be called to obtain the name of the control that the container has assigned to it. This name can then be used in error messages displayed to the user.

Parameters: none.

Return Value

The return value is a Cstring object that contains the ambient display name of the OLE control. The default name is a zero-length string.

OLE_COLOR COleControl::AmbientForeColor( );

This container defines the ambient ForeColor property and provides it to all controls.

Parameters: none.

Return Value

This function returns the value of the container's ambient ForeColor property if it exists as an OLE_COLOR data type.

If the ambient property is not supported, this function returns the system-defined Windows foreground color.

LPFONTDISP COleControl::AmbientFont( );

The ambient Font property is available to all controls. It is defined by the control's container.

Parameters: none.

Return Value

This function returns a pointer to the container's ambient Font dispatch interface. The default value is NULL. If the return value is not equal to NULL, you are responsible for releasing the font by calling its IUnknown::Release member function.

LCID AmbientLocaleID( );

The control can use the LocaleID to adapt its user interface for specific locales.

Parameters: none.

Return Value

The return value is the value of the container's LocaleID property, if it exists. If the property is not supported by the container, the function returns 0.

CString COleControl::AmbientScaleUnits( );

The container's ambient ScaleUnits property is useful in displaying positions or dimensions in a unit, such as twips or centimeters.

Parameters: none.

Return Value

The return value is a string containing the ambient ScaleUnits of the container. A zero-length string is returned by the function if the property is not supported.

BOOL COleControl::AmbientShowGrabHandles ( );

This function should be called to determine whether the container allows the control to display grab handles for itself when active.

Parameters: none.

Return Value

The return value is nonzero if grab handles should be displayed; otherwise, 0 is returned. The function returns nonzero if the ambient GrabHandles property is not supported.

BOOL COleControl::AmbientShowHatching( );

This function should be called to determine whether the container allows the control to display itself with a hatched pattern when UI-active.

Parameters: none.

Return Value

The return value is nonzero if the hatched pattern should be shown; otherwise, 0 is returned. The function returns nonzero if the ambient ShowHatching property is not supported.

short COleControl::AmbientTextAlign( );

This function should be called to determine the ambient text alignment preferred by the control container. This property, which is defined by the container, is available to all embedded controls.

Parameters: none.

Return Value

The return value is the status of the container's ambient TextAlign property. If this property is not supported, this function returns 0.

The following is a list of valid return values:

0	General alignment (numbers to the right, text to the left)
1	Left-justify

2   Center
3   Right-justify

BOOL COleControl::AmbientUIDead( );

This function should be called to determine if the container wants the control to acknowledge user-interface actions. For example, a container might set this to TRUE in design-mode.

Parameters: none.

Return Value

The return value is nonzero if the control should respond to user-interface actions; otherwise, the return value is 0. The function returns 0 if the property is not supported.

BOOL COleControl::AmbientUserMode( );

This function should be called to determine if the container is in user mode or design mode. For example, in user mode the container might set the ambient property UserMode to TRUE.

Parameters: none.

Return Value

The return value is nonzero if the container is in user mode. If the container is in design mode, the return value is 0. The function returns 0 if the property is not supported.

BOOL COleControl::GetAmbientProperty (DISPID *dwDispid*, VARTYPE *vtProp*, void* *pvProp*);

This function should be called to get the value of an ambient property of the container. To use GetAmbientProperty to retrieve the ambient DisplayName and ScaleUnits properties, you must set vtProp to VT_BSTR and pvProp to CString*. If you are retrieving the ambient Font property, you must set vtProp to VT_FONT and pvProp to LPFONTDISP*.

Parameters:

dwDispid: This parameter is a DWORD that is the dispatch ID of the desired ambient property.

vtProp: This parameter is a variant type tag. It specifies the type of the value to be returned in pvProp.

pvProp: This parameter is a pointer to the address of the variable that will receive the property value or return value. The type of this pointer must match the type that is specified by vtProp.

vtPropType of pvProp
VT_BOOLBOOL*
VT_BSTRCString*
VT_I2 short*
VT_I4 long*
VT_R4 float*
VT_R8 double*
VT_CY CY*
VT_COLOROLE_COLOR*
VT_DISPATCH   LPDISPATCH*
VT_FONTLPFONTDISP*

Return Value

The return value is nonzero if the ambient property is supported; otherwise, the return value is 0 (not supported).

Event-Firing Methods

This group of COleControl member functions is used for firing events. All of the stock events have an associated member function. This should make the events easy to commit to memory. The current implementation of the event-firing methods all call the FireEvent function to dispatch their events. This member function is not generally called directly. ClassWizard, which comes with Visual C++, is usually used to generate the desired event type for you. It also generates a new member function that will call FireEvent for you. The definitions of the event-firing methods are detailed in the following subsections.

void COleControl::FireClick( );

This function is called by the framework when the mouse is clicked over an active control. You can determine when the event is fired if this event is defined as a custom event.

To automatically fire a Click event, the control's event map must have a stock Click event defined.

Parameters: none.

void COleControl::FireDblClick( );

This function is called by the framework when the mouse is double-clicked over an active control. You can determine when the event is fired if this event is defined as a custom event.

To automatically fire a DoubleClick event, the control's event map must have a stock DoubleClick event defined.

void COleControl::FireError(SCODE *scode*, LPCTSTR *lpszDescription*, UINT *nHelpID* = 0);

This function can be called to fire the stock Error event—to signal that an error has occurred within your control. The stock Error event, unlike other stock events, is never fired by the framework.

Parameters:

> scode: This parameter is the status code value to be reported. If you would like to see a complete list of possible codes, see the article "OLE Controls: Advanced Topics" in *Programming with MFC*. *Programming with MFC* is available on the Visual C++ version 4.0 and higher CD-ROM.
>
> lpszDescription: A string that hold the description of the error being reported.
>
> nHelpID: The Help ID of the error being reported.

void FireEvent(DISPID *dispid*, BYTE FAR* *pbParams*, ...);

Call this function to fire a user-defined event from your control. This function can be called with any number of optional arguments and normally should not be called directly. Instead, you will usually call the event-firing functions generated by the Developer Studio's ClassWizard.

Parameters:

> dispid: This parameter is the dispatch ID of the event to be fired.
>
> pbParams: This parameter is a descriptor for the event's parameter types.

The pbParams argument is list of VTS_ symbols separated by spaces. One or more of these values can specify the function's parameter list. The possible values are listed here:

Symbol	Parameter type
VTS_COLOR	OLE_COLOR
VTS_FONT	IFontDisp*
VTS_HANDLE	HWND
VTS_PICTURE	IPictureDisp*
VTS_OPTEXCLUSIVE	OLE_OPTEXCLUSIVE*
VTS_TRISTATE	OLE_TRISTATE
VTS_XPOS_HIMETRIC	OLE_XPOS_HIMETRIC
VTS_YPOS_HIMETRIC	OLE_YPOS_HIMETRIC
VTS_XPOS_PIXELS	OLE_XPOS_PIXELS
VTS_YPOS_PIXELS	OLE_YPOS_PIXELS
VTS_XSIZE_PIXELS	OLE_XSIZE_PIXELS
VTS_YSIZE_PIXELS	OLE_XSIZE_PIXELS
VTS_XSIZE_HIMETRIC	OLE_XSIZE_HIMETRIC
VTS_YSIZE_HIMETRIC	OLE_XSIZE_HIMETRIC

void COleControl::FireKeyDown(USHORT* pnChar, short nShiftState);

This function is called by the framework when a key is pressed while the control is user-interface (UI) active. You can determine when the event is fired by defining it as a custom event.

For the automatic firing of a KeyDown event to occur, the control must have a stock KeyDown event defined in its event map.

Parameters:

pnChar: This parameter is a pointer to the virtual key code value of the pressed key.

nShiftState: This parameter contains a combination of the following flags:

SHIFT_MASK: The Shift key was pressed during the action.

CTRL_MASK: The Ctrl key was pressed during the action.

ALT_MASK: The Alt key was pressed during the action.

void FireKeyUp(USHORT* pnChar, short nShiftState);

This function is called by the framework when a key is released while the control is UI-active. You can determine when the event is fired by defining this event as a custom event.

For the automatic firing of a KeyUp event to occur, the control must have a stock KeyUp event defined in its event map.

Parameters:

> pnChar: This parameter is a pointer to the virtual key code value of the released key.

> nShiftState: This parameter contains a combination of the following flags:

>> SHIFT_MASK: The Shift key was pressed during the action.

>> CTRL_MASK: The Ctrl key was pressed during the action.

>> ALT_MASK: The Alt key was pressed during the action.

void COleControl::FireKeyPress(USHORT* pnChar);

This function is called by the framework when a key is pressed and released while the custom control is UI-active. You can determine when the event is fired by defining this event as a custom event.

For the automatic firing of a KeyPress event to occur, the control must have a stock KeyPress event defined in its event map. The recipient of the event can modify pnChar. To examine the modified character, override the OnKeyPress event.

Parameters:

> pnChar: This parameter is a pointer to the character value of the key pressed.

void COleControl::FireMouseDown(short nButton, short nShiftState, OLE_XPOS_PIXELS x, OLE_YPOS_PIXELS y);

This function is called by the framework when a mouse button is pressed while over an active custom control. You can determine when the event is fired by defining it as a custom event.

For the automatic firing of a MouseDown event to occur, the control must have a stock MouseDown event defined in its event map.

Parameters:

> nButton: This parameter is the numeric value of the mouse button pressed. It is a variable of the data type short and can represent one of the following values:

>> LEFT_BUTTON: The left mouse button was pressed.

>> MIDDLE_BUTTON: The middle mouse button was pressed.

>> RIGHT_BUTTON: The right mouse button was pressed.

nShiftState: This parameter is a variable of the data type short and contains a combination of the following flags:

> SHIFT_MASK: The Shift key was pressed during the action.

> CTRL_MASK: The Ctrl key was pressed during the action.

> ALT_MASK: The Alt key was pressed during the action.

x: This parameter is a variable of the data type OLE_XPOS_PIXELS and represents the x-coordinate of the cursor when a mouse button is pressed. The coordinate is relative to the upper-left corner of the control window.

y: This parameter is a variable of the data type OLE_XPOS_PIXELS and represents the y-coordinate of the cursor when a mouse button is pressed. The coordinate is relative to the upper-left corner of the control window.

void COleControl::FireMouseUp(short *nButton*, short *nShiftState*, OLE_XPOS_PIXELS *x*, OLE_YPOS_PIXELS *y*);

This function is called by the framework when a mouse button is released while over an active custom control. You can determine when the event is fired by defining it as a custom event.

For the automatic firing of a MouseUp event to occur, the control must have a stock MouseUp event defined in its event map.

Parameters:

> nButton: This parameter is the numeric value of the mouse button released. It is a variable of the data type short and can represent one of the following values:

>> LEFT_BUTTON: The left mouse button was pressed.

>> MIDDLE_BUTTON: The middle mouse button was pressed.

>> RIGHT_BUTTON: The right mouse button was pressed.

> nShiftState: This parameter is a variable of the data type short and contains a combination of the following flags:

>> SHIFT_MASK: The Shift key was pressed during the action.

>> CTRL_MASK: The Ctrl key was pressed during the action.

>> ALT_MASK: The Alt key was pressed during the action.

x: This parameter is a variable of the data type OLE_XPOS_PIXELS and represents the x-coordinate of the cursor when a mouse button is released. The coordinate is relative to the upper-left corner of the control window.

y: This parameter is a variable of the data type OLE_XPOS_PIXELS and represents the y-coordinate of the cursor when a mouse button is released. The coordinate is relative to the upper-left corner of the control window.

void COleControl::FireMouseMove(short nButton, short nShiftState, OLE_XPOS_PIXELS x, OLE_YPOS_PIXELS y);

This function is called by the framework when the mouse is moved while over an active custom control. You can determine when the event is fired by defining it as a custom event.

For the automatic firing of a MouseMove event to occur, the control must have a stock MouseMove event defined in its event map.

Parameters:

nButton: This parameter is the numeric value of the mouse button pressed. It is a variable of the data type short and can represent one of the following values:

LEFT_BUTTON: The left mouse button was pressed.

MIDDLE_BUTTON: The middle mouse button was pressed.

RIGHT_BUTTON: The right mouse button was pressed.

nShiftState: This parameter is a variable of the data type short and contains a combination of the following flags:

SHIFT_MASK: The Shift key was pressed during the action.

CTRL_MASK: The Ctrl key was pressed during the action.

ALT_MASK: The Alt key was pressed during the action.

x: This parameter is a variable of the data type OLE_XPOS_PIXELS and represents the x-coordinate of the cursor when a mouse button is pressed. The coordinate is relative to the upper-left corner of the control window.

y: This parameter is a variable of the data type OLE_XPOS_PIXELS and represents the y-coordinate of the cursor when a mouse button is pressed. The coordinate is relative to the upper-left corner of the control window.

Stock Methods/Properties

The following group of member functions of COleControl allows you to set and examine the values of the of the stock properties and methods. Each of the functions first asks the control site for permission to alter the value of a stock property. If the container responds with *yes,* the property is changed and the control notifies the container of this change. The stock methods/property functions and their purposes are listed in the following subsections.

void COleControl::DoClick( );

This function is used to simulate a mouse click action on the control. The function accomplishes this task by calling the overridable COleControl::OnClick member function. In addition to calling the OnClick member function, a stock Click event will be fired, if supported by the control.

This function is supported by the COleControl base class as a stock method called DoClick. For more information, see the article "Methods" in *Programming with MFC. Programming with MFC* is available on the Visual C++ version 4.0 and higher CD-ROM.

Parameters: none.

void COleControl::Refresh( );

This function is called to force a repaint of the OLE control and is supported by the COleControl base class as the stock method Refresh. The stock method allows users of your OLE control to repaint the control at a specific time. For more information on this method, refer to the article "Methods" in *Programming with MFC. Programming with MFC* is available on the Visual C++ version 4.0 and higher CD-ROM.

Parameters: none.

OLE_COLOR COleControl::GetBackColor( );

This function provides the implementation of the Get function for your control's stock BackColor property.

Parameters: none.

Return Value

The function returns a value that specifies the current background color as an OLE_COLOR value, if successful. A call to TranslateColor with this return value as the parameter will translate the OLE_COLOR value to a COLORREF value.

void COleControl::SetBackColor(OLE_COLOR *dwBackColor*);

This function is can be called to set the stock BackColor property value of your control.

Parameters:

> dwBackColor: This parameter is an OLE_COLOR value to be used for background drawing of your control.

short COleControl::GetBorderStyle( );

This function provides the implementation for the Get function of your control's stock BorderStyle property.

Parameters: none.

Return Value

If the control has a normal border, the return value is 1 and 0 if the control has no border.

void COleControl::SetBorderStyle(short *sBorderStyle*);

Call this function to set the stock BorderStyle property value of your control. The control window will then be re-created, and the OnBorderStyleChanged member function will be called.

Parameters:

> sBorderStyle: This parameter is of the type short and determines the new border style for the control; 0 indicates no border, and 1 indicates a normal border.

BOOL COleControl::GetEnabled( );

This function provides the implementation of the Get function of your control's stock Enabled property.

Parameters: none.

Return Value

The return value is nonzero if the control is enabled; otherwise, the return value is 0.

void COleControl::SetEnabled(BOOL *bEnabled*);

You should call this function to set the stock Enabled property value of your control. After setting this property, the OnEnabledChange member function is called.

Parameters:

bEnabled: This parameter is a Boolean that is set to TRUE if the control is to be enabled; otherwise, it is set to FALSE.

OLE_COLOR COleControl::GetForeColor( );

This function provides the implementation of the Get function of the stock ForeColor property.

Parameters: none.

Return Value

The return value specifies the current foreground color as an OLE_COLOR value, if successful. A call to TranslateColor with this return value as the parameter will translate the OLE_COLOR value to a COLORREF value.

void COleControl::SetForeColor(OLE_COLOR *dwForeColor*);

This function should be called to set the stock ForeColor property value of your control.

Parameters:

dwForeColor: This parameter is an OLE_COLOR value to be used as the foreground color when drawing your control.

LPFONTDISP COleControl::GetFont( );

This function provides the implementation for the Get function of the stock Font property. It is the caller's responsibility to release the object when finished.

Parameters: none.

Return Value

The return value is a pointer to the font dispatch interface of the control's stock Font property.

void COleControl::GetFontTextMetrics (LPTEXTMETRIC *lptm*, CFontHolder& *fontHolder*);

You should call this function to measure the text metrics of any CFontHolder object owned by the control. Such a font can be selected for use by calling the COleControl::SelectFontObject function. GetFontTextMetrics will initialize the TEXTMETRIC structure pointed to by lptm with valid metrics information about fontHolder's font if successful; otherwise, it will fill the structure with zeros. Use this function instead of ::GetTextMetrics when painting your control, because it might be required to render itself into a metafile, like any other OLE-embedded object.

Parameters:

lptm: This parameter is a pointer to a TEXTMETRIC structure.

fontHolder: This parameter is a reference to a CFontHolder object.

void COleControls::GetStockTextMetrics (LPTEXTMETRIC *lptm*);

You should call this function to measure the text metrics for the control's stock Font property. This font can be selected with the SelectStockFont function. The GetStockTextMetrics function will initialize the TEXTMETRIC structure pointed to by lptm with valid metrics information if successful; otherwise, it will fill the structure with zeros. Use this function instead of ::GetTextMetrics when painting your control, because it might be required to render itself into a metafile, like any other OLE-embedded object.

Parameters:

lptm: This parameter is a pointer to a TEXTMETRIC structure.

CFontHolder& COleControl::InternalGetFont ( );

This function should be called to access the stock Font property of your control.

Parameters: none.

Return Value

The function returns a reference to a CFontHolder object. This object contains the stock Font object.

void COleControl::SetFont(LPFONTDISP *pFontDisp*);

This function should be called to set the stock Font property of your control.

Parameters:

pFontDisp: This parameter is a pointer to a Font dispatch interface.

CFont* COleControl::SelectStockFont(CDC* *pDC*);

This function should be called to select the stock Font property into a device context.

Parameters:

pDC: This parameter is a pointer to the device context into which the font will be selected.

Return Value

This function returns a pointer to the previously selected CFont object. CDC::SelectObject should be used to select this font back into the device context when you are finished.

OLE_HANDLE COleControl::GetHwnd( );

This function provides the implementation for the Get function of the stock hWnd property.

Parameters: none.

Return Value

The function returns the OLE control's window handle, if it exists. Otherwise, NULL is returned.

BSTR COleControl::GetText( );

This function provides the implementation for the Get function of the stock Text or Caption property. Note that the caller of this function is responsible for calling SysFreeString on the string returned. SysFreeString must be called in order to free the resource associated with the string.

Parameters: none.

Return Value

This function returns the current value of the control text string. If a text string is not present, a zero-length string is returned.

const CString&
COleControl::InternalGetText( );

You should call this function to access the stock Text or Caption property of your control.

Parameters: none.

Return Value

The return value is a constant reference to the control's text string.

void COleControl::SetText(LPCTSTR*pszText*);

This function should be called to set the value of your control's stock Caption or Text property.

---

note ▼

The stock Caption and stock Text properties are both mapped to the same value. If you make changes to either property, the change will be reflected in both properties. To avoid confusion, a control should support either the stock Caption or stock Text property, but not both.

Parameters:

pszText: This parameter is a pointer to a character string.

OLE Control-Sizing Methods

The control-sizing methods are used to get and set the size of the control. In addition to this functionality, the position of the control can be retrieved or specified.

void COleControl::GetControlSize(int* *pcx*, int* *pcy*);

This function should be used to retrieve the size of the OLE control window.

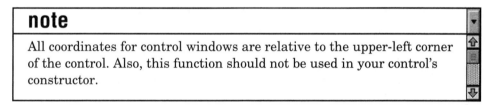

> **note**
>
> All of the control's window coordinates are relative to the upper-left corner of the control.

Parameters:

pcx: This parameter is a pointer to an integer that specifies the width of the control in pixels.

pcy: This parameter is an integer that specifies the height of the control in pixels.

BOOL COleControl::SetControlSize(int cx, int cy);

You should call this function to set the size of the OLE control window. This function also notifies the container that the control site is changing.

> **note**
>
> All coordinates for control windows are relative to the upper-left corner of the control. Also, this function should not be used in your control's constructor.

Parameters:

cx: This parameter is an integer that specifies the new width of the control in pixels.

cy: This parameter is an integer that specifies the new height of the control in pixels.

Return Value

The return value for the function will be nonzero if the call was successful; otherwise, the return value will be 0.

BOOL COleControl::GetRectInContainer (LPRECT lpRect);

This function can be called to obtain the coordinates of the control's rectangle. The control's rectangle will be relative to the container and expressed in device units. The rectangle is valid only if the control is in-place active.

Parameters:

> lpRect: A pointer to a LPRECT data type that specifies the rectangle struc-
> ture into which the control's coordinates will be copied.

Return Value

The function will return a nonzero if the control is in-place active; otherwise, 0 will
be returned.

BOOL COleControl::SetRectInContainer(LPRECT *lpRect*);

You should call this function to set the coordinates of the control's rectangle. The
coordinates should be relative to the container and expressed in device units. If
the control is open, it will be resized; otherwise, the container's OnPosRectChanged
function is called.

Parameters:

> lpRect: A pointer to an LPRECT data type that specifies the control's new
> coordinates relative to the container.

Return Value

The function will return a nonzero value if the call was successful; otherwise, 0
will be returned.

OLE Data-Binding Methods

Data binding is a powerful use of OLE/ActiveX controls. This feature allows a
property of a control to bind with a field in a database. When the property in the
control is altered, the control sends a notification to the database and requests
that the field be updated. The database then notifies the control of the success or
failure of the operation. The following group of member functions of COleControl
allows you to request permission to change the values of a bound property. In
addition to that functionality, there is a function to allow the control to send a
notification of a change in the value of a bound property. These functions are
detailed in the following subsections.

void COleControl::BoundPropertyChanged (DISPID *dispid*);

This function should be called to signal that the bound property value has
changed. This function must be called every time the value of the property is
altered, even when the change was not made through the property's set method.

> **note**
>
> Pay close attention to bound properties, which are mapped to member variables. Any time such a member variable changes, `COleControl::BoundPropertyChanged` must be called.

Parameters:

> `dispid`: This parameter is the dispatch ID of a bound property of the control.

BOOL COleControl::BoundPropertyRequestEdit (DISPID *dispid*);

You should call this function to request permission from the `IPropChangeNotify` interface to change a bound property value provided by the control. The control must not let the value of the property change if permission is denied. This can be accomplished by simply ignoring the action that attempted to alter the value of the property.

Parameters:

> `dispid`: This property is the dispatch ID of a bound property of the control.

Return Value

The return value is nonzero if the change is permitted; in all other cases, 0 is returned. The default value returned is nonzero.

Simple Frame Methods

Only one function exists in this category. This function is used to enable the simple frame characteristic of an OLE control. The function is detailed on the following subsection.

void COleControl::EnableSimpleFrame( );

You can call this function to enable the simple frame attribute for an OLE control. This attribute allows a control to support visual containment of other controls. This is not true OLE containment. For example, a group box could contain serveral controls inside of itself, such as multiple edit controls. These controls would not be OLE contained even though they are in the same group box.

Parameters: none.

OLE Control Site Methods

OLE controls use a pair of interfaces to communicate between the control and its container. The control implements an interface IOleControl, and the container implements the IOleControlSite interface on its site objects.

ControlInfoChanged encapsulates part of the functionality or the IOleControl interface. GetExtendedControl, LockInPlaceActive, and TransformCoords all encapsulate a great deal of the IOleControlSite interface. The purpose of each of these functions is detailed in the following subsections.

void COleControl::ControlInfoChanged( );

You should call this function when the set of mnemonics that the control supports has changed. When the container of the control recieves this notification, it obtains the new set of mnemonics by making a call to the method IOleControl::GetControlInfo.

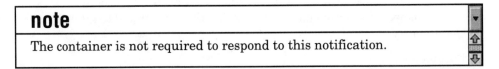

note

The container is not required to respond to this notification.

LPDISPATCH COleControl::GetExtendedControl ( );

Call this function to obtain a pointer to an object maintained by the container that represents the control with an extended set of properties. The function that calls this function is responsible for releasing the pointer when finished with the object. Note that the container is not required to support this object.

Parameters: none.

Return Value

The return value is a pointer to the container's extended control object. If there is no control object available, the value returned is NULL. The object can be manipulated through its IDispatch interface. QueryInterface can be used to obtain any other available interfaces that are provided by the object.

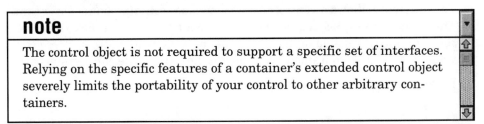

note

The control object is not required to support a specific set of interfaces. Relying on the specific features of a container's extended control object severely limits the portability of your control to other arbitrary containers.

BOOL COleControl::LockInPlaceActive(BOOL *bLock*);

This function is to be called to prevent the container from deactivating your control. The control should be locked only for short periods, such as while firing an event.

> ## note
>
> Each time the control is locked, the locking must be paired with an unlocking of the control when finished.

Parameters:

> bLock: This parameter is set to TRUE if the in-place active state of the control is to be locked; otherwise, it is set to FALSE if it is to be unlocked.

Return Value

This function returns a nonzero value if the lock was successful; otherwise, 0 is returned.

void COleControl::TransformCoords(POINTL FAR* *lpptlHimetric*, POINTF FAR* *lpptfContainer*, DWORD *flags*);

You should call this function to transform coordinate values between the container's native units and HIMETRIC units.

Parameters:

> lpptlHimetric: This parameter is a pointer to a POINTL structure containing coordinates in HIMETRIC units.
>
> lpptfContainer: This parameter is a pointer to a POINTF structure containing coordinates in the container's unit size.
>
> flags: This parameter is a combination of the following values:
>
> XFORMCOORDS_POSITION: A position in the container.
>
> XFORMCOORDS_SIZE: A size in the container.
>
> XFORMCOORDS_HIMETRICTOCONTAINER: Transforms HIMETRIC units to the container's units.
>
> XFORMCOORDS_CONTAINERTOHIMETRIC: Transforms the container's units to HIMETRIC units.

The flags XFORMCOORDS_POSITION and XFORMCOORDS_SIZE indicate whether the coordinates should be treated as a position or a size. The remaining flags indicate the direction of transformation.

Modal Dialog Methods

The modal dialog methods are useful in helping the control's container to properly enable and disable its top-level windows. Before a control displays a modal dialog box, the container must be allowed to disable all of its top-level windows. After a modal dialog box has been closed, the container must enable all of its top-level windows. The functions that provide these implementations are detailed below.

void COleControl::PreModalDialog( );

This function must be called prior to displaying any modal dialog box so that the container can disable all its top-level windows. After the modal dialog box has been displayed, you must call PostModalDialog.

Parameters: none.

void COleControl::PostModalDialog( );

This function must be called after displaying any modal dialog box so that the container can enable any top-level windows disabled by PreModalDialog. This function should be paired with a call to PreModalDialog.

Parameters: none.

Overridable Methods

The overridable methods are a collection of general-purpose functions to take care of a variety of tasks for an OLE control. These tasks range from displaying error messages and getting messages strings to providing overridden functionality usually found in the CWnd class. Overridden functions such as OnDraw or OnEdit can be enhanced implementations, which provide OLE specific capabilities. These functions and explanations are detailed on the following pages.

virtual void COleControl::DisplayError (SCODE *scode*, LPCTSTR *lpszDescription*, LPCTSTR *lpszSource*, LPCTSTR *lpszHelpFile*, UINT *nHelpID*);

The framework calls this function after the stock Error event has been handled. This function will not be called if the stock Error event handler has suppressed the display of the error. The default behavior displays a message box containing the description of the error. The description is contained in `lpszDescription`.

You should override this function if you would like to customize how errors are displayed.

Parameters:

> `scode`: This parameter is the status code value to be reported.
>
> `lpszDescription`: This parameter is a pointer to the string describing the error being reported.
>
> `lpszSource`: This parameter is a pointer to a string. The string contains the name of the module generating the error. The name is usually the name of the OLE control module.
>
> `lpszHelpFile`: This parameter is a pointer to a string that contains the name of the help file containing a description of the error.
>
> `nHelpID`: This parameter represents the Help Context ID of the error being reported.

virtual void COleControl::DoPropExchange (CPropExchange* *pPX*);

This function is called by the framework when loading or storing a control from a persistent storage representation—for example, a stream or property set. Normally, this function makes calls to the property exchange family of functions. It uses these functions to store or load specific, user-defined properties.

You should override this function to serialize the user-defined stock properties of your control. The stock properties of your control will be serialized by the overridden version of this function with a call to `COleControl::DoPropExchange`.

Parameters:

> `pPX`: This parameter is a pointer to a `CPropExchange` object. This is a framework supplied object used to establish the context of the property exchange and its direction.

virtual HRESULT COleControl::GetClassID (LPCLSID *pclsid*) = 0;

The framework calls this function to retrieve the OLE class ID of the control. This function is usually implemented by the `IMPLEMENT_OLECREATE_EX` macro.

Parameters:

> `pclsid`: This parameter is a pointer to the location of the class ID.

Return Value

The function will return a nonzero value if the call was successful; otherwise, 0 will be returned.

virtual void COleControl::GetMessageString (UINT *nID*, CString& *rMessage*) const;

The framework will call this function to obtain a string that describes the purpose of the menu item identified by nID. This string can be used to obtain a message for display in a status bar while the menu item is highlighted. This function's default implementation will attempt to load a string resource identified by nID.

Parameters:

nID: A menu item ID.

rMessage: This parameter is a reference to a CString object. It is through this object that a string will be returned.

virtual BOOL COleControl::IsSubclassedControl( );

The framework calls this function to check if the control subclasses a Windows control. If your OLE control subclasses a Windows control, you must override this function and return TRUE.

Parameters: none.

Return Value

The return value is nonzero if the control is subclassed; otherwise, the return value is 0.

virtual void COleControl::OnClick(USHORT *iButton*);

The framework calls this function when a mouse button has been clicked or the DoClick stock method has been invoked. The default implementation simply calls COleControl::FireClick. If you would like to modify or extend the default handling, override this member function.

Parameters:

iButton: This parameter is the index of a mouse button. It can have one of the following values:

LEFT_BUTTON: The left mouse button was clicked.

MIDDLE_BUTTON: The middle mouse button was clicked.

RIGHT_BUTTON: The right mouse button was clicked.

virtual BOOL COleControl::OnDoVerb(LONG *iVerb*, LPMSG *lpMsg*, HWND *hWndParent*, LPCRECT *lpRect*);

The framework calls this function when the container calls the IOleObject::DoVerb member function. The default implementation of COleControl::OnDoVerb uses the ON_OLEVERB and ON_STDOLEVERB message map entries to determine the proper function to invoke.

Return Value

The return value is nonzero if the call was successful; otherwise, 0 is returned.

Parameters:

iVerb: This integer is the index of the control verb to be invoked.

lpMsg: This parameter is a pointer to the Windows message that caused the verb to be invoked.

hWndParent: This is a handle to the parent window of the control. If the window is created from the execution of a verb, hWndParent should be used as the window's parent.

lpRect: This parameter points to a RECT structure into which the coordinates of the control will be copied. These coordinates will be relative to the container.

virtual void COleControl::OnDraw(CDC* *pDC*, const CRect& *rcBounds*, const CRect& *rcInvalid*);

The framework calls this function to draw the OLE control in the specified bounding rectangle using the specified device context.

Parameters:

pDC: This parameter represents a pointer to the device context in which the drawing occurs.

rcBounds: This parameter is the rectangular area of the control which includes the border.

rcInvalid: This parameter represents the rectangular area of the control that is invalid.

virtual void COleControl::OnDrawMetafile (CDC* *pDC*, const CRect& *rcBounds*);

The framework calls this function to draw the OLE control in the specified bounding rectangle using the specified metafile device context. The default implementation calls the OnDraw function.

Parameters:

pDC: A pointer to the device context in which the drawing occurs.

rcBounds: This parameter is the rectangular area of the control that includes the border.

virtual BOOL COleControl::OnEdit(LPMSG *lpMsg*, HWND *hWndParent*, LPCRECT *lpRect*);

This function can be called to cause the control to be UI-activated. Calling this function has the same effect as invoking the control's OLEIVERB_UIACTIVATE verb.

Parameters:

lpMsg: This parameter points to the Windows message that invoked the verb.

hWndParent: A handle to the parent window of the control.

lpRect: This parameter points to the rectangle used by the control in the container.

Return Value

The return value is an OLE result code, which is nonzero if the call is not successful; otherwise, 0 is returned.

virtual BOOL COleControl::OnEnumVerbs (LPENUMOLEVERB FAR* *ppenumOleVerb*);

The framework calls this function in response to the container's call to the IOleObject::EnumVerbs member function. The default implementation enumerates the ON_OLEVERB entries in the message map.

Parameters:

ppenumOleVerb: This parameter points to the IEnumOLEVERB object that enumerates the control's verbs.

Return Value

If verbs are available, the return value is nonzero; otherwise, the return value is 0.

virtual void COleControl::OnEventAdvise (BOOL *bAdvise*);

The framework calls this function when an event handler is connected to or disconnected from an OLE control.

Parameters:

> bAdvise: A value of TRUE indicates that an event handler has been connected to the control. A value of FALSE indicates that an event handler has been disconnected from the control.

virtual BOOL COleControl::OnGetColorSet (DVTARGETDEVICE FAR* *ptd*, HDC *hicTargetDev*, LPLOGPALETTE FAR* *ppColorSet*);

The framework calls this function in response to the container calling the IOleObject::GetColorSet member function. IOleObject::GetColorSet is called by the container to obtain all the colors needed to draw the OLE control. The container can use the color sets obtained to set the color palette. You should override this function to do any special processing of this request because the default implementation returns FALSE.

Parameters:

> ptd: This parameter is a pointer to the target device for which the picture should be rendered. If this value is NULL, the picture should be rendered for a default target device. This is usually a display device.

> hicTargetDev: This parameter specifies the information context for the target device indicated by ptd. This parameter does not necessarily need to be a device context. If ptd is NULL, hicTargetDev should also be NULL.

> ppColorSet: A pointer to the location into which the set of colors that would be used should be copied. If the function does not return the color set, NULL is returned.

Return Value

The return value is nonzero if a valid color set is returned; otherwise, 0 is the return value.

virtual void COleControl::OnKeyDownEvent (USHORT *nChar*, USHORT *nShiftState*);

After the stock KeyDown event has been processed, the framework calls this function. If your control needs access to the key information after the event has been fired, override this function.

Parameters:

> nChar: This parameter represents the virtual key code value of the pressed key.

> nShiftState: This parameter contains a combination of the following flags:

> SHIFT_MASK: The Shift key was pressed during the action.

> CTRL_MASK: The Ctrl key was pressed during the action.

> ALT_MASK: The Alt key was pressed during the action.

virtual void COleControl::OnKeyPressEvent (USHORT *nChar*);

After the stock KeyPress event has been fired, the framework calls this function. You should override this function if you want notification after this event occurs.

note
It is possible that the container prior to calling COleControl::OnKeyPressEvent might have modified the nChar value.

Parameters:

> nChar: This parameter represents the virtual key code value of the pressed key.

virtual void OnKeyUpEvent(USHORT *nChar*, USHORT *nShiftState*);

After the stock KeyDown event has been processed, the framework calls this function. If your control needs access to the key information after the event has been fired, override this function.

Parameters:

> nChar: This parameter represents the virtual key code value of the pressed key.

nShiftState: This parameter contains a combination of the following flags:

SHIFT_MASK: The Shift key was pressed during the action.

CTRL_MASK: The Ctrl key was pressed during the action.

ALT_MASK: The Alt key was pressed during the action.

virtual BOOL OnProperties(LPMSG *lpMsg*, HWND *hWndParent*, LPCRECT *lpRect*);

This is called by the framework when the container has invoked the control's properties verb. The default implementation displays a modal property dialog box.

Parameters:

lpMsg: This parameter points to the Windows message that invoked the verb.

hWndParent: A handle to the parent window of the control.

lpRect: This parameter points to the rectangle used by the control in the container.

Return Value

The return value is an OLE result code. Therefore, nonzero will be returned if the call is not successful; otherwise, 0 is returned.

virtual void COleControl::OnResetState( );

When the control's properties should be set to their default values, the framework calls this function. The default implementation calls COleControl::DoPropExchange, passing a CPropExchange object. This causes properties to be set to their default values. You should override this function to insert initialization code for the OLE control.

Change Notification Methods

The change notification methods are used to notify the control of a change in the value of a control's stock property. These functions must be overridden by the control for the control to receive notification of a change in the value of a stock property. The methods and explanations of their functionality are detailed in the following subsections.

virtual void COleControl::OnBackColorChanged( );

This function is called by the framework when the stock BackColor property value has changed. If you want notification after this property has changed, you must override this function. The default implementation of this function calls InvalidateControl.

Parameters: none.

virtual void COleControl::OnBorderStyleChanged( );

This function is called by the framework when the stock BorderStyle property value has changed. If you want notification after this property has changed, you must override this function. The default implementation of this function calls InvalidateControl.

Parameters: none.

virtual void COleControl::OnEnabledChanged ( );

This function is called by the framework when the stock Enabled property value has changed.

If you want notification after this property has changed, you must override this function. The default implementation of this function calls InvalidateControl.

Parameters: none.

virtual void COleControl::OnFontChanged( );

When the stock Font property value has changed, this function is called by the framework. To receive notification after this property has changed, you must override this function. The default implementation of this function calls InvalidateControl. The default implementation also sends a WM_SETFONT message to the control's window if the control subclasses a Windows control.

Parameters: none.

virtual void COleControl::OnForeColorChanged( );

This method is called by the framework when the stock ForeColor property value has changed. If you want notification after this property has changed, you must override this function. The default implementation of this function calls `InvalidateControl`.

Parameters: none.

virtual void COleControl::OnTextChanged( );

When the stock `Caption` or `Text` property value has changed, this function is called by the framework. If you want notification after this property has changed you must override this function. The default implementation of this function calls `InvalidateControl`.

Parameters: none.

OLE Interface Notification Methods

The interface notification methods provide functionality to notify the control or container to status changes in events, data, general information, properties, and dimensions of an OLE control. These functions are used to allow the control and the container to effectively communicate this information to each other. The functions are listed below. Each function is followed by a description of its purpose.

virtual void COleControl::OnAmbientPropertyChange (DISPID *dispID*);

When an ambient property of the container has changed value, the framework calls this function. To receive notification of a change in the value of an ambient property, you should override this function in your control.

Parameters:

dispID: This parameter refers to the dispatch ID of the ambient property that has changed or `DISPID_UNKNOWN` if multiple properties have changed.

virtual void COleControl::OnFreezeEvents (BOOL *bFreeze*);

After the container calls the interface method, the `IOleControl::FreezeEvents` framework calls this function. If you want additional behavior while event handling is frozen or unfrozen, you should override this function. The default implementation of this function does nothing.

Parameters:

bFreeze: This parameter is set to TRUE if the control's event handling is frozen; otherwise, the parameter's value is FALSE.

virtual void COleControl::OnGetControlInfo (LPCONTROLINFO *pControlInfo*);

When the control's container has requested information about the control, the framework calls this function. The information passed back through pControlInfo mainly consists of a description of the control's mnemonic keys. You should override this function if your control needs to process mnemonic keys. The default implementation fills pControlInfo with default information.

Parameters:

pControlInfo: This parameter is a pointer to a CONTROLINFO structure to be filled in.

virtual void COleControl::OnMnemonic(LPMSG *pMsg*);

This function is called by the framework when the container has detected a press of a mnemonic key of the OLE control.

Parameters:

pMsg: This parameter is a pointer to the Windows message generated by a mnemonic keypress.

virtual BOOL COleControl::OnRenderData (LPFORMATETC *lpFormatEtc*, LPSTGMEDIUM *lpStgMedium*);

This function is called by the framework to obtain data in a specified format. The specified format was stored in the control object prior to calling this function by using the DelayRenderData or the DelayRenderFileData member functions. These functions, as their names imply, delay the rendering of your data. If the storage medium supplied is either a file or memory, the default implementation of this function calls OnRenderFileData or OnRenderGlobalData, respectively.

You will need to override this function to provide your data in the requested format and medium. You might consider overriding one of the other variations of this function, OnRenderGlobalData, or OnRenderFileData. Override OnRenderGlobalData if your data is small and its size does not vary. Don't override OnRenderFileData if your data is in a file, is large, or varies in size.

> **note**
>
> STGMEDIUM should be allocated and filled as specified by lpFormatEtc->tymed if lpStgMedium->tymed is TYMED_NULL. If lpStgMedium->tymed is not TYMED_NULL, STGMEDIUM should be filled in place with the data.

Parameters:

> lpFormatEtc: This parameter is a pointer to a FORMATETC structure that specifies the format in which information is requested.
>
> lpStgMedium: This parameter is a pointer to a STGMEDIUM structure in which the data is to be returned.

Return Value

The default implementation of this function renders the appropriate data and returns nonzero if the requested data format is CF_METAFILEPICT or the persistent property set format. Otherwise, it does nothing and returns 0.

virtual BOOL COleControl::OnRenderFileData (LPFORMATETC *lpFormatEtc*, CFile* *pFile*);

This function is called by the framework to retrieve data in the specified format when the storage medium is a file. The specified format was stored in the control object prior to calling this function by using the DelayRenderData.

You must override this function to provide your data in the requested format and medium. With OnRenderData, you might want to override another version of this function instead. This will depend on your data. To handle multiple storage mediums, you should override OnRenderData. Override OnRenderFileData if your data is in a file, is large, or varies in size.

> **note**
>
> The default implementation of this function simply returns FALSE. Therefore, it is required that you override this function if you want to retrieve data in the specified format.

Return Value

The function returns a nonzero value upon successful completion; otherwise, it returns 0.

Parameters:

lpFormatEtc: This parameter is a pointer to a FORMATETC structure specifying the format in which information is requested.

pFile: This parameter is a pointer to a CFile object in which the data is to be rendered.

virtual BOOL COleControl:: OnRenderGlobalData(LPFORMATETC *lpFormatEtc*, HGLOBAL* *phGlobal*);

The framework calls this function to retrieve data in the specified format when the specified storage medium is global memory. The specified format was stored in the control object prior to calling this function by using the DelayRenderData member function for delayed rendering.

If phGlobal is NULL, a new HGLOBAL should be allocated and returned in phGlobal. Otherwise, the HGLOBAL specified by phGlobal should be filled with the retrieved data. The memory block for phGlobal cannot be reallocated to a larger size. Therefore, care must be taken that the amount of data placed in the HGLOBAL does not exceed the current size of its memory block that was passed in.

You must override this function to provide your data in the requested format and medium. As in the case of OnRenderData, you might want to override another version of this function instead. This will depend on your data. To handle multiple storage mediums, you should override OnRenderData. Override OnRenderFileData if your data is in a file, is large, or varies in size.

> ### note
>
> The default implementation of this function simply returns FALSE. Therefore, it is required that you override this function if you want to retrieve data in the specified format.

Parameters:

lpFormatEtc: This parameter is a pointer to a FORMATETC structure specifying the format in which information is requested.

phGlobal: This parameter is a pointer to a handle to global memory. This pointer will provide the memory in which the data is to be returned. If no memory has been allocated, this parameter can be NULL.

Return Value

The function returns a nonzero value upon successful completion; otherwise, it returns 0.

virtual void COleControl::OnSetClientSite ( );

This function is called by the framework after the control's IOleControl::SetClientSite method has been called by the container. You can override this function to do any special processing for this function.

Parameters: none.

virtual BOOL COleControl::OnSetData (LPFORMATETC *lpFormatEtc*, LPSTGMEDIUM *lpStgMedium*, BOOL *bRelease*);

The framework will call this function to replace the control's data with the data specified. The default implementation of this function modifies the control's state accordingly if the data is in the persistent property set format. If bRelease is TRUE, a call to ReleaseStgMedium is made; otherwise the default implementation does nothing.

If you would like to replace the control's data with the specified data, override this function.

Parameters:

lpFormatEtc: This parameter is pointer to a FORMATETC structure specifying the format of the data.

lpStgMedium: This parameter is pointer to a STGMEDIUM structure in which the data resides.

bRelease: This parameter is set to TRUE if the control should free the storage medium. If the control should not free the storage medium, the parameter's value is set to FALSE.

Return Value

This function returns a nonzero if successful; otherwise, a value of 0 is returned.

virtual BOOL COleControl::OnSetExtent (LPSIZEL *lpSizeL*);

The framework will call this function when the control's extent needs to be changed. This is a result of a call to IOleObject::SetExtent method. The default implementation of OnSetExtent will handle the resizing of the control's extent. Then, if the control is in-place active, a call to the container's OnPosRectChanged is then made. If you would like to alter the default resizing of your control, override this function.

Return Value

This function returns nonzero if the size change was accepted; otherwise, it returns 0.

Parameters:

lpSizeL: A pointer to the SIZEL structure. This structure uses long integers to represent the width and height of the control, expressed in HIMETRIC units.

virtual BOOL COleControl::OnSetObjectRects (LPCRECT lpRectPos, LPCRECT lpRectClip);

This function is called by the framework to implement a call to IOleInPlaceObject::SetObjectRects. The default implementation will automatically handle the resizing and repositioning of the control's window and return TRUE. If you are not satisfied with the default behavior of this function you can override its implementation.

Parameters:

lpRectPos: This parameter is a pointer to a RECT structure indicating the control's new position and size relative to the container.

lpRectClip: Another pointer to a RECT structure. This parameter indicates a rectangular area to which the control is to be clipped.

Return Value

The function will return a nonzero value if the repositioning was accepted; otherwise, 0 will be returned.

In-Place Activation Methods

In-place activation is a user interface extension of the embedding feature of OLE controls. A container and a control use a collection of interfaces and protocols to merge their various user interface elements, and to display those elements in the container's frame and window directly.

Displaying those elements usually involves the creation of a shared menu that contains items from both the container and the object. To accomplish this, there is a negotiation process through which the control is granted space in the container to create toolbars and other frame and document window decorations. Other concerns such as a protocol for handling both the container and the object's accelerators, handling Undo operations, context-sensitive help, window resizing, and so on are all taken care of in the negotiation process. Because this chapter covers MFC, it will not go into all of the specifics of the negotiation process. Instead, this chapter examines the functions provided in the COleControl class to handle the an OLE control's in-place activation issues. These methods are detailed in the following subsections.

virtual HMENU COleControl::OnGetInPlaceMenu( );

This function is called by the framework when the control is UI-activated. This function obtains the menu to be merged into the container's existing menu and returns a handle to the menu. To learn more about merging OLE resources, see the article titled "Menus and Resources" in *Programming with MFC*. *Programming with MFC* is available on the Visual C++ version 4.0 and higher CD-ROM.

Parameters: none.

Return Value

The function's return value is the handle of the control's menu, or NULL if the control has none. The default implementation of this function always returns NULL.

virtual void COleControl::OnHideToolBars ( );

The framework calls this function when the control is UI-deactivated. The implementation that you provide should hide all toolbars displayed by the overridden implementation of OnShowToolbars. The default implementation does nothing.

Parameters: none.

virtual void OnShowToolBars( );

The framework calls this function when the control is UI-activated. The default implementation does nothing. You should override this function to show toolbars.

Parameters: none.

Property Browsing Methods

The property browsing methods provide an interface for you to manipulate display strings and values for the control's properties. These functions are useful for obtaining property strings and their predefined values. The ability to retrieve a class ID of a property page that implements editing of the specified property is also provided. The methods to implement this functionality are examined in the following subsections.

virtual BOOL COleControl::OnGetDisplayString(DISPID *dispid*, CString& *strValue*);

This function is called by the framework to obtain a string that represents the current value of the property identified by dispid. You should override this function if there is a property for your control that has a value that cannot be directly converted to a string. This is useful if you want the property's value to be displayed in a property browser that is supplied by the control's container.

Parameters:

> dispid: This parameter represents the dispatch ID of a property of the control.
>
> strValue: This parameter is a reference to a CString object. This object will be used to return a string.

Return Value

The return value is nonzero if a string has been returned in strValue; otherwise, 0 is returned.

virtual BOOL OnGetPredefinedStrings(DISPID *dispid*, CStringArray* *pStringArray*, CDWordArray* *pCookieArray*);

This function is used by the framework to retrieve a collection of predefined strings representing the possible values for a property.

If your control has a property with a set of possible values that can be represented by strings, override this function. For each element added to pStringArray, you should add a corresponding element (known as a *cookie*) to pCookieArray. A cookie value is nothing more than a value that can be associated with the corresponding string. These values can later be passed by the framework to the COleControl::OnGetPredefinedValue function.

Parameters:

dispid: This parameter represents the dispatch ID of a property of the control.

pStringArray: This parameter represents a string array to be filled in with return values.

pCookieArray: This parameter is a DWORD array that is to be filled in with return values.

Return Value

The return value will be nonzero if elements have been added to pStringArray and pCookieArray.

virtual BOOL OnGetPredefinedValue(DISPID *dispid*, DWORD *dwCookie*, VARIANT FAR* *lpvarOut*);

This function is called by the framework to obtain the cookie value corresponding to one of the predefined strings previously returned by an override of COleControl::OnGetPredefinedStrings.

Parameters:

dispid: This parameter represents the dispatch ID of a property of the control.

dwCookie: This parameter represents the cookie value previously returned by an override of COleControl::OnGetPredefinedStrings.

lpvarOut: This parameter is a pointer to a VARIANT structure through which a property value will be returned.

Return Value

The return value will be nonzero if a value has been returned in lpvarOut; in all other cases, the value will be 0.

virtual BOOL OnMapPropertyToPage(DISPID *dispid*, LPCLSID *lpclsid*, BOOL* *pbPageOptional*);

The framework calls this function to retrieve the class ID of a property page that implements the editing of the specified property. You can use this function as a way to invoke your control's property pages for the container's property browser.

Parameters:

dispid: This parameter represents the dispatch ID of a property of the control.

lpclsid: This parameter is a pointer to a CLSID structure. It is through this pointer that a class ID will be returned.

pbPageOptional: This parameter returns an indicator of whether use of the specified property page is optional.

Return Value

If a class ID has been returned in lpclsid, the function returns a nonzero value; otherwise, the function returns 0.

Update/Painting Methods

Only one function is available in this category. Its purpose is detailed in the following subsection.

BOOL COleControl::IsOptimizedDraw( );

This function should be called to determine whether the container supports optimized drawing for the current drawing operation. The control does not need to select old objects (such as pens, brushes, and fonts) into the device context when drawing is finished if optimized drawing is supported.

Parameters: none.

Return Value

The return value is TRUE if the container supports optimized drawing for the current drawing operation; otherwise, FALSE is returned.

Windowless Operations Methods

The following functions are used for windowless controls. OLE controls can be used in-place active without a window and provide significant advantages.

One such advantage is that windowless controls can be transparent and non-rectangular. This basically means that it is entirely possible that you could create a control that had a circular shape. Such a control would also benefit from having a reduced creation time and instance size. Because a significant portion of the code to support a window is not present, your control will be smaller and load quicker.

The functions and their descriptions are listed on the following pages.

BOOL COleControl::ClipCaretRect(LPRECT lpRect);

You should call this function to adjust the caret rectangle if it is entirely or even partially covered by overlapping, opaque objects. A windowless object cannot safely show a caret if the caret is partially or totally hidden by overlapping objects. The object first must check for that case by using ClipCaretRect to get the caret adjusted to guarantee it fits in the clipping region.

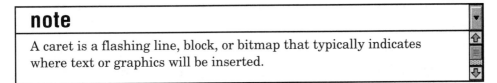

note

A caret is a flashing line, block, or bitmap that typically indicates where text or graphics will be inserted.

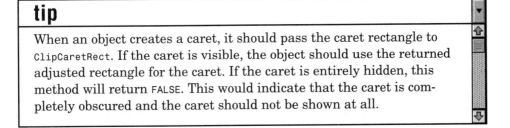

tip

When an object creates a caret, it should pass the caret rectangle to ClipCaretRect. If the caret is visible, the object should use the returned adjusted rectangle for the caret. If the caret is entirely hidden, this method will return FALSE. This would indicate that the caret is completely obscured and the caret should not be shown at all.

Parameters:

> lpRect: On input, this parameter is a pointer to a RECT structure that contains the caret area to be adjusted. On output, the parameter points to an adjusted caret area. If the caret rectangle is completely covered, the parameter points to NULL.

Return Value

If the function is successful, a nonzero value is returned; otherwise 0 is returned.

CWnd* COleControl::GetCapture( );

Call this function if you want to determine whether the COleControl object has the mouse capture. A windowless activated control receives the mouse capture when SetCapture is called.

Parameters: none.

Return Value

The function returns the this pointer if the control is activated, windowless, and the control currently has the mouse capture. NULL is returned if it does not have the capture. In all other cases, the function returns the CWnd object that has the mouse capture. The control's container determines whether or not the control has the mouse capture.

virtual void COleControl::GetClientRect (LPRECT lpRect) const;

You should call this function to retrieve the size of the control's client area.

Parameters:

> lpRect: This parameter points to a RECT structure, which contains the dimensions of the windowless control's client area. The control's client area is the control's size minus window borders, frames, scrollbars, and so on. The lpRect parameter is used to indicate the size of the control's client rectangle.

CDC* COleControl::GetDC(LPCRECT lprcRect = NULL, DWORD dwFlags = OLEDC_PAINTBKGND);

This function is called to provide a means for a windowless object to get a screen device context from its container. After painting, the ReleaseDC member function must be called to release the context. Control objects should pass the rectangle they want to draw into in their own client coordinates when calling GetDC. GetDC will translate these to coordinates of the container client area. To prevent objects from inadvertently drawing where they are not supposed to, the object should not request a desired drawing rectangle larger than its own client area rectangle.

Parameters:

> lprcRect: This parameter is a pointer to the rectangle that the windowless control wants to redraw. The rectangle is in the client coordinates of the control. A value of NULL indicates that the control wants to redraw using the full object's extent.

`dwFlags`: This parameter indicates the drawing attributes of the device context. Choices are as follows:

`OLEDC_NODRAW`: This flag indicates that the object won't use the device context to perform any drawing. Instead, it will get information about the display device. The container should pass the window's DC without further processing.

`OLEDC_PAINTBKGND`: This flag requests that the container paint the background before returning the DC. This flag should be used by an object if it is requesting a DC for redrawing an area with a transparent background.

`OLEDC_OFFSCREEN`: This flag informs the container that the object wants to render into an off-screen bitmap that should then be copied to the screen. This flag should be used by an object when the drawing operation it is about to perform will generate a lot of flicker. The container is not obligated to honor this request. If this flag is not set, the container needs to hand back an on-screen DC. This allows objects to perform direct screen operations.

Return Value

If successful, this function returns a pointer to the display device context for the container `CWnd` client area. Otherwise, the return value is `NULL`. The returned display device context can be used in following GDI function calls to draw in the client area of the container's window.

CWnd* COleControl::GetFocus( );

You should call this function to determine whether the `COleControl` object has the focus. An activated windowless control will receive the focus when `SetFocus` is called.

Parameters: none.

Return Value

The function returns the `this` pointer if the control is activated, windowless, and the control currently has the keyboard focus. `NULL` is returned if it does not have the focus. In all other cases, the function returns the `CWnd` object that has the keyboard focus. The control's container determines whether or not the control has the focus.

virtual IDropTarget* COleControl::GetWindowlessDropTarget( );

If you want a windowless control to be the target of an OLE drag-and-drop operation, you should override this function. This would normally mean that the control's window needs to be registered as a drop target. The container of the control will use its own window as the drop target because the control doesn't have a window of its own. The container will just simply delegate pass calls at the appropriate times to the IDropTarget interface that the control implements. A short example is as follows:

```
IDropTarget* CMyActiveXCtrl::GetWindowlessDropTarget()
{
    // increment the reference count
    m_xActiveXDropTarget.AddRef();
    // return an interface pointer.
    return &m_xActiveXDropTarget;
}
```

Return Value

This function returns a pointer to the control object's IDropTarget interface. A windowless object cannot register an IDropTarget interface. But to participate in drag and drop, a windowless object can still implement the interface. The interface then becomes the return value for GetWindwolessDropTarget.

Parameters: none.

void COleControl::InvalidateRgn(CRgn* pRgn, BOOL bErase = TRUE);

You should call this function to invalidate the container window's client. The client area invalidated will be within the given region. This function can be used to redraw windowless controls within the container. The invalidated region, along with all other areas in the update region, is marked for painting. This happens when the next WM_PAINT message is sent.

Parameters:

pRgn: This parameter is a pointer to a CRgn object. This object identifies the display region of the OLE object to invalidate in client coordinates of the containing window. If this parameter's value is NULL, the area invalidated is the entire object.

bErase: This parameter specifies whether the background within the invalidated region is to be erased. If TRUE, the background of the region is erased. If FALSE, the background will remain unchanged.

virtual BOOL COleControl:: OnWindowlessMessage(UINT *msg*, WPARAM *wParam*, LPARAM *lParam*, LRESULT* *plResult*);

This function is called by the framework in response to the container's `IOleInPlaceObjectWindowless::OnWindowMessage` request. This function processes the window messages for windowless controls and should be used for window messages other than keyboard and mouse messages.

A windowless OLE object gets messages from its container, through the `IOleInPlaceObjectWindowless::OnWindowMessage` method, which is an extension of `IOleInPlaceObject` for windowless support.

Parameters:

> `msg`: This parameter is a message identifier as passed by Windows.
>
> `wParam`: This parameter is a `WPARAM` as passed by Windows. It specifies additional information specific to the message. The contents of this parameter depend on the value of the `msg` parameter.
>
> `lParam`: This parameter is an `LPARAM` as passed by Windows. It specifies additional information specific to the message. The contents of this parameter depend on the value of the `msg` parameter.
>
> `plResult`: This parameter is a pointer to a Windows result code. It specifies the result of the message processing and depends on the message sent.

Return Value

The return value will be nonzero if successful; otherwise, it will be 0.

int COleControl::ReleaseDC(CDC* *pDC*);

This function is called when you want to release the display device context of a container of a windowless control. This function will free the device context for use by other applications.

---

note

For each call to `GetDC`, the application must call `ReleaseDC`.

Parameters:

> `pDC`: This parameter identifies the container device context to be released.

Return Value

The return value will be nonzero if successful; otherwise, it will be 0.

void COleControl::ScrollWindow(int *xAmount*, int *yAmount*, LPCRECT *lpRect* = NULL, LPCRECT *lpClipRect* = NULL);

You should call this function to allow a windowless OLE object to scroll. The scrolled area will be within its in-place active image on the screen.

Parameters:

xAmount: This parameter specifies the amount of horizontal scrolling in device units. To scroll to the left, this parameter must be a negative value.

yAmount: This parameter specifies the amount of vertical scrolling in device units. To scroll upward, this parameter must be a negative value.

lpRect: This parameter points to a CRect object or RECT structure. It specifies the portion of the OLE object's client area to scroll. The coordinates are specified in client coordinates of the containing window. If lpRect is NULL, the entire OLE object's client area is scrolled.

lpClipRect: This parameter points to a CRect object or RECT structure. It specifies the rectangle to clip to. Only the pixels inside the rectangle are scrolled. Regions outside the rectangle are not affected even if they are in the lpRect rectangle. No clipping is performed on the scroll rectangle if lpClipRect is NULL.

CWnd* COleControl::SetCapture( );

This function causes the control's container window to take possession of the mouse capture on the control's behalf. This is done only if the control is activated and windowless. Otherwise, calling this function will cause the control itself to take possession of the mouse capture.

Parameters: none.

Return Value

The return value will be a pointer to the CWnd window object that previously received mouse input.

CWnd* COleControl::SetFocus( );

This function causes the control's container window to take possession of the input focus on the control's behalf. The input focus directs keyboard input to the container's window causing the container to dispatch all subsequent keyboard messages to the OLE object that called SetFocus. The window that previously had the input focus, if any, loses it. This is done only if the control is activated and windowless. Otherwise, if the control is not windowless, calling this function will cause the control itself to take possession of the input focus.

Parameters: none.

Return Value

The return value is a pointer to the CWnd window object that previously had the input focus. NULL will be the return value if there is no such window.

Asynchronous Control Methods

Asynchronous control functions are used to determine or set a control's readiness state. By keeping track of its readiness state, a control can determine whether it has enough critical data loaded to become interactive.

long COleControl::GetReadyState( );

You should call this function to retrieve the ready state of the control object.

> **note**
>
> Most simple controls never need to distinguish between the LOADED and INTERACTIVE states. However, more complex controls might support data path properties and might not be ready to be interactive until a certain amount of data is received asynchronously. In any case, a control should attempt to become interactive as soon as possible.

Parameters: none.

Return Value

The readiness state of the control is returned, which is one of the following values:

READYSTATE_UNINITIALIZED: The default initialization state.

READYSTATE_LOADING: The control is currently loading its properties.

READYSTATE_LOADED: The control has loaded its properties, and the control has been initialized.

READYSTATE_INTERACTIVE: The control has enough data to be interactive, but not all the asynchronous data is loaded yet.

READYSTATE_COMPLETE: The control has all its data and can be interactive.

void COleControl::InternalSetReadyState (long *lNewReadyState*);

You should call this function to retrieve the ready state of the control object.

> **note**
>
> Most simple controls never need to distinguish between the LOADED and INTERACTIVE states. However, more complex controls might support data path properties and not be ready to be interactive until a certain amount of data is received asynchronously. In any case, a control should attempt to become interactive as soon as possible.

Parameters:

lNewReadyState: This parameter indicates the readiness state to set for the control. Only one of the following values are valid:

READYSTATE_UNINITIALIZED: The default initialization state.

READYSTATE_LOADING: The control is currently loading its properties.

READYSTATE_LOADED: The control has loaded its properties, and the control has been initialized.

READYSTATE_INTERACTIVE: The control has enough data to be interactive, but not all the asynchronous data is loaded yet.

READYSTATE_COMPLETE: The control has all its data and can be interactive.

void COleControl::Load(LPCTSTR *strNewPath*, CDataPathProperty& *prop*);

This function should be called when you want to reset any previous data loaded asynchronously. It should also be called to initiate a new loading of the control's asynchronous property.

Parameters:

strNewPath: This parameter is a pointer to a string that contains the path that references the absolute location of the asynchronous control property.

prop: A CDataPathProperty object that implements an asynchronous control property.

Inactive Pointer Handling Functions

This group of functions provides the control builder with a means of receiving mouse input while the control is inactive. Functions also exist to translate point coordinates between the client and control. The functions are described in the following subsections.

virtual void COleControl::ClientToParent(LPCRECT *lprcBounds*, LPPOINT *pPoint*) const;

Call this function to translate the coordinate of a point in the OLE control client area into the control's container coordinates. When passed in, pPoint is relative to the origin of the client area of the OLE control. When the function exits, pPoint is relative to the origin of the control's container.

Parameters:

> lprcBounds: This parameter is a pointer to the bounds of the OLE control within the container. The bounds are of entire control area including borders and scrollbars.

> pPoint: This parameter is a pointer to the OLE client area point to be translated into the coordinates of the container.

virtual DWORD COleControl::GetActivationPolicy( );

You should override this function if you want to alter the default activation behavior of a control. The control must support the IPointerInactive interface.

The container will transfer WM_MOUSEMOVE and WM_SETCURSOR messages to the control when the IPointerInactive interface is enabled. The implementation of this interface provided by COleControl will dispatch the messages through the control's message map. The messages will be dispatched after the mouse coordinates are adjusted appropriately.

Parameters: none.

Return Value

The return value can be any combination of flags from the POINTERINACTIVE enumeration. The possible flags are

> POINTERINACTIVE_ACTIVATEONENTRY: This flag indicates the object should be in-place activated when the mouse enters it during a mouse move operation.

> POINTERINACTIVE_DEACTIVATEONLEAVE: This flag indicates the object should be deactivated when the mouse leaves the object during a mouse-move operation.

POINTERINACTIVE_ACTIVATEONDRAG: This flag indicates the object should be in-place activated when the mouse is dragged over it during a drag-and-drop operation.

virtual void COleControl::GetClientOffset(long* *pdxOffset*, long* *pdyOffset*) const;

An OLE control occupies a rectangular area within its container. The client area of the control is the area of the control excluding borders and scrollbars. GetClientOffset retrieves the difference between the upper-left corner of the control's area and the upper-left corner of its client area. You need to override this function if your control has non-client elements other than the standard borders and scrollbars. In the overriden function you can make the proper calculations to return the correct difference.

Parameters:

pdxOffset: This parameter is a pointer to the horizontal offset of the OLE control's client area.

pdyOffset: This parameter is a pointer to the vertical offset of the OLE control's client area.

virtual void COleControl:: OnInactiveMouseMove(LPCRECT *lprcBounds*, long *x*, long *y*, DWORD *dwKeyState*);

The control's container calls COleControl::OnInactiveMouseMove. It is called for the inactive object under the mouse pointer on receipt of a WM_MOUSEMOVE message.

> **note**
>
> The window client coordinates, pixels, are used to pass the mouse cursor position.

Parameters:

lprcBounds: The control's bounding rectangle represented in client coordinates of the containing window. This parameter contains the object's exact size and position on the screen when the WM_MOUSEMOVE message was received.

x: This parameter contains the x-coordinate of the mouse location in client coordinates of the containing window.

y: This parameter contains the y coordinate of the mouse location in client coordinates of the containing window.

dwKeyState: This parameter is used to identify the current state of the keyboard modifier keys. Valid values can be a combination of the flags MK_CONTROL, MK_SHIFT, MK_ALT, MK_BUTTON, MK_LBUTTON, MK_MBUTTON, and MK_RBUTTON.

virtual BOOL COleControl:: OnInactiveSetCursor(LPCRECT *lprcBounds*, long *x*, long *y*, DWORD *dwMouseMsg*, BOOL *bSetAlways*);

The control's container calls COleControl::OnInactiveSetCursor. It is called for the inactive object under the mouse pointer on receipt of a WM_SETCURSOR message.

> **note**
>
> The window client coordinates, pixels, are used to pass the mouse cursor position.

Parameters:

lprcBounds: The control's bounding rectangle represented in client coordinates of the containing window. This parameter contains the object's exact size and position on the screen when the WM_MOUSEMOVE message was received.

x: This parameter contains the x coordinate of the mouse location in client coordinates of the containing window.

y: This parameter contains the y coordinate of the mouse location in client coordinates of the containing window.

dwMouseMsg: This parameter contains the identifier of the mouse message for which a WM_SETCURSOR occurred.

bSetAlways: Used to specify whether or not the object must set the cursor. The object must set the cursor if this parameter is TRUE; if FALSE, this function is not obligated to set the cursor.

Return Value

If the function returns successfully, the return value will be nonzero; otherwise 0 is returned.

virtual UINT COleControl::ParentToClient(LPCRECT *lprcBounds*, LPPOINT *pPoint*, BOOL *bHitTest* = FALSE) const;

Call this function to translate the coordinate of a point in the control's container into the OLE control client coordinates. When passed in, pPoint is relative to the origin of the control's container. Upon exiting, the function pPoint is relative to the origin client area of the OLE control.

Parameters

lprcBounds: This parameter is a pointer to the bounds of the OLE control within the container. The bounds are of the entire control, including borders and scrollbars.

pPoint: This parameter is a pointer to the container point. This is the point to be translated into the coordinates of the client area of the control.

bHitTest: bHitTest specifies whether or not hit testing is to be done on the point.

Return Value

The function returns HTNOWHERE if bHitTest is FALSE. If bHitTest is TRUE, the function returns the location in which the container point landed in the client area of the OLE control. The location is one of the following mouse hit-test values:

HTBORDER: The point is in the border of a window that does not have a sizing border.

HTBOTTOM: The point is in the lower horizontal border of the window.

HTBOTTOMLEFT: The point is in the lower-left corner of the window border.

HTBOTTOMRIGHT: The point is in the lower-right corner of the window border.

HTCAPTION: The point is in a title bar area.

HTCLIENT: The point is in a client area.

HTERROR: The point falls on the screen background or on a dividing line between windows

HTGROWBOX: The point is in a size box.

HTHSCROLL: The point is in the horizontal scrollbar.

HTLEFT: The point is in the left border of the window.

HTMAXBUTTON: The point is in a Maximize button.

HTMENU: The point is in a menu area.

HTMINBUTTON: The point is in a Minimize button.

HTNOWHERE: The point falls on the screen background or on a dividing line between windows.

HTREDUCE: The point is in a Minimize button.

HTRIGHT: The point is in the right border of the window.

HTSIZE: The point is in a size box (same as HTGROWBOX).

HTSYSMENU: The point is in a Control menu or in a Close button in a child window.

HTTOP: The point is in the upper horizontal border of the window.

HTTOPLEFT: The point is in the upper-left corner of the window border.

HTTOPRIGHT: The point is in the upper-right corner of the window border.

HTTRANSPARENT: The point is in a window currently covered by another window.

HTVSCROLL: The point is in the vertical scrollbar.

HTZOOM: The point is in a Maximize button.

IviewObject Interface Notification Overridables

These functions are useful in determining the control's viewable extents. They are also useful for hit detection of rectangles and points in the controls viewable area. The four functions in this category are detailed in the following subsections.

virtual BOOL COleControl::OnGetColorSet (DVTARGETDEVICE FAR* *ptd*, HDC *hicTargetDev*, LPLOGPALETTE FAR* *ppColorSet*);

The framework calls this function in response to the container calling the IOleObject::GetColorSet member function. IOleObject::GetColorSet is called by the container to obtain all the colors needed to draw the OLE control. The container can use the color sets obtained to set the color palette. You should override this function to do any special processing of this request because the default implementation returns FALSE.

Parameters:

ptd: This parameter is a pointer to the target device for which the picture should be rendered. A value of NULL indicates that the picture should be rendered fo the default device, typically a display device.

hicTargetDev: This parameter specifies the information context for the target device indicated by ptd. This parameter does not necessarily need to be a device context. If ptd is NULL, hicTargetDev should also be NULL.

ppColorSet: A pointer to the location into which the set of colors that would be used should be copied. If the function does not return the color set, NULL is returned.

Return Value

The return value is nonzero if a valid color set is returned; otherwise, 0 is returned.

virtual BOOL COleControl:: OnGetNaturalExtent(DWORD *dwAspect*, LONG *lindex*, DVTARGETDEVICE* *ptd*, HDC *hicTargetDev*, DVEXTENTINFO* *pExtentInfo*, LPSIZEL *psizel*);

This function is called by the framework when the container makes an IviewObjectEx::GetNaturalExtent request. You should override this function to return the object's display size. The returned size should be closest to the proposed size and extent mode in the DVEXTENTINFO structure. This function's default implementation returns FALSE and does not make any adjustments to the size.

Parameters:

dwAspect: This parameter specifies how the object is to be represented. Representations can be content, an icon, a thumbnail, or a printed document. Valid values are taken from the enumeration DVASPECT or DVASPECT2.

lindex: A long integer value that indicates the portion of the object that is of interest. Currently, only -1 is valid.

ptd: This parameter is a pointer to the DVTARGETDEVICE structure that defines the target device for which the object's size should be returned.

hicTargetDev: This parameter specifies the information context for the target device indicated by the ptd parameter. The object can extract device metrics and test the device's capabilities from this context. If ptd is NULL, the object should ignore the value in the hicTargetDev parameter.

pExtentInfo: A pointer to the DVEXTENTINFO structure that specifies sizing data.

psizel: A pointer to sizing data returned by the control object. If the dimension was not adjusted, the returned sizing data is set to -1.

Return Value

A nonzero value is returned if the function successfully returns or if the function adjusts the display size of the object. Otherwise, 0 is returned.

virtual BOOL COleControl::OnGeewExtent (DWORD *dwDrawAspect*, LONG *lindex*, DVTARGETDEVICE* *ptd*, LPSIZEL *lpsizel*);

You should override this function if your control's opaque and transparent parts have different dimensions and the control uses two-pass drawing. The function is called by the framework in response to a container's IviewObjectEx::GetExtent request.

Parameters:

dwDrawAspect: This parameter is a DWORD describing which form or aspect of an object is to be displayed. Valid values for this parameter are found in the enumeration DVASPECT or DVASPECT2.

lindex: This parameter is a long that contains the portion of the object that is of interest. Only -1 is currently valid.

ptd: This parameter is a pointer to the DVTARGETDEVICE structure. The structure defines the target device for which the object's size should be returned.

lpsizel: A pointer to sizing data returned for the control object.

Return Value

If extent information is successfully returned, the return value is nonzero. Otherwise, the function's return value is 0.

virtual BOOL COleControl::OnGetViewRect (DWORD *dwAspect*, LPRECTL *pRect*);

This method is called by the framework in response to a container's IviewObjectEx::GetRect request. You should override this function if your control's opaque and transparent parts have different dimensions and use two-pass drawing.

Parameters:

dwDrawAspect: This parameter is a DWORD describing which form or aspect of an object is to be displayed. Values for this parameter are found in the enumeration DVASPECT or DVASPECT2. The valid values are as follows:

DVASPECT_CONTENT: The bounding rectangle of the whole object. The top-left corner is at the object's origin, and its size is equal to the extent returned by GetViewExtent.

DVASPECT_OPAQUE: Objects that have a rectangular opaque region return that rectangle. All others fail.

DVASPECT_TRANSPARENT: A rectangle covering all transparent or irregular parts.

pRect: This value is a pointer to the RECT structure specifying the rectangle in which the object should be drawn. This parameter is used to control the stretching and positioning of the object.

Return Value

The return value is nonzero if the rectangle sized to the object is successfully returned. Otherwise, 0 is the return value.

virtual DWORD COleControl::OnGetViewStatus ( );

The framework calls this function in response to a container's IviewObjectEx::GetViewStatus request. If your control uses two-pass drawing, you should override this function. The default implementation returns VIEWSTATUS_OPAQUE.

Parameters: none.

Return Value

The function's return value will be one of the values of the VIEWSTATUS enumeration if successful. Otherwise, 0 will be returned. Possible values from the VIEWSTATUS enumeration are any combination of the following:

VIEWSTATUS_OPAQUE: The object is completely opaque. If this bit is not set, the object contains transparent parts.

VIEWSTATUS_SOLIDBKGND: The object has a solid background that is not a brush pattern. This bit is meaningful only if VIEWSTATUS_OPAQUE is set. It only applies to content-related aspects and not to DVASPECT_ICON or DVASPECT_DOCPRINT.

VIEWSTATUS_DVASPECTOPAQUE: The object supports DVASPECT_OPAQUE. Any IviewObjectEx methods that support a drawing aspect as a parameter can be called with this aspect.

VIEWSTATUS_DVASPECTTRANSPARENT: The object supports DVASPECT_TRANSPARENT. All IviewObjectEx methods that support a drawing aspect as a parameter can be called with this aspect.

virtual BOOL COleControl::OnQueryHitPoint (DWORD *dwAspect*, LPCRECT *pRectBounds*, POINT *ptlLoc*, LONG *lCloseHint*, DWORD* *pHitResult*);

The framework calls this function in response to a container's IviewObjectEx::QueryHitPoint request. This function examines whether a control object's display rectangle overlaps the given point.

Parameters:

dwAspect: This parameter specifies how the object is to be represented. Representations can be content, an icon, a thumbnail, or a printed document. Valid values are taken from the enumeration DVASPECT or DVASPECT2.

pRectBounds: This parameter points to a RECT structure. This structure specifies the bounding rectangle of the OLE control client area.

ptlLoc: A pointer to the POINT structure. The structure specifies the point to be checked for a hit. The point is specified in OLE client area coordinates.

lCloseHint: This parameter defines what close is to the point being checked for a hit.

pHitResult: A pointer to the result of the hit query. A result can be one of the following values:

HITRESULT_OUTSIDE: ptlLoc is completely outside the OLE object and not close.

HITRESULT_TRANSPARENT: ptlLoc is within the bounds of the OLE object. It is not close to the image.

HITRESULT_CLOSE: ptlLoc is inside or outside the OLE object. It is close enough to the object to be considered inside. Objects that are small, thin, or detailed can use this value.

HITRESULT_HIT: ptlLoc is within the image of the object. Therefore, a hit has occurred.

Return Value

If a hit result is successfully returned, the function's return value is nonzero; otherwise, the return value is 0. Think of a hit as an overlap with the OLE control display area.

virtual BOOL OnQueryHitRect(DWORD *dwAspect*, LPCRECT *pRectBounds*, LPCRECT *prcLoc*, LONG *lCloseHint*, DWORD* *pHitResult*);

The framework calls this function in response to a container's `IviewObjectEx::QueryHitRect` request. This function examines whether a control object's display rectangle overlaps any point in the given rectangle. You should override to test hits for non-rectangular objects.

Parameters:

`dwAspect`: This parameter specifies how the object is to be represented. Representations can be content, an icon, a thumbnail, or a printed document. Valid values are taken from the enumeration `DVASPECT` or `DVASPECT2`.

`pRectBounds`: This parameter points to a `RECT` structure. This structure specifies the bounding rectangle of the OLE control client area.

`ptlLoc`: A pointer to the `RECT` structure. The structure specifies the rectangle to be checked for a hit. The rectangle's coordinates are specified in OLE client area coordinates.

`lCloseHint`: Not used.

`pHitResult`: A pointer to the result of the hit query. A result can be one of the following values:

`HITRESULT_OUTSIDE`: The rectangle is completely outside of the OLE object.

`HITRESULT_HIT`: There is at least one point in the rectangle that hits the object.

Return Value

The return value is nonzero if a hit result is successfully returned. In all other cases, the return value is 0.

Summary

As you can see, the `COleControlModule` and `COleControl` classes encapsulate an enormous amount of functionality. This encapsulation simplifies the creation and maintenance of the controls. The `COleControl` class provides easy access to the most of powerful features of OLE/COM designed for controls. As the functionality of ActiveX controls and OLE/COM becomes more complex, you can expect the Microsoft Foundation Classes to provide even greater support for ActiveX controls. Hopefully, this chapter serves as a reference to the functionality provided by MFC to build and maintain ActiveX controls.

8

Custom Interfaces

by Daniel N. Leeks

This chapter discusses the basics of constructing custom interfaces for ActiveX controls. At the heart of these implementations is the IUnknown class. The basics of creating custom interfaces that support the IUnknown interface are explored in the following pages. To give you a taste of implementing custom interfaces from scratch, a brief overview is presented that does not utilize the MFC/OLE interface maps. Implementing custom interfaces utilizing the MFC/OLE IUnknown class and C++ multiple inheritance is examined.

Creating a Custom COM Interface

The OLE Component Object Model, or COM, defines a standard for how cooperating objects communicate with one another. This standard defines what an object looks like, which includes how its methods are dispatched. All COM-compatible objects are defined from one base class, IUnknown. OLE refers to all classes derived from IUnknown as *interfaces*. The IUnknown interface is usually referred to as a C/C++ class but is not specific to any one language. IUnknown can be implemented in any language that can support the binary layout of a COM object, such as C, Pascal, or Delphi.

The following is a simplified version of the IUnknown class, which is defined in MFC. For simplicity, certain necessary calling convention details have been omitted.

```
Class Iunknown
{
public:
    virtual ULONG AddRef() = 0;
    virtual ULONG Release() = 0;
    virtual HRESULT QueryInterface(REFIID iid, void**    ppvObj) = 0;
};
```

Memory management of the object is controlled by the AddRef and Release member functions. To keep track of objects, COM uses reference counting. COM objects, unlike objects in C++, are never referenced directly. They are referenced through a pointer. When an object is referenced, the AddRef function increments the reference count on the object. When the owner is done using the object, the Release member is called. Together, AddRef and Release maintain a reference count on the object. The object is never deleted until its reference count reaches 0. Simple implementations of AddRef and Release are shown here:

```
ULONG CTestObj::AddRef()
{
    // Increment and return the reference count
    return ++m_dwRef;
}
ULONG CTestObj::Release()
{
// Decrement and return the reference count if nonzero

    if( --m_dwRef == 0 )
    {
        // Zero references on this object; delete it
        delete this;
        return 0;
    }
    return m_dwRef;
}
```

The QueryInterface member function provides quite a bit more functionality. It allows you to obtain a pointer to a different interface on the same object. The interface obtained is normally an IUnknown derived interface that provides additional functionality. This functionality is provided through a new member function or method. An example of another interface would be

```
class IIpxInterface : public Iunknown
{
public:
    virtual void IpxObject() = 0;
}
```

> ### note
>
> COM interfaces never contain member variables. Also, all member
> functions are declared as pure-virtual.

If you have only an IUnknown pointer, you could get a IIpxInterface pointer by
calling IUnknown::QueryInterface using the IID for IIpxInterface. IIDs are 128-bit
numbers that uniquely identify an interface. Each interface that is defined has
its own unique IID. An example to retrieve an IIpxInterface pointer using a
pointer to an IUnknown named pUnknown could be

```
IIpxInterface* pIpx = NULL
if ( pUnknown->QueryInterface(IID_IIpxInterface, (void**)&pPrint) == NOERROR )
{
    pIpx->IpxObject();
    // Release the pointer obtained when finished
    pIpx->Release();
}
```

That doesn't appear to be too difficult, does it? Now let's look at how to create an
object that supports both the IIpxInterface and IUnknown interfaces. To accomplish
this, we would simply have an object that inherits IIpxInterface. This would work
because IIpxInterface is derived directly from IUnknown. Therefore, the new object
automatically supports IUnknown. A simple example might look something like
this:

```
class CIpxObj : public CIpxInterface
{
    virtual ULONG AddRef();
    virtual ULONG Release();
    virtual HRESULT QueryInterface(REFIID iid, void** ppvObj);
    virtual void IpxObject();
};
```

AddRef and Release could be implemented in the same fashion as illustrated above.
CIpxObj::QueryInterface would be implemented as follows:

```
HRESULT CPrintObj::QueryInterface(REFIID iid, void** ppvObj)
{
    if (iid == IID_IUnknown ¦¦ IID == iid_IIpxInterface)
    {
        // The interface is one this object supports
        *ppvObj = this;
        AddRef();
        return NOERROR;
    }
    // Error: The interface is not supported
    return ResultFromScode(E_NOINTERFACE);
}
```

This function is fairly straightforward. If the interface is one that the object supports, a pointer to the object is returned and the reference count is incremented. Otherwise, the object returns an error code signifying that the interface is not supported. The function `CIpxObj::IpxObject` would also have to be implemented. This would be necessary because it was provided by `IIpxInterface` as a virtual function.

Multiple Interface Support

Suppose you wanted to create a custom class that supported two completely different interfaces that were both derived from `IUnknown`. There are several ways, such as inheritance, to implement such support, but consider the following:

```
class IIpxInterface : public Iunknown
{
public:
    virtual void IpxObject() = 0;
}
class INetInterface : public Iunknown
{
public:
    virtual void NetObject() = 0;
}
class CNetIpxObj
{
public:
    CNetIpxObj();
    ULONG AddRef();
    ULONG Release();
    HRESULT QueryInterface(REFIID iid, void**);
    DWORD m_dwRef;

class CNetObj : public CNetInterface
{
    CNetIpxObj* m_pParent;
    virtual ULONG AddRef();
    virtual ULONG Release();
    virtual HRESULT QueryInterface(REFIID iid, void** ppvObj);
    virtual void NetObject();
} m_netObj;

class CIpxObj : public CIpxInterface
{
    CNetIpxObj* m_pParent;
    virtual ULONG AddRef();
    virtual ULONG Release();
    virtual HRESULT QueryInterface(REFIID iid, void** ppvObj);
    virtual void IpxObject();
}m_ipxObj;

};
```

To complete this example, I have included the entire implementation of the preceding class in the following code. It should be noted that most of the implementation for the IUnknown interface is placed in the CNetIpxClass. The IUnknown implementation could have been placed in the CNetIpxObj::CNetObj and CNetIpxObj::CIpxObj classes, but this would have created more code and more complexity than necessary. It also would have made it more likely for the code to have bugs in the AddRef and Release implementations.

```
CNetIpxObj::CNetIpxObj()
{
    m_IpxObj.m_pParent = this;
    m_NetObj.m_pParent = this;
}

ULONG CNetIpxObj::AddRef()
{
    return ++m_dwRef;
}

CNetIpxObj::Release()
{
    if (--m_dwRef == 0)
    {
        delete this;
        return 0;
    }
    return m_dwRef;
}

HRESULT CNetIpxObj::QueryInterface(REFIID iid, void** ppvObj)
{
    if (iid == IID_IUnknown || iid == IID_INetInterface)
    {
        *ppvObj = &m_NetObj;
        AddRef();
        return NOERROR;
    }
    else if (iid == IID_IIpxInterface)
    {
        *ppvObj = &m_IpxObj;
        AddRef();
        return NOERROR;
    }
    return ResultFromScode(E_NOINTERFACE);
}

ULONG CNetIpxObj::CIpxObj::AddRef()
{
    return m_pParent->AddRef();
}

ULONG CNetIpxObj::CIpxObj::Release()
{
    return m_pParent->Release();
}
```

```
HRESULT CNetIpxObj::CIpxObj::QueryInterface(
    REFIID iid, void** ppvObj)
{
    return m_pParent->QueryInterface(iid, ppvObj);
}

ULONG CNetIpxObj::CNetObj::AddRef()
{
    return m_pParent->AddRef();
}

ULONG CNetIpxObj::CNetObj::Release()
{
    return m_pParent->Release();
}

HRESULT CNetIpxObj::CNetObj::QueryInterface(
    REFIID iid, void** ppvObj)
{
    return m_pParent->QueryInterface(iid, ppvObj);
}
```

Summary

This chapter discussed the basics of implementing custom interfaces for ActiveX controls. Most custom interfaces inherit the IUnknown interface. They provide extended functionality for the interface through the use of methods. This chapter examined the technique of utilizing the MFC/OLE IUnknown calls and C++ multiple inheritance. This chapter also covered the technique of using contained classes to provide multiple interfaces for an object.

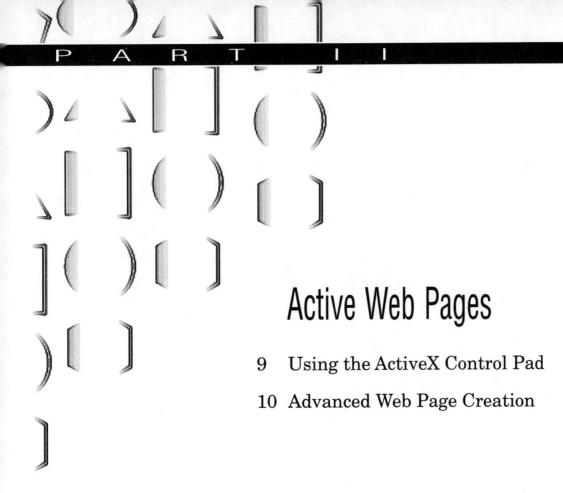

Active Web Pages

9

Using the ActiveX Control Pad

by Mahendra Palsule

The World Wide Web has made a dramatic impact on the computing paradigm in the last couple of years. It has changed the way people access information and communicate with each other. This is largely due to the development of technologies that enable the Web to interact with the user, leading to a more meaningful and fulfilling Web surfing experience.

Leading the way toward making the Web a powerful medium for accessing information, experiencing multimedia content, and enabling integration of the Web with the desktop is Microsoft's ActiveX technology. The core component of the ActiveX set of technologies is ActiveX controls, which are used to author Web pages with active content.

The Microsoft Internet Explorer 3.0 Web browser and the Mosaic Web browser support Web pages with active content developed using ActiveX controls. NCompass Labs, Inc., has developed an add-on to the Netscape Navigator Web browser called ScriptActive that adds ActiveX and VBScript support to the Navigator Web browser. More information about ScriptActive can be found at the NCompass Web site at http://www.ncompasslabs.com.

Microsoft Internet Explorer 3.0 will be available for the Macintosh and the various UNIX platforms soon, making ActiveX technology truly universal in appeal.

Web Pages with ActiveX Controls

ActiveX controls are software components that can be used to develop interactive, advanced Web pages that incorporate multimedia support, interface with back-end databases, and receive input from the user. The process of authoring ActiveX Web pages begins with the third-party developers who develop ActiveX controls for use by Web designers and Web authors. These controls are distributed with a developer's license to Web site developers, who then incorporate the functionality provided by the controls into their Web pages.

ActiveX controls are source-code–independent, and they can work with other controls developed in different languages. It is the Webmaster who orchestrates the interaction of the controls with each other and with the user.

ActiveX controls are binary objects having properties, events, and methods:

- Properties define the appearance or behavior of the control. They can be set at design time and can also be changed at runtime.

- Events are triggered during runtime. An event may be generated in response to user input or other criteria such as time elapsed, and so on. The events are notified to the browser, which can then respond to the event. Scripts that are invoked in response to specific events are called "event handlers."

- Methods incorporate the functionality of the ActiveX control. Methods are invoked by the browser, and the ActiveX control performs the appropriate function as required.

The communication between the browser and the ActiveX control is achieved through the use of snippets of code in a scripting language such as Visual Basic Scripting Edition (VBScript) or JavaScript.

Embedding ActiveX Controls in Web Pages

Web pages incorporate ActiveX controls using the HTML <OBJECT> tag. The syntax for the <OBJECT> tag when used for embedding ActiveX controls is as follows:

```
<OBJECT
CLASSID="CLSID:class-identifier"
CODEBASE="URL where control can be downloaded from"
DATA="url to control's object date"
ID=control_name
ALIGN=TEXTTOP ¦ MIDDLE ¦ TEXTMIDDLE ¦ BASELINE ¦ TEXTBOTTOM ¦ LEFT ¦ CENTER ¦
RIGHT
WIDTH=width of control
HEIGHT=height of control
BORDER=TRUE ¦ FALSE
>
```

```
<PARAM NAME="parameter name" VALUE="parameter value">
.
.   (list of name-value pairs for controls having multiple parameters)
.
<PARAM NAME="parameter name" VALUE="parameter value">
</OBJECT>
```

The class identifier is a unique 128-bit value that identifies each ActiveX control uniquely. This 128-bit value is stored in the registry on the system on which the ActiveX control was installed and registered. The Web developer has to specify this class identifier in the HTML syntax for incorporating the control in the HTML document.

Interactive Web Pages Overview of Scripting

Events that are generated by ActiveX controls are handled by procedures of code that are embedded in the HTML file in the form of a script. The two popular scripting languages are Visual Basic Scripting Edition (VBScript) and JavaScript.

The HTML syntax for embedding scripts in Web pages is

```
<SCRIPT LANGUAGE = "VBScript">
<!--
Sub SomeSubroutine(SomeParameter)
.
.
.
End Sub
-->
</SCRIPT>
```

ActiveX Control Pad

Using ActiveX controls in Web authoring involves carefully noting the class identifier for each ActiveX control, specifying the property values for the control by enlisting them in the <PARAM> and <VALUE> tag pairs, and writing the necessary scripts to achieve the required interactivity. This process becomes extremely unwieldy after a while, especially if you are working with a considerable number of controls.

Another obstacle that Web designers are confronted with is that they cannot specify precise positioning information for various ActiveX controls on a Web page using pure HTML 3.2. HTML 3.2 does not support specifying coordinates for placing objects on Web pages.

Microsoft, sticking to its commitment to making life easier for developers, has come to the rescue. Recognizing the need for a development environment for authoring HTML pages using ActiveX controls, it has developed the first version of what is called the ActiveX Control Pad.

The ActiveX Control Pad provides an integrated development environment for authoring Web pages with active content. The ActiveX Control Pad Version 1.0 has the following features:

- Text Editor: Used for simple editing of HTML pages. It doesn't have special HTML editing features, and it is a simple text editor.
- Object Editor: With the Object Editor you can insert ActiveX controls in the HTML file open in the Text Editor. The Object Editor has a Properties window, which provides a visual representation of the properties of the ActiveX control so that you can edit the properties easily.
- Script Wizard: Makes adding simple scripts to HTML files a snap. Using its powerful intuitive interface, you can easily specify the actions to be taken in response to specific events, and the Script Wizard takes care of writing the script for you. The Script Wizard can be configured to generate either VBScript or JavaScript.
- 2D-Style Page Editor: A WYSIWYG (what you see is what you get) page editor for creating special 2D layout regions within an HTML page. The 2D-style region provides precise placement control of the controls used on the HTML page.
- ActiveX controls: The ActiveX Control Pad comes with an assortment of ActiveX controls free for incorporating in your ActiveX Web pages.

This chapter takes a tour of the ActiveX Control Pad and shows you how it makes authoring Web pages with active content easier than ever.

---

note

The ActiveX Control Pad does not support authoring HTML pages with Java applets in version 1.0. Microsoft will incorporate support for Java applets in a future Version of the ActiveX Control Pad. You can expect the newer version with support for Java applets soon after Visual J++ is released.

Getting Started

Let's begin by looking at the basic features of the ActiveX Control Pad. We will first familiarize ourselves with the ActiveX Control Pad environment and proceed to develop a simple HTML page with an ActiveX control.

Installing the ActiveX Control Pad

The ActiveX Control Pad is available on the accompanying CD-ROM. There are different versions for Windows 95 and Windows NT 4.0, so be careful to use the appropriate version. For using the ActiveX Control Pad, you must have the Microsoft Internet Explorer 3.0 browser installed on your system. If you do not have Internet Explorer 3.0 installed, the Setup will not install the ActiveX Control Pad. If you have not already done so, you can install Microsoft Internet Explorer 3.0 from the accompanying CD-ROM.

Double-click SETUPPAD.EXE to start the setup and installation program. The installation routine will check for the presence of Internet Explorer 3.0 and then guide you through the installation process. The ActiveX Control Pad is installed by default in the C:\PROGRAM FILES\ActiveX Control Pad folder. The ActiveX Control Pad will copy the required program files and online help, and it will register the various ActiveX controls that are bundled with it on your system.

Launching the ActiveX Control Pad

You can start the ActiveX Control Pad from the Start | Programs | Microsoft ActiveX Control Pad menu. The Control Pad opens up with a blank new HTML file, as shown in Figure 9.1.

Figure 9.1.
*ActiveX Control Pad
with blank new HTML
file.*

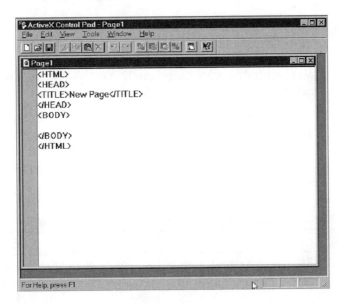

You are now ready to begin using the Control Pad to author ActiveX Web pages.

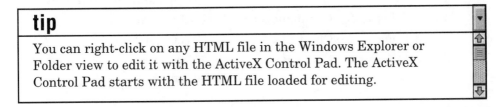

tip

You can right-click on any HTML file in the Windows Explorer or Folder view to edit it with the ActiveX Control Pad. The ActiveX Control Pad starts with the HTML file loaded for editing.

The Control Pad is a Multiple Document Interface (MDI) application, so you can edit multiple HTML files at the same time. This means you can cut, copy, and paste HTML tags, objects, and 2D layout regions across multiple files and edit them at the same time.

The Text Editor

The Text Editor has a vertical pane on the left of the HTML document where the ActiveX Control Pad places icons for easy access to ActiveX controls and 2D layout regions that are embedded in the HTML file.

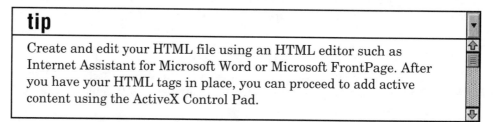

tip

Create and edit your HTML file using an HTML editor such as Internet Assistant for Microsoft Word or Microsoft FrontPage. After you have your HTML tags in place, you can proceed to add active content using the ActiveX Control Pad.

Adding ActiveX Controls

Place the cursor in the HTML file where you want to insert the ActiveX control. Select Insert ActiveX Control on the Edit menu. The Control Pad shows a list box displaying all the controls registered on your system.

Table 9.1 lists the controls supplied with the ActiveX Control Pad. The examples in this chapter use several of the controls listed. It is easy to use any ActiveX control once you are familiar with a few of them. You can experiment with the Hot Spot and Web Browser controls yourself, after you have finished reading this chapter.

Table 9.1. ActiveX controls included with the ActiveX Control Pad.

Control	Description
Microsoft ActiveX Image 1.0	Displays images in common graphics file formats, including BMP, JPEG, and GIF
Microsoft ActiveX Hot Spot 1.0	Creates regions within an image to respond in different ways
Microsoft Forms 2.0 CommandButton	Pushbutton control
Microsoft Forms 2.0 CheckBox	Checks an option
Microsoft Forms 2.0 ComboBox	Selects from drop-down list of options

Control	Description
Microsoft Forms 2.0 Frame	Groups related controls together
Microsoft Forms 2.0 Image	Displays, crops, sizes images
Microsoft Forms 2.0 Label	Labels for text and icons
Microsoft Forms 2.0 ListBox	Selects from a scrollable list of options
Microsoft Forms 2.0 MultiPage	Displays multiple pages
Microsoft Forms 2.0 OptionButton	Chooses between multiple options
Microsoft Forms 2.0 ScrollBar	Basic horizontal and vertical scrollbars
Microsoft Forms 2.0 SpinButton	Button with Up and Down arrows
Microsoft Forms 2.0 TabStrip	Property-sheet style tabs for displaying multiple pages
Microsoft Forms 2.0 TextBox	Multiline text input and display
Microsoft Forms 2.0 ToggleButton	Button with two possible states
Microsoft Web Browser	Views ActiveX documents such as Microsoft Word documents, Microsoft Excel spreadsheets, and so on

Select the Microsoft Forms 2.0 CommandButton control from the list and select OK. The Control Pad brings up the Object Editor to let you set the control's properties.

Using the Object Editor and Properties Window

Figure 9.2 shows the Object Editor invoked along with the Properties window for editing the control and its properties.

The control is shown on a grid, and the properties of the control are listed in the Properties window. You can adjust the size of the button by dragging the selection border drawn around the button. If you click on the button, you can edit the caption of the button. Many ActiveX controls support in-place editing. You can double-click on the button to toggle the display of the Properties window. You can also access the Properties window by right-clicking the control.

The Properties window lists the property names and values in a tabular form and enables you to edit them by double-clicking the property and clicking the Apply button. You can also set many properties by selecting appropriate values from the drop-down list at the top.

Figure 9.2.
Object Editor with the Microsoft Forms 2.0 CommandButton control.

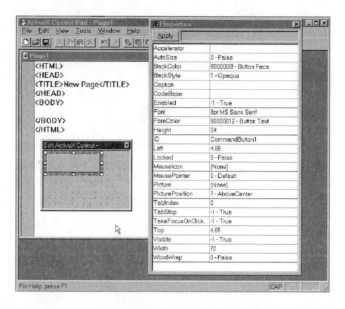

After you finish setting the properties for the control, close the Object Editor window, and voilá! The ActiveX Control Pad inserts the appropriate HTML syntax for embedding the control using the <OBJECT> tag. The Control Pad locates the class identifier for the control from the registry and automatically sets the CLASSID for you. The properties you have set for the control are specified in pairs of PARAM NAME and PARAM VALUE tags. Figure 9.3 shows the HTML file in the Text Editor with the <OBJECT> tag inserted by the Object Editor.

Figure 9.3.
HTML file with embedded CommandButton ActiveX control.

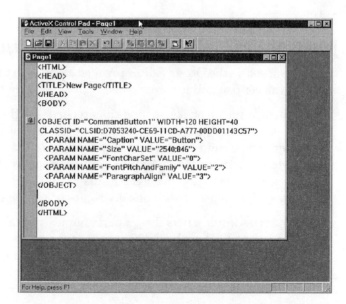

The vertical pane to the left of the HTML file provides you with a visual cue of the objects inserted in the HTML file. You can see a cube icon in Figure 9.3 to the left of the <OBJECT> tag in the Text Editor. If you scroll through the file, the Control Pad automatically repositions the icon adjacent to the <OBJECT> tag. You can click the cube icon to launch the Object Editor again, whenever you want to revise the control's properties.

ActiveX Control Pad thus maps a visual interface on top of the stream metaphor of HTML.

Using the Script Wizard

To experience the ease of using the Script Wizard, first add a TextBox ActiveX control to your HTML file. After adding the CommandButton control described in the previous section, repeat the procedure just described to add a TextBox control to the HTML file. The ActiveX Control Pad assigns the default Object IDs of CommandButton1 and TextBox1 to the controls, respectively. Set the CAPTION of CommandButton1 as Click Me. You can also customize the font face and size of the caption. After you have both controls embedded in your HTML file, invoke the Script Wizard from either the Tools menu or the toolbar icon. The Script Wizard starts as shown in Figure 9.4.

Figure 9.4.
The Script Wizard window.

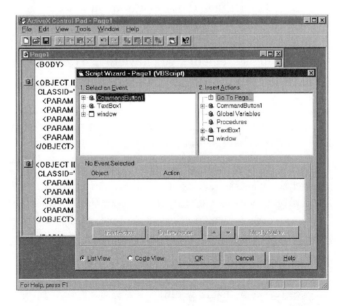

The Script Wizard consists of three panes, with a command panel at the bottom.

The left pane is the Event Pane, which displays a tree view of the objects and events to which you can assign scripts. The objects are listed in alphabetical order by ID name, and the events of that object are listed under that branch of the tree.

To assign an action to a particular event, locate the object and click the event that you want to script. Thus, you can choose the event handler you want to script.

The right pane is the Action Pane, which displays the various actions you can perform and the properties you can change in response to each event. If you have global variables and procedures in the script on your page, they are also listed in the Action Pane. To associate an action with the event you have selected, double-click the action. If you want to change the property of some object, double-clicking brings up a dialog box in which you can enter the new property value.

To define new global variables or write procedures, right-click in the Action Pane and select the appropriate option from the pop-up menu.

The bottom pane is the Script Pane, which lists in a sequential manner the actions you have assigned to specific events, giving you a lucid interpretation of the actions you have selected. You can reorder the sequence of actions, insert and delete actions, and modify property values by using the command buttons in the Script Pane. The Script Pane displays this simple list of actions, called List View by default. However, if you are comfortable with writing and editing scripts, you can also display the event handler script by selecting the Code View radio button.

You would use Code View when writing event handlers that do the following:

- Invoke methods that have numbers or names of arguments different from the event handler itself.

- Require control of the flow of execution. Thus, if you use conditional or looping statements, you have to use Code View.

---

note

The ActiveX Control Pad does not support scripting of HTML `<AHREF="...">` or `<FRAMESET>` tags.

Select the `MouseUp` event of `CommandButton1` in the Event Pane and double-click the `Text` property of `TextBox1` in the Action Pane. Enter `Hello World` in the dialog box that appears. Close the Script Wizard, and you can see the following VBScript code added to your HTML file:

```
<SCRIPT LANGUAGE="VBScript">
<!--
Sub CommandButton1_MouseUp(Button, Shift, X, Y)
TextBox1.Text = "Hello World!"
end sub
-->
</SCRIPT>
```

Save the file as `HELLO.HTM` and view it in Internet Explorer 3.0. When you press the button, the text box displays `Hello World`.

You can return to the Script Wizard for editing the event handler directly by clicking the yellow icon next to the <SCRIPT> tag. The Script Wizard displays the Event Pane with a solid icon next to the MouseUp event of CommandButton1 in the event hierarchy indicating the presence of an event handler. Script Wizard also adds the event handler to the Procedures in the Action Pane.

Switch to Code View to see the event handler code in the Script Pane.

```
Sub CommandButton1_MouseUp(Button, Shift, X, Y)
TextBox1.Text = "Hello World!"
```

The Sub statement is shown in a title at the top with the body of the event handler underneath. Notice that no End Sub statement is displayed. Script Wizard adds the End Sub statement for you after you finish writing the body of the event handler.

caution
When working in Code View, do not type the End Sub statement at the end of your event handler, as this will result in duplicate End Sub statements being added to the script.

You can change the display font of the Script Pane Code View by right-clicking in the Script Pane.

You have just used the ActiveX Control Pad to develop an interactive Web page, using ActiveX technology, without writing code, with point-and-click ease!

Script Wizard can generate both VBScript and JavaScript code. You can select the code it generates from the Tools l Options menu. However, you may not mix both languages in the same HTML file. If you have scripts in both languages in your HTML file, when you start Script Wizard, it will assume the language of the first <SCRIPT> block to be the default scripting language of the entire HTML file.

note
The ActiveX Control Pad does not support scripts external to the HTML file using the SRC= attribute of the HTML <SCRIPT> tag.

HTML Layout Control

Traditional HTML lacks 2D layout specification. In other words, there is no way for the Web author to specify the exact placement of images, text, and objects on an HTML page. For the most part, the browser is in control, not the author.

Frames and tables have enhanced the interface of Web sites, but they are a far cry from the advanced layout capabilities that have turned desktop publishing into an industry.

Authors need to be able to specify exact placement of text, images, and other controls on a Web page to create well-defined interfaces. For more sophisticated Web page design, they need to be able to overlap text and images, use transparency effects, and specify the layering of the objects that are placed on the Web page.

As you might expect, these capabilities are soon to be incorporated in the W3C HTML specification. The World Wide Web Consortium, which defines HTML standards, has published a preliminary draft specification for 2D layout capabilities by evolving the stylesheet and frameset specifications. Microsoft has given ActiveX Web authors a head start in this direction by developing a special ActiveX control for 2D HTML layout.

HTML Layout Control Overview

The HTML Layout control is an ActiveX control that acts as a container for other ActiveX controls. It specifies a 2D layout region within the HTML file in which it is placed. The HTML Layout control uses a separate file for referencing the controls that are placed within the layout. This file is a simple text file with an .ALX extension and is stored along with the HTML file. The HTML Layout control is inserted in the HTML file using the <OBJECT> tag.

> **note**
>
> This is an early implementation of the 2D layout capabilities to be supported in future HTML specifications. These layout specifications will be incorporated into native HTML syntax and will not require a separate file. Microsoft has promised to adhere to the W3C standards and incorporate layout support natively in Microsoft Internet Explorer in future versions accordingly.

Multiple HTML layout regions can be incorporated into a single HTML file. Multiple instances of the HTML Layout control are created, and they can be individually aligned or placed in tables, and so on. These Layout controls behave independently of each other and do not support scripting across multiple layout regions. This means that events occurring in one layout region are not visible to controls in other layout regions within the same HTML document.

Using the 2D-Style Layout Editor

This section explores how to incorporate a 2D-style layout region in an HTML file using the ActiveX Control Pad.

Start the ActiveX Control Pad from the Windows Start menu and when the new HTML file is being displayed in the Text Editor, select Edit I Insert HTML Layout. In the dialog box that appears, you can select a name and location for the .ALX file that would contain the 2D layout information. This file would normally be located in same directory as the source HTML file. Specify new.alx for the filename, and Control Pad confirms whether you want to create a new file. Click OK, and the HTML Layout control is inserted in the HTML file.

Click the icon next to the <OBJECT> tag, and the ActiveX Control Pad launches the HTML Layout Editor as shown in Figure 9.5.

Figure 9.5.
*The HTML Layout
Editor.*

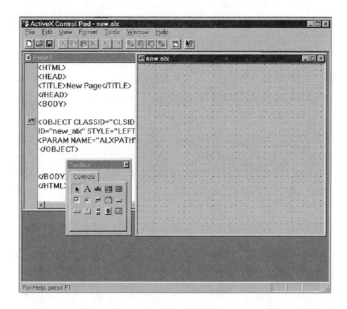

The HTML Layout Editor consists of a 2D region in which you can place the controls shown on a floating toolbox. The toolbox contains the ActiveX controls that you can place within the layout. This is similar to designing a form in Visual Basic.

You can specify default properties such as the background color of the Layout region by either right-clicking on the empty region or selecting Properties from the View menu. You can place a control in the 2D region by selecting it from the toolbox and drawing it on the region. The Properties window displays the properties of the control that has the focus. You can also access the properties of a particular control by right-clicking the control. Experiment with using the various controls provided with the ActiveX Control Pad.

As you become comfortable with using the Layout Editor, you will soon realize the incredible power you have for creating an attractively designed Web page. You can design an interface with command buttons, labels, text boxes, and list boxes. You can determine the exact placement of images and text, overlap controls, and set the layering of controls. Some of the subtle properties that are very effective in creating good Web pages are

- BackStyle: Used to add transparency effects.
- ControlTipText: Specifies the tooltip text that appears when the user brings the mouse over the control.
- Picture: Used to display images over controls such as buttons. Some controls also support tiling of the image.
- Accelerator: Enables the user to navigate quickly using accelerator key combinations.
- MouseIcon: Used to change the mouse pointer when the mouse is over the control.

After you finish drawing your controls, you can jump directly to the Script Wizard or return to Text Editor to view your HTML file. The Control Pad will prompt you to save the file. The Text Editor window reappears, and the source HTML file now includes the <OBJECT> tag for the HTML Layout control, as shown in the following code:

```
<HTML>
<HEAD>
<TITLE>New Page</TITLE>
</HEAD>
<BODY>

<OBJECT CLASSID="CLSID:812AE312-8B8E-11CF-93C8-00AA00C08FDF"
ID="new_alx" STYLE="LEFT:0;TOP:0">
<PARAM NAME="ALXPATH" REF VALUE="new.alx">
 </OBJECT>


</BODY>
</HTML>
```

When the browser parsing this file encounters the <OBJECT> tag, it instantiates the HTML Layout control. The HTML Layout control loads the .ALX file specified in the ALXPATH parameter. The HTML Layout control in conjunction with the browser then displays the controls embedded in the .ALX file using the exact 2D layout as specified by you, the author.

> **note**
>
> The complete URL for the ALXPATH parameter should be specified unless the .ALX file resides in the same directory as the source HTML file or in a directory underneath it.

You can view the resulting page by opening the source HTML file in Internet Explorer 3.0.

> **tip**
>
> You can change the alignment of the HTML Layout region within the source file by surrounding in regular HTML formatting tags (such as <CENTER> or <p align = "right"> ... </p>) the <OBJECT> tag for the HTML Layout control. This is not achieved by setting the LEFT: and TOP: attributes of the STYLE parameter in the <OBJECT> tag used to insert the layout region.

Next, take a closer look at the .ALX file created for the Layout control.

The .ALX File

The .ALX file is a text file and can be edited with a regular text editor. The .ALX file specifies the layout within the fixed 2D region—the controls embedded in it as well as the scripts associated with those controls. The layout is specified using the <DIV> tag, which is used by the W3C as a block tag for containing divisions in an HTML document. The <DIV> tag is used as shown in the following:

```
<DIV [ID=Layout_ID] STYLE = "layout-style-attributes">
   object-blocks
</DIV>
```

The <DIV> tag has two attributes:

- ID attribute, which is optional but useful for referencing the layout control in scripts.
- STYLE attribute, which specifies the style for the division.

The STYLE attribute has the following attributes:

- LAYOUT: This is defined as FIXED for the 2D layout region.
- HEIGHT: The height of the layout region in pixels.
- WIDTH: The width of the layout region in pixels.
- BACKGROUND: The background color of the region in HEX digits.

Inside the <DIV> tag are the <OBJECT> blocks specifying the controls placed within the 2D region.

caution

The <OBJECT> tag may not be used to insert images, documents, or applets inside the .ALX file. The HTML Layout control implementation currently supports only ActiveX controls conforming to the ActiveX controls '96 specification for windowless, transparent controls.

One or more <SCRIPT> blocks may be inserted before or after the <DIV> block, but not within it.

The limitation of this preliminary implementation of the layout region in the form of a separate .ALX file is that a transparent object hierarchy including the source HTML file and the controls within the layout region is no longer present.

The browser parses the HTML source file before the Layout control renders the layout specified in the .ALX file. Hence, you cannot access any properties, events, or methods of the objects in the layout from scripts in the source HTML document.

Similarly, the scripts in the .ALX file cannot access all the methods and events of the window object of the HTML file. Scripts can only access the window.location.href property of the source HTML file so that the controls placed in the layout region can trigger navigation of the browser window.

note

Some ways to bypass the inherent limitation of the .ALX layout implementation have been tried with mixed results, particularly for accessing the properties or methods of ActiveX controls in the .ALX layout file from the source HTML file.

In some circumstances, adding an OnLoad="InitALX" attribute to the <OBJECT> tag for the HTML Layout or referencing the ActiveX control in the layout file.ALX as Control_ID.FILE.property may seem to work, but these are not officially supported and thus are not recommended.

Using HTML Layout Control Effectively

The HTML Layout control can be used to create a layout template that you can reuse in multiple Web pages. You might use this for making navigation toolbars, consistent interfaces for query forms, and style templates for electronic Web magazines (ezines).

You can achieve a dramatic improvement in the look of your Web pages by using transparent overlapping images. A basic understanding of images used in the ActiveX Control Pad gives you the power to use these techniques effectively.

Several controls in the toolbox, such as the CheckBox, CommandButton, and so forth, enable you to specify a PICTURE property. The PICTURE property specifies images that are embedded in the .ALX file. Embedded images of the .bmp, .cur, .wmf, .jpg, .gif, and .ico image file types are read by the PICTURE property, converted into text format, and stored with the DATA attribute. You should consider the size of the images you select for the PICTURE property because using many large images will bloat the .ALX file. Use the PICTURE property for small icons and graphics so that the .ALX file is not large, and the user does not have to download a separate image file.

The other way you can use images on your Web page is to use the Image control. The Image control is different from the other controls because it references the image URL specified in its PicturePath property at runtime. The PicturePath property of the Image control can load .bmp, .jpg, .gif, and .wmf format image files, but the user has to download the external image from the separate file at runtime.

Transparent images are ones in which a particular pixel color is rendered with the color of the background by the browser. Embedded images in the ActiveX Control Pad are always transparent, whether the source file format supports transparency or not. In the case of file formats that do not support transparency, such as .bmp and .wmf, the HTML Layout control assumes the color of the lower-left pixel of the image to be the transparent color. Transparency in external images is determined by the file format of the image. The GIF89a image specification supports transparent images, but .jpg does not.

> **note**
>
> The HTML Layout control does not support animated GIF89a files.

If your Web page uses controls that are large in dimensions, you might want to improve the performance of your Web page by increasing the size of the off-screen buffer used for painting your page. The number of pixels reserved for off-screen painting is specified by the DrawBuffer property of the HTML Layout control. The default size allows for 32,000 pixels, which is fine for most Web pages. If you use larger images, however, you can specify a higher value.

You saw how the HTML Layout control in conjunction with the ActiveX Control Pad lets Web authors develop interactive Web pages with precise control placement. The next section consolidates your knowledge of the ActiveX Control Pad and the HTML Layout control as you develop a simple ActiveX puzzle.

ActiveX Web Puzzle

After seeing the power and ease of use of the ActiveX Control Pad, it is time to develop a sample application of this powerful tool. Remember the game in which the numbers 1 to 8 appear randomly in a 3×3 matrix, and the player has to sort them using the empty slot in the matrix? Figure 9.6 shows just such a puzzle developed with the ActiveX Control Pad supplied on the accompanying CD-ROM. You can copy the source files from the SOURCE\VOL3\CHAP09\ directory on the CD-ROM.

Figure 9.6.
A puzzle developed using the ActiveX Control Pad.

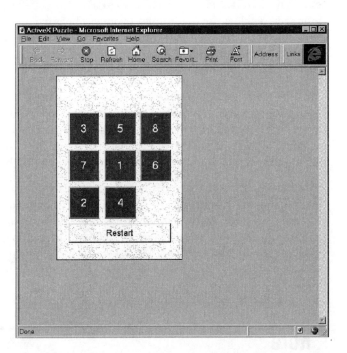

Developing such an application for the Web is quite easy using the ActiveX Control Pad. Continue through the steps needed to develop the puzzle.

Implementation Strategy

Here's an overview of the technique required for implementing the puzzle. The game starts with initializing the digits in a random order on the game board. A mouse click on a button horizontally or vertically adjacent to the empty slot should move the button into the slot, and all other invalid mouse clicks should be ignored. At every click, the program needs to check whether the puzzle is solved. It will also provide for restarting the game whenever desired.

The straightforward way of using eight buttons and moving them at every mouse click leads to the complexity of tracking the coordinates of buttons. A trick to avoid this is to use nine buttons instead of eight and simply change their captions. An invisible button simulates the empty slot. On a valid mouse click, you change the caption of the invisible button to that of the clicked button and toggle the visibility of the two buttons.

To track the progress of the puzzle, you will maintain an array of eight Boolean values. Each element of the array corresponds to a button, and its value depends on whether the button is in the proper place. After the initialization in a random state, you evaluate the state and initialize the array.

You also keep a count of the number of moves so that you can display the number of moves in which the puzzle was solved.

Creating the Layout

Start by creating the layout for the puzzle using the ActiveX Control Pad. In a new HTML file, insert an HTML Layout control and name the file PUZZLE.ALX. Insert nine CommandButton controls, arranging them in a matrix similar to that shown in Figure 9.6. Change the default IDs for the buttons to CB1, CB2, and so on, up to CB9.

Add two labels for displaying the winning message and the number of clicks at the top and then change their default IDs to LblWon and LblClicks. Next, draw the Restart command button below the button array, setting its ID to btnRestart.

For enhancing the aesthetics of this puzzle, you can add an Image control for displaying a background image. Add an Image control, setting its Picture property to point to an image file. If you have an image that is small in size, you can set the PictureTilingMode to True. The Image control is drawn in front of the other controls, so right-click it and choose Send to Back from the pop-up menu. Now select the LblWon, btnRestart, and LblClicks controls and change their BackStyle property to transparent.

> **tip**
>
> Press the Control key while clicking for selecting multiple non-adjacent controls so that you can edit properties of multiple controls at a time.

Adjust the BackColor and ForeColor of the buttons in the grid to a suitable color. Close the Layout Editor and save PUZZLE.ALX. Also save the source HTML file as PUZZLE.HTM.

The resulting source HTML file, PUZZLE.HTM, is shown in Listing 9.1.

Listing 9.1. The source HTML file for the ActiveX Puzzle (PUZZLE.HTM).

```
<HTML>
<HEAD>
<TITLE>New Page</TITLE>
</HEAD>
<BODY>
<CENTER>
    <OBJECT ID="puzzle_alx"
     CLASSID="CLSID:812AE312-8B8E-11CF-93C8-00AA00C08FDF">
        <PARAM NAME="ALXPATH" REF VALUE="puzzle.alx">
    </OBJECT>
</CENTER>
</BODY>
</HTML>
```

You are done with the layout of your puzzle! Now you can add the scripting to make it functional.

Scripting the Puzzle

Before we embark on writing the script for the puzzle, make sure you are comfortable with using VBScript.

While PUZZLE.ALX is open in the Layout Editor, start Script Wizard by clicking on the Script Wizard toolbar icon or by right-clicking in the background of the .ALX file and selecting Script Wizard... from the pop-up menu.

Start by defining the global variables to use. In the Action Pane right-click pop-up menu, choose Add Global Variable. Enter two variables in this way, named Click and Right(8). Click counts the number of moves, and Right is the array in which you maintain the progress of the game.

Next, script the custom procedures. Three procedures are used:

1. Call_To_Start_Fresh() initializes the puzzle.
2. Display_Buttons_At_Random() does just that.
3. Is_Over() checks whether the puzzle is solved.

Choose Add Procedure from the Action Pane pop-up menu, and add the three procedures shown in Listing 9.2.

Listing 9.2. Procedures for the puzzle.

```
' This Subroutine is used to to Initialize the Game
Sub Call_To_Start_Fresh()
Dim t

' Array Right() is Initialized to False :0:
    for t=1 to 8
        Right(t) = 0
    Next
```

```
' Subroutine Display_Buttons_At_Random is used to
' initially start the game in random state
Call Display_Buttons_At_Random()

' Make the Label for "You Have Won" Invisible
    LblWon.Visible = False
    LblClicks.Visible = False
    LblClicks.Caption = ""
    Click = 0
' To check whether the game has been won by randomize!
    Call Is_Over()

End Sub

' Subroutine Display_Buttons_At_Random is used to
' Initially Start the game in random state
Sub Display_Buttons_At_Random()

Dim Number(8)
Dim Random_Number
Dim Button
Dim j
Dim Re_Generate

Button=1
j=1
Re_Generate=True
while Button <= 8
    While Re_Generate = True
        Re_Generate = False
        Randomize
        Random_Number= Int((8 * Rnd)+1)
        while Re_Generate = False And j <= Button-1
            if Number(j) = Random_Number then
                Re_Generate = True
            End if
            j = j + 1
        Wend
        j=1
        if Re_Generate = False then
            Number(Button) = Random_Number
            Button = Button + 1
        End If
    Wend
    Re_Generate = True
Wend

' Make all buttons visible except the last
CB1.Visible = True
CB2.Visible = True
CB3.Visible = True
CB4.Visible = True
CB5.Visible = True
CB6.Visible = True
CB7.Visible = True
CB8.Visible = True
CB9.Visible = False
```

continues

Listing 9.2. continued

```
' Assign the generated random numbers to all buttons
CB1.Caption = CStr(Number(1))
CB2.Caption = CStr(Number(2))
CB3.Caption = CStr(Number(3))
CB4.Caption = CStr(Number(4))
CB5.Caption = CStr(Number(5))
CB6.Caption = CStr(Number(6))
CB7.Caption = CStr(Number(7))
CB8.Caption = CStr(Number(8))
end sub

' Subroutine to check whether the puzzle is solved
Sub Is_Over()
Dim Total
Dim Num
If CB1.Caption = "1" then
    Right(1) = 1
End If
If CB2.Caption = "2" then
    Right(2) = 1
End If
If CB3.Caption = "3" then
    Right(3) = 1
End If
If CB4.Caption = "4" then
    Right(4) = 1
End If
If CB5.Caption = "5" then
    Right(5) = 1
End If
If CB6.Caption = "6" then
    Right(6) = 1
End If
If CB7.Caption = "7" then
    Right(7) = 1
End If
If CB8.Caption = "8" then
    Right(8) = 1
End If

for i=1 to 8
    Total = Total + Right(i)
Next
If Total = 8 then
    LblWon.Visible = True
    btnRestart.Caption = "Play Again  ?"
    If Click <> 0 then
        LblClicks.Visible = True
        LblClicks.Caption = "            in " & CStr(Click) & " clicks"
    End If
End If
End Sub
```

After entering the procedures, you'll add the event handlers for the MouseUp event of the buttons in the grid. Here's what the event handler does:

- Checks whether the button is in place and updates the score
- Checks whether an adjacent button is invisible and toggles the visibility of both buttons, while transferring its caption

The number of possible moves for a button is dependent on its location in the grid, for example, CB1 can move only to CB2 and CB4, whereas CB2 can move to CB1, CB5, and CB3. The third possibility is the center button, for which there are four possible moves.

The event handler for the button CB5 is shown in Listing 9.3; it is pretty simple to add similar ones for the other buttons.

Listing 9.3. Event handlers for MouseUp event of buttons in the puzzle.

```
Sub CB5_MouseUp(Button, Shift, X, Y)
If CB5.Caption = "5" then
    Right(5) = 1
End If
If CB5.Visible = True then
    If CB2.Visible = False then
        CB2.Visible = True
        CB2.Caption = CB5.Caption
        CB5.Caption = ""
        CB5.Visible = False
        Click = Click + 1
    End If
    If CB4.Visible = False then
        CB4.Visible = True
        CB4.Caption = CB5.Caption
        CB5.Caption = ""
        CB5.Visible = False
        Click = Click + 1
    End If
    If CB6.Visible = False then
        CB6.Visible = True
        CB6.Caption = CB5.Caption
        CB5.Caption = ""
        CB5.Visible = False
        Click = Click + 1
    End If
    If CB8.Visible = False then
        CB8.Visible = True
        CB8.Caption = CB5.Caption
        CB5.Caption = ""
        CB5.Visible = False
        Click = Click + 1
    End If
End If
If CB5.Caption = "5" then
    Right(5) = 1
else
    Right(5) = 0
End If
Call Is_Over()
End Sub
```

Finally, you call the initialization procedure from the OnLoad event of the HTML Layout control and also handle the MouseUp event for the Restart button, as shown in Listing 9.4.

Listing 9.4. HTML Layout OnLoad and Restart button MouseUp event handlers.

```
' Subroutine called when the Layout is loaded
Sub Layout1_OnLoad()
Call Call_To_Start_Fresh()
End Sub

' Subroutine to be called when Button for "Re-start" or "Play Again" is Pressed
Sub btnRestart_MouseUp(Button, Shift, X, Y)
Call Call_To_Start_Fresh()
LblWon.Visible = False
btnRestart.Caption = "Restart"
End Sub
```

After you have the scripts in place, save the files PUZZLE.ALX and PUZZLE.HTM and double-click PUZZLE.HTM to start Microsoft Internet Explorer. Figure 9.7 shows the winning screen after the puzzle is solved.

Enjoy the game!

Figure 9.7.
The ActiveX Puzzle winning screen.

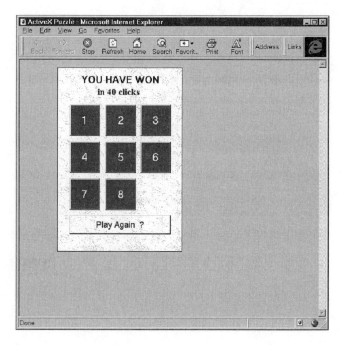

ActiveX Search Page

The ActiveX Puzzle application demonstrates the power of the Layout control in creating interactive Web pages. Now, see how you can use the ActiveX Control Pad to utilize the Internet Explorer Object Model interface for adding advanced capabilities to your Web pages.

A fairly common Web application is an all-in-one Internet search page in which the user can type his keywords and select the source and/or type of search. Normal HTML forms that accomplish this generally present a cluttered interface to the user, because they are limited by the HTML form object implementation.

Using ActiveX, however, you can develop a sophisticated interface using ActiveX controls in HTML layout regions, and create an intuitive interface for the user. Your search page needs to collect data from the user and pass it on to the search engine of the user's choice.

\source\vol3\
chap-09

To demonstrate how you can accomplish this using the ActiveX Control Pad, you'll develop a sample search page from which the user can select the search engine from a drop-down list box and enter his query keywords. When he activates the Go button, your Web page will pass the keywords along with any optional parameters to the appropriate search engine server. The browser will navigate to the site and display the query results on that site. The ActiveX Search page as seen in Internet Explorer is shown in Figure 9.8. The source files for the ActiveX Search page can be found on the CD-ROM accompanying this book in the \source\vol3\chap-09 directory.

For your sample search page, allow the user to choose his search site between Yahoo!, WebCrawler, DejaNews, and AltaVista. Note that your Web page has to supply the query data to the server script executing on these Web sites. In order to interface your page correctly with the server application on the search site, emulate the form used by that search site. Further, some search sites support additional parameters for customizing the results. For instance, the popular DejaNews Usenet search enables you to specify the number of hits requested, and AltaVista enables you to return results in Standard, Compact, or Detailed form.

note

The server applications of search engines are modified from time to time, and if you are interested in implementing an ActiveX search interface on the Web, you should constantly monitor the sites accordingly.

Figure 9.8.
The ActiveX search page.

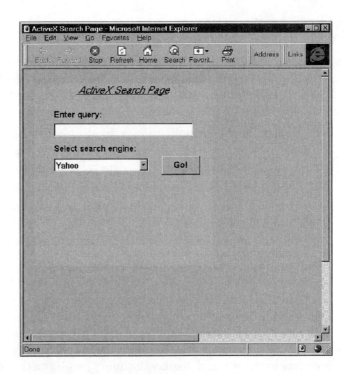

Emulating an HTML Form Through ActiveX

The HTML Form object lies below the Document object in the Object Scripting Model. The HTML form that you create in your source file would have to be filled with the data from the controls in the HTML Layout control. You create hidden input fields in your HTML form and transfer the data using scripts. When the user clicks the Go button, you trigger the SUBMIT event of the Form object.

Because each search engine uses a different form, you include an HTML form for each of them, with the appropriate number of input fields, which are given specific names used by the search engine. The trick to discovering the number and names of input fields required by a search engine is to view the HTML source of the query page of the Web site.

To demonstrate the advantages of using ActiveX to create a form rather than use pure HTML forms, the next step is to alter the interface at runtime according to the search engine selected by the user. If this is done, the user easily can utilize the custom options that a particular search engine supports.

Developing the ActiveX Search Page

The source for the HTML file with unique forms for each search engine is shown in Listing 9.5.

Listing 9.5. Source HTML file for ActiveX search page (SEARCH.HTM).

\source\vol3\
chap-09\
source.htm

```
<HTML>
<HEAD>
<TITLE>ActiveX Search Page</TITLE>
</HEAD>
<BODY>
<!-- form for search in DejaNews -->
<FORM NAME="SearchFormIdDeja" METHOD=POST

ACTION="http://xp5.dejanews.com/dnquery.xp">
    <INPUT TYPE="hidden" NAME="query">
    <INPUT TYPE="hidden" NAME="defaultOp" VALUE="AND">
    <INPUT TYPE="hidden" NAME="svcclass" VALUE="dncurrent">
    <INPUT TYPE="hidden" NAME="maxhits">
</FORM>

<!-- form for search in AltaVista -->
<FORM NAME="SearchFormIdAlta" METHOD=GET

ACTION="http://www.altavista.digital.com/cgi-bin/query">
    <INPUT TYPE="hidden" NAME="pg" VALUE=q>
    <INPUT TYPE="hidden" NAME="what">
    <INPUT TYPE="hidden" NAME="fmt">
  <INPUT TYPE="hidden" NAME="q">
</FORM>

<!-- form for search in Yahoo -->
<FORM NAME="SearchFormIdYahoo" METHOD=GET

ACTION="http://search.yahoo.com/bin/search">
    <INPUT TYPE="HIDDEN" NAME="p">
</FORM>

<!-- form for search in WebCrawler -->
<FORM NAME="SearchFormIdCrawler"  METHOD="POST"

ACTION="http://www.webcrawler.com/cgi-bin/WebQuery" >
    <INPUT TYPE="hidden" NAME="searchText">
    <INPUT TYPE="hidden" NAME="maxHits">
    <INPUT TYPE="hidden" NAME="mode">
</FORM>

<!-- HTML Layout for ActiveX Search Page -->
<OBJECT CLASSID="CLSID:812AE312-8B8E-11CF-93C8-00AA00C08FDF"
ID="query_alx" STYLE="LEFT:0;TOP:0">
<PARAM NAME="ALXPATH" REF VALUE="query.alx">
</OBJECT>

</BODY>
</HTML>
```

Creating the Layout for the ActiveX Search Page

The complete layout is illustrated in Figure 9.9.

Figure 9.9.
*Layout for ActiveX
search page.*

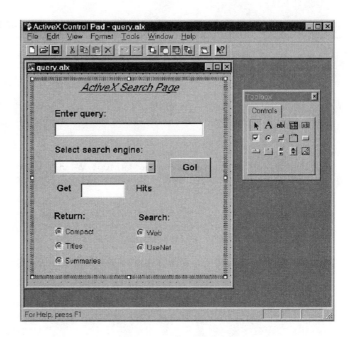

The layout development for the ActiveX search page is fairly straightforward.
Table 9.2 lists and describes the controls used in the layout.

Table 9.2. Controls used in the ActiveX search page.

Control_ID	Description
btnGo	Command button for starting the search
lblEngine	"Select Engine" label
lblGet	"Get" label
lblHits	"Hits" label
lblQuery	"Enter Query" label
lblReturn	"Return:" label
lblSearch	"Search:" label
lblTitle	"ActiveX Search Page" label
lbNames	Drop-down list of Web search engines
optbtnHitType1	Option (radio) button for selecting format of hits
optbtnHitType2	Option (radio) button for selecting format of hits
optbtnHitType3	Option (radio) button for selecting format of hits
optbtnNews	Option (radio) button for selecting Usenet search

Control_ID	Description
optbtnWeb	Option (radio) button for selecting Web search
txtboxHits	Text box for specifying number of hits to return
txtboxQuery	Text box for entering the query text

A colorful background is selected for lblTitle, and the labels are made transparent for an enhanced appearance. You are now ready to add scripts.

Scripting the ActiveX Search Page

You'll proceed by first adding the global variables as before. Add query_string, mode_str, maxhits_str, what_str = "Web" as four global variables, from the pop-up menu in the Action Pane. The global variables are used as follows:

- query_string contains the text of the query.
- mode_str defines the type of hits desired for WebCrawler and AltaVista searches.
- maxhits_str specifies the maximum number of hits to return for WebCrawler and DejaNews searches.
- what_str selects Web or Usenet search for AltaVista.

The HTML Layout OnLoad event handler adds the names of the search engines to the list box at runtime and selects the first as default. This is shown in the following:

```
Sub Layout1_OnLoad()
    call lbNames.AddItem("Yahoo")
    call lbNames.AddItem("Web Crawler")
    call lbNames.AddItem("DejaNews UseNet")
    call lbNames.AddItem("Altavista")
    lbNames.Value = "Yahoo"
end sub
```

The script for handling the Change event for the drop-down list box, radio buttons, and text boxes is shown in Listing 9.6.

Listing 9.6. Change event handlers for ActiveX search page controls.

```
Sub lbNames_Change()
 optbtnHitType1.Visible = True
 Dim comp
 comp = StrComp(lbnames.Value,"WebCrawler")
 if comp = 0 then
     optbtnHitType1.Caption = "Compact"
     optbtnHitType1.Visible = True
     optbtnHitType2.Caption = "Titles"
     optbtnHitType2.Visible = True
```

continues

Listing 9.6. continued

```
        optbtnHitType3.Caption = "Summaries"
        optbtnHitType3.Visible = True
        optbtnHitType1.Value = True
        optbtnWeb.Visible = False
        optbtnNews.Visible = False
        optbtnHitType3.Value = True
        lblReturn.Visible = True
        lblGet.Visible = True
        lblHits.Visible = True
        txtboxHits.Visible = True
        lblSearch.Visible = False
    End If

    comp = StrComp(lbnames.Value,"Yahoo")
    if comp = 0 then
        optbtnHitType1.Visible = False
        optbtnHitType2.Visible = False
        optbtnHitType3.Visible = False
        optbtnWeb.Visible = False
        optbtnNews.Visible = False
        lblReturn.Visible = False
        lblGet.Visible = False
        lblHits.Visible = False
        txtboxHits.Visible = False
        lblSearch.Visible = False
    End If

    comp = StrComp(lbnames.Value,"DejaNews UseNet")
    if comp = 0 then
        optbtnHitType1.Visible = False
        optbtnHitType2.Visible = False
        optbtnHitType3.Visible = False
        optbtnWeb.Visible = False
        optbtnNews.Visible = False
        lblReturn.Visible = False
        lblGet.Visible = True
        lblHits.Visible = True
        txtboxHits.Visible = True
        lblSearch.Visible = False
    End If

    comp = StrComp(lbnames.Value,"Altavista")
    if comp = 0 then
        optbtnHitType1.Caption = "Standard"
        optbtnHitType1.Visible = True
        optbtnHitType2.Caption = "Compact"
        optbtnHitType2.Visible = True
        optbtnHitType3.Caption = "Detailed"
        optbtnHitType3.Visible = True
        optbtnHitType1.Value = True
        optbtnWeb.Visible = True
        optbtnNews.Visible = True
        lblReturn.Visible = True
        lblGet.Visible = False
        lblHits.Visible = False
        lblSearch.Visible = True
```

```
      optbtnWeb.Value = True
      txtboxHits.Visible = False
 End If
end sub

Sub optbtnHitType3_Change()
 Dim comp
 comp = StrComp(lbnames.Value,"Altavista")
 if comp = 0 then
      mode_str = "d"
 else
      mode_str = optbtnHitType3.Caption
 End If
end sub

Sub optbtnHitType2_Change()
 Dim comp
 comp = StrComp(lbnames.Value,"Altavista")
 if comp = 0 then
      mode_str = "c"
 else
      mode_str = optbtnHitType2.Caption
 End If
end sub

Sub optbtnHitType1_Change()
 Dim comp
 comp = StrComp(lbnames.Value,"Altavista")
 if comp = 0 then
      mode_str = "."
 else
      mode_str = optbtnHitType1.Caption
 End If
end sub

Sub txtboxQuery_Change()
     query_string = txtboxQuery.Value
end sub

Sub txtboxHits_Change()
     maxhits_str = txtboxHits.Value
end sub
```

The Change event handlers for the type of results desired adapt the mode_str variable to the appropriate value. The Change event handlers for the txtboxQuery, and txtboxHits text boxes update the query_string and maxhits_str global variables, respectively.

The search engine drop-down list box determines the controls that are visible after a particular search engine is selected. The Yahoo! search doesn't support any parameters; WebCrawler enables you to select the format of the results and the number of hits. Similarly, DejaNews supports specifying the number of hits returned, whereas with AltaVista you choose the format of the results and the search field (Web or Usenet).

The lbNames_Change event handler makes the appropriate controls visible when a particular search engine is selected. Selection among the type of results desired (mode_str) is implemented by handling the Change event for each of the option buttons, whereas the field of query for the AltaVista search is scripted using MouseUp event handlers. This is because mode_str is used by both WebCrawler and AltaVista, whereas the Web/Usenet choice of option buttons is relevant only to AltaVista.

Finally, the MouseUp event handlers for the AltaVista Usenet/Web option buttons and the Go button are given in Listing 9.7.

Listing 9.7. MouseUp event handlers for ActiveX search page controls.

```
Sub optbtnNews_MouseUp(Button, Shift, X, Y)
    what_str = "news"
end sub

Sub optbtnWeb_MouseUp(Button, Shift, X, Y)
    what_str = "web"
end sub

Sub btnGo_MouseUp(Button, Shift, X, Y)
 Dim frmSearchFormIdDeja
 Dim frmSearchFormIdYahoo
 Dim frmSearchFormIdCrawler
 Dim frmSearchFormIdAlta
 Dim comp
 comp = StrComp(lbnames.Value,"DejaNews UseNet")
 if comp = 0 then
     Set frmSearchFormIdDeja = Document.SearchFormIdDeja
     frmSearchFormIdDeja.query.Value = query_string
     frmSearchFormIdDeja.maxhits.Value = maxhits_str
     frmSearchFormIdDeja.Submit
 End If

 comp = StrComp(lbnames.Value,"Yahoo")
 if comp = 0 then
     Set frmSearchFormIdYahoo = Document.SearchFormIdYahoo
     frmSearchFormIdYahoo.p.Value = query_string
     frmSearchFormIdYahoo.Submit
 End If

 comp = StrComp(lbnames.Value,"Web Crawler")
 if comp = 0 then
     Set frmSearchFormIdCrawler = Document.SearchFormIdCrawler
     frmSearchFormIdCrawler.searchText.Value = query_string
     frmSearchFormIdCrawler.mode.Value = mode_str
     frmSearchFormIdCrawler.maxHits.Value = maxhits_str
     frmSearchFormIdCrawler.Submit
 End If

 comp = StrComp(lbnames.Value,"AltaVista")
 if comp = 0 then
```

```
      Set frmSearchFormIdAlta = Document.SearchFormIdAlta
      frmSearchFormIdAlta.what.Value = what_str
      frmSearchFormIdAlta.fmt.Value = mode_str
      frmSearchFormIdAlta.q.Value = query_string
      frmSearchFormIdAlta.Submit
  End If
end sub
```

The MouseUp event handler for the Go button checks for the string in the search engine drop-down list box, and accordingly it sets the hidden form variables to the global variables. After the required fields of the form are initialized, it calls the SUBMIT method for the form, submitting the query to the search engine.

You can test the ActiveX search page by copying the source files to a Web server and browsing the SEARCH.HTM file using Internet Explorer 3.0.

This example shows you the ready-made functionality that the ActiveX controls supplied with the ActiveX Control Pad offer for developing customized superior interfaces for your Web pages. Now take a cursory look at some additional controls that Microsoft provides for developing superlative Web pages.

Additional ActiveX Controls Supplied by Microsoft

The ActiveX controls shipped with the ActiveX Control Pad are standard controls that can be used for most application interfaces ported to the Web. However, to develop powerful compelling Web pages, you can make use of additional ActiveX controls that are offered by Microsoft. These controls can be downloaded from the Internet at Microsoft's ActiveX controls Web page at http://www.microsoft.com/intdev/controls/ctrlref.htm. Table 9.3 lists sample controls available on the ActiveX controls Web page.

Table 9.3. Additional ActiveX controls available on the ActiveX controls Web page.

Control	Description
ActiveMovie	Displays sound and video data with support for different file formats and streaming
Animated Button	Used for displaying various frame sequences of an .AVI file depending on the button state
Chart	Displays charts in different styles such as bar-chart, pie-chart, and so on
Gradient	Draws shaded transition between colors

continues

Table 9.3. continued

Control	Description
Label	Draws text in angles and along user-defined curves
Marquee	Displays scrolling and/or bouncing URLs
Menu	Displays a menu button or a pull-down menu
Pop-up Menu	Displays a pop-up menu
Pop-up Window	Displays specified HTML documents in a pop-up window
Preloader	Downloads a URL in the background to store in cache
Stock Ticker	Displays changing data in text or XRT format at regular intervals
Timer	Generates periodic events
View Tracker	Detects whether control is in the viewable area

Along with the previously mentioned ActiveX controls, there are several controls from third-party vendors which are available at the ActiveX Component Gallery on the World Wide Web. The ActiveX Component Gallery at `http://www.microsoft.com/activex/controls` is an impressive assortment of powerful controls.

The next section addresses a few issues relevant to publishing Web pages developed using ActiveX controls supplied along with ActiveX Control Pad or from third-party vendors.

Using Custom or Third-Party ActiveX Controls

There are over a thousand ActiveX controls available today, and you can expect this figure to rise astronomically as ActiveX gains momentum. In order to use these custom controls to publish active Web pages, there is an important property that has to be specified in the <PARAM> attribute of the <OBJECT> tag used for the control. This is the CODEBASE property.

When users browse a Web page developed with an ActiveX control that is not installed on their system, the CODEBASE property identifies the source URL where the browser can locate the ActiveX control and automatically download it. Depending on the browser's security settings, the browser will either ask the user before installing the control or install the control automatically and then display the Web page.

If you are using one of the controls shipped along with the ActiveX Control Pad, you can download the `Mspert10.cab` file from Microsoft's Web site at `http://activex.microsoft.com/controls/mspert10.cab`. Copy this file to the Web server on which you are publishing your Web page. To set the browser for automatic downloading, you need to point the CODEBASE attribute of the controls that you use to point to this file on your server. Alternatively, you can set CODEBASE to point to Microsoft's Web site, but this would require additional overhead for the browser to establish a connection with Microsoft's Web server.

> ## caution
>
> If you use ActiveX controls on your server and point the CODEBASE attribute to your server, be sure that the control is digitally signed and certified. Refer to the Microsoft ActiveX Code Signing Documentation in the ActiveX Software Developer's Kit (SDK) for details.

When using ActiveX controls from the Component Gallery or a third-party ActiveX control, be sure to refer to the documentation of the control and specify the CODEBASE attribute correctly. Otherwise, users who do not have the control installed on their system may be unable to view your Web page.

Some examples of ActiveX controls shipping today are

- Macromedia's ActiveShockwave plays multimedia movies developed in Macromedia authoring tools like Director.
- Adobe Acrobat displays documents in Adobe Acrobat format.
- Black Diamond Consulting's SurroundVideo displays a 360° interactive panoramic view.
- Progressive Networks RealAudio Player plays streaming audio over the Internet at low-bandwidth connections.

You can download and look for many more ActiveX controls in the ActiveX Component Gallery at `http://www.microsoft.com/activex/controls`. New controls are being added to the ActiveX Component Gallery frequently.

These examples should give you a glimpse of the exciting possibilities offered by ActiveX technology.

Summary

This chapter gave you a glimpse of how you can exploit the power of ActiveX using the first development environment for using ActiveX controls to build Web pages, the ActiveX Control Pad.

10

Advanced Web Page Creation

by James Mohler

Most developers find that the general block- and text-level tags of the HTML language make it difficult to design and create pages that are formatted the same way across platforms and across browsers. Often text and graphic elements shift slightly when viewed in various browsers (or on various platforms), causing unintentional misalignment of elements on the page. The same is true of the ActiveX and VBScript controls that are integrated within pages. Precise placement of controls is generally as difficult as precise placement of graphics and text. Creating advanced Web pages—those with a complex design or other complex features—can be difficult with basic HTML block tags such as <OL>, <IMG>, and <P>.

Within the HTML language, there are two major page-formatting structures that can be used to create advanced Web pages that remain relatively stable from browser to browser and from platform to platform: The structure tags for HTML tables and HTML frames allow more precise control over the formatting of page elements—more than the other tags found in the language. Both tables and frames are designed so that a page or site developer can easily control and lay out the structure of a page and its various elements.

note

One topic of Web pages and the HTML language discussed extensively, particularly by ratifying bodies such as the World Wide Web Consortium (W3C) and other involved institutions, is focused on structure versus appearance. Many developers would like to see the HTML language include tags that make it easier to control the appearance of Web pages. The entire debate involving which tags should and should not be included in the official HTML language surrounds structure versus appearance. People whose jobs depend upon precise layout of Web pages argue for more control over appearance, whereas those who are familiar with SGML (the precursor and "parent" of HTML) argue for less appearance control and more focus on document structure. For the time being, HTML is still predominantly focused on being a semantic language in which pages are defined by structure rather than appearance. This is why most of the tags, barring tables and frames, allow little placement dependability when viewed across browsers and platforms: HTML semantically describes structure rather than precisely defining appearance. However, more tags are being added for more design and appearance control.

Formatting Pages with Tables and Frames

In reality, tables were not originally designed to house entire groups of text and graphics, but they do provide one of the best ways to exhibit more control over the appearance of a Web page. You'll find that most of the time it is difficult to get graphics and text formatted the way you like with the standard block- and text-level tags. Using tables is a unique way of creating and formatting Web pages with relative consistency. Tables give you more accurate control over the way elements appear on the page. They also give you the ability to format your pages consistently across your entire site.

One of the newest features in the Web world is the support of framed documents. As a means of combating the "structure" point of view (desiring more control over appearance of Web pages), the makers of some of the most familiar browsers have begun creating their own extensions to the HTML language. These extensions are the "unofficial" HTML tags, ones not officially supported by all browsers.

Prior to the <FRAMESET> tag, all Web documents were known as *body documents*, or documents that had a body section. Each browser window contained one and only one Web page. Today, however, the framing convention, invented by Netscape and now supported by Internet Explorer as well, has added a new twist to documents that can be viewed inside a browser.

In this chapter, you'll look at both tables and frames to see how they can be used for more precise control over the pages you create. No matter whether you are dealing with intermingled text and graphics or ActiveX or VBScript controls, tables and frames can give you a better means of controlling the layout and design of your pages.

In the first part of this chapter you'll focus on using tables to format your pages. Sure, tables were originally designed to house data, but as you surf the Web you'll find ingenious solutions that integrate tables with many of the other tags that are part of the HTML language. Tables can internally utilize all of the HTML tags in addition to table-specific tags.

In the second part of this chapter you'll look at how you can use frames in your Web pages. From how they work to creating the programming for them, you'll see that frames can be a good addition to your Web site. Yet there are some design considerations you must ponder before cranking out a framed page.

Basic Uses for Tables

Tables have a wide variety of uses in a Web page. They can be used for their original purpose, that of tabular data, or they can also be used to help format graphics as well as entire pages of information. Let's look at the basic tags that are used for an HTML table. In our example, you'll begin by looking at how to create an embossed graphic using a table.

The <TABLE> tag is used to house all of the data for a particular table in the HTML code. The <TR> tag, or table row, is used within the <TABLE>...</TABLE> tags to define the rows for the table. The <TD> tag, or table data cell, is used within the <TR>... </TR> tags to define the cells within the table row.

The three previous tags are the minimum tags required to create a simple table. When tables are created, the developer usually begins by defining the first row's data cell and then the items that appear beneath it. Creating tables one column at a time is much easier than trying to develop the whole thing at once. But before you are introduced to the various attributes associate with these tags and an extensive example, let's look at these three tags in a simple example.

Creating Embossed Effects

One of the most basic yet most effective uses of a table is to create a simple border for a graphic or other element. To introduce the concepts and basic tags involved, you'll begin with a simple exercise of creating a table with a single data cell that contains a graphic.

To create the image shown in Figure 10.1, enter the code shown in Listing 10.1.

Figure 10.1.
Creating an embossed outline graphic using a table.

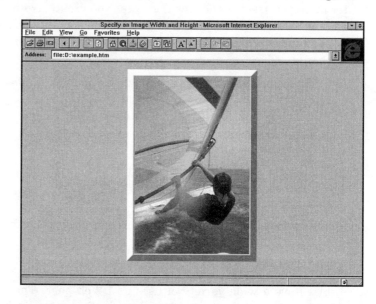

Listing 10.1. The code to create the embossed table graphic.

```
<!DOCTYPE "HTML 3.2 //EN">
<HTML>
  <HEAD>
    <TITLE>Creating an Embossed Image</TITLE>
  </HEAD>
  <BODY>
    <CENTER>
      <TABLE BORDER=14>
          <TR>
          <TD><IMG SRC="windsurf.gif"></TD>
          </TR>
      </TABLE>
    </CENTER>
  </BODY>
</HTML>
```

Notice the relationship between the code and the image in Figure 10.1. In the code, you see a table defined with a single row and one data cell. Note that the table's single cell conforms to the size of the graphic that is placed within it. By default, the data cells of a table will always conform to the size of the object inserted within it. Also notice the border that has been added with the BORDER attribute of the <TABLE> tag. This is one of the most common uses of the <TABLE> tag.

Now let's make it more interesting by adding a second row to the table containing a title for the graphic, as shown in Figure 10.2. The code for the page now looks like Listing 10.2.

Figure 10.2.
Adding a title to the graphic.

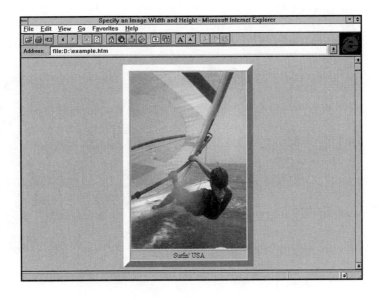

Listing 10.2. The code for adding a second row for the graphic's caption.

```
<!DOCTYPE "HTML 3.2 //EN">
<HTML>
  <HEAD>
    <TITLE> Using Tables </TITLE>
  </HEAD>
  <BODY>
    <CENTER>
      <TABLE BORDER=14>
        <TR>
        <TD><IMG SRC="windsurf.gif"></TD>
        </TR>
      <TR>
        <TD ALIGN=CENTER>Surfin' USA</TD>
        </TR>
      </TABLE>
    </CENTER>
  </BODY>
</HTML>
```

As you can see from Listing 10.2, adding another `<TR>` section or table row adds another row to the table. This is how you build the Y dimension of your tables—by adding more rows.

Now let's add more a second graphic and caption to the table. To do this, add another `<TD>` or table data cell to the right of the existing one in the first row as shown in Figure 10.3. The code that we have added looks like Listing 10.3.

Figure 10.3.
Adding another column to the table.

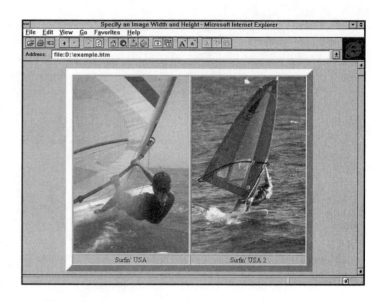

Listing 10.3. Adding a second graphic and caption.

```
<!DOCTYPE "HTML 3.2 //EN">
<HTML>
  <HEAD>
    <TITLE>Using Tables</TITLE>
  </HEAD>
  <BODY>
    <CENTER>
      <TABLE BORDER=14>
        <TR>
        <TD><IMG SRC="windsurf.gif"></TD>
        <TD><IMG SRC="windsur2.gif"></TD>
        </TR>
        <TR>
        <TD ALIGN=CENTER>Surfin' USA</TD>
        <TD ALIGN=CENTER>Surfin' USA 2</TD>
        </TR>
        </TABLE>
      </CENTER>
  </BODY>
</HTML>
```

Using the previous examples, you can see how tables are built. The `<TABLE>`...
`</TABLE>` tags are what mark both the beginning and the end of the table elements.
The `<TR>`...`</TR>` tags define the rows of the table, and the `<TD>`...`</TD>` tags define
the cells in the row, which consequently define the number of columns for each
row.

Basic Tags and Attributes

As you read, the `<TABLE>`...`</TABLE>` tags define the beginning and ending of the table. The `<TABLE>` tag has several attributes that can be used to set options for the entire table, including the following:

- `ALIGN`—Allows text to flow around the table much like text flowing around an image. Valid entries for the `ALIGN` attribute include `LEFT` and `RIGHT`.

- `BORDER`—Sets the thickness for the borders of the table boundaries. The default for this attribute is `0`, so not putting any value causes the table borders to be invisible.

- `CELLSPACING`—Defines the thickness of the cells within the table. The default is `CELLSPACING=2`.

- `CELLPADDING`—Defines how close a cell border can come to the edges of the object inside the cell. The default is `CELLPADDING=1`.

- `WIDTH`—Attempts to specify the desired width of the table either in pixels or as a percentage. However, a value defined with this attribute can be overridden by the values set in other attributes (see `WIDTH` attribute of `<TR>`, `<TD>` , and `<TH>` in the "Row, Cell, and Table Head Attributes" section).

- `HEIGHT`—Attempts to specify the desired width of the table either in pixels or as a percentage. As with the `WIDTH` attribute, a value defined with this attribute can be overridden by the values set in other attributes (see `HEIGHT` attribute of `<TR>`, `<TD>`, and `<TH>` in the "Row, Cell, and Table Head Attributes" section).

As you continue on by looking at the attributes for rows, cells, and table heads, keep in mind that attributes set for the `<TABLE>` tag affect the entire table. Attributes set per row, cell, or table head (`<TR>`, `<TD>`, and `<TH>`, respectively) affect only those items.

Row, Cell, and Table Head Attributes

As mentioned previously, the `<TR>`...`</TR>` tags define the individual rows for the table and the `<TD>`...`</TD>` tags define the cells for the table. In addition to these two items, the `<TH>` tag creates a table header cell for the particular row of data cells. The text contained in these cells is rendered in boldface text.

The attributes that can be used with these remaining table tags apply to all three tags, `<TR>`, `<TD>`, and `<TH>`. The attributes for these tags include the following:

- `ALIGN`—Specifies the alignment of the text or elements within the cell. Valid entries include `ALIGN=LEFT`, `RIGHT`, and `CENTER`; the default is `ALIGN=LEFT`.

- VALIGN—Specifies the vertical alignment of the text or elements within the cell. The default is ALIGN=MIDDLE. Valid entries include VALIGN=TOP, MIDDLE, BOTTOM, and BASELINE.

The following attributes apply only to the <TD> and <TH> tags:

- WIDTH—Specifies a width for the element in pixels or as a percentage. Specifying a width will affect all the cells in the particular column. Therefore, if multiple cells use the WIDTH attribute, the widest cell setting will be used. Note that if the compilation of the cell widths exceeds that specified in the WIDTH attribute of the <TABLE> tag, the cumulative widths specified per cell will override the WIDTH specified in the <TABLE> tag.

- HEIGHT—Specifies a height for the cell in pixels or as a percentage. Specifying a height will affect all the cells in the particular row. Therefore, if multiple cells use the HEIGHT attribute, the tallest cell setting will be used. Note that if the compilation of the cell heights exceeds that specified in the HEIGHT attribute of the <TABLE> tag, the cumulative heights specified per cell will override the HEIGHT specified in the <TABLE> tag.

- COLSPAN—Specifies the number of columns that the cell spans.

- ROWSPAN—Specifies the number of rows that the cell spans.

- NOWRAP—Disables the text-wrapping feature.

Now that you have looked at the various table tags and attributes, let's look at how to build a table using them. Because I have an interest in wildlife, we'll be formatting a chart involving the wild game local to central Indiana. The chart that I want to create will show eight counties in central Indiana and the population of the eight most common game animals, as shown in Figure 10.4.

To begin this chart, first lay out the rows and the row header for the counties. The code looks like Listing 10.4.

Listing 10.4. The beginning code for the game table.

```
<!DOCTYPE "HTML 3.2 //EN">
<HTML>
  <HEAD>
    <TITLE>Central Indiana Wildlife</TITLE>
  </HEAD>
<BODY>
  <TABLE BORDER=4>
    <TR>
        <TH>Counties</TH>
    </TR>
    <TR>
```

```
            <TD>Boone</TD>
          </TR>
                ...
                ...
                ...
          <TR>
            <TD>Tipton</TD>
          </TR>
          </TABLE>
        </CENTER>
      </BODY>
    </HTML>
```

Figure 10.4.

The table showing the population of wild game in eight counties in central Indiana.

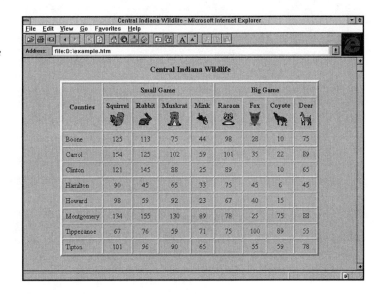

Figure 10.5 shows an example of what this code generates. As you can see, the best way to begin the code for the table is by establishing the first column for the table. Subsequent columns will be added to the code later. Much like any other programming or scripting language, adding too much new code at a time can make it difficult to find errors or bugs.

Now let's go back and add the second column of data. The code looks like Listing 10.5.

Listing 10.5. Adding the second column to the table.

```
<!DOCTYPE "HTML 3.2 //EN">
<HTML>
  <HEAD>
    <TITLE>Central Indiana Wildlife</TITLE>
```

continues

Listing 10.5. continued

```
    </HEAD>
    <BODY>
      <TABLE BORDER=4>
        <TR>
      <TH>Counties</TH>
          <TH ALIGN=CENTER>Squirrel</TH>
        </TR>
        <TR>
          <TD>Boone</TD>
          <TD ALIGN=CENTER>125</TD>
        </TR>
              . . .
              . . .
              . . .
        <TR>
          <TD>Tipton</TD>
          <TD ALIGN=CENTER>101</TD>
        </TR>
        </TABLE>
      </CENTER>
    </BODY>
  </HTML>
```

Figure 10.5.
The beginnings of the
table.

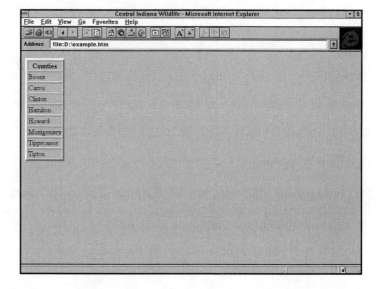

After I have added the second column, the table looks like Figure 10.6. Now I'll finish out the chart with the rest of the data. After I have entered all my data, my table looks pretty good, as shown in Figure 10.7; but there are a few things that I can do to make it look a little better.

Figure 10.6.
*Adding the second
column.*

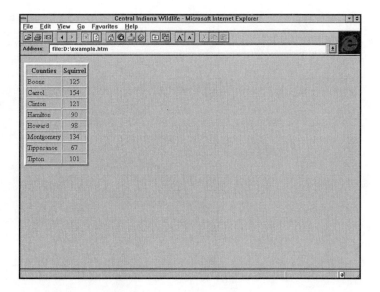

Figure 10.7.
*The table after all the
data is entered.*

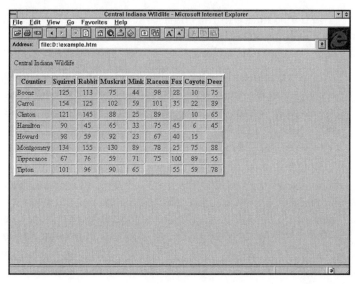

You'll see in the image that there are a few things that I can do to make my table look a little prettier. First, notice that all the cell borders come pretty close to the edges of my data. The first thing I'll do is add some space between the text and the data in my cells using the CELLPADDING attribute for the <TABLE> tag. Adding a cell padding of 6 makes the table spread out a little, as shown in Figure 10.8.

Figure 10.8.
Adding some visual space around the data using the CELLPADDING *attribute.*

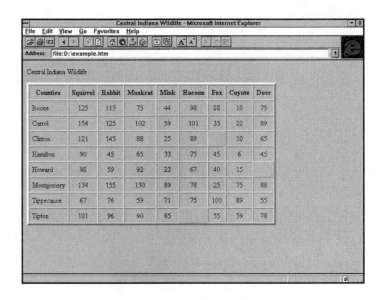

Counties	Squirrel	Rabbit	Muskrat	Mink	Racoon	Fox	Coyote	Deer
Boone	125	113	75	44	98	28	10	75
Carrol	154	125	102	59	101	35	22	89
Clinton	121	145	88	25	89		10	65
Hamilton	90	45	65	33	75	45	6	45
Howard	98	59	92	23	67	40	15	
Montgomery	134	155	130	89	78	25	75	88
Tippecanoe	67	76	59	71	75	100	89	55
Tipton	101	96	90	65		55	59	78

You'll also notice in the chart that there are a few cells without data. The chart will look much better if blank space is inserted within it so that it looks recessed like the rest of the chart.

When you are dealing with tables, there are two predominant methods of forcing a blank cell to recess. The first is the use of the nonbreaking space; to create this character, define it using its entity designation of . The second way of achieving this is to use a line break, or <BR>. Let's fix these blank cells. (See Figure 10.9.) Some browsers do not support special characters, so I am going to use the <BR> tag to create the recess.

The next thing I would like to do to finish off my table is add some spanning table data cells. I want to highlight the difference between what Hoosiers see as "big" game and "small" game. To do this I'll use two spanning cells, as shown in Figure 10.10. Notice the new row (<TR> tag) that has been added at the beginning of the chart. To make these data cells span multiple columns, use the COLSPAN attribute for the <TD> tag to make each cell span four columns.

If you look closely at Figure 10.10, you'll see that Counties appears to be a Small Game, which is not what I really want. To fix this, I'll move the data cell for Counties up to the top row that I just created and set its ROWSPAN attribute to 2. Now it will span two rows. By doing this it makes up for the "missing" row in the next set of cells. My chart now looks like Figure 10.11. You'll note that I have also centered the chart and its title to make things look a little better as well.

Figure 10.9.
Fixing a blank cell with a special character ( ) or a <BR> tag.

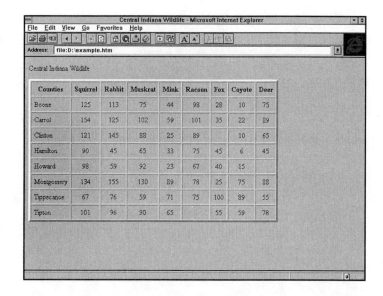

Figure 10.10.
Creating two spanning cells for the various types of game.

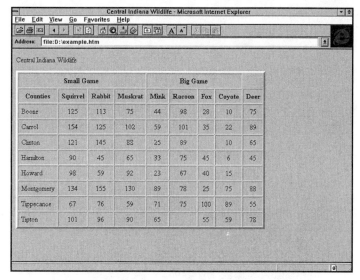

The finished code from Figure 10.11 ends up looking like Listing 10.6.

Figure 10.11.
The "finished" chart.

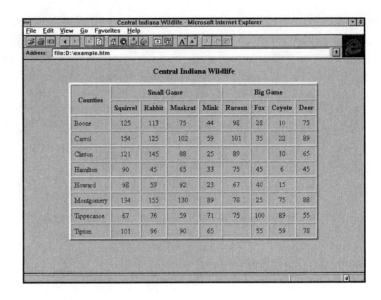

Listing 10.6. The finished table code.

```
<!DOCTYPE "HTML 3.2 //EN">
<HTML>
  <HEAD>
    <TITLE>Central Indiana Wildlife</TITLE>
  </HEAD>
  <BODY>
    <H3 ALIGN=CENTER> Central Indiana Wildlife</H3>
    <CENTER>
    <TABLE BORDER=4  CELLPADDING=6>
      <TR>
        <TH ROWSPAN=2>Counties</TH>
    <TH ALIGN=CENTER COLSPAN=4> Small Game </TH>
    <TH ALIGN=CENTER COLSPAN=4> Big Game </TH>
      </TR>
      <TR>
    <TH ALIGN=CENTER>Squirrel</TH>
    <TH ALIGN=CENTER>Rabbit</TH>
    <TH ALIGN=CENTER>Muskrat</TH>
    <TH ALIGN=CENTER>Mink</TH>
    <TH ALIGN=CENTER>Racoon</TH>
    <TH ALIGN=CENTER>Fox</TH>
    <TH ALIGN=CENTER>Coyote</TH>
    <TH ALIGN=CENTER>Deer</TH>
      </TR>
      <TR>
        <TD>Boone</TD>
        <TD ALIGN=CENTER>125</TD>
    <TD ALIGN=CENTER>113</TD>
    <TD ALIGN=CENTER>75</TD>
    <TD ALIGN=CENTER>44</TD>
    <TD ALIGN=CENTER>98</TD>
    <TD ALIGN=CENTER>28</TD>
    <TD ALIGN=CENTER>10</TD>
```

```
<TD ALIGN=CENTER>75</TD>
  </TR>
  <TR>
    <TD>Carrol</TD>
    <TD ALIGN=CENTER>154</TD>
<TD ALIGN=CENTER>125</TD>
<TD ALIGN=CENTER>102</TD>
<TD ALIGN=CENTER>59</TD>
<TD ALIGN=CENTER>101</TD>
<TD ALIGN=CENTER>35</TD>
<TD ALIGN=CENTER>22</TD>
<TD ALIGN=CENTER>89</TD>
  </TR>
  <TR>
    <TD>Clinton</TD>
    <TD ALIGN=CENTER>121</TD>
<TD ALIGN=CENTER>145</TD>
<TD ALIGN=CENTER>88</TD>
<TD ALIGN=CENTER>25</TD>
<TD ALIGN=CENTER>89</TD>
<TD ALIGN=CENTER><BR></TD>
<TD ALIGN=CENTER>10</TD>
<TD ALIGN=CENTER>65</TD>
  </TR>
  <TR>
    <TD>Hamilton</TD>
    <TD ALIGN=CENTER>90</TD>
<TD ALIGN=CENTER>45</TD>
<TD ALIGN=CENTER>65</TD>
<TD ALIGN=CENTER>33</TD>
<TD ALIGN=CENTER>75</TD>
<TD ALIGN=CENTER>45</TD>
<TD ALIGN=CENTER>6</TD>
<TD ALIGN=CENTER>45</TD>
  </TR>
  <TR>
    <TD>Howard</TD>
    <TD ALIGN=CENTER>98</TD>
<TD ALIGN=CENTER>59</TD>
<TD ALIGN=CENTER>92</TD>
<TD ALIGN=CENTER>23</TD>
<TD ALIGN=CENTER>67</TD>
<TD ALIGN=CENTER>40</TD>
<TD ALIGN=CENTER>15</TD>
<TD ALIGN=CENTER><BR></TD>
  </TR>
  <TR>
    <TD>Montgomery</TD>
    <TD ALIGN=CENTER>134</TD>
<TD ALIGN=CENTER>155</TD>
<TD ALIGN=CENTER>130</TD>
<TD ALIGN=CENTER>89</TD>
<TD ALIGN=CENTER>78</TD>
<TD ALIGN=CENTER>25</TD>
<TD ALIGN=CENTER>75</TD>
<TD ALIGN=CENTER>88</TD>
```

continues

Listing 10.6. continued

```
           </TR>
           <TR>
             <TD>Tippecanoe</TD>
             <TD ALIGN=CENTER>67</TD>
       <TD ALIGN=CENTER>76</TD>
       <TD ALIGN=CENTER>59</TD>
       <TD ALIGN=CENTER>71</TD>
       <TD ALIGN=CENTER>75</TD>
       <TD ALIGN=CENTER>100</TD>
       <TD ALIGN=CENTER>89</TD>
       <TD ALIGN=CENTER>55</TD>
           </TR>
           <TR>
             <TD>Tipton</TD>
             <TD ALIGN=CENTER>101</TD>
       <TD ALIGN=CENTER>96</TD>
       <TD ALIGN=CENTER>90</TD>
       <TD ALIGN=CENTER>65</TD>
       <TD ALIGN=CENTER><BR></TD>
       <TD ALIGN=CENTER>55</TD>
       <TD ALIGN=CENTER>59</TD>
       <TD ALIGN=CENTER>78</TD>
           </TR>
           </TABLE>
         </CENTER>
      </BODY>
   </HTML>
```

As you can see, building a chart from ground zero is pretty easy, as long as you add things one part at a time. If you just start pounding in the code for a table, it's likely you'll end up with all sorts of crazy things going on. Start by entering a single column, add the next one, and so on. Finish out the chart by adding any other tags, special formatting, or adjustments that you desire.

Before we leave the chart that you just created, let's make it a little more interesting by incorporating some graphics into the chart. Incorporating any of the other HTML tags, particularly text-level tags, VBScript, or ActiveX controls is quite easy when you've got the basic structure of your table.

We'll add some graphics so that the chart looks like Figure 10.12. The code is really quite simple: All you have to do is integrate some <IMG> tags into the <TH>, table headers, of the chart. The only thing that is modified is the second row of data cells. You'll also see in the code that I have added line breaks so the graphic appears below the chart text that appears in the cell. The modified chart code looks like Listing 10.7.

Figure 10.12.
Adding graphics to the already formatted chart is quite easy.

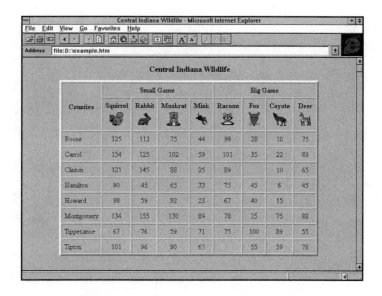

Listing 10.7. The finished chart, complete with graphics.

```
...
<TR>
    <TH ALIGN=CENTER>Squirrel<BR><IMG SRC="squirrel.gif"></TH>
    <TH ALIGN=CENTER>Rabbit<BR><IMG SRC="rabbit.gif"></TH>
    <TH ALIGN=CENTER>Muskrat<BR><IMG SRC="rat.gif"></TH>
    <TH ALIGN=CENTER>Mink<BR><IMG SRC="mink.gif"></TH>
    <TH ALIGN=CENTER>Racoon<BR><IMG SRC="racoon.gif"></TH>
    <TH ALIGN=CENTER>Fox<BR><IMG SRC="fox.gif"></TH>
    <TH ALIGN=CENTER>Coyote<BR><IMG SRC="coyote.gif"></TH>
    <TH ALIGN=CENTER>Deer<BR><IMG SRC="deer.gif"></TH>
</TR>
...
```

Formatting Pages

Now that you've seen the basics of creating tables, let's examine some of the other things that you can do with them. As you are working with the HTML language you'll find that it is often difficult to get graphics, text, and other elements just the way you want them on the Web page with the standard block tags. When you use a table, you can force the text and graphics to conform to its data cells, thus giving you more control and formatting capabilities. Figure 10.13 shows an example of a Web that uses a table to format the various graphics and text in a very structured way. Consequently, this page looks consistent across platforms and browsers.

Figure 10.13.
Laying out a page with a table.

Can you see how the table is used to lay out the data inside it? Let's look at the basic table that is used to lay it out. The code looks like Listing 10.8.

Listing 10.8. The code behind the table used to format the Web page.

```
<!DOCTYPE "HTML 3.2 //EN">
<HTML>
  <HEAD>
    <TITLE>Example Layout</TITLE>
  </HEAD>
  <BODY>
    <TABLE BORDER=6>
      <TR>
        <TD COLSPAN=3 WIDTH=596 HEIGHT=97><H3 ALIGN=CENTER> --BANNER-- </H3>
        </TD>
      </TR>
      <TR>
        <TD WIDTH=196 HEIGHT=49><H2 ALIGN=CENTER> Advertisement </H2></TD>
 <TD COLSPAN=2 WIDTH=400 HEIGHT=49><H2 ALIGN=CENTER>Area Banner</H2>
      </TR>
      <TR>
        <TD WIDTH=196 HEIGHT=49><H2 ALIGN=CENTER> Advertisement </H2></TD>
 <TD ROWSPAN=3 WIDTH=256 HEIGHT=404><H2 ALIGN=CENTER> Information </H2></TD>
        <TD ROWSPAN=3 WIDTH=144 HEIGHT=404><H2 ALIGN=CENTER> Subjects </H2></TD>
      </TR>
      <TR>
 <TD WIDTH=196 HEIGHT=49><H2 ALIGN=CENTER> Advertisement </H2></TD>
      </TR>
      <TR>
 <TD WIDTH=196 HEIGHT=306><H2 ALIGN=CENTER> Menu </H2></TD>
      </TR>
    </TABLE>
  </BODY>
</HTML>
```

If you turn on all the table borders and look at the previous code in the browser, you can see how easy it is to make templates that can be used to format pages like this. Figure 10.14 shows what a blank template page would look like for the SportsLine page.

Figure 10.14.
A blank template for the previous page.

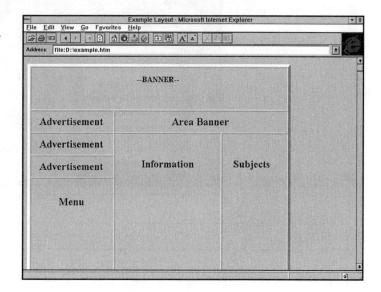

Structuring Data

As you are creating a table to structure your data, make sure that you build the table a column at a time. Often developers begin creating tables by inserting multiple columns at a time as well as various formatting attributes. You'll find that it is much easier to add a column at a time until the entire table is built. Then go back and add special formatting such as ALIGN, COLSPAN, ROWSPAN, and CELLPADDING attributes, or VBScript and ActiveX controls.

You may also want to use code generators such as FrontPage or PageMill to generate your tables. You'll still probably have to add some of these things through hard coding, but using a generator will help you get the basic structure created pretty quickly.

Structuring Graphics

In addition to structuring a page of graphics and text, you can also integrate other features such as interactive form elements or other controls. Figure 10.15 shows an example of a Web page composed of graphics and interactive form elements. For the developers of this page, probably the hardest part of the whole page layout was getting the images the right sizes.

Figure 10.15.
Almost any other tag can be used with tables.

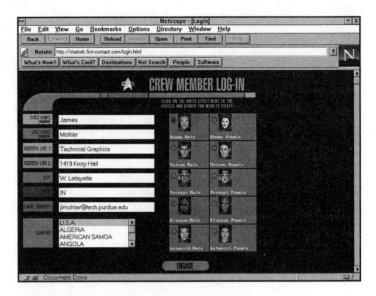

---

note

If you want to do something like Figure 10.15, make sure you either sketch it out or lay it out in a image editor. Then simply construct that table around the preformatted graphics. Remember that table data cells always attempt to size themselves around the contents of the cell. You can partially control this through the CELLPADDING, HEIGHT, and WIDTH attributes. In addition, the cell borders have been turned off to aid in the look of the page. You can always make the table borders "invisible" to your audience by turning off the cell borders with the BORDER attribute.

Tips for Successful Tables

Working with tables can be one of the most frustrating things in HTML. However, there are several things you can do to make it a little easier. Following these steps to create your table:

1. Lay out a single column of cells first.
2. Add in subsequent columns of data cells.
3. Make sure all the columns are inserted prior to using text-level tags or other block-level tags.
4. Insert any block-level tags such as lists or paragraphs that occur within a cell.

5. Insert any text-level tags that you want to add to format text or to insert graphics.

6. Create any hyperlinks that you want to appear in the table or document.

7. Adjust any formatting that applies to the entire table such as justification, height, or width attributes.

Frames

As you saw in the "Basic Uses for Tables" section, you can create Web documents that are formatted using tables; however, tables must be designed around the audience's display size. If your audience views a table that was designed for a screen size larger than their current setting, they must horizontally scroll to view all of the table. Note that this is an unwritten cardinal sin.

However, frames can help you overcome the display problems with tables, *if* you create them correctly. What's worse than horizontally scrolling to see an entire table? Having to horizontally scroll three separate windows or frames in a document to see each of the items displayed in those windows.

---

note

Frames are a browser convention. This means they are not included in the "official" HTML tags established by the World Wide Web Consortium. Therefore, some browsers still do not support them. The big two, Netscape and Explorer, both do so. Explorer actually gives you a few more options than does Netscape. If your audience uses one of these two browsers, you don't necessarily have to be concerned. However, in the "Dealing with Nonframe Browsers" section, you'll discover a way of creating a Web page that will work in browsers that do not support frames.

Working with Frames

So what's the whole point to using frames in your Web pages? Well, predominantly frames can be used to divide your screen into various windows, as shown in Figure 10.16. The windows each contain a single Web page, and they can actually be any size you want. However, you must still work within the limitations of your audience's screen size. If you specify a frames page that is too big for the current display, the browser will scale the windows to fit them into the browser work area.

Figure 10.16.
Dividing the browser work area into multiple windows using browser frames.

In reality, being able to open multiple pages into a browser is not anything new. By now you've probably been to a site that has automatically opened a new browser window to load a document. (See Figure 10.17.) In most of the modern operating systems such as Windows 95 and Windows NT, you can open multiple browser windows that can each contain a different document. For the blessed few that have (and can afford) indulgently fast Internet connections, you can even be downloading multiple pages at a time or surfing in two windows at once.

Figure 10.17.
Opening multiple browser windows and documents.

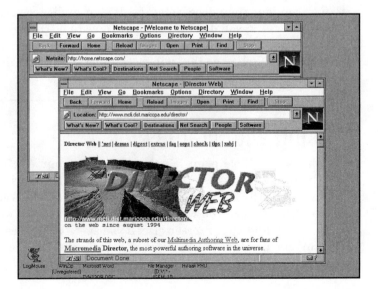

However, frames enable you to do two distinct things. First, a Web page that is divided into frames gives the audience the ability to size the frames, as shown in Figure 10.18. When a page is laid out using frames, simply dragging the frame's border resizes the window. This works much the same way as dragging any window in the Windows, Macintosh, or other GUI environment.

Figure 10.18.
*Sizing the windows
established in framed
pages.*

The second thing that frames allow is the ability to have one window control the contents that are displayed in another window. For example, you can create a frame that houses a menu for the contents of your site. Clicking one of the hotlinks in the menu causes the contents of another window to change. Many of the examples on the Web that work this way are graphics related. For example, a site designed to distribute clip art or other graphic images may use a menu down one side of the screen to control what is seen in another window, as shown in Figure 10.19.

Figure 10.19.
*Using a menu in a frame
to control the contents of
another frame.*

Because each window of a framed Web page houses a separate HTML file, the windows can actually contain anything. Each window is linked to a different Web document, which can contain any of the HTML tags. Figure 10.20 shows an example of a graphics-intense Web page that uses frames.

Even though the user can size the frames, keep in mind that the pages you link to the various windows must be designed around the size of the frame. In Figure 10.20, the developer of this page had to design all of the graphics for the window pages so that they would fit into the windows without the audience having to horizontally scroll. Just as with other pages, you'll have to design your graphics and text elements around the size of the area in which the page is to be displayed.

Figure 10.20.
Any tags can be included in the Web documents that appear in the frames.

Structure

Up to this point, all the HTML documents you've seen in this chapter have contained a body section. However, in documents that use frames, the frames section (denoted by the <FRAMESET> tag) replaces the body section (denoted by the <BODY> tag) of the document. As the browser loads a frames document, the frames document only contains the information to set up the frames and what pages go into those frames. The body for a frames document is actually contained in the pages that are inserted into the frames, not in the frames document itself.

If you load a Web page that has frames defined without loading the pages that go into the frames, you have a bunch of blank frames, which isn't worth a whole lot. Just keep in mind that the body of a Web page that uses frames is contained in the pages that are loaded in the frames, not in the page that defines or lays out the frames. This will become clearer as you begin looking at the code for a frames document.

Defining Frames

The primary tag that is used to create a frames document is the <FRAMESET> tag. As mentioned in the "Structure" section, this tag replaces the normal <BODY>... </BODY> tags found in an HTML document. A document that uses the <FRAMESET> tag, the one that defines the layout of the windows, only contains information relevant to the actual windows or frames. The content for the frames is defined in any number of other HTML files and is stored externally.

Special Features

One of the special features of a frames document is the capability to open another browser window; this makes two instances, or copies, of the browser run simultaneously. Using this feature keeps the current document where it is. Normally, choosing a new link replaces the items shown in the browser's work area. Opening a new window leaves the current window where it is; the new window jumps to the specified URL.

Basic Frame Tags and Attributes

As mentioned in the "Defining Frames" section, the primary tag to create frames is the <FRAMESET> tag. The <FRAMESET>...</FRAMESET> tags are the containers for the definition of a framed page. The <FRAMESET>...</FRAMESET> tags replace the <BODY>... </BODY> tags in the HTML document. Note that the <FRAMESET> tag contains only information about how the screen should be subdivided into windows. Valid attributes for the <FRAMESET> tag include the following:

- ROWS—Defines the number and size of row frames that should be created in the browser work area. Valid entries include absolute (pixels), relative (wild card characters), and percentages of the screen.

- COLS—Defines the number and size of column frames that should be created in the browser work area. Valid entries include absolute (pixels), relative (wild card characters), and percentages of the screen.

As you use the <FRAMESET> tag, the ROWS and COLS attributes can use absolute dimensions, relative dimensions, or percentages to define the sizes of the windows that appear in the document. For example, you can specify that a series of frames be created by setting the COLS attribute to 150,150,150,150; these are absolute dimensions. However, specifying absolute dimensions can be detrimental if a user accesses your page at a screen size smaller than you anticipated. In our example, the user's browser would have to have 600 pixels to be able to display your frames as you created them. If the browser has less than 600 pixels, it will automatically scale the windows to fit in the user's screen, which can cause problems (that is, horizontal scrolling). A better way of defining frames is to use either the relative or percentage specification. No matter how you define your frames, you have to allow enough give and take in the pages shown in the frames for variability in the frame sizes.

The percentage specification is pretty easy to understand. To create a page that defines a series of column frames, each occupying 25% of the screen, you would enter COLS=25%,25%,25%,25%. This allows the browser to show the frames no matter what the display setting. However, as mentioned in the "Frames" section, the pages that are shown in these frames must allow enough variability so that the user will *never* have to horizontally scroll. As you examine some pages with frames you'll understand this better.

tip

If you choose to use the relative dimensioning, understand that it works the same way as percentages. A relative dimension may look like COLS=1*,3*,6*, which is the same as saying 10 percent, 30 percent, 60 percent. I find in most of my frame pages, as well as ones on the Net, that percentages are most commonly used.

After you have defined the containers for the frames setup, you must define the contents and other attributes of the frames themselves using the <FRAME> tag. The <FRAME> tag defines one frame or window in a frames document.

After you have defined a window, you can also use the following attributes to control how the window or frame behaves:

- SRC—Defines the Web page that will appear in the frame.
- NAME—Defines a name for the individual frame. This attribute is used to allow one frame to control another through a TARGET specification.
- SCROLLING—Defines whether the frame should have scrollbars or not. Valid entries for this attribute are SCROLLING=YES, NO, and AUTO. The default is AUTO.
- MARGINWIDTH—Defines the left and right margins for the frame in pixels. This attribute cannot be 0.
- MARGINHEIGHT—Defines the top and bottom margins for the frame in pixels. This attribute cannot be 0.
- NORESIZE—Disables the user's ability to size the frame.

Now that you have looked at the various frames tags and attributes, let's see how they actually work. You'll begin by looking at the basics of creating frames. Then you'll look at how to control one frame with another as well as how to open new browser windows using frames. You'll conclude with a neat trick for updating two frames based on another.

Creating Basic Frames

To begin working with frames, let's start with a simple example. First, divide the screen into two columns. You will need three HTML files to do this example: The first is the frames document, which defines how the screen will be laid out, and the other two are the actual documents that are inserted into the frames.

Figure 10.21 shows an example of the frames document. Notice the source code for this file shown in Listings 10.9 and 10.10. The <FRAMESET> tag contains the definitions for the frames. The document uses the COLS attribute to define two frames that each take up 50 percent of the screen. The code for the content of Frame A looks like Listing 10.9 and that for the content of Frame B looks like Listing 10.10.

Figure 10.21.
A simple frames document.

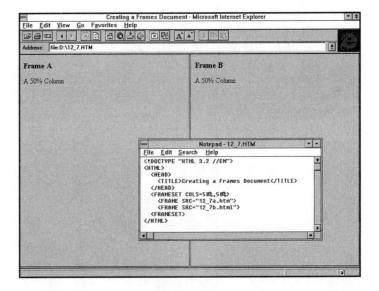

Listing 10.9. The code for Frame A.

```
<!DOCTYPE "HTML 3.2 //EN">
<HTML>
  <HEAD>
    <TITLE>Page A </TITLE>
```

continues

Listing 10.9. continued

```
  </HEAD>
  <BODY>
    <H3> Frame A </H3>
    <P> A 50% Column </p>
  </BODY>
</HTML>
```

Listing 10.10. The code for Frame B.

```
<!DOCTYPE "HTML 3.2 //EN">
<HTML>
  <HEAD>
    <TITLE>Page B</TITLE>
  </HEAD>
  <BODY>
    <H3> Frame B </H3>
    <P> A 50% Column </p>
  </BODY>
</HTML>
```

From this example you can see that any frame setup includes the frames document and an HTML file for each window. Now let's divide the two columns into two rows, as shown in Figure 10.22. The code for this frames document looks like Listing 10.11.

Figure 10.22.
Dividing the two columns into rows.

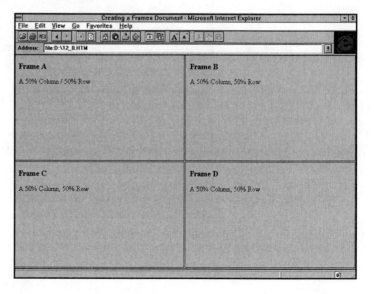

Listing 10.11. The code for dividing the two columns into rows.

```
<!DOCTYPE "HTML 3.2 //EN">
<HTML>
  <HEAD>
    <TITLE>Creating a Frames Document</TITLE>
  </HEAD>
  <FRAMESET COLS=50%,50%>
    <FRAMESET ROWS=50%,50%>
      <FRAME SRC="12_7a.htm">
      <FRAME SRC="12_7c.htm">
    </FRAMESET>
    <FRAMESET ROWS=50%,50%>
      <FRAME SRC="12_7b.html">
      <FRAME SRC="12_7d.html">
    </FRAMESET>
  <FRAMESET>
</HTML>
```

As you can see from this example, you can nest the <FRAMESET> container. In the example, the first <FRAMESET> tag defines two columns that are 50 percent of the screen. The second <FRAMESET> tag defines the divisions for the first column—two 50 percent rows. The third <FRAMESET> tag defines the divisions within the second column—again two 50 percent rows.

note

If you decide that you want to use frames in your pages, make sure that you lay them out on grid paper before you create the pages that go inside the frames. You must create the inserted pages at the size of the frame; elements that are larger than the frame will require scrolling. Designing on grid paper will help you determine how big the frames actually are.

In the previous example, any links to other pages that appear in the windows (that is, links in page A, B, C, or D) will cause the page to be loaded into the respective frame. In Figure 10.23, I have added a clickable link to Netscape's home page into page A. This creates a fundamental problem if I use the code that was set up previously for the frames document.

If page A has a clickable link, when the user clicks that link, the linked page will automatically load into that window, as shown in Figure 10.24. If no other attributes are used for the frame, it will load the page into the frame by default. The problem is that links that occur within your framed pages may not be designed to fit in your frame size. What you really want is to load the externally linked page into a new window so that the user will see it at its true size.

Figure 10.23.
Putting a clickable link into page A.

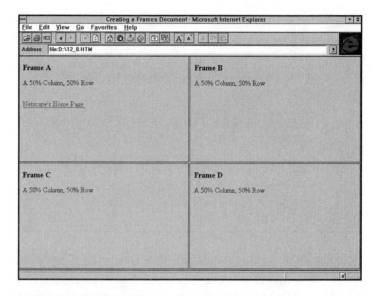

Figure 10.24.
The page is forced to load into the frame.

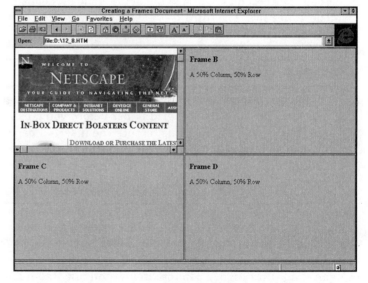

To make a new window open, acknowledge the TARGET attribute for the <A> tag. The TARGET attribute is usually only used with frames documents; however, with the _blank option, you can also use it in normal body documents (nonframes documents).

The TARGET attribute is predominantly used to allow one frame to update the contents of another frame. (You'll see this in the "Interaction Between Frames" section.) However, with the TARGET attribute, there are also several implicit names that you can use. These implicit names are simply predefined objects that you can reference when using frames documents. Implicit names for targets begin with an underscore and include the following:

- _self—Makes the browser update the frame that the page occurs in.
- _parent—Makes the browser update the parent of the current frame, assuming one exists.
- _top—Makes the browser update the entire browser work area.
- _blank—Makes the browser open a new window in which to display the page.

As you can see, there are several predetermined references that you can use as targets for your links. The one we are concerned with in this example is the _blank setting.

To get the Netscape link to load into a new browser window, simply add a TARGET statement for the page in which the link or <A HREF> occurs. From the code in Listing 10.9, change the code for Page A so that it includes a target specification like Listing 10.12.

Listing 10.12. The revised code for Page A.

```
<!DOCTYPE "HTML 3.2 //EN">
<HTML>
  <HEAD>
    <TITLE>Page A </TITLE>
  </HEAD>
  <BODY>
    <H3> Frame A </H3>
    <P> A 50% Column, 50% Row <BR><BR><BR>
    <A HREF="http://www.netscape.com" TARGET="_blank"> Netscape's Home Page
</A></p>
  </BODY>
</HTML>
```

Now when the user clicks the link in Frame A, a new browser window is opened for the document, as shown in Figure 10.25.

tip

Keep in mind that you can use the TARGET="_blank" attribute in both frames and body documents. However, having every link set this way may frustrate your users. Use it cautiously and only when there is a real need to open a new browser window.

Figure 10.25.
Using the
`TARGET="_blank"`
attribute causes a new
window to be opened.

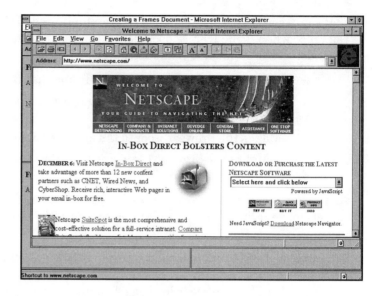

Figure 10.25.
Using the
`TARGET="_blank"`
attribute causes a new
window to be opened.

Interaction Between Frames

You have seen how the basics of the frames document works; now let's do some things that are a little more complicated. What if you want to have one window control another (for example, having a clickable link in one frame's page change the contents of another frame)? Or, what if you want one frame controlling two other frames? To have one page update another requires the use of frame names and target specifications. If each frame is named, you can target a frame for update using links in other frames.

Controlling One Frame

Let's use an example in which you create a menu on the left side of the screen that controls images that are displayed on the right side of the screen. You'll also have a graphic banner at the top that is frozen with no scrollbars and nonmovable frames. Figure 10.26 shows an example of what you will be creating.

To begin setting up this page, the first thing you must do is create the frames document itself using the <FRAMESET> tag and the ROWS and COLS attributes. However, first you must look at the document and see how the screen needs to be divided. Remember that you can define rows and columns, but the order in which you define them in the code is what determines how the frames will look. To determine how to divide the screen, look at what you want to create and determine whether the columns or rows extend over the entire screen. This will show you whether you need to define the rows or the columns first using the <FRAMESET> tag.

Figure 10.26.
*Controlling one frame
with another.*

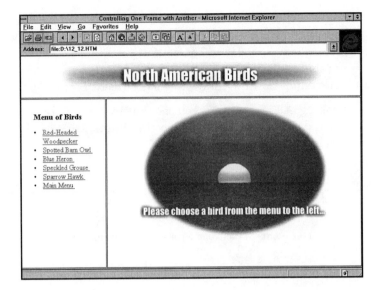

The code in Listing 10.13 means that the screen is first divided into two 50 percent columns. Then the first column is divided into two rows: One is 10 percent and the other is 90 percent. The second column is defined by the remaining <FRAME> tag at 100 percent.

Listing 10.13. The code for defining columns and then rows.

```
...
<FRAMESET COLS 50%, 50%>
    <FRAMESET ROWS 10%, 90%>
        <FRAME SRC="URL">
    </FRAMESET>
    <FRAME SRC="URL">
</FRAMESET>
...
```

Listing 10.14 shows how to define rows and then columns.

Listing 10.14. The code for defining rows and then columns.

```
...
<FRAMESET COLS 50%, 50%>
    <FRAMESET ROWS 10%, 90%>
        <FRAME SRC="URL">
    </FRAMESET>
    <FRAME SRC="URL">
</FRAMESET>
...
```

Notice that this code defines two 50 percent columns. The first 50 percent column is divided into a 10 percent row and a 90 percent row; the remaining 50 percent column is assigned to 100 percent using the last <FRAME> tag in the code. So you can see that the way that you define your frames using the COLS and ROWS attributes determines how the final frames document is created.

Looking at Figure 10.27, you see that the rows extend over the entire screen, so you'll define the rows and then the columns. The code for this page looks like Listing 10.15.

Listing 10.15. The code for Figure 10.27.

```
<!DOCTYPE "HTML 3.2 //EN">
<HTML>
  <HEAD>
    <TITLE>Controlling One Frame with Another</TITLE>
  </HEAD>
  <FRAMESET ROWS=20%,80%>
      <FRAME SRC="banner.htm">
    <FRAMESET COLS=25%,75%>
      <FRAME SRC="menu.htm">
      <FRAME SRC="screen.htm" NAME="screen">
    </FRAMESET>
  </FRAMESET>
</HTML>
```

In this code you see that the rows have been defined first because they extend over the entirety of the screen. The 20 percent row is assigned to the HTML file called BANNER, a 100 percent row. The second row, which is 80 percent, is further divided into two columns. The 25 percent column is assigned to the HTML file called MENU.HTM, and the 75 percent column is assigned to the HTML file called SCREEN.HTM. Note that you want the user to be able to choose items in the menu frame and have the browser update the screen frame. To do this, give the screen frame a name as is done in the code. Giving a frame a name gives documents in other windows the capability to target the named frame.

To demonstrate this, let's look at the code for MENU.HTM. This file shows you how to target frames using anchors. The code for this page looks like Listing 10.16.

Listing 10.16. The code for targeting frames with anchors.

```
<!DOCTYPE "HTML 3.2 //EN">
<HTML>
  <HEAD>
    <TITLE>Bird Menu</TITLE>
  </HEAD>
  <BODY BGCOLOR="#FFFFFF">
    <UL>
      <LH><H3> Menu of Birds </H3>
```

```
<LI><A HREF="bird1.htm" TARGET="screen"> Red-Headed Woodpecker</A></LI>
    <LI><A HREF="bird2.htm" TARGET="screen"> Spotted Barn Owl </A></LI>
    <LI><A HREF="bird3.htm" TARGET="screen"> Blue Heron </A></LI>
    <LI><A HREF="bird4.htm" TARGET="screen"> Speckled Grouse </A></LI>
    <LI><A HREF="bird5.htm" TARGET="screen"> Sparrow Hawk </A></LI>
    <LI><A HREF="screen.htm" TARGET="screen"> Main Menu </A></LI>
  </UL>
 </BODY>
</HTML>
```

In the anchor tags of this code, you can see that targets have been specified. Any time the user on these links, he or she will see the respective document in the frame called screen. Figure 10.27 shows a new screen displayed in the frame called screen.

Figure 10.27.
One frame updates another using the TARGET attribute for the anchor tag.

Controlling Two Frames

Now that you've seen how to control one frame, let's look at a way of updating two or more frames based on the interaction with the contents of another frame.

In Figure 10.28 you see what you are going to be creating. You want to modify the previous frames document code so that the menu now controls both the image screen and the text about the particular bird (both frames in the right-hand column). When you understand how it's done, you'll see how easy it really is.

Figure 10.28.
Frames within frames.

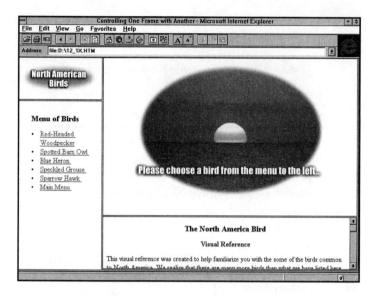

To make this whole thing work you're going to use an indirectly nested frame. In our previous birds example, the frames document alone defined all of the frames and subframes to be arranged on the screen; every subframe was defined in the frames document, so it would be called *directly nested*. You can also make references within a frames document to another frames document; these frames documents are called *indirectly nested*. This is what you will do to create a document that updates two frames simultaneously. The code for your frames document will look like Listing 10.17.

Listing 10.17. The code for indirectly nested frames.

```
<!DOCTYPE "HTML 3.2 //EN">
<HTML>
  <HEAD>
    <TITLE>Controlling Two Frames with Another</TITLE>
  </HEAD>
  <FRAMESET COLS=25%,75%>
    <FRAMESET ROWS=20%,80%>
      <FRAME SRC="sm_ban.htm">
      <FRAME SRC="menu.htm">
    </FRAMESET>
    <FRAME SRC="split.htm" NAME="split">
  <FRAMESET>
</HTML>
```

Let's look closely at this code compared with Figure 10.28. You'll see that it begins by defining two columns, a 25 percent and a 75 percent column. Note that the first 25 percent column is divided into 20 percent and 80 percent rows and that the

HTML files associated with them are listed using the <FRAME> tags immediately after.

The next part is the important part. Notice that the 75 percent column is assigned to the file called SPLIT.HTM. The column should be divided into two rows, yet it has only referenced one HTML file instead of two files. Also note that this column is named SPLIT. The reason it looks this way is because the row definitions for that column are in the file called SPLIT.HTM rather than in the code of this document. This is how you get two frames to update simultaneously: You update the indirectly nested frames document (SPLIT.HTM) rather than focusing on the two files that appear in the subdivided frames. Let's look inside the file called SPLIT.HTM. Its code looks like Listing 10.18.

Listing 10.18. The code for SPLIT.HTM.

```
<!DOCTYPE "HTML 3.2 //EN">
<HTML>
  <HEAD>
    <TITLE>The Split Window</TITLE>
  </HEAD>
  <FRAMESET ROWS=75%,25%>
      <FRAME SRC="s_screen.htm">
      <FRAME SRC="s_text.htm">
  </FRAMESET>
</HTML>
```

Notice in this file that there are definitions for the two rows you saw in the column of the frames document. Through this example, you can see that a frames document can actually be embedded into another frames document. This means that when a user clicks an option in the menu contained in the "master" frames document, it updates the 75 percent column with another frames document, causing both windows to be updated simultaneously. Let's take a look at it graphically.

Note that the overall file is the master frames document and that it has indirectly nested the file called SPLIT.HTM into the right-hand column. SPLIT.HTM contains the row divisions and the <FRAME> references to the content that will appear in the rows in that column. When a user clicks an item in the menu, the master frames document updates the right-hand side of the screen with a new file called SPLIT2.HTM. SPLIT2.HTM contains the same row divisions as SPLIT1.HTM; however, it references two different HTML files. The code for SPLIT2.HTM looks like Listing 10.19.

Listing 10.19. The code for `SPLIT2.HTM`.

```
<!DOCTYPE "HTML 3.2 //EN">
<HTML>
  <HEAD>
    <TITLE>Controlling One Frame with Another</TITLE>
  </HEAD>
  <FRAMESET ROWS=75%,25%>
      <FRAME SRC="s_bird2.htm">
      <FRAME SRC="s_text2.htm">
  </FRAMESET>
</HTML>
```

Clicking an item in the bird menu would update both the picture of the bird and the text associated with it by replacing SPLIT1.HTM in the master frames document with SPLIT2.HTM, as shown Figure 10.29. Note that for each menu item you have three HTML files: the nested frames document (SPLIT1.HTM, SLIT2.HTM, SPLIT3.HTM, and so on), the HTML file that contains the image, and the HTML file that contains the text describing the image. Using this technique requires many more HTML files but is extremely effective in Web pages.

Figure 10.29.
Updating both frames.

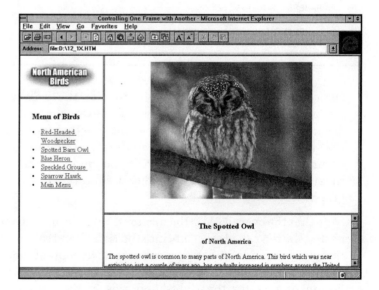

So why do you have to go through all this to update multiple frames? Well, to have one frame update another, you must use the NAME attribute with the <FRAME> tag and the TARGET attribute with the <A HREF> tag. Note that you can only have one TARGET in the <A HREF> tag, but each frame must have a name. To update multiple windows in any other way would require the ability to assign multiple targets for an <A HREF>, which you cannot do. By using an intermediate frames document, you can allow an anchor TARGET to update multiple frames.

Dealing with Nonframe Browsers

To deal with non–frame-capable browsers you must be aware of the <NOFRAMES> tag. The <NOFRAMES> tag allows the developer to specify an alternative body section within a frames document for browsers that cannot utilize frames.

In the examples in this chapter, if you used the <NOFRAMES> tag—which I strongly recommend—it would be inserted into the frames document itself. To include this in the frames document used in the "Controlling Two Frames" section, the code would look like Listing 10.20.

Listing 10.20. The code for using the <NOFRAMES> tag.

```
<!DOCTYPE "HTML 3.2 //EN">
<HTML>
  <HEAD>
    <TITLE>Controlling Two Frames with Another</TITLE>
  </HEAD>
  <FRAMESET COLS=25%,75%>
    <FRAMESET ROWS=20%,80%>
      <FRAME SRC="sm_ban.htm">
      <FRAME SRC="menu.htm">
    </FRAMESET>
    <FRAME SRC="split.htm" NAME="split">
  <FRAMESET>
    <NOFRAMES>
      <BODY>

        ...
        Insert alternative body content here for non-frames browsers.
        ...
      </BODY>
  </NONFRAMES>
</HTML>
```

Summary

In this chapter you have looked at how to use tables to format data and pages, and covered the basics of using frames in your Web documents. Realistically, you can use tables and frames to format just about anything you want from text, graphics, multimedia, and scripted elements. Most developers use tables to format pages that have many in-line graphics and text that must flow consistently and aesthetically together. Frames are generally used to enhance the interactive structure of Web documents. Tables give you far better control over how text flows around graphics as well as how graphics are placed on the screen, but they can require horizontal scrolling if viewed on a smaller screen size than that for which they were designed.

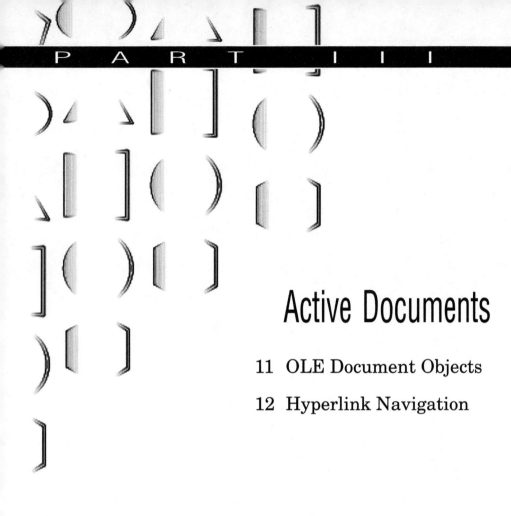

Active Documents

OLE Document Objects

by Dan Wygent

Using the Internet Explorer browser to surf my corporate intranet, I found a hyperlink to a CAD drawing and got curious. To satisfy my curiosity, I clicked the hyperlink. Almost instantly the drawing displayed inside the Internet Explorer (IE) browser window (as shown in Figure 11.1) with merged menus and Imagineer's toolbar.

The file was an Intergraph Imagineer CAD drawing with the .IGR filename extension. Because Imagineer can act as an ActiveX Document, the IE activated Imagineer in a mode Microsoft refers to as *Visual Editing inside of IE*.

I was truly pleased to see Imagineer work as an ActiveX Document (or *DocObject*) just as Microsoft Office's Word for Windows will act as an ActiveX Document. To have a CAD drawing product go ActiveX made me really start thinking ahead. Seeing Imagineer as a DocObject suggests that other products will soon follow suit by providing ActiveX Document capabilities for their file formats.

This fits right in with Microsoft's vision of an Active Desktop, in which every application, every file format, can be displayed as an ActiveX Document. From this vision two questions arise:

- How do you use these capabilities to enhance your product's work flow?
- How do you build an ActiveX Document application quickly and safely?

Figure 11.1.
*Intergraph Imagineer
CAD drawing in Internet
Explorer.*

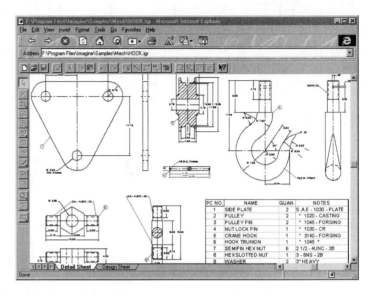

An answer to the work flow question can be illustrated by showing you what Intergraph's Imagineer product can do as an ActiveX Document within Microsoft's Internet Explorer. The second is more a question of basic object-oriented programming (OOP) methodology, now that Microsoft Foundation Classes (MFC) provide ActiveX document server support. You will discover this basic OOP methodology in the context of building on top of an MFC AppWizard-generated project. But before we start into MFC's implementation for ActiveX document server support, we must cover the specifications of the ActiveX Document interfaces.

So to reiterate, first you'll see an example of how to use an ActiveX Document in a work flow. Then I give you some basics on why you should use MFC, followed by ActiveX Document interface specifications. Finally, I will lay out the OOP methodology behind MFC's implementation for ActiveX document server support.

DocObject Work-Flow Possibilities

The key to successfully providing ActiveX Document support in your application is to define a work flow that adds value to your product. The added value should come in the form of ease of use and higher productivity for the user. Let's identify what ActiveX Documents can be used for before we try to define a work flow.

As mentioned in the introduction, an ActiveX Document is displayed in Visual Editing mode inside another application. There are two main ActiveX Document containers in which DocObjects do Visual Editing: The first is the Microsoft Office

Binder, and the other—more important and pertinent—is the IE. The IE, an ActiveX container, can display ActiveX Documents in Visual Editing mode when the user clicks a hyperlinked file whose associated application can act as a DocObject. The IE, and the Office Binder DocObject container, basically provide a host for the ActiveX Document to run and display in. Figures 11.2, 11.3, and 11.4 show how two applications (container and server) merge into a single application. Figure 11.2 shows Imagineer running stand-alone, Figure 11.3 shows IE running stand-alone, and Figure 11.4 shows Imagineer running in the context of the IE. The callouts in Figure 11.4 specify which application is responsible for each portion of the merged graphical user interface.

Figure 11.2.
Imagineer as a stand-alone application.

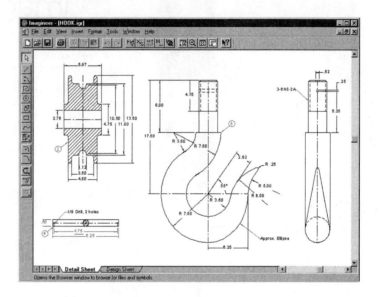

The DocObject server basically provides a way to view or edit a particular file format in the context of another application, an ActiveX Document container. This is similar to the "Open" verb in OLE terminology. As stated in the introduction, Microsoft has coined the term "Visual Editing" to describe this cross between opening and editing with one application in another application's frame. The difference is that a DocObject server will take over the entire viewing window, whereas a regular OLE server will be edited where it is displayed, that is, "in place." Also, the menu merging between the container application and the running ActiveX Document server is slightly different from earlier OLE menu merging. In particular, the help pull-down menu is merged to have submenus for container and server help commands.

This should give you an idea about what a DocObject does. Let's look at an excellent example that illustrates a work flow centered on this Visual Editing technology. Intergraph's Imagineer Technical CAD drawing product leverages not just the DocObject technology, but the other OLE technology made available by ActiveX and the Internet Explorer. To start with, you saw Imagineer embedded inside the IE. But, as you see in Figure 11.5, Imagineer also has an instance of an IE browser window embedded.

Figure 11.3.
IE as a stand-alone application.

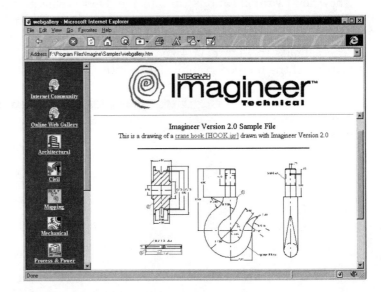

Internet Explorer menus

Imagineer menus

Merged help menu

Internet Explorer toolbars

Figure 11.4.
IE and Imagineer DocObject container and server applications merged.

Imagineer toolbars

Imagineer display

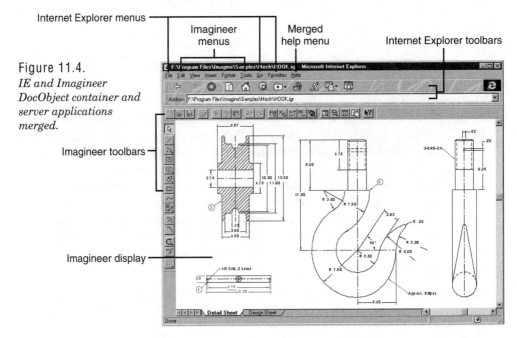

Figure 11.5.
Imagineer DocObject
with IE embedded.

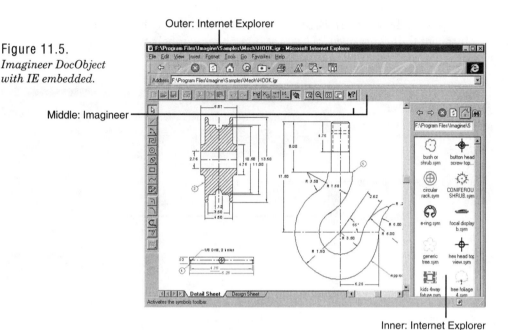

This second embedded IE provides the following capabilities:

- Hyperlinked tutorials
- Symbols and files for file-view drag-and-drop

With the hyperlinked tutorials, the user is slow-walked through creating CAD drawings. As the user moves through each step in the embedded IE, VBScript code drives Imagineer with OLE Automation. In each step, a portion of the tutorial's final CAD drawing is completed until the whole drawing has been created. An intermediate step is illustrated in Figure 11.6.

The work flow in this case is that if you wish to come up to speed quickly, you work through the tutorials needed for the task at hand. Suppose you want to create a line and associate its endpoint with a tangent to a circle; their dimensions will depend on a tangent keypoint on the circle. You just bring up the tutorial for that type of operation, and it seamlessly guides you through the simple steps required for such an operation.

In the next work-flow case, Imagineer symbol files (CAD symbols such as a door or a window) are displayed in the embedded IE. The embedded IE displays these symbols in an IE file view with large icons. Figure 11.7 shows a completed symbol drag-and-drop operation.

The work flow in this case is that you can use the embedded IE to browse your company intranet to find the drawing or symbol you need. When you find what you want, just drag it into Imagineer's drawing window and bingo—you have a completed drawing. It is also likely that there will be external sites on the Internet that contain collections of Imagineer symbols that can just as simply be dragged and dropped into your drawing window.

Figure 11.6.
Embedded IE HTML tutorial drives drawing in Imagineer with VBScript.

Partially completed drawing

HTML tutorial

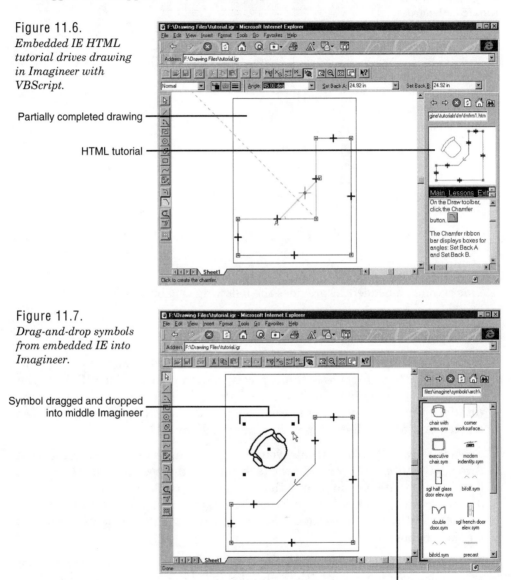

Figure 11.7.
Drag-and-drop symbols from embedded IE into Imagineer.

Symbol dragged and dropped into middle Imagineer

Symbol file view

The whole-work flow idea is to leverage the OLE capabilities given to us by ActiveX in new and useful ways—making our jobs easier and therefore more productive.

Leveraging MFC DocObjects

The current software evolution/revolution seems centered around ActiveX and the Internet. It is expected that many developers will want their products to support the ActiveX Document interfaces. Moreover, in recent years there has been a surge in OLE development. Therefore, many products are already in a good position to add support for ActiveX Document interfaces. This is even easier if your product already leverages off the Visual C++ (VC++) MFCs. Actually the term *leverage* really implies parentage in, or subclassing from, the MFC Document-View architecture (but more on that in the following paragraphs). Right now you need to realize the power and flexibility that the Visual C++ Application Wizard (AppWizard) provides. The AppWizard's MFC framework uses OOP methodologies, allowing you to create an ActiveX Document application with ease.

What you get by using the MFC DocObject framework is an ActiveX Document server application executable built from a set of MFC subclasses created automatically by the AppWizard. Microsoft uses the OOP methodology of subclassing to specify parent classes with DocObject support. The subclasses created by the AppWizard, when you specify you want ActiveX document server support, use MFC's DocObject support classes. If you do not specify ActiveX document server support in the AppWizard, you end up with a different set of parent classes. The MFC's DocObject support classes still define a Document-View architecture that is at the heart of what MFC has given us in the past. The difference is that activation model supports (DocObject) Visual Editing in addition to what has been supported in the past.

This set of parent MFC DocObject-support classes is really the only major difference between a normal MFC AppWizard application and one with DocObject support. To provide DocObject support using the MFC framework, Microsoft basically just added a new set of intermediate (or parent) classes for your application's classes to subclass from. When you select the ActiveX document server option, the AppWizard just uses these MFC DocObject support parent classes for your Document-View parent classes. Figure 11.8 illustrates how these new classes fit in with previous levels of MFC parent classes and what each level of parentage supplies.

Two nice things about using MFC's Document-View architecture are that you are buffered from underlying changes and you get new capabilities with very little development effort. Let me explain these concepts a bit more. The idea of subclassing to get capabilities the parent class provides is not a new one; it is the main idea behind doing OOP.

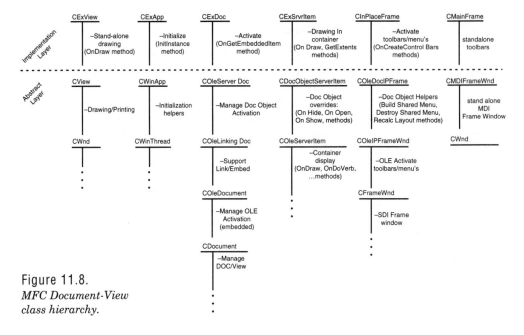

Figure 11.8.
*MFC Document-View
class hierarchy.*

The great thing about subclassing is that if a developer changes the code in the parent class, he or she doesn't (usually) have to change anything in the subclass; the subclass instantly receives the benefits (or detriments if a bug is introduced!) of the new code in the parent class. In addition, if a change is made at an even lower level, the chances are that any required change will be taken care of by one of the intermediate parent classes. Again the developer is buffered from underlying changes.

In the future, when Microsoft adds even more capabilities to the Document-View architecture, you can get those capabilities for little, if any, development cost. Typically in the past, MFC has just added another layer of abstraction by adding a new set of intermediate parent classes. For DocObject support, MFC added a new set of (abstract) parent classes to handle the differences in creation and activation. The new set of MFC classes integrate the additional DocObject-OLE interfaces in this abstraction layer to buffer applications from change. So if you already have an MFC AppWizard-generated application, virtually all you may need to do is change your parent classes to use these new MFC DocObject-support classes.

> ## tip
>
> You should always save your original MFC AppWizard-generated project before making any changes. In addition, write down the answers you gave along the way. The point in doing this is that later on when the AppWizard adds support for another feature, you can go through the wizard, generate a base application with this additional support, and compare the differences with the original. The differences you find will guide you through adding this support manually. Perhaps in some future release of Visual C++, Microsoft might provide an upgrade wizard, but for now it may be wise to practice this tidbit of wizardry on your own!

This OOP methodology of using special parent classes provides the capabilities that you need with little effort in recoding. The Imagineer product uses the same OOP methodology to provide and manage common functionality used by multiple applications. There was a need for specialized initialization and display code, and it was needed by more than one application. What was needed was a set of Document-View subclasses that could act as another layer of abstraction from the MFC classes. That is exactly what was done: The new set of classes provided the common functionality for each application. The new set of classes fits right in between the AppWizard-generated classes and the MFC DocObject-support classes, as illustrated in Figure 11.9.

Figure 11.9.
Imagineer's Document-View class hierarchy.

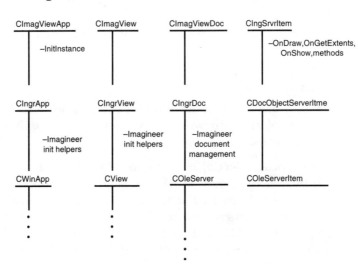

Again, this buffers the various applications from extreme changes in implementation and provides a clear migration path for future enhancements to both MFC's and Imagineer's framework. So all the applications built on top of Imagineer, which is built on top of MFC, will not suffer the slings and arrows of continuous code, or even design, changes.

ActiveX Document Specifications

You should now understand what to do with a DocObject in terms of work flow and have a feel for what MFC provides for DocObject support. Let's look at the specifications for the OLE interfaces required of a DocObject. There are two sides of the DocObject coin: the server side and the container side. Each side has DocObject interfaces that must be implemented. For instance, the IE has implemented the container-side ActiveX Document interfaces, and Imagineer has implemented the server-side ActiveX Document interfaces. Imagineer, being the server, serves up a picture into the browser window of the IE DocObject-container. The server also occupies most of the container's pull-down menu and adds its own toolbars to the frame while it (Imagineer as a DocObject Server) is active. All of this activity occurs through the interfaces described in the following "ActiveX Document Server-Side Interfaces" section.

ActiveX Document Server-Side Interfaces

The interfaces that the ActiveX Document server must implement are listed as follows:

- `IOleDocument`—Represents the document (one-to-one relationship with the document)
- `IOleDocumentView`—Represents a view (many-to-one relationship with the document)
- `IEnumOleDocumentViews`: Represents all of the views of the document (one-to-one relationship with the document). Only required if multiple views are supported.

For a particular DocObject, or document instance, there is one `IOleDocument` object. This `IOleDocument` object, which represents the actual document, is referred to as *the document*. Each document has one or more `IOleDocumentView` interfaces. Each one of these objects represents one view; each of these views is merely a different representation of the data in the document. For instance, the document may be viewed with different levels of detail. One view may have a high level of detail presented by zooming in on a CAD drawing of a house to look at the kitchen with all display layers turned on. Another view might be viewing the entire drawing with only an outline layer of detail displayed. These various views or representations of the data that your DocObject application can present are the views that are specified by the IOleDocumentView interfaces object.

If your server does maintain a set of views, then the IEnumOleDocumentViews interface can be implemented in your DocObject server. The container may initially ask your document for a status flag that indicates, among other things, whether your ActiveX Document server can provide more than one view. The ActiveX Document container may also ask your document to return this document view enumeration, an enumeration of IOleDocumentView interface objects. If your DocObject has only one view, then it returns that one view (IOleDocumentView interface object) and NULL for the enumeration. If multiple views are maintained, then your DocObject application should return its IEnumOleDocumentViews interface object.

---

note

The idea of multiple views really applies to CAD products like Imagineer, but there has not yet been any kind of implementation of a standard GUI to allow the user to enumerate the views. The use of multiple views in DocObject containers appears to be left for specific applications. Neither the IE nor the Office Binder use multiple views (yet). One area where it has been considered is in the OLE for Design and Modeling specification (OLE for D&M). An OLE for D&M server serves up a 3D picture using an OpenGL interface wrapper for the rendering. The IOleDocumentView interface could have been used to allow the user to pick a view to be placed. The OLE for D&M DocObject server would use a small storage in the container to save information describing the view selected. The view information saved could be parameters used to drive the display in OpenGL. This was still under consideration as of this writing. To find out more about OLE for D&M browse http://www.dmac.org. To contact the Design and Modeling council, e-mail owner-dmac@list.intergraph.com and put the word "subscribe" in the body of the e-mail message to subscribe to the OLE for D&M mailing list.

ActiveX Document Container-Side Interfaces

On the client side—the container—there is an interface called IOleDocumentSite. It's just what it sounds like: the server's "view site" within the container. This interface represents where the server's ActiveX Document will "live" in the client's application, or where the DocObject will be placed. The IOleDocumentSite isn't really used in that manner, but rather tells your DocObject application that it's supposed to act like a DocObject and not like the typical OLE 2.0 server object. This makes a difference when the container asks your ActiveX Document to activate; you can tell the container to activate with a particular—favorite or default—view.

Optional Interfaces

There are a few other optional, yet important, DocObject interfaces that are part of the ActiveX DocObject specification. The following is a brief description of each of these interfaces:

- The IPrint interface is used for printing through the client. In the Office Binder, in particular, it's used to create the binder in hard-copy form, which would have a real-life binder layout.

- The IContinueCallback interface, used with the IPrint interface, is designed to facilitate a generalized callback interface for a continue/interrupt paradigm yet to be implemented anywhere but in the IPrint interface.

- The IOleCommandTarget must be used to perform a command handshake between client and server. In the specification, it's referred to as the "command dispatch interface" used for executing and querying commands.

OLE Interfaces

It is important to understand that being an OLE Document Object implies support and use of some standard OLE interfaces. The nice thing about OLE is that, even with the flurry of extensions for specific needs—like DocObjects—everything still fits into the OLE scenario. What I mean is that the scenario for activating a DocObject server is similar to the scenario for activating an OLE server. For instance, the IOleObject and IPersistFile interfaces are used slightly out of context from the way they are used in standard OLE. But the difference really makes sense in the context of what an ActiveX Document needs in order to activate. Specifically, the IPersistFile::Load() method is used, just as in OLE, by the container to supply the filename to the server. On the other hand, the IOleObject::SetClientSite() method is used by OLE Document Objects specifically to obtain the "view site" interface pointer (and therefore to know it is to act as a DocObject).

Although different from typical OLE, these are logical uses of existing OLE technology. And everything still works for all the previous OLE scenarios. From my perspective, this is significant in that OLE interfaces have in the past been thought out carefully to provide a steady migration path for additions to the OLE specification. Adding features like DocObject support without breaking existing OLE applications would be almost inconceivable otherwise.

Interface and Method Specifics

Now that you know the basics, let's cover a few essential details. The following provides a method level of detail of the essential DocObject server-side interfaces:

- IOleDocument This represents the file, or rather the "document." For both the Binder and IE, all QueryInterface() calls go through this interface. It represents the DocObject, is one-to-one with the file, and (possibly) one-to-many with views of the file. It has the following interface methods:

  CreateView() Returns a view object (IOleDocumentView), possibly pre-initializing it with a saved-view state stored in a stream (IStream) passed in. The view site (IOleInPlaceSite) may also be passed in.

  Parameters

  [in] IOleInPlaceSite *pIPSite

  [in] IStream *pstm

  [in] DWORD dwReserved

  [out] IOleDocumentView **ppView

  GetDocMiscStatus() Returns a status flag (actually a bit mask), duplicated in the object's registry under the DocObject key. The client is responsible for using this status to determine how to communicate with the DocObject. The values listed in Table 11.1 can be combined with the | (OR) operator to create the status mask.

  Parameter

  [out] DWORD *pdwStatus

Table 11.1. The values that may be assigned to the status word returned.

DOCMISC *enumerations*	=	*Meaning*	*Interfaces*
DOCMISC_CANCREATEMULTIPLEVIEWS	1	Supports multiple views	IEnumOleDocumentViews interface supported
DOCMISC_SUPPORTCOMPLEXRECTANGLES	2	Can use complex rectangles for scrollbar	IOleDocumentView's SetRectComplex interface scrollbar method not construction implemented

continues

Table 11.1. continued

DOCMISC_CANTOPENEDIT	4	Cannot "open" stand-alone view application	IOleDocumentView's open interface method not implemented
DOCMISC_NOFILESUPPORT	8	Cannot read/ write file	IPersistFile interface not implemented, only IPersistStorage interface implemented

EnumViews() Returns either an enumeration of view objects (IEnumOleDocumentViews) if your DocObject wishes to support more than one view, or a single-view object (IOleDocumentView) if not.

Parameter

[out] IEnumOleDocumentViews **ppEnum

[out] IOleDocumentView **ppView

- IOleDocumentView Represents a single view of your document. If your DocObject supports multiple views, there is a many-to-one relationship of views to document; otherwise, it's a one-to-one relationship. According to the specification, "This interface provides all the necessary operations for a container to manipulate, manage, and activate a view."

SetInPlaceSite() Saves the view site's (IOleInPlaceSite) interface pointer in the container.

Parameter

[in] IOleInPlaceSite *pIPSite

GetInPlaceSite() Returns the view site's (IOleInPlaceSite) interface pointer in the container.

Parameter

[out] IOleInPlaceSite **ppIPSite

GetDocument() Returns an (IUnknown) interface pointer to the DocObject.

Parameter

[out] IUnknown **ppunk

SetRect() Sets the view's rectangle for display inside the container or client.

Parameter

[in] `LPRECT prcView`

`GetRect()`   Returns the view's rectangle for display inside the container or client. An error (`E_UNEXPECTED`) is returned if no view rectangle has yet been set.

Parameter

[out] `LPRECT prcView`

`SetRectComplex()`   Same as `SetRect()` with additional rectangles for vertical and horizontal scrollbars.

Parameters

[in] `LPRECT prcView`

[in] `LPRECT prcHScroll`

[in] `LPRECT prcVScroll`

[in] `LPRECT prcSizeBox`

`Show()`   Either "Show" or "Hide." This is the same idea as OLE's "Show" and "Hide" verbs. To "Show" means to in-place activate the view without a user-interface activation *and* to show, or display, the view window. To "Hide" means to deactivate the user interface *and* hide the view.

Parameter

[in] `BOOL fShow`

`UIActivate()`   Activate or deactivate the user interface. Activating involves the menu merging/sharing, setting up the toolbar and accelerators, and so forth.

Parameter

[in] `BOOL fUIActivate`

`Open()`   Same as OLE's "Open" verb. Invokes the native application as a separate process or in a pop-up window.

Parameter

void—no parameters

`CloseView()`   Close down the view by hiding the view and user interface by calling `Show(FALSE)` and releasing the view site's (`IOleInPlaceSite`) interface pointer in the container by calling `SetInPlaceSite(NULL)`.

Parameter

[in] `DWORD dwReserved`

`SaveViewState()`   Save view-specific data to a stream for use in reinitializing the view at a later time by `ApplyViewState()`. According to the DocObject specification: "Instructs the view to save its state into the given stream, where the state includes properties like the view type, zoom factor, insertion point, and so on."

Parameter

[in] `IStream *pstm`

`ApplyViewState()`   Reinitialize the view from data in a stream previously saved by `SaveViewState()`. According to the DocObject specification: "Instructs a view to reinitialize itself according to the data in a stream that was previously written through `IOleDocumentView::SaveViewState`."

Parameter

[in] `IStream *pstm`

`Clone()`   Create and return another view object exactly like itself.

Parameters

[in] `IOleInPlaceSite *pIPSiteNew`

[out] `IOleDocumentView **ppViewNew`

- `IOleObject`   This is the main interface used by containers to communicate to all OLE objects. The only interface methods of interest to this discussion are `SetClientSite()` and `DoVerb()`.

   `SetClientSite()`   This interface method is called by the container to set up the view site interface pointer. If the view site passed in has the `IOleDocumentSite` interface, then the server is supposed to act as a DocObject (set a Boolean flag) as opposed to an ordinary OLE server.

   `DoVerb()`   For a DocObject Server (a Boolean flag was set in the `SetClientSite()` method), this interface method is called by the container to allow your document to specify which view to use. This view would typically be the default or favorite view.

- `IPersistFile`   This interface is a standard OLE server interface. The `Load()` interface method is called by the client with the filename to use for initialization.

- `IPersistStorage`   This interface, also a standard OLE interface, is used for OLE embedding (as opposed to linking). The container calls the `Save()` interface method with a pointer to a structured storage (`IStorage`) to let the OLE server save—or embed—its data in the container's document. Likewise, the `Load()` interface method is later called to let the OLE server initialize itself from the embedded data.

OOP, MFC, and COM/OLE Methodology

To actually do some useful OOP with COM and OLE, you need to start with MFC and build up. "Building up" means using the OOP methodology of adding at least one layer of abstract classes. An abstract class is used as a parent to an implementation class but is rarely created directly. There is almost always a little extra application-specific functionality to add at your implementation layer to make it work properly. The implementation layer is the top layer of classes that are actually created, or in OOP terminology, *instantiated*. The implementation classes are just what they sound like—the implementation code that your application is directly responsible for implementing. The lower layers of abstract classes provide common functionality and buffer implementation classes from changes at lower layers.

What all of this amounts to on your end is deciding what common functionality you want to provide. If you are developing a suite of applications, then you should provide an additional layer of abstraction. As stated in the previous paragraph, your added abstract classes would provide any common functionality that is needed.

In the case of the Imagineer product, we used this methodology. In our toolkit, we have an additional layer of abstraction where we provide support for reading Imagineer's .IGR file format and provide a common display path. There are many other pieces of common functionality implemented at this highest—or last—layer of abstract classes. This has saved a considerable amount of recoding effort in our suite of applications based on Imagineer. So virtually all a new Imagineer-based application has to do is subclass and go, because most of the implementation specifics have been done in Imagineer's abstract classes.

The nice part of this OOP methodology is that any number of applications can be completed very cost effectively. Simply put, inherit the common functionality provided by layers of abstract classes, and implement anything left over. These layers of abstraction make application building simple, with an added bonus of low maintenance costs. The class definitions of each abstract layer don't change much, if at all. However, the actual code developed for the abstract classes can change to react to changes at lower layers, so the abstract layers effectively buffer the actual applications from changes at those lower levels.

Imagineer Viewer Application

As a proof of concept, I built an Imagineer IGR Viewer application that simply displays Imagineer files. This application was written initially using the MFC AppWizard and specifying the ActiveX document server option. All I did to create a working application was change it to use the abstract classes provided by

Imagineer. Imagineer's abstract classes are, in turn, subclassed from the MFC DocObject support classes. This buys DocObject support plus Imagineer file reading and display support for next to nothing.

To describe the process of creating this viewer application, we will step through creating a new application with the MFC AppWizard. Make certain that you select the ActiveX document server checkbox so that your application uses MFC's DocObject support classes. When you are done, copy this project to a save directory; you can look back at this later to see the minimal changes that had to be made.

The following steps will guide you through the AppWizard. (Make certain you write down the steps you take for future reference. Also save the ReadMe.txt file, which contains related useful information.):

1. Bring up Visual C++, choose File | New (or Ctrl+N), and select the Project Workspace option from the New dialog box. This will bring up the New Project Workspace dialog box. Select MFC AppWizard (exe), enter the name Ex, and click the Create button to start the MFC AppWizard.

2. Check either the "Multiple documents" (default) or "Single document" checkbox depending on which you prefer, then click the Next button. Click the Next button again on this database support step, taking the default of "none."

3. Check the "Both container and server" option, then select the "ActiveX document server" option checkbox. Make sure the "Yes, please" checkbox is selected under the "Would you like support for OLE compound files?" option checkbox; then click the Next button. Figure 11.10 shows how this dialog should look with everything checked off. Note in Figure 11.10 I also have the "OLE automation" and the "OLE controls" option checkboxes selected, but these are not required.

4. Click the "Advanced..." button to bring up the Advanced Options dialog box. On the Document Template Strings option tab in the "File extension" field, enter .DVW. Now click the Close button to close the Advanced Options dialog box, then click the Next button.

5. Click the Next button to go to the next step, taking the defaults for source file comments and using the shared MFC library. If you want to change the default names of classes or source files, this dialog is the place to do it. When you are done changing names, click the Finish button to bring up the New Project Information dialog box. Finally, click the OK button to complete the wizardry.

Figure 11.10.
*MFC AppWizard step 3
of 6 dialog with the
"ActiveX document
server" option checkbox
selected.*

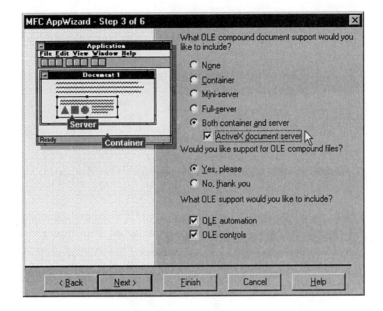

You can compile this application and run it stand-alone without a file, but you
cannot open and display a file yet. Now you have to change the parent class
specified in a few instances and add just a bit of code, and then you'll be able to
open and display files. In addition, you'll be able to Visual Edit as a DocObject in
the IE.

To change the class hierarchy so you can use the Imagineer classes, edit and
change the parent classes as indicated in the following files:

- `Ex.h`: Change parent from `CWinApp` to `CIngrApp`
  class `CExApp : public CIngrApp`

- `ExDoc.h`: Change parent from `COleServerDoc` to `CIngrDoc`
  class `CExDoc : public CIngrDoc`

- `ExView.h`: Change parent from `CView` to `CingrView`
  class `CExView : public CIngrView`

The Imagineer toolkit provides a complete implementation of a "DocObject server
item," subclassed from `CDocObjectServerItem`. The `SrvrItem.cpp` and `SrvrItem.h` files
can be deleted from the project. Wherever the code refers to the AppWizard-
created `CExSrvrItem` class, change to use the `CIngrSrvrItem` instead. The following
code snippets show what the `GetEmbeddedItem()` and `OnGetEmbeddedItem()` methods
look like after this change:

In `exdoc.h`:

```
class CIngrSrvrItem; // forward declaration of class
class CExDoc : public CIngrDoc {
```

```
    .
    .
    .
public:
   CIngrSrvrItem* GetEmbeddedItem()
     {return (CIngrSrvrItem*)COleServerDoc::GetEmbeddedItem();}
     .
     .
     .
}
```

In exdoc.cpp:

```
COleServerItem* CExDoc::OnGetEmbeddedItem() {
   CIngrSrvrItem * pItem = new CIngrSrvrItem (this);
}
```

First we'll discuss what support the MFC framework provides for OLE Document Objects. Then we'll take a peek at what Imagineer's abstraction layer does to complete a Document-View puzzle. This should give you the ability to analyze how to design an abstraction layer of your own.

The three MFC classes that provide most of what we need follow:

- COleServerDoc—Represents the entire document. Manages the DocObject-style Visual Editing (activation).

- CDocObjectServerItem—Overrides OLE verb methods for OLE Document Object–style of Visual Editing. Defers to parent class COleLinkingDoc if not in a DocObject container for normal OLE Edit or Open verbs.

- COleDocIPFrame—Provides helper methods for toolbar/menu creation for DocObject activation.

For DocObject activation, your AppWizard-generated implementation classes are subclassed from these three classes. The Imagineer toolkit classes provide much of the needed implementation that you normally would have to code yourself. In particular, the Imagineer classes provide code for reading/saving files, displaying files, and a platform for adding commands easily. There are four main Imagineer subclasses, which provide the following functionality:

- CIngrDoc—Manages an Imagineer document and provides specific OLE interfaces.

- CIngrSrvrItem—Implements and overrides methods for display as either an OLE or DocObject server in an OLE container.

- CIngrApp—Imagineer-specific initialization helper methods.

- CIngrView—Imagineer-specific window setup.

Using this framework, the IGR Viewer can read and display Imagineer (.IGR) files with very little implementation code of its own. The IGR Viewer is included on the CD that accompanies this book, as well as a variety of Imagineer files (.IGR) and symbols (.SYM) included for you to test the IGR Viewer. In addition, because the IGR Viewer was built to support the ActiveX Document server interfaces, it can be activated in the IE. You will find some HTML files that allow you to perform the DocObject style of Visual Editing. Experience the DocObject-in-IE scenario for yourself and realize its usefulness.

Summary

You should now be able to take the ideas presented in these two abstract framework layers and design a framework layer of your own. In your own abstract framework, you must decide what functionality you need for reading, writing, and displaying your file format. While you are designing this, try to determine how these capabilities relate to initialization, reading, and displaying. The way the Imagineer framework was laid out should help you determine these relationships.

For instance, the initialization usually will go in the CWinApp subclass. Proprietary code for managing and reading your document's file format fits with a COleServerDoc subclass. Specific functionality needed in relation to activation and displaying as a DocObject, in a container such as the Internet Explorer, should be in a subclass of the CDocObjectServerItem class.

When you have an MFC-based application with ActiveX Document support, you must think about a work flow that you can use with your DocObject application. The work flow used by Intergraph's Imagineer CAD product fits right in with Microsoft's vision of an Active Desktop. Tighter integration through the Active Desktop's seamless view makes DocObject server products more useful and therefore more appealing. All DocObject-enabled applications will integrate as if they were one. This ease of use and tight integration provided by DocObject servers and containers is just what users are calling for these days. So get started now on a design using the methodology and work flow presented here. Your DocObject server application will join Microsoft Office, Intergraph Imagineer, and many other DocObject servers on the Active Desktop very soon.

Hyperlink Navigation

by Laurent Poulain

Microsoft has decided to open itself to the Internet/intranet world and has oriented its whole strategy around this key idea. Thus, it is already getting its products ready to fully integrate the Internet philosophy:

- Windows 97 will be document- and Internet-oriented, with the Internet Explorer (that is, the Web browser) merged with the Microsoft Explorer (that is, the file manager). Word documents, HTML (HyperText Markup Language) pages, or any type of document should be accessible through this new Explorer, whether they are on the local hard disk, on a corporate network, or on the Internet. Of course, any HTML page can be visualized by the Explorer.

- ActiveX technology was designed for this purpose, too. ActiveX controls are designed to "activate the Internet," that is, to enhance HTML's rather limited functionality.

- OLE Document object (DocObject for short), part of the ActiveX technology, allows a document to be fully embedded within a container, as if the container were recognizing the DocObject as a native format. Internet Explorer 3.0 (Microsoft's latest state-of-the-art

Web browser) already supports this technology, and thus it can display DocObjects (provided the corresponding DocObject server is on the local hard disk) the same way it displays HTML pages.

So far, what this gives you is an Internet-oriented environment where you can display and edit any OLE Document object stored anywhere on the local hard disk or on the Internet. In Microsoft's vision, DocObject replaces HTML as the standard Web document format. HTML pages are now considered as standard DocObjects (whose server is the Internet Explorer). The next step is to enable every DocObject to provide the functionality that is the base technology of HTML and is responsible for the Web's success—hyperlinking.

A hyperlink is a reference to another location (it can be a document, a file, or whatever else) generally represented in an HTML page by colored, underlined text. The user can access this reference by simply clicking the text. A hyperlink enables you to jump from one document to another through a simple click. Though it was greatly popularized by the World Wide Web, hyperlinking has been used for a long time (for example, in Windows online help).

OLE hyperlinks enable DocObjects or ActiveX controls to fully support hyperlinking. As a result, an OLE hyperlinks-compliant document can contain hyperlinks to other existing documents, objects, and applications. This technology also enables a document to use Web browser features.

Definitions

Before going any further, you may want to review the definition of a few key terms, along with an example:

- Hyperlink reference: A reference or pointer to another file or location. A hyperlink is composed of a hyperlink target and a hyperlink location. A relative reference is just the path from the hyperlink container to the hyperlink target, whereas an absolute reference contains the full path to find the hyperlink target.

- Hyperlink: A hyperlink reference with a friendly name. A hyperlink could be considered as the object that represents what you see; it has a friendly name (what is displayed by the user interface), and a reference (the file pointed by the hyperlink).

- Hyperlink container: A document containing a hyperlink reference. A DocObject or an ActiveX control-enhanced HTML page containing hyperlink reference(s) is an example of containers.

- Friendly name: The string that graphically represents the hyperlink on a hyperlink container. The friendly name is the text generally represented in colored, underlined text.

- Hyperlink target: A hyperlink container/document/file pointed by a hyperlink reference.

- Location (within the target): A hyperlink reference can point to a location within a target (such as a given bookmark of an HTML page). When no location is defined within the target, the hyperlink points to the top of the target document. A hyperlink reference location is coded in HTML as a `#location` (for example, `http://www.mysite.com/hello.html#links`).

- Hyperlink jump: "Jumping" from the hyperlink container that contains the hyperlink to the hyperlink target.

- Internal jump: The jump is within the same document, but generally at a different location within this document (a jump within the same document and at the same location has no interest).

- Hyperlink navigation: Hyperlink jumping.

- Hyperlink frame: The outer frame that contains the hyperlink container. In this chapter, the hyperlink frame will be referenced as a Web browser for better understanding (especially when the hyperlink frame uses a Web browser's specific features).

- Navigation stack: The stack where the hyperlink frame (that is, a Web browser) writes all the hyperlink references of the previous HTML pages/documents/files displayed. Each time the user has the browser display a new page (either by directly specifying its address or through a hyperlink jump), the browser adds the new page on top of the stack. Whenever the user selects the browser's Go Back command, the navigation stack's current hyperlink reference (that is, the hyperlink reference corresponding to the page being displayed) is moved back one element in the stack (the top element of the stack isn't removed, so that the Go Forward command can be used).

- Hyperlink browse context: Portion of code and data (that is, in implementation terms, objects) of the hyperlink frame that manages the navigation stack.

- Fully integrated hyperlink navigation: Hyperlink navigation using the browse context.

- Browse context's current hyperlink: The hyperlink reference whose hyperlink target is being displayed.

In order to make everything clear, take a look at the concrete example shown in Figure 12.1.

Figure 12.1.
*A hyperlink frame
(Internet Explorer)
displaying a hyperlink
container (the HTML
page).*

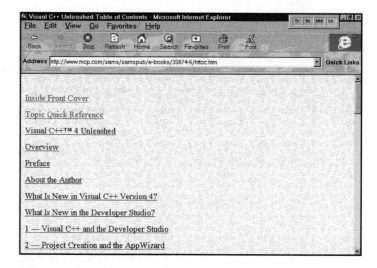

In Figure 12.1, the hyperlink frame (Internet Explorer 3.0) contains a hyperlink container (the HTML page whose Internet address is `http://www.mcp.com/sams/samspub/e-books/30874-6/httoc.htm`, as shown in the Address combo box). This page contains several hyperlinks (represented as the underlined blue or red sentences). These hyperlinks are composed of a friendly name (for example, "Topic: Quick Reference") and of a hyperlink reference (the relative reference `vcuif.htm#13`, as shown in the bottom of the Internet Explorer window). These references point to the hyperlink target (the HTML page whose address is `http://www.mcp.com/sams/samspub/e-books/30874-6/vcuif.htm`). The location within the target is symbolized by `#13` and points to a hyperlink target's bookmark.

The Internet Explorer also manages a navigation stack, which is the list of all the previously displayed HTML pages (the friendly names of the stack's elements are represented in the Go menu bar, as shown in Figure 12.2). This navigation stack is managed by the browse context (some Internet Explorer code and data devoted to this task), thus enabling the user to use buttons such as Back or Forward.

The hyperlink navigation performed between Figures 12.1 and 12.2 is a fully integrated one. Indeed, the navigation stack is updated after the jump, as shown in Figure 12.2.

Figure 12.2.
After the jump, the navigation stack has been updated accordingly, as the menu shows (numbers 1 to 4).

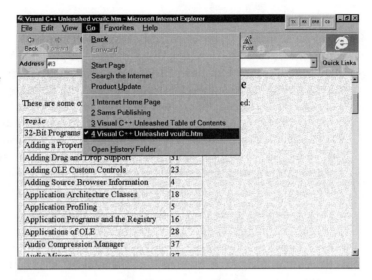

What's the Use of OLE Hyperlinking?

Of course, hyperlinking implementation may not seem to be a big deal. After all, the OLE Hyperlink API provides only the hyperlink jump itself; the programmer still has to determine when to launch it (depending on user-created events).

But OLE hyperlinking first of all allows an easy implementation. Indeed, using the Simple Hyperlink Navigation API, the programmer implements a hyperlink jump with just one function call. Furthermore, using the full Hyperlink Navigation API, the programmer can implement a hyperlink navigation that is fully integrated within an OLE hyperlink-compliant Web browser. That is, when the programmer's OLE hyperlinking-compliant document "jumps" to another document within a hyperlink frame, the jump is notified to the frame's browse context (if any). This means that the navigation stack is updated accordingly, and that the previous document can still be retrieved by using the browser's Go Back command. A hyperlink container can behave like an HTML page. Its URL (Uniform Resource Locator) will be added automatically in the navigation stack.

Furthermore, a hyperlink container can control the hyperlink frame's browse context. It can have access to commands such as Go Back or Go Forward, and even to the entire navigation stack (either for visualization purposes or for modifying one).

For example, take a regular HTML page containing a link to a DocObject. In order to go back to the main page, this DocObject can use the browser's Go Back command rather than displaying a hyperlink pointing to the main page. This avoids adding extra copies of the same hyperlink reference in the navigation stack. If such a feature isn't a big deal for an HTML page because browser-widespread scripting languages such as Visual Basic Script and JavaScript provide functions for these types of tasks, OLE hyperlinking is the only way for a DocObject to access these Web browser's commands. (Indeed, a DocObject can't call Visual Basic Script or JavaScript code.) Furthermore, an ActiveX control may want to directly implement such a feature instead of calling some external script code.

But OLE hyperlinking provides more functionality than just using the browser's popular commands. Indeed, it provides access to the browser's navigation stack. For example, a DocObject (or an ActiveX control enhanced HTML page) can retrieve the navigation stack, filter its elements that comply with a given set of specifications, and show them to the user. When the user chooses a given hyperlink, the DocObject just sends it to the Web browser (actually, it sends only the hyperlink position within the navigation stack). The browse context will just move the current hyperlink pointer in the stack, without having to reload the referenced hyperlink target.

Hyperlink Navigation API and Simple Hyperlink Navigation API

OLE hyperlinks come with two APIs: the Hyperlink Navigation API and the Simple Hyperlink Navigation API. Both have their advantages and their drawbacks and are used for different purposes.

Simple Hyperlink Navigation API

The Simple Hyperlink Navigation API is a reduced set of the full Hyperlink Navigation API and allows basic hyperlinking programming on the hyperlink container side (there is no such thing as simple hyperlinking on the hyperlink frame side). This API is the minimum requirement a DocObject or ActiveX control needs to implement OLE hyperlinking. Even people who are interested in the full Hyperlink Navigation API should first have a look at this API. The advantages of this API are

- It is easy to implement: The API is reduced to a few functions, is not difficult to use, and is very fast to implement.

- It is not subject to change: This API is not in flux like the full Hyperlink Navigation API, which can be changed by Microsoft at any time. Actually, Microsoft currently encourages developers to use the Simple Hyperlink Navigation API.

The Simple Hyperlink Navigation API consist of six global functions:

```
HlinkSimpleNavigateToString()
HlinkSimpleNavigateToMoniker()
HlinkNavigateString()
HlinkNavigateMoniker()
HlinkGoBack()
HlinkGoForward()
```

It also includes an enumeration:

```
typedef enum tagHLNF {
    HLNF_INTERNALJUMP,
    HLNF_OPENINNEWWINDOW
} HLNF;
```

A Word About the Examples

Because this API is simple, an example is given after each function description. All the examples assume that they are executed within an OLE Document object (or DocObject). In order to better understand the code, first review some of the argument types that may be required:

- IUnknown*: Described as "a pointer to the document or object initiating the hyperlink," this argument may sometimes be optional (that is, it can take a NULL value) and sometimes not. Contrary to what you might think, this argument is not the this pointer cast into an IUnknown* type. It must be a pointer to any interface of the document. Remember that in the ActiveX philosophy, you have a hand on an object if you got a pointer to just one of its interfaces, whatever it is (you can always retrieve the desired interface by calling the IUnknown::QueryInterface() interface member function). In the examples, the value passed is (IUnknown*)&m_xOleDocument. Indeed, assuming the code is executed within a DocObject, an IOleDocument interface is supposed to be implemented. It means a class is defined to implement this interface, along with a member variable defined as an IOleDocument, which will contain the object interface. If the class is named XOleDocument, the variable is named m_xOleDocument.

- LPCWSTR: This is a string. However, it is not a regular ASCII string, but a Unicode, character string of 16 bits (LPCWSTR is defined as const unsigned short*). You can't pass a regular C text string. You first have to convert it into a Unicode text string by calling ToWideChars(). Note that there are several other ways to convert ANSI text into Unicode text.

- `Moniker*`: The creation of a moniker isn't detailed here, as it would mean implementing a whole class. The examples just refer to a `moniker` variable, defined as a `Moniker*`.

HlinkSimpleNavigateToString()

This function performs a hyperlink jump. The hyperlink target is determined by a Unicode string.

```
HRESULT HlinkSimpleNavigateToString(LPCWSTR, LPCWSTR, LPCWSTR,
                                    IUnknown*, IBindCtx*,
                                    IBindStatusCallBack*,
                                    DWORD, DWORD);
```

Argument type	Description
LPCWSTR	Hyperlink target. A NULL value means the navigation is an internal jump.
LPCWSTR	Location within the hyperlink target (optional, may be NULL).
LPCWSTR	Frame within the hyperlink target (optional, may be NULL).
IUnknown*	The IUnknown pointer to the document that is initiating the hyperlink. A NULL value means the hyperlink was initiated from a non–OLE-compliant application.
IBindCtx*	The bind context that will be used for any moniker binding during this navigation.
IBindStatusCallback*	The bind status callback that will be used for any asynchronous moniker binding during this navigation. A NULL value means that the hyperlink initiator isn't interested in having information such as status or navigation progress.
DWORD	HLNF enumeration values.
DWORD	Reserved for a future use. Must be zero.

Returned value	Meaning
S_OK	The operation succeeded.
E_INVALIDARG	Some arguments are invalid.
Other	Other error.

```
HRESULT hr;
WCHAR text[21];
MultiByteToWideChar(CP_ACP, MB_PRECOMPOSED,
                    "D:\\download\\nt40.htm", 21, text, 21);
```

```
hr = HlinkSimpleNavigateToString(text, NULL, NULL,
                                 (IUnknown*)&m_xOleDocument,
                                 NULL, NULL, 0, 0);
```

HlinkSimpleNavigateToMoniker()

This function performs a hyperlink jump. Contrary to HlinkSimpleNavigateToString(), the hyperlink target is not set by a text string, but by a moniker.

```
HRESULT HlinkSimpleNavigateToMoniker(IMoniker*, LPCWSTR, LPCWSTR,
                                     IUnknown*, IBindCtx*,
                                     IBindStatusCallBack*,
                                     DWORD, DWORD);
```

Argument type	Description
IMoniker*	Hyperlink target. A NULL value means the navigation is within a document.
LPCWSTR	Location within the hyperlink target (optional, may be NULL).
LPCWSTR	Frame within the hyperlink target (optional, may be NULL).
IUnknown*	The IUnknown pointer to the document that is initiating the hyperlink. A NULL value means the hyperlink was initiated from a non–OLE-compliant application.
IBindCtx*	The bind context that will be used for any moniker binding during this navigation.
IBindStatusCallback*	The bind status callback that will be used for any asynchronous moniker binding during this navigation. A NULL value means that the hyperlink initiator isn't interested in having information such as status or navigation progress.
DWORD	HLNF enumeration values.
DWORD	Reserved for a future use. Must be zero.

Returned value	Meaning
S_OK	The operation succeeded.
E_INVALIDARG	Some arguments are invalid.
Other	Other error.

```
HRESULT hr;

hr = HlinkSimpleNavigateToMoniker(moniker, NULL, NULL,
                                  (IUnknown*)&m_xOleDocument,
                                  NULL, NULL, 0, 0);
```

HlinkNavigateString()

This function is a macro that expands itself into a `HlinkSimpleNavigateToString()` call, where most arguments are NULL.

```
HRESULT HlinkNavigateString(IUnknown*, LPCWSTR);
```

Argument Type	Description
IUnknown*	The IUnknown pointer to the document that is initiating the hyperlink. A NULL value means the hyperlink was initiated from a non-OLE-compliant application.
LPCWSTR	Hyperlink target.

Returned Value	Meaning
S_OK	The operation succeeded.
E_INVALIDARG	Some arguments are invalid.
Other	Other error.

```
HRESULT hr;
WCHAR text[21];
MultiByteToWideChar(CP_ACP, MB_PRECOMPOSED,
                "D:\\download\\nt40.htm", 21, text, 21);

hr = HlinkNavigateString((IUnknown*)&m_xOleDocument, text);
```

HlinkNavigateMoniker()

This function is a macro that expands itself into a `HlinkSimpleNavigateToMoniker()` call, where most arguments are NULL.

```
HRESULT HlinkNavigateMoniker(IUnknown*, IMoniker*);
```

Argument type	Description
IUnknown*	The IUnknown pointer to the document that is initiating the hyperlink. A NULL value means the hyperlink was initiated from a non–OLE-compliant application.
IMoniker*	Hyperlink target.

Returned value	Meaning
S_OK	The operation succeeded.
E_INVALIDARG	Some arguments are invalid.
Other	Other error.

```
HRESULT hr;

hr = HlinkNavigateString((IUnknown*)&m_xOleDocument, moniker);
```

HlinkGoBack()

This function asks the hyperlink frame (that is, the Web browser) to jump backward in the navigation stack. Here, only the argument that points to the document or object initiating the hyperlink jump, cannot be NULL. Furthermore, this function will work only if this same document or object is contained in an OLE hyperlink-compliant container, such as Internet Explorer 3.0.

```
HRESULT HlinkGoBack(IUnknown*);
```

Argument type	Description
IUnknown*	Pointer to the document or object initiating the hyperlink jump.

Returned value	Meaning
S_OK	The operation succeeded.
E_INVALIDARG	The argument is invalid.
Other	Other error.

```
HRESULT hr;

hr = HlinkGoBack((IUnknown*)&m_xOleDocument);
```

HlinkGoForward()

This function asks the hyperlink frame (that is, the Web browser) to jump forward in the navigation stack. Here, the only argument that points to the document or object initiating the hyperlink jump cannot be NULL. Furthermore, this function will work only if this same document or object is contained in an OLE hyperlink-compliant container, such as Internet Explorer 3.0.

```
HRESULT HlinkGoBack(IUnknown*);
```

Argument type	Description
IUnknown*	Pointer to the document or object initiating the hyperlink jump.

Returned value	Meaning
S_OK	The operation succeeded.
E_INVALIDARG	The argument is invalid.
Other	Other error.

```
HRESULT hr;

hr = HlinkGoForward((IUnknown*)&m_xOleDocument);
```

Hyperlink Navigation API

The Hyperlink Navigation API allows many more possibilities than the Simple Hyperlink Navigation API does. It is composed of several global functions, enumerations, structures, and interfaces. As a result, the HLINK.H file (the hyperlink API include file) from the ActiveX SDK is different from the file provided with Visual C++ 4.1. This means a given program may not compile when the HLINK.H is changed (for example, when the Visual C++ HLINK.H file is replaced by ActiveX SDKs), even if the changes are only minor. You can even expect this file to change during the next Visual C++ releases.

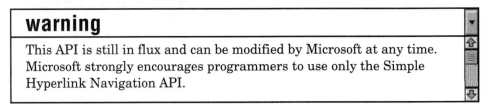

warning

This API is still in flux and can be modified by Microsoft at any time. Microsoft strongly encourages programmers to use only the Simple Hyperlink Navigation API.

OLE Hyperlink Components

In order to implement the Hyperlink Navigation API, the programmer first needs to understand which are OLE Hyperlink components and how they interact with each other. OLE Hyperlink is composed of two programs: the hyperlink frame program and the hyperlink container program. Typically, the hyperlink frame program is a DocObject client and the hyperlink container program is a DocObject server (be careful not to mix a Hyperlink container and a DocObject container). Thus, the frame program can display not only its own native format, but also multiple hyperlink container formats.

The Hyperlink Frame Program

This program manages an outer frame that contains and shows hyperlink container(s). It is called through its IHlinkTarget interface, which must be supported by the class derived from COleClientItem.

This program also contains the hyperlink browse context. This component manages the navigation stack; it notes every hyperlink jump and stores all the containers' references into the stack. It can also allow the user to look at the stack and go to specific hyperlink references within it. The browse context is controlled through its unique IHlinkBrowseContext interface, which must be supported by the class implementing it. This class is typically created for this sole purpose and has its interface pointer given away through the hyperlink frame.

The Hyperlink Container Program

This program manages the hyperlink document being displayed. It can manage either a hyperlink container (that is, a document being displayed) or a hyperlink target (that is, a document pointed at by a hyperlink). For example, the hyperlink container program corresponding to HTML pages is the OLE server part of the Internet Explorer.

This program doesn't always need to implement interfaces. Indeed, it is controlled through the standard OLE and DocObject interfaces. However, if the program wants its documents to be included in the navigation stack by the browse context after a hyperlink jump, it must implement the IHlinkTarget interface.

The hyperlink target can also support the IPersistMoniker interface rather than IPersistFile. Thus, the target can support asynchronous download as a persistence mechanism.

The hyperlink container, as its name implies, contains some hyperlinks and hyperlink sites. A hyperlink site is used by the hyperlink to get the container moniker. Thus, the hyperlink can notice an internal jump by comparing the target moniker to the container moniker and perform the necessary optimizations.

Hyperlinks manage the reference to a document (or more generally, any kind of application/document/file). A hyperlink is composed of the hyperlink target (stored as a moniker) and the location within this target (stored as a string). The graphical representation of the hyperlink (such as its friendly name) is up to the container itself. A hyperlink is controlled through its IHlink interface.

How Everything Works Together

This section examines how OLE hyperlinking works when a hyperlink navigation occurs. Both simple hyperlink navigation and fully integrated hyperlink navigation will be detailed. Both types of navigation are basically the same; the last type of navigation just performs some extra work in order to have the browse context integrate the hyperlink references that are navigated to. The following section describes the major steps of hyperlink navigation. The numbers indicate the order in which the steps are executed over time and are common to both types of navigation.

As you can see, the hyperlink container calls the hyperlink frame, sending it the desired hyperlink reference interface. The frame then calls the hyperlink reference, which calls the hyperlink target. Then, the target notifies the frame that the navigation successfully performed. This notification is useful for asynchronous navigation, where it is the only way for the frame to know when the navigation is over.

How Simple Hyperlinking Navigation Works

This section describes how the different components interact when a simple hyperlink jump occurs. Of course, only the global function call must be implemented (provided the hyperlink frame already exists). In this example, neither the hyperlink container nor the hyperlink target uses (or is even aware of) the frame's browse context.

- The hyperlink container: The hyperlink navigation begins when the hyperlink container calls the global `HlinkSimpleNavigateToString()` Simple Hyperlinking Navigation API function, which calls the hyperlink frame's `IHlinkFrame::Navigate()` interface member function. It is up to the hyperlink container to determine whenever it must launch any hyperlink jump, as the container is called by OLE when an event (for example a mouse click on colored, underlined text representing a hyperlink) occurs within the container's view.

- `IHlinkFrame::Navigate()`: The frame can perform tasks such as asking confirmation, displaying a progress indicator, managing its hyperlinks history, and so forth. Finally, it calls the hyperlink's `IHlink::Navigate()` interface member function.

- `IHlink::Navigate()`: The hyperlink gives control to the hyperlink target by calling its `IHlinkTarget::Navigate()` interface member function.

- `IHlinkTarget::Navigate()`: The hyperlink target is passed the location string and interprets it (which means the interpretation is at its own discretion). Finally, the target notifies the frame that the hyperlink jump was performed by calling the `HlinkOnNavigate()` global function, which will call the frame's `IHlinkFrame::OnNavigate()` member function.

- `IHlinkFrame::OnNavigate()`: The frame is notified that the navigation is over and can now update its window.

How Fully Integrated Hyperlink Navigation Works

This kind of navigation allows the integration of navigated hyperlinks within the browse context. All tasks described in the previous section are supposed to be performed here, too.

- The hyperlink container: In order to start the navigation, the container needs three interfaces: the hyperlink to navigate interface, the hyperlink frame's interface, and its browse context interface.

  The hyperlink may be either created (through the `HlinkCreateFromData()`, `HlinkCreateFromMoniker()`, or `HlinkCreateFromString()` global functions) or loaded from persistent storage (through the `OleLoadFromStream()` function).

The container can then associate it with a hyperlink site by calling its `IHlink::SetHlinkSite()` member function.

The container either retrieves its frame's browse context through the `IHlinkFrame::GetBrowseContext()` member function or creates it by calling the `HlinkCreateBrowseContext()` global function. The container registers itself with the browse context by calling the `IHlinkBrowseContext::Register()` member function. It then calls `IHlinkBrowseContext::OnNavigateHlink()` to tell the browse context to add the hyperlink to the navigation stack.

Finally, it calls the `HlinkNavigate()` global function, which calls the frame's `IHlinkFrame::Navigate()` function.

- `IHlinkFrame::Navigate()`: As with the Simple Hyperlink Navigation API, this function calls the hyperlink's `IHlink::Navigate()` function.

- `IHlink::Navigate()`: If passed the `HLNF_USERBROWSECONTEXTCLONE` value, the hyperlink clones the browse context by calling `IHlinkBrowseContext::Clone()`.

For the sake of performance, the hyperlink must determine whether it is in the presence of an internal jump by comparing the moniker it was passed and the container's moniker returned by the hyperlink site. If the jump is internal, the hyperlink target's interface is retrieved by asking the hyperlink site to return the `IHlinkTarget` interface of the container (as the container is the target).

If the jump is not an internal one, the function must call the target's moniker `Imoniker::BindToObject()` function to retrieve the target interface, and then call `IHlinkTarget::SetBrowseContext()`, so that the target registers with the browse context.

Eventually, it calls the `IHlinkTarget::Navigate()` function to perform the jump within the target.

- `IHlinkTarget::SetBrowseContext()`: This function is called for a non-internal jump. The target must first revoke any registration with a browse context by calling `IHlinkBrowseContext::Revoke()` and `IHlinkBrowseContext::Release()`. Then, the target must register with the browse context passed as an argument by calling `IHlinkBrowseContext::AddRef()` and `IHlinkBrowseContext::Register()`.

- `IHlinkTarget::Navigate()`: This function is called to perform the internal jump part of the hyperlink navigation (even if it is the whole navigation). It is up to the target to interpret the location and to display itself properly. It then calls the `IHlinkOnNavigate()` global function to notify the hyperlink frame that the navigation has performed. This function calls `IHlinkFrame::OnNavigate()` and `IHlinkBrowseContext::OnNavigateHlink()`.

- `IHlinkFrame::OnNavigate()`: The hyperlink frame now knows that the navigation is over.
- `IHlinkBrowseContext::OnNavigateHlink()`: Finally, the browse context is notified that the hyperlink navigation is over, so that it can update the navigation stack accordingly.

The Enumerations/Structures

The interfaces of the Hyperlink Navigation API often use enumerations and/or structures either as input or output arguments. Some of the following enumerations can take several values; some can take only a single value.

The HLNF Enumeration

These values give some information about a hyperlink navigation.

Name	Description
HLNF_INTERNALJUMP	Indicates that the navigation is an internal jump. This value allows some internal jump-specific optimization, such as avoiding re-loading the document. The system will have the hyperlink automatically send this value to IHlink::Navigate() if the moniker is NULL.
HLNF_NAVIGATINGBACK	Indicates that the navigation occurs because the Go Back command was selected. The position in the navigation stack should be moved back one element, without altering the stack. The hyperlink frame and hyperlink container send this value to IHlink::Navigate().
HLNF_NAVIGATINGFORWARD	Indicates that the navigation occurs because the Go Forward command was selected. The position in the navigation stack should be moved forward one element, without altering the stack. The hyperlink frame and hyperlink container send this value to IHlink::Navigate().
HLNF_USERBROWSECONTEXTCLONE	When IHlink::Navigate() is passed this value, it should clone the browse context passed-in argument by calling IHlinkBrowseContext::Clone(). This new browse context will always be used during the rest of the hyperlink navigation.

Name	Description
HLNF_OFFSETWINDOWORG	When IHlinkTarget::Navigate() is passed this value, it should alter its window position according to the information contained by the HLBWINFO returned by HlinkBrowseContext:: GetBrowseContextWindowContext(). This value is generally used with the HLNF_USERBROWSECONTEXTCLONE value to implement the Open in New Window command.
HLNF_OPENINNEWWINDOW	Using this value is like using both HLNF_USERBROWSECONTEXTCLONE and HLNF_OFFSETWINDOWORG values.
HLNF_CREATENOHISTORY	When IHlinkBrowseContext::OnNavigateHlink() is passed this value, it should not add the hyperlink to the navigation stack.
HLNF_NAVIGATINGTOSTACKITEM	Same as HLNF_CREATENOHISTORY. Furthermore, IHlinkBrowseContext::OnNavigateHlink() should set the passed hyperlink as the browse context's current hyperlink. This value is used when the user decides to jump to a hyperlink from the navigation stack: though the navigation occurs, the navigation stack should not be altered—only the position on the stack.

The HLINKWHICHMK Enumeration

A single value from this enumeration is used by the IHlinkSite::GetMoniker() interface member function to know whether it must return a moniker for the container or a base moniker specific to the site.

Name	Description
HLINKWHICHMK_CONTAINER	Returns the moniker for the hyperlink container corresponding to a particular hyperlink site.
HLINKWHICHMK_BASE	Returns the base moniker corresponding to a particular hyperlink site.

The HLINKGETREF Enumeration

A single value from this enumeration is used by the IHlink::GetMonikerReference() and IHlink::GetStringReference() interface functions to know whether they must return the absolute or relative reference for the hyperlink target.

Name	Description
HLINKGETREF_DEFAULT	Returns the default reference for hyperlink target.
HLINKGETREF_ABSOLUTE	Returns the absolute reference for hyperlink target.
HLINKGETREF_RELATIVE	Returns the relative reference for hyperlink target.

The HLFNAMEF Enumeration

A single value from this enumeration is used by IHlink::GetFriendName() to know which type of friendly name to return.

Name	Description
HLFNAMEF_TRYCACHE	Returns the friendly name that is cached on the Hlink interface object.
HLFNAMEF_TRYFULLTARGET	Returns the full display name of the hyperlink target.
HLFNAMEF_TRYPRETTYTARGET	Returns a beautiful version of the full display name of the hyperlink target.
HLFNAMEF_TRYWIN95SHORTCUT	Returns the version of the full display name of the hyperlink target without any path or extension.
HLFNAMEF_DEFAULT	Returns the cached friendly name.

The HLINKMISC Enumeration

A single value of this enumeration is returned by IHlink::GetMiscStatus() to tell whether a hyperlink is relative or absolute.

Name	Description
HLINKMISC_ABSOLUTE	The hyperlink contains an absolute reference to the hyperlink target.
HLINKMISC_RELATIVE	The hyperlink contains a relative reference to the hyperlink target.

The HLITEM Structure

This structure is used by the IEnumHLITEM interface, which belongs to enumerators returned by IHlinkBrowseContext::EnumNavigationStack().

Name	Type	Description
uHLID	ULONG	The hyperlink ID.
szFriendlyName	LPWSTR	The friendly name of the hyperlink.

The HLBWIF Enumeration

Values from this enumeration are passed in an HLBWINFO structure, which is associated with each browse context. The HLIBWINFO structure is accessed by calling IHlinkBrowseContext::GetBrowseWindowContext() and IHlinkBrowseContext:: SetBrowseWindowContext().

Name	Description
HLBWIF_HASFRAMEWNDINFO	The browse context has available frame-level window positioning information.
HLBWIF_HASDOCWNDINFO	The browse context has available document-level window positioning information.
HLBWIF_FRAMEWNDMAXIMIZED	The browse context's frame-level windows should appear maximized. Always used with HLBWIF_HASFRAMEWNDINFO.
HLBWIF_DOCWNDMAXIMIZED	The browse context's document-level windows should appear maximized. Always used with HLBWIF_HASDOCWNDINFO.

The HLBWINFO Structure

This structure contains information about the locations and sizes of frame-level and document-level windows within a browse context. This structure is returned from the browse context by calling IHlinkBrowseContext::GetBrowseWindowContext() and is then sent to the browse context by calling IHlinkBrowseContext:: SetBrowseWindowContext(). This structure is used by a hyperlink target during IHlinkTarget::Navigate() so it can reposition its user interface.

Name	Type	Description
cbSize	ULONG	Size of the structure in bytes.
grfHLBWIF	DWORD	HLBWIF enumeration values.
rcFramePos	RECTL	If grfHLBWIF has the FLBWIF_HASFRAMEWNDINFO value, this variable contains the rectangle in screen coordinates of current frame-level windows within the browse context. If grfHLBWIF has the FLBWIF_FRAMEWNDMAXIMIZED value, this means the frame-level windows are currently maximized, and rcDocPos represents the non-maximized size of the document-level windows.

continues

Name	Type	Description
rcDocPos	RECTL	If grfHLBWIF has the FLBWIF_HASDOCWNDINFO value, this contains the rectangle in screen coordinates of current document-level windows within the browse context. If grfHLBWIF has the FLBWIF_DOCWNDMAXIMIZED value, this means the document-level windows are currently maximized, and rcFramePos represents the non-maximized size of the document-level windows.

The HLID Constants

Some specific hyperlinks are identified by an HLID constant rather than by an IHlink interface pointer. Thus, the hyperlink frame can perform specific optimization.

Name	Description
HLID_PREVIOUS	Indicates the hyperlink before the current one in the navigation stack. If such a hyperlink does not exist (either the current hyperlink is the first one in the navigation stack or the stack is empty), methods such as IHlinkBrowseContext::GetHlink() return NULL and E_FAIL.
HLID_NEXT	Indicates the hyperlink past the current one in the navigation stack. If such a hyperlink does not exist (either the current hyperlink is the last one in the navigation stack or the stack is empty), methods such as IHlinkBrowseContext::GetHlink() return NULL and E_FAIL.
HLID_CURRENT	Indicates the current hyperlink in the navigation stack. This value can be used when the hyperlink has to be physically navigated again. For example, a page can have to be reloaded (to implement a Reload command), a sound sample may have to be replayed, and so on.
HLID_STACKBOTTOM	Indicates the first hyperlink of the navigation stack. If the stack is empty, methods such as IHlinkBrowseContext::GetHlink() return NULL and E_FAIL.

Name	Description
HLID_STACKTOP	Indicates the last hyperlink of the navigation stack. If the stack is empty, methods such as IHlinkBrowseContext::GetHlink() return NULL and E_FAIL.

The HLQF Enumeration

A single value of this enumeration is used by IHlinkBrowseContext::QueryHlink() to know which kind of hyperlink test it must perform.

Name	Description
HLQF_ISVALID	Instructs to test the validity of a particular hyperlink.
HLQF_ISCURRENT	Instructs to test whether a particular hyperlink is the browse context's current hyperlink.

The HLSR Enumeration

A single value from this enumeration is used by the HlinkGetSpecialReference() or HlinkSetSpecialReference() global functions to know which value to set or get.

Name	Description
HLSR_HOME	Hyperlink reference to the user's home page.
HLSR_SEARCHPAGE	Hyperlink reference to the user's search page.
HLSR_HISTORYFOLDER	Hyperlink reference to the user's history folder page.

The CF_HYPERLINK Clipboard Format

This format consists of a serialized hyperlink. When used with IDataObject, this format is passed under TYMED_ISTREAM or TYMED_HGLOBAL mediums. The OleSaveToStreamEx() function stores a hyperlink into an IStream, provided the hyperlink supports the OLE IPersistStream interface.

The Global Functions

The full Hyperlink Navigation API provides a set of global functions. This allows the creation of a hyperlink from different types of data, and the initiation of a hyperlink navigation.

HlinkCreateBrowseContext()

This function creates an empty browse context instance, whose interface is returned through the last argument.

```
HRESULT HlinkCreateBrowseContext(IUnknown*, REFIID, void**);
```

Argument type	Description
IUnknown*	IUnknown interface of the object controlling the new browse context. A NULL value (the most common) means that the browse context isn't aggregated.
REFIID	Which type of browse context's interface to return, typically IID_IHlinkBrowseContext.
void**	Where to send the browse context REFIID interface.

Returned value	Meaning
S_OK	The browse context was created successfully.
E_OUTOFMEMORY	Not enough memory for creating the browse context.
E_INVALIDARG	At least one argument is invalid.

HlinkQueryCreateFromData()

This function determines whether a hyperlink can be created from the IDataObject interface passed-in argument—that is, if

- The IDataObject offers CF_HYPERLINK on either TYMED_ISTREAM or TYMED_HGLOBAL.
- The IDataObject offers Win95 shortcut data (this format isn't yet determined).

Here, the result is returned by the function itself, not through any argument.

```
HRESULT HlinkQueryCreateFromData(IDataObject*);
```

Argument type	Description
IDataObject*	The source data interface.

Returned value	Meaning
S_OK	Yes, a hyperlink can be created from the given IDataObject.
E_OUTOFMEMORY	No, a hyperlink can't be created because the IDataObject doesn't fulfill the requirements.
E_INVALIDARG	The argument is invalid.

HlinkCreateFromData()

This function creates a hyperlink from the `IDataObject` passed as the first argument. The created hyperlink is returned through the last argument.

This function can be called after a cut-and-paste operation from the Clipboard, in which case the `IDataObject` interface is retrieved by calling `OleGetClipboard()`. It can be also called after a drag-and-drop operation, in which case the `IDataObject` interface is retrieved by calling `IDropTarget::Drop()`, where the `IDropTarget` interface is the one registered to the target drag-and-drop window.

```
HRESULT HlinkCreateFromData(IDataObject*, IHlinkSite*, DWORD,
                            IUnknown*, REFIID, void**);
```

Argument type	Description
IDataObject*	Source data from which the hyperlink must be created.
IHlinkSite*	The hyperlink site associated with the new hyperlink.
DWORD	Additional hyperlink site data.
IUnknown*	IUnknown interface of the object controlling the new hyperlink. A NULL value (the most common) means the hyperlink object isn't aggregated.
REFIID	Which hyperlink interface the function must return, generally IID_IHlink.
void**	Where to send the hyperlink's desired interface.

Returned value	Meaning
S_OK	The hyperlink was successfully created.
E_NOINTERFACE	The hyperlink does not support the desired interface.
E_INVALIDARG	At least one argument is invalid.

HlinkCreateFromMoniker()

This function creates a hyperlink from a moniker whose `IMoniker` interface is passed as the first argument. The created hyperlink is returned through the last argument. This function is faster than `HlinkCreateFromString()` if the moniker is already defined.

It is generally called when the program wants to create a hyperlink from an already existing hyperlink. It can retrieve the already existing hyperlink moniker's interface and target location through `Hlink::GetMonikerReference()` and its friendly name through `GetFriendlyName()`.

```
HRESULT HlinkCreateFromMoniker(IMoniker*, LPCWSTR, LPCWSTR,
                               IHlinkSite*, DWORD, IUnknown*,
                               REFIID, void**);
```

Argument type	Description
IMoniker*	The interface of the moniker from which the hyperlink must be created.
LPCWSTR	Location of the new hyperlink within the hyperlink target. May not be NULL.
LPCWSTR	The new hyperlink's friendly name.
IHlinkSite*	The hyperlink site to be associated with the hyperlink.
DWORD	Additional hyperlink site data.
IUnknown*	IUnknown interface of the object controlling the new hyperlink. A NULL value (the most common) means the hyperlink object isn't aggregated.
REFIID	The hyperlink's interface to be returned, generally IID_IHlink.
void**	Where to return the desired hyperlink interface.

Returned value	Meaning
S_OK	The hyperlink was created successfully.
E_INVALIDARG	At least one argument is invalid.

HlinkCreateFromString()

This function creates a hyperlink from strings representing the hyperlink target, the location within this target, and the friendly name. The created hyperlink is returned through the last argument. This function is slower than HlinkCreateFromMoniker() because it must parse the text strings and create a moniker. The HlinkCreateFromMoniker() function should be called if the hyperlink target's moniker already exists.

```
HRESULT HlinkCreateFromString(LPCWSTR, LPCWSTR, LPCWSTR,
                              IHlinkSite*, DWORD, IUnknown*,
                              REFIID, void**);
```

Argument type	Description
LPCWSTR	String describing the hyperlink target.
LPCWSTR	Location of the new hyperlink within the hyperlink target. May not be NULL.

Argument type	Description
LPCWSTR	The new hyperlink's friendly name.
IHlinkSite*	The hyperlink site to be associated with the hyperlink.
DWORD	Additional hyperlink site data.
IUnknown*	IUnknown interface of the object controlling the new hyperlink. A NULL value (the most common) means that the hyperlink object isn't aggregated.
REFIID	The hyperlink's interface to be returned, generally IID_IHlink.

Returned value	Meaning
S_OK	The hyperlink was created successfully.
E_INVALIDARG	At least one argument is invalid.

HlinkGetSpecialReference()

This function retrieves the current user's global home, search, or history page as a string. The result is returned through the second argument, and it can be turned into a hyperlink by calling the HlinkCreateFromString() global function.

```
HRESULT HlinkGetSpecialReference(DWORD, LPCWSTR*);
```

Argument type	Description
DWORD	An HLSR enumeration value. Determines whether the function must return the home page, search page, or history page.
LPCWSTR*	Where to send the required page as a string.

Returned value	Meaning
S_OK	The function retrieved the page successfully.
E_INVALIDARG	At least one argument is invalid.

HlinkSetSpecialReference()

This function sets the current user's global home, search, or history page as a string.

```
HRESULT HlinkSetSpecialReference(DWORD, LPCWSTR);
```

Argument type	Description
DWORD	An HLSR enumeration value. Determines whether the function must set the home page, search page, or history page.
LPCWSTR	Where to send the required page as a string.

Returned value	Meaning
S_OK	The operation succeeded.
E_INVALIDARG	At least one argument is invalid.

HlinkNavigateToStringReference()

This function performs a hyperlink navigation by regrouping common function calls. It creates a hyperlink from a string by calling HlinkCreateFromString(), performs hyperlink navigation by calling HlinkNavigate(), and then releases the hyperlink by calling Hlink::Release().

```
HRESULT HlinkNavigateToStringReference(LPCWSTR, LPCWSTR,
                    IHlinkSite*, DWORD, IHlinkFrame*, DWORD,
                    IBindCtx*, IBindStatusCallback*
                    IHlinkBrowseContext*);
```

Argument type	Description
LPCWSTR	String describing the hyperlink target.
LPCWSTR	Location within the hyperlink target.
IHlinkSite*	The hyperlink site to be associated with the hyperlink.
DWORD	Additional site data.
IHlinkFrame*	Hyperlink frame of the hyperlink container. A NULL value means the container doesn't have any frame.
DWORD	HLNF enumeration values.
IBindCtx*	The bind context to use for every moniker that will be created during the navigation. May not be NULL.
IBindStatusCallback*	The bind status callback to use for asynchronous moniker binding. A NULL value means the caller doesn't need to know information such as cancellation, progress state, and so on.
IHlinkBrowseContext*	The browse context to use for this navigation.

Returned value	Meaning
S_OK	The hyperlink jump was performed success-fully.
E_INVALIDARG	At least one argument is invalid.

HlinkNavigate()

This function calls `IHlinkFrame::Navigate()` if it is passed a hyperlink frame as argument, and calls `IHlink::Navigate()` if it is passed only a hyperlink as argument.

```
HRESULT HlinkNavigate(IHlink*, IHlinkFrame*, DWORD, IBindCtx*,
                IBindStatusCallback*, IHlinkBrowseContext*);
```

Argument type	Description
IHlink*	The hyperlink to navigate to.
IHlinkFrame*	The hyperlink frame of the hyperlink container. A NULL value means the hyperlink container doesn't have any frame.
DWORD	HLNF enumeration values.
IBindCtx*	The bind context to use for every moniker that will be created during the navigation. May not be NULL.
IBindStatusCallback*	The bind status callback to use for asynchronous moniker binding. A NULL value means the caller doesn't need to know information such as cancellation, progress state, and so forth.
IHlinkBrowseContext*	The browse context to use for this navigation.

Returned value	Meaning
S_OK	The hyperlink navigation succeeded.
E_INVALIDARG	At least one argument is invalid.

HlinkOnNavigate()

This function encapsulates functions during `IHlinkTarget::Navigate()` execution. It calls `IHlinkBrowserContext::OnNavigateHlink()` and `IHlinkFrame::OnNavigate()` if the hyperlink target has a hyperlink frame.

```
HRESULT HlinkOnNavigate(IHlinkFrame*, IHlinkBrowseContext*, DWORD,
                IMoniker*, LPCWSTR, LPCWSTR);
```

Argument type	Description
IHlinkFrame*	Hyperlink frame of the hyperlink container. A NULL value means the container doesn't have any frame.
IHlinkBrowseContext*	The browse context to use for this navigation.
DWORD	HLNF enumeration values.
IMoniker*	The hyperlink target's moniker. May not be NULL.
LPCWSTR	Location within the hyperlink target.
LPCWSTR	The friendly name of the hyperlink.

Returned value	Meaning
S_OK	The hyperlink navigation succeeded.
E_INVALIDARG	At least one argument is invalid.

IHlinkSite Interface

This interface is used by a hyperlink site and allows the site's associated hyperlink to retrieve information about the container.

```
BEGIN_INTERFACE_PART(HlinkSite, IHlinkSite)
    INIT_INTERFACE_PART(CMyDocObject, HlinkSite)
    STDMETHOD(GetMoniker)(DWORD, DWORD, DWORD, Moniker**);
    STDMETHOD(GetInterface)(DWORD, DWORD, REFIID, void**);
    STDMETHOD(OnNavigateComplete)(DWORD, HRESULT, LPCWSTR);
END_INTERFACE_PART(HlinkSite)
```

IHlinkSite::GetMoniker()

This member function retrieves the moniker of the hyperlink site's container, which is returned through the last argument.

```
STDMETHOD(GetMoniker)(DWORD, DWORD, DWORD, Moniker**);
```

Argument type	Description
DWORD	Hyperlink associated with the site. This value was given by IHlink::SetHlinkSite().
DWORD	An OLEGETMONIKER enumeration value. It means the function must not create a moniker, even if it doesn't already exist. An OLEGETMONIKER_FORCEASSIGN value means the function should create a moniker if it doesn't already exist.

Argument type	Description
DWORD	An OLEWHICHMK enumeration value. It means the hyperlink site must return the container's moniker.
IMoniker**	Where to send the container's moniker interface pointer.

Returned value	Meaning
S_OK	The moniker was returned successfully.
E_INVALIDARG	At least one argument is invalid.

IHlinkSite::GetInterface()

This member function retrieves a hyperlink site's container interface, which is returned through the last argument.

If a hyperlink, while comparing the target's moniker to the container's moniker (returned by IHlinkSite::GetMoniker()), finds that the navigation is an internal jump, it retrieves the hyperlink target's IHlinkTarget interface by calling this function.

This function differs slightly from IUnknown::QueryInterface(). First, it may return an interface based on the hyperlink passed-in argument. Second, the returned interface may not belong to the hyperlink site.

```
STDMETHOD(GetInterface)(DWORD, DWORD, REFIID, void**);
```

Argument type	Description
DWORD	Hyperlink associated with the site. This value was given by IHlink::SetHlinkSite().
DWORD	Reserved for future use. Must be zero.
REFIID	The desired interface's IID.
void**	Where to send the container's desired interface pointer.

Returned value	Meaning
S_OK	The interface was returned successfully.
E_NOINTERFACE	The desired interface isn't supported by the container.
E_INVALIDARG	At least one argument is invalid.

IHlinkSite::OnNavigationComplete()

This member function is called whenever a hyperlink jump has been performed. This function can be useful when the jump is executed asynchronously, because it's the only way for the site to know when the navigation has completed.

```
STDMETHOD(OnNavigateComplete)(DWORD, HRESULT, LPCWSTR);
```

Argument Type	Description
DWORD	Hyperlink associated with the site. This value was given by Ihlink::SetHlinkSite().
HRESULT	Result of the hyperlink navigation. Must be S_OK, E_ABORT, or E_FAIL.
LPCWSTR	A text string describing, in case of a problem, the failure that occurred.

Returned Value	Meaning
S_OK	The operation succeeded.
E_INVALIDARG	At least one argument is invalid.

IHlink Interface

This interface is used by a hyperlink. It allows hyperlink-specific information management (that is, either retrieving or setting) of data such as its moniker, its hyperlink site, its friendly name, and so forth.

```
BEGIN_INTERFACE_PART(Hlink, IHlink)
    INIT_INTERFACE_PART(CMyDocObject, Hlink)
    STDMETHOD(GetHlinkSite)(IHlinkSite**, DWORD*);
    STDMETHOD(SetHlinkSite)(IHlinkSite*, DWORD);
    STDMETHOD(GetMonikerReference)(DWORD, IMoniker**, LPWSTR*);
    STDMETHOD(GetStringReference)(DWORD, LPWSTR*, LPWSTR*);
    STDMETHOD(GetFriendlyName)(DWORD, LPCWSTR*);
    STDMETHOD(SetFriendlyName)(LPCWSTR);
    STDMETHOD(GetTargetFrameName)(LPCWSTR*);
    STDMETHOD(SetTargetFrameName)(LPCWSTR);
    STDMETHOD(GetAdditionalParams)(LPCWSTR*);
    STDMETHOD(SetAdditionalParams)(LPCWSTR);
    STDMETHOD(Navigate)(DWORD, IBindCtx*, IBindStatusCallback*,
                        IHlinkBrowseContext*);
    STDMETHOD(GetMiscStatus)(DWORD*);
END_INTERFACE_PART(Hlink)
```

IHlink::GetHlinkSite()

This member function retrieves the hyperlink's associated site, along with its data, which are returned through the two arguments.

```
STDMETHOD(GetHlinkSite)(IHlinkSite**, DWORD*);
```

Argument type	Description
IHlinkSite**	Where to send the hyperlink-associated site's interface. A NULL value is not accepted.
DWORD*	Where to send further site data. A NULL value is not accepted.

Returned value	Meaning
S_OK	The hyperlink site was returned successfully.
E_INVALIDARG	At least one argument is invalid.

IHlink::SetHlinkSite()

This member function associates the hyperlink with a hyperlink site whose interface is passed in the first argument. A hyperlink must be associated with a hyperlink site in order to work properly when IHlink::Navigate() is called.

```
STDMETHOD(SetHlinkSite)(IHlinkSite*, DWORD);
```

Argument type	Description
IHlinkSite*	Hyperlink site's interface.
DWORD	Further site's data.

Returned value	Meaning
S_OK	The hyperlink site was associated successfully.
E_INVALIDARG	At least one argument is invalid.

IHlink::GetMonikerReference()

This member function retrieves the container's moniker and the location within the target container, which are returned through the last two arguments.

Implementation note: the moniker passed in the second argument can bind to the target by calling IMoniker::BindToObject(). Once the hyperlink jump succeeds, this function can perform an internal hyperlink jump to go to the location, by calling Hlink::Navigate().

```
STDMETHOD(GetMonikerReference)(DWORD, IMoniker**, LPWSTR*);
```

Argument type	Description
DWORD	An HLINKGETREF enumeration value.
IMoniker**	Where to send the container's moniker interface pointer.
LPWSTR*	Location within the hyperlink target.

Returned value	Meaning
S_OK	The moniker was retrieved successfully.
E_INVALIDARG	At least one argument is invalid.

IHlink::GetStringReference()

This member function retrieves the container's address and location as strings, which are returned through the last two arguments.

```
STDMETHOD(GetStringReference)(DWORD, LPWSTR*, LPWSTR*);
```

Argument type	Description
DWORD	An HLINKGETREF enumeration value.
LPWSTR*	Where to send the string.
LPWSTR*	Where to send the location.

Returned value	Meaning
S_OK	The string reference was retrieved successfully.
E_INVALIDARG	At least one argument is invalid.

IHlink::GetFriendlyName()

This member function retrieves the friendly name of the hyperlink reference, which is returned through the last argument. This function is called by the hyperlink container when updating its user interface.

Note that the friendly name returned from the hyperlink may differ from the one returned from the target, as the hyperlink may cache it.

```
STDMETHOD(GetFriendlyName)(DWORD, LPCWSTR*);
```

Argument type	Description
DWORD	An HLFNAMEF enumeration value. Indicates which friendly name must be returned.
LPWSTR*	Where to send the friendly name.

Returned value	Meaning
S_OK	The friendly name was returned successfully.
E_INVALIDARG	At least one argument is invalid.

IHlink::SetFriendlyName()

This member function sets the friendly name of a hyperlink reference.

```
STDMETHOD(SetFriendlyName)(LPCWSTR);
```

Argument type	Description
LPCWSTR	Where to send the friendly name.

Returned value	Meaning
S_OK	The friendly name was set successfully.
E_INVALIDARG	Invalid argument.

IHlink::GetTargetFrameName()

This member function retrieves the name of the target frame (as in HTML framesets). The name is returned through the single argument and is useless if the container doesn't support framesets.

```
STDMETHOD(GetTargetFrameName)(LPCWSTR*);
```

Argument type	Description
LPCWSTR*	Where to send the target frame name.

Returned value	Meaning
S_OK	The target frame name was returned successfully.
E_INVALIDARG	Invalid argument.

IHlink::SetTargetFrameName()

This member function sets the target frame name. The name is useless if the container doesn't support framesets.

```
STDMETHOD(SetTargetFrameName)(LPCWSTR);
```

Argument type	Description
LPCWSTR	Target frame name.

Returned value	Meaning
S_OK	The target frame name was set successfully.
E_INVALIDARG	Invalid argument.

IHlink::GetAdditionalParams()

This member function retrieves additional parameters or properties of the hyperlink, which are returned through the single argument. The parameter string's format is designed as follows:

```
<ID1="value1"><ID2="value2">...<Idn="valuen">
```

Most of the parameters saved in this string are specific to the hyperlink frame.

```
STDMETHOD(GetAdditionalParams)(LPCWSTR*);
```

Argument type	Description
LPCWSTR*	Where to send the parameter string.

Returned value	Meaning
S_OK	The parameter string was retrieved successfully.
E_INVALIDARG	Invalid argument.

IHlink::SetAdditionalParams()

This member function sets additional parameters or properties of the hyperlink. The string format is described in IHlink::SetAdditionalParams().

```
STDMETHOD(SetAdditionalParams)(LPCWSTR);
```

Argument type	Description
LPCWSTR	Parameter string.

Returned value	Meaning
S_OK	The parameters were passed successfully.
E_INVALIDARG	At least one argument is invalid.

IHlink::Navigate()

This member function performs a hyperlink jump.

```
STDMETHOD(Navigate)(DWORD, IBindCtx*, IBindStatusCallback*,
                    IHlinkBrowseContext*);
```

Argument type	Description
DWORD	HLNF enumeration values.
IBindCtx*	The bind context to use for every moniker that will be created during the navigation. May not be NULL.

Argument type	Description
IBindStatusCallback*	The bind status callback to use for asynchronous moniker binding. A NULL value means the caller doesn't need to know information such as cancellation, progress state, and so on.
IHlinkBrowseContext*	The browse context that will be used during this hyperlink navigation.

Returned value	Meaning
S_OK	The navigation succeeded.
HLINK_S_NAVIGATEDTOLEAFNODE	To be determined.
E_INVALIDARG	At least one argument is invalid.

IHlink::GetMiscStatus()

Asks if the hyperlink is an absolute or relative link. The answer is returned through the single argument.

```
STDMETHOD(GetMiscStatus)(DWORD*);
```

Argument type	Description
DWORD*	Where to send an HLINKMISC enumeration value.

Returned value	Meaning
S_OK	Argument succeeds.
E_INVALIDARG	Invalid argument.

IHlinkTarget Interface

This interface is used to access a hyperlink container, typically when it is viewed as a hyperlink target (hence the interface name).

```
BEGIN_INTERFACE_PART(HlinkTarget, IHlinkTarget)
    INIT_INTERFACE_PART(CMyDocObject, HlinkTarget)
    STDMETHOD(GetBrowseContext)(IHlinkBrowseContext**);
    STDMETHOD(SetBrowseContext)(IHlinkBrowseContext*);
    STDMETHOD(Navigate)(DWORD, IBindCtx*, IBindStatusCallback*,
                        IHlink*);
    STDMETHOD(GetMoniker)(LPCWSTR, DWORD, IMoniker**);
    STDMETHOD(GetFriendlyName)(LPCWSTR, LPWSTR*);
END_INTERFACE_PART(HlinkTarget)
```

IHlinkTarget::GetBrowseContext()

This member function retrieves the browse context of the target. This function returns the desired interface through the argument and calls `HlinkBrowseContext::AddRef()` in order to tell the browse context the target is holding a reference to it.

This function doesn't need to be implemented for simple hyperlinking.

```
STDMETHOD(GetBrowseContext)(IHlinkBrowseContext**);
```

Argument type	Description
IHlinkBrowseContext**	Where to send the browse context interface.

Returned value	Meaning
S_OK	The browse context was returned successfully.
E_NOTIMPL	Browse context retrieval not supported.
E_INVALIDARG	At least one argument is invalid.

IHlinkTarget::SetBrowseContext()

This member function sets the hyperlink target's browse context. This function will typically release its previous browse context (if any) by calling `IHlinkBrowseContext::Release()` and hold a reference to the browse context passed-in argument by calling `IHlinkBrowseContext::AddRef()`.

This function doesn't need to be implemented for simple hyperlinking.

```
STDMETHOD(SetBrowseContext)(IHlinkBrowseContext*);
```

Argument type	Description
IHlinkBrowseContext*	The new browse context interface pointer.

Returned value	Meaning
S_OK	The browse context is set successfully.
E_NOTIMPL	The hyperlink target does not understand browse context.
E_INVALIDARG	At least one argument is invalid.

IHlinkTarget::Navigate()

This function navigates to the location and shows it if not visible (that is, display it onscreen). Note that if the target supports browse context, it calls `IHlinkBrowseContext::OnNavigateHlink()` to notify about a hyperlink jump.

This function doesn't need to be implemented for simple hyperlinking.

```
STDMETHOD(Navigate)(DWORD, IBindCtx*, IBindStatusCallback*,
                    IHlink*);
```

Argument type	Description
DWORD	HLNF enumeration values.
LPCWSTR	Location within the hyperlink target.

Returned value	Meaning
S_OK	The navigation succeeded.
E_INVALIDARG	At least one argument is invalid.

IHlinkTarget::GetMoniker()

This member function returns a moniker pointing to the hyperlink target for the given hyperlink location. The moniker's interface is returned through the last argument.

```
STDMETHOD(GetMoniker)(LPCWSTR, DWORD, IMoniker**);
```

Argument type	Description
LPCWSTR	Location within the hyperlink target.
DWORD	An OLEGETMONIKER enumeration. Must be either OLEGETMONIKER_ONLYIFTHERE (if the moniker does not exist, return E_FAIL) or OLEGETMONIKER_FORCEASSIGN (if the moniker does not exist, create it).
IMoniker**	Where to send the resulting moniker.

Returned value	Meaning
S_OK	The moniker was returned successfully.
E_FAIL	The moniker does not exist and the OLEGETMONIKER_ONLYIFTHERE flag was set.
E_INVALIDARG	At least one argument is invalid.

IHlinkTarget::GetFriendlyName()

This member function retrieves the friendly name, which is returned through the last argument.

```
STDMETHOD(GetFriendlyName)(LPCWSTR, LPWSTR*);
```

Argument type	Description
LPCWSTR	The location within the target.
LPWSTR*	Where to return the friendly name. This string must be allocated by the function by calling CoTaskMemFree() and freed by the function's caller through CoTaskMemFree().

Returned value	Meaning
S_OK	The friendly name was retrieved successfully.
E_OUTOFMEMORY	Not enough memory to create the friendly name string.
E_INVALIDARG	At least one argument is invalid.

IHlinkFrame Interface

This interface is used by the hyperlink frame. It is used mostly for browse context management (either retrieving or setting the browse context).

```
BEGIN_INTERFACE_PART(HlinkTarget, IHlinkTarget)
    INIT_INTERFACE_PART(CMyDocObject, HlinkTarget)
    STDMETHOD(GetBrowseContext)(IHlinkBrowseContext**);
    STDMETHOD(SetBrowseContext)(IHlinkBrowseContext*);
    STDMETHOD(Navigate)(DWORD, IBindCtx*, IBindStatusCallback*,
                        IHlink*);
    STDMETHOD(OnNavigate)(DWORD);
END_INTERFACE_PART(HlinkTarget)
```

IHlinkFrame::GetBrowseContext()

This member function retrieves the hyperlink frame browse context, which is returned through the function's single argument.

This function doesn't need to be implemented for simple hyperlinking.

```
STDMETHOD(GetBrowseContext)(IHlinkBrowseContext**);
```

Argument type	Description
IHlinkBrowseContext**	Where to send the browse context interface pointer.

Returned value	Meaning
S_OK	The browse context was retrieved successfully.
E_NOTIMPL	Browse context retrieval not supported.
E_INVALIDARG	At least one argument is invalid.

IHlinkFrame::SetBrowseContext()

This member function sets the hyperlink frame browse context.

This function doesn't need to be implemented for simple hyperlinking.

```
STDMETHOD(SetBrowseContext)(IHlinkBrowseContext*);
```

Argument type	Description
IHlinkBrowseContext*	The browse context interface.

Returned value	Meaning
S_OK	The given browse context was set successfully.
E_NOTIMPL	Browse context setting not supported.
E_INVALIDARG	At least one argument is invalid.

IHlinkFrame::Navigate()

This member function performs a hyperlink navigation. It is called by the IHlink::Navigate() interface member function when it is given a non-NULL IHlinkFrame pointer. The goal of this function is to allow the hyperlink frame to perform some action during the hyperlink jump.

```
STDMETHOD(Navigate)(DWORD, IBindCtx*, IBindStatusCallback*,
                    IHlink*);
```

Argument type	Description
DWORD	HLNF enumeration values.
IBindCtx*	The bind context to use for every moniker that will be created during the hyperlink jump.
IBindStatusCallback*	The bind status callback to use for every asynchronous moniker that will be created during the hyperlink jump.
IHlink*	The hyperlink to navigate to.

Returned value	Meaning
S_OK	The hyperlink jump succeeded.
E_INVALIDARG	At least one argument is invalid.
Other	From IHlink::Navigate().

IHlinkFrame::OnNavigate()

This member function is called to notify the hyperlink frame that the navigation succeeded. This allows a hyperlink frame to update its window. This function is called by the hyperlink target during `IHlinkTarget::Navigate()` using the global function `HlinkOnNavigate()`.

```
STDMETHOD(OnNavigate)(DWORD);
```

Argument type	Description
DWORD	HLNF enumeration values.

Returned value	Meaning
S_OK	The navigation succeeded.
E_INVALIDARG	Invalid argument.

IHlinkBrowseContext Interface

This interface is returned by the hyperlink frame and is used for browse context management.

```
BEGIN_INTERFACE_PART(HlinkBrowseContext, IHlinkBrowseContext)
    INIT_INTERFACE_PART(CMyDocObject, HlinkBrowseContext)
    STDMETHOD(Register)(DWORD, IUnknown*, IMoniker*, DWORD*);
    STDMETHOD(GetObject)(IMoniker*, IUnknown**);
    STDMETHOD(Revoke)(DWORD);
    STDMETHOD(GetBrowseWindowInfo)(HLBWINFO*);
    STDMETHOD(SetBrowseWindowInfo)(HLBWINFO*);
    STDMETHOD(EnumNavigationStack)(IEnumHLITEM**);
    STDMETHOD(QueryHlink)(ULONG);
    STDMETHOD(GetHlink)(ULONG, Iklink**);
    STDMETHOD(SetCurrentHlink)(ULONG);
    STDMETHOD(OnNavigateHlink)(DWORD, IMoniker*, LPCWSTR, LPCWSTR);
    STDMETHOD(Clone)(IUnknown*, REFIID, IUnknown**);
    STDMETHOD(Close)(DWORD);
END_INTERFACE_PART(HlinkBrowseContext)
```

IHlinkBrowseContext::Register()

This member function registers an object with the browse context. The browse context maintains a table of moniker-object bindings. This table can be accessed for navigation to hyperlink targets already registered. When a hyperlink jump occurs, the browse context looks at this table and checks whether the hyperlink target is already registered and running. If so, it doesn't have to reload the same document object. This function returns a registration ID (through the last argument), which can be used to revoke the registration.

```
STDMETHOD(Register)(DWORD, IUnknown*, IMoniker*, DWORD*);
```

Argument type	Description
DWORD	Reserved for future use. Must be zero.
IUnknown*	The object to register.

Argument type	Description
IMoniker*	The moniker that points to the object being registered.
DWORD*	Where to send the output value—that is, the registration ID.

Returned value	Meaning
S_OK	The object was registered successfully.
MK_S_MONIKERALREADYREGISTERED	The object was registered successfully. However, another object has already been registered with the same moniker.
E_OUTOFMEMORY	Not enough memory to register the object.
E_INVALIDARG	At least one argument is invalid.

IHlinkBrowseContext::GetObject()

This member function retrieves the object corresponding to the moniker passed in the first argument. The resulting object is returned through the last argument.

```
STDMETHOD(GetObject)(IMoniker*, IUnknown**);
```

Argument type	Description
IMoniker*	Identifies the object to retrieve.
IUnknown**	Where to send the object's IUnknown interface pointer.

Returned value	Meaning
S_OK	The object was retrieved successfully.
S_FALSE	There was no object corresponding to the moniker being passed.
E_INVALIDARG	At least one argument is invalid.

IHlinkBrowseContext::Revoke()

This member function cancels the object whose registration ID is the one passed-in argument. This ID is given by IHlinkBrowseContext::Register().

```
STDMETHOD(Revoke)(DWORD);
```

Argument type	Description
DWORD	Registration ID of the object to be revoked.

Returned value	Meaning
S_OK	The object was successfully removed from registration.
E_INVALIDARG	Invalid argument.

IHlinkBrowseContext::GetBrowseWindowInfo()

This member function retrieves the HLBWINFO structure currently associated with the browse context, which is returned only through the function argument. This function is generally called by a hyperlink target during IHlinkTarget::Navigate() in order to draw its user interface.

```
STDMETHOD(GetBrowseWindowInfo)(HLBWINFO*);
```

Argument type	Description
HLBWINFO*	Where to return the HLBWINFO structure containing window information.

Returned value	Meaning
S_OK	The HLBWINFO structure was returned successfully.
E_INVALIDARG	Invalid argument.

IHlinkBrowseContext::SetBrowseWindowInfo()

This member function is the opposite of IHlinkBrowseContext::GetBrowseWindowInfo(). It sets the browse context window information from a HLBWINFO structure passed-in argument. This function is generally used by the hyperlink target and the hyperlink container when the window is resized.

```
STDMETHOD(SetBrowseWindowInfo)(HLBWINFO*);
```

Argument type	Description
HLBWINFO*	The HLBWINFO structure containing window information

Returned value	Meaning
S_OK	The window settings were updated.
E_INVALIDARG	Invalid argument.

IHlinkBrowseContext::EnumNavigationStack()

This member function creates an HLITEM enumerator that will browse a sequence of HLITEM structures. The sequence structures will contain information about the navigation stack's hyperlinks and associated friendly names. This function returns through the argument of the enumerator's interface—that is, `IEnumHLITEM`.

```
STDMETHOD(EnumNavigationStack)(IEnumHLITEM**);
```

Argument type	Description
`IEnumHLITEM**`	Where to send the enumerator's interface.

Returned value	Meaning
`S_OK`	The enumerator was created successfully.
`E_INVALIDARG`	Invalid argument.

IHlinkBrowseContext::QueryHlink()

This member function tests the validity of a hyperlink. It is generally called by the hyperlink frame to determine the validity of commands such as Go Forward or Go Back by passing `HLID_NEXT` and `HLID_PREVIOUS`. The `HLQF` enumeration must be either `HLQF_ISVALID` or `HLQF_ISCURRENT`. An `HLQF_ISVALID` value means the function must check whether the hyperlink (whose ID is passed in the second argument) is valid within the browse context. An `HLQF_ISCURRENT` value means the function must check if the hyperlink is the current browse context hyperlink.

```
STDMETHOD(QueryHlink)(DWORDULONG);
```

Argument type	Description
`DWORD`	An `HLQF` enumeration value.
`ULONG`	Identifies the hyperlink to check. Can be an `HLID` constant.

Returned value	Meaning
`S_OK`	The test succeeded.
`E_FALSE`	The test failed.
`E_INVALIDARG`	The `HLQF` value is invalid.

IHlinkBrowseContext::GetHlink()

This member function retrieves from the browse context the hyperlink whose ID is passed as the first argument. The resulting hyperlink `IHlink` interface is returned through the second argument.

```
STDMETHOD(GetHlink)(ULONG, IHlink**);
```

Argument type	Description
ULONG	Identifies the hyperlink to retrieve. Can be an HLID constant.
IHlink**	Where to send the interface of the hyperlink to retrieve.

Returned value	Meaning
S_OK	The hyperlink was retrieved successfully.
E_FAIL	The desired hyperlink does not exist.
E_INVALIDARG	Invalid IHlink** argument.

IHlinkBrowseContext::SetCurrentHlink()

This member function sets as current hyperlink in the browse context of the hyperlink whose ID is passed in argument.

```
STDMETHOD(SetCurrentHlink)(ULONG);
```

Argument type	Description
ULONG	Identifies the hyperlink to set as current browse context hyperlink. Can be an HLID constant.

Returned value	Meaning
S_OK	The hyperlink was successfully set as current hyperlink.
E_FAIL	The desired hyperlink does not exist.
E_INVALIDARG	Invalid argument.

IHlinkBrowseContext::OnNavigateHlink()

This member function is called by the hyperlink target during IHlinkTarget::Navigate() to notify the browse context that a hyperlink jump has been performed.

```
STDMETHOD(OnNavigateHlink)(DWORD, IMoniker*, LPCWSTR, LPCWSTR);
```

Argument type	Description
DWORD	HLNF enumeration values.
IMoniker*	The moniker of the hyperlink target.
LPCWSTR	The location within the hyperlink target. May not be NULL.
LPCWSTR	The friendly name of the location within the hyperlink target. May not be NULL.

Returned value	Meaning
S_OK	A hyperlink jump has been performed successfully.
E_INVALIDARG	At least one argument is invalid.

IHlinkBrowseContext::Clone()

This member function clones the browse context. The clone is returned through the last argument.

```
STDMETHOD(Clone)(IUnknown*, REFIID, IUnknown**);
```

Argument type	Description
IUnknown*	IUnknown interface of the object controlling the new browse context. A NULL value (the most common) means the browse context isn't aggregated.
REFIID	Interface ID of the created browse context. Generally IID_IHlinkBrowseContext.
IUnknown**	Where to return the new browse context desired interface.

Returned value	Meaning
S_OK	The new browse context was created successfully.
E_INVALIDARG	At least one argument is invalid.

IHlinkBrowseContext::Close()

This member function closes the browse context. It releases all the hyperlink targets that are still registered through IHlinkBrowseContext::Register().

```
STDMETHOD(Close)(DWORD);
```

Argument type	Description
DWORD	Reserved for a future use. Must be zero.

Returned value	Meaning
S_OK	The browse context has been closed successfully.
E_INVALIDARG	Invalid argument.

IEnumHLITEM Interface

This interface is a standard OLE enumeration interface. When the
`IHlinkBrowseContext::EnumNavigationStack()` function is called, it creates an `HLITEM`
structure's enumerator and returns its `IEnumHLITEM` interface. The created enumerator is controlled through this interface and can browse an `HLITEM` sequence.

```
BEGIN_INTERFACE_PART(EnumHLITEM, IEnumHLITEM)
    INIT_INTERFACE_PART(CMyDocObject, EnumHLITEM)
    STDMETHOD(Next)(ULONG, HLITEM*, ULONG*);
    STDMETHOD(Skip)(ULONG);
    STDMETHOD(Reset)(void);
    STDMETHOD(Clone)(IEnumHLITEM**);
END_INTERFACE_PART(EnumHLITEM)
```

IEnumHLITEM::Next()

This member function retrieves a given number (passed as the first argument) of
`HLITEM` structures. These structures will be copied in an `HLITEM` array (passed as the
second argument).

```
STDMETHOD(Next)(ULONG, HLITEM*, ULONG*);
```

Argument type	Description
ULONG	Number of HLITEM structures to retrieve.
HLITEM*	Array where the HLITEM structures will be copied.
ULONG*	Where to send the actual number of HLITEM copied, in case fewer elements are left than requested.

Returned value	Meaning
S_OK	The structures were returned successfully.
S_FALSE	Some structures were returned successfully. However, fewer elements were left than requested.
E_INVALIDARG	At least one argument is invalid.

IEnumHLITEM::Skip()

This member function skips a given number of elements.

```
STDMETHOD(Skip)(ULONG);
```

Argument type	Description
ULONG	The number of elements to skip.

Returned value	Meaning
S_OK	The given number of elements that were skipped.
S_FALSE	There were fewer elements left in the sequence than requested. The enumerator is now at the end of the sequence.

IEnumHLITEM::Reset()

This member function sets the enumerator at the beginning of the sequence.

```
STDMETHOD(Reset)(void);
```

Returned value	Meaning
S_OK	The enumerator was set successfully.

IEnumHLITEM::Clone()

This member function clones the enumerator. The clone will have the same state—that is, the same position in the sequence.

```
STDMETHOD(Clone)(IEnumHLITEM**);
```

Argument type	Description
IEnumHLITEM**	Where to send the created enumerator's interface pointer.

Returned value	Meaning
S_OK	The enumerator was cloned successfully.
E_OUTOFMEMORY	Not enough memory to create a new enumerator.
E_INVALIDARG	Invalid argument.

Summary

OLE Hyperlinking Navigation brings to ActiveX what made the Web successful: hyperlinks—that is, how to jump from one document to another by a simple mouse click. This technology allows either a DocObject or an ActiveX control to simply implement hyperlinks and to interact with the Web browser. Hyperlinking Navigation comes with two sets of APIs. The first set is a simple API that enables quick hyperlinking implementation. The second API, which is far larger, implements many more features, such as greater interaction with the Web browser than with the simple API. However, this API is tougher to implement and, most important of all, still subject to change.

This chapter first explained exactly what OLE hyperlinking Navigation is, how it works, and what you can do with it. It then described the differences between the two APIs. Finally, it explained each API in detail.

VBScript

13

Overview of VBScript

by Sanjaya Hettihewa

VBScript has been designed to make it easier to develop client-side Web applications that run on the Web browser. A long time ago (which translates to about a year when you're talking about the Internet), people were discovering the virtues of providing dynamic information to users browsing a Web site. CGI applications were typically used to create Web pages that displayed dynamic information. Although this method worked well in some cases, it did not work well for some people. The development of a CGI application typically meant learning a programming language such as C or C++, compiling the CGI application, transferring it to the CGI directory of a Web server, and testing the CGI application for bugs. Even the slightest change to the application meant recompiling the entire application, and repeating the process of copying the application to a CGI directory and testing the application for bugs. To solve this problem, Web scripting languages such as JavaScript and VBScript were developed to aid in the development of client-side and server-side CGI applications.

Although Web scripting languages are widely used in the development of client-side CGI applications that run on the Web browser, Web scripting languages are also highly suitable for developing sophisticated server-side CGI applications. For example, Microsoft's latest server-side Web development application, Microsoft Visual InterDev, uses VBScript to interact with various objects on the Web server. Therefore, skills you learn in this chapter can be used not only to develop interactive client-side Web applications but also to develop server-side Web applications in the form of Active Server Pages. The purpose of this chapter is to introduce you to VBScript and discuss how various capabilities of VBScript can be used to develop interactive Web applications.

Why Use VBScript?

VBScript is a powerful, lightweight, easy-to-use, freely available, cross-platform, and cross-language scripting language for the Internet developed by Microsoft. It is designed to leverage skills and investments of millions of Visual Basic programmers to the Internet. Before proceeding any further, let's quickly examine why VBScript is a powerful, lightweight, easy-to-use, freely available, cross-platform, and cross-language scripting language.

- VBScript is powerful: Various capabilities of VBScript can be used to develop richly interactive Web pages that respond to user input intelligently. For example, when a user submits a form, a VBScript subroutine can be triggered to verify that the form is properly filled in with valid values. In the case of a server-side CGI application, VBScript can be used to process data submitted by users with the aid of ActiveX controls specially designed for Microsoft Active Server Pages.
- VBScript is lightweight: VBScript code is lightweight, fast, and has been optimized to be transmitted via the Internet. Because VBScript code is lightweight, it can be quickly transmitted to users browsing a Web site—even via relatively slow Plain Old Telephone Service (POTS) links to the Internet.
- VBScript is easy to use: Compared with scripting languages such as JavaScript, VBScript is easier to use because it is based on the easy-to-learn BASIC (Beginner's All-Purpose Symbolic Instruction Code) language.
- VBScript is freely available: Microsoft has made VBScript freely available to software vendors so that they can add scripting capabilities to their applications with the aid of VBScript.
- VBScript is cross-platform: By the time you read this book, VBScript will be functioning on UNIX as well as Macintosh computers, in addition to Windows 95 and Windows NT computers.
- VBScript is cross-language: VBScript supports languages, such as C++ and Java, that allow objects to be compiled as ActiveX controls.

VBScript has been designed to leverage the skills of millions of Visual Basic programmers to the Internet. VBScript can be used to easily create active and intelligent Web pages. Because VBScript is supported by Microsoft, in the near future you will also see a great deal of integration between VBScript and Internet Explorer, Windows NT/95, Microsoft Office, and Microsoft BackOffice.

VBScript is a subset of Microsoft Visual Basic and is upwardly compatible with Visual Basic for Applications (VBA). VBA is shipped with Microsoft Office applications to make it easier for developers to build custom solutions using Microsoft Office applications. The scripting, automation, and customization capabilities for Web browsers and Web servers are a major feature of VBScript. If you are already familiar with Visual Basic, very shortly you will be able to leverage your skills to the Internet by using VBScript. Even if you are not familiar with another programming language, after reading this section you will be able to create interactive Web pages with VBScript. Familiarity with a programming language, however, will make it easier for you to grasp various concepts, such as type casting, control structures, and Boolean arithmetic. Visit the Microsoft VBScript home page for the most up-to-date information about VBScript.

> **note**
>
> Visit the Microsoft VBScript information Web site for the latest information about VBScript:
>
> ```
> http://www.microsoft.com/VBScript
> ```

But What About JavaScript?

I am sure you must have heard about JavaScript by now. You might have already developed JavaScript applications on your own to solve various tasks, and you might be wondering why you should bother to learn JavaScript if you know VBScript or vice versa.

If you know neither scripting language, you should start with VBScript and learn how VBScript is used to develop interactive Web applications. As mentioned earlier, VBScript is easy to learn, and you can use it to start developing interactive Web applications in no time—even if you are new to programming.

If you are familiar with Visual Basic or Visual Basic for Applications, you already know VBScript, and you will easily be able to leverage your skills to the Internet by using VBScript. Except for a few differences in the language and the availability of additional objects for obtaining information about Web transactions, VBScript is very similar to Visual Basic and Visual Basic for Applications.

If you know JavaScript, learning VBScript will make it easier for you to learn Visual Basic and Visual Basic for Applications. Visual Basic 5.0 can easily be used to develop ActiveX controls. Information presented in this chapter will help you learn VBScript and leverage your VBScript skills when you are developing ActiveX controls with Visual Basic.

After learning VBScript and JavaScript, you can select the language you are most comfortable with when developing Web applications.

How VBScript Works

VBScript programs are defined between the two HTML tags <SCRIPT LANGUAGE=VBS> and </SCRIPT>. Browsers that support VBScript read the VBScript application contained between these two HTML tags and execute it after checking the code for any syntax errors. VBScript works as shown in Figure 13.1.

Figure 13.1.
How VBScript works.

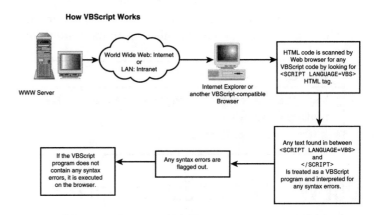

As you can see in Figure 13.1, a VBScript application is part of a regular HTML file. When a Web browser that supports VBScript encounters the <SCRIPT LANGUAGE=VBS> HTML tag, all text between that tag and </SCRIPT> is treated as a VBScript application and is checked for syntax errors. If the application does not contain any syntax errors, it is executed on the Web browser. If any syntax errors are detected, they are flagged by the VBScript interpreter, as shown in Figure 13.2.

Figure 13.2.
*Syntax errors in
VBScript programs are
flagged by the VBScript
interpreter.*

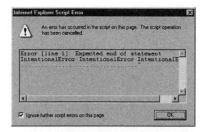

Dealing with Technologically Challenged Web Browsers

To hide VBScript code from "technologically challenged" Web browsers, VBScript code can be enclosed in two HTML comment tags, as shown in Listing 13.1. This technique prevents technologically challenged Web browsers from attempting to display the VBScript application as if it were part of the HTML code of the Web page.

Listing 13.1. Hiding VBScript code from technologically challenged Web browsers.

```
<SCRIPT LANGUAGE=VBS>
<!-- To hide VBScript code from technologically challenged
     Web browsers
... VBScript code ...
!-->
</SCRIPT>
```

Hello World!

Writing the classic Hello World! application with VBScript is simple. For the purpose of this example, you will see how to create a Web page similar to the one shown in Figure 13.3. This Web page will have three buttons. The first button will display a message box with a greeting, the second button will display the current time, and the third button will display today's date.

If you want to experiment with the VBScript application shown in Figure 13.3, you can find it in the CD-ROM that accompanies this resource library in the directory \Chap-17\Hello.htm. Various key elements of the Hello World! VBScript application are outlined next.

Figure 13.3.
The classic Hello World!
application written with
VBScript.

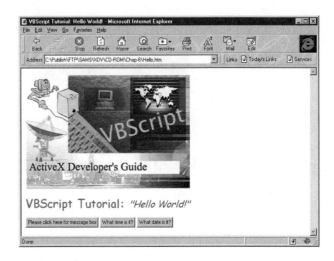

The Hello World! Dialog Box

The Hello World! dialog box shown in Figure 13.4 is displayed each time a user clicks the Please click here for message box button shown in Figure 13.3. If you look at the HTML page of the VBScript application (see lines 22 and 23 of Listing 13.5), you will see that the command button associated with the Hello World! dialog box is named. As shown in line 1 of Listing 13.2, the OnClick event of the BtnHello command button is associated with the BtnHello_OnClick subroutine. Each time a user clicks the Please click here for message box button shown in Figure 13.3, the Web browser invokes the BtnHello_OnClick subroutine, and any VBScript code defined in that subroutine is executed.

The BtnHello_OnClick subroutine is a simple VBScript subroutine. The first three lines of code create strings displayed in the dialog box shown in Figure 13.4. Note how the string concatenation operator (&) is used in line 4 to merge two strings and assign the result to a variable. The result is then displayed in the message box shown in Figure 13.4.

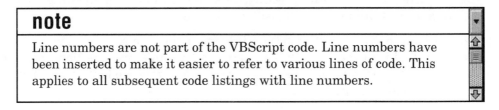

note

Line numbers are not part of the VBScript code. Line numbers have been inserted to make it easier to refer to various lines of code. This applies to all subsequent code listings with line numbers.

Listing 13.2. The `BtnHello_OnClick` subroutine.

```
1: Sub BtnHello_OnClick
2:  titleString = "ActiveX Developer's Guide"
3:  helloString = "Hello world! Welcome to the fun filled "
4:  helloString = helloString & "world of VBScript programming!"
5:  MsgBox helloString, 0, titleString
6: End Sub
```

Figure 13.4.
The Hello World! dialog box.

The Time Dialog Box

The `BtnTime_OnClick` subroutine is very similar to the `BtnHello_OnClick` subroutine. The only difference is that instead of concatenating two strings, it concatenates a string with the result of a function. The `time` function returns the current time. As shown in Figure 13.5, line 3 of Listing 13.3 displays the current time in a dialog box. The `BtnTime_OnClick` subroutine is associated with the `OnClick` event of the `BtnTime` command button.

Listing 13.3. The `BtnTime_OnClick` subroutine.

```
1: Sub BtnTime_OnClick
2:  timeString = "So, you want to know the time? The time is " & time
3:  MsgBox  timeString , 0, "Time Dialog Box"
4: End Sub
```

Figure 13.5.
The Time dialog box.

The Date Dialog Box

The date dialog box displays the current date in a dialog box, as shown in Figure 13.6. As you can see in line 2 of Listing 13.4, the result of one function (`date`) can be used as an argument (`input`) of another function (`DateValue`).

Listing 13.4. The `BtnDate_OnClick` subroutine.

```
1: Sub BtnDate_OnClick
2:  dateString = "Today's date is " & DateValue(date)
3:  MsgBox  dateString , 0, "Date Dialog Box"
4: End Sub
```

Figure 13.6.
The Date dialog box.

For your reference, the full source code of the Hello World! application is shown in Listing 13.5.

Listing 13.5. The Hello World! Web page.

```
 1: <!--
 2: © 1996 Sanjaya Hettihewa
 3: http://www.NetInnovation.com/sanjaya
 4: !-->
 5:
 6: <HTML>
 7: <HEAD>
 8: <TITLE>VBScript Tutorial: Hello World!</TITLE>
 9: </HEAD>
10:
11: <BODY BGCOLOR="#FFFFFF" TEXT="#0000FF"
12:       LINK="#B864FF" VLINK="#670000" ALINK="#FF0000">
13:
14: <IMG SRC="vbscript.jpg"><P>
15:
16: <B><FONT FACE="Comic Sans MS" SIZE=6 COLOR=RED>
17: VBScript Tutorial: <FONT></B>
18: <I><FONT FACE="Comic Sans MS" SIZE=5 COLOR=BLUE>
19:  "Hello World!" </I><P><FONT>
20:
21: <form>
22: <INPUT TYPE=BUTTON VALUE="Please click here for message box"
23:        NAME="BtnHello">
24: <INPUT TYPE=BUTTON VALUE="What time is it?"
25:        NAME="BtnTime">
26: <INPUT TYPE=BUTTON VALUE="What date is it?"
27:        NAME="BtnDate">
28: </form>
29:
30: <SCRIPT LANGUAGE="VBScript">
31: <!-- To hide VBScript code from technologically challenged browsers
32:
33: Sub BtnHello_OnClick
34:   titleString = "ActiveX Developer's Guide"
35:   helloString = "Hello world! Welcome to the fun filled "
36:   helloString = helloString & "world of VBScript programming!"
37:   MsgBox helloString, 0, titleString
38: End Sub
39:
40: Sub BtnTime_OnClick
41:   timeString = "So, you want to know the time? The time is " & time
42:   MsgBox  timeString , 0, "Time Dialog Box"
43: End Sub
44:
45: Sub BtnDate_OnClick
46:   dateString = "Today's date is " & DateValue(date)
```

```
47:  MsgBox  dateString , 0, "Date Dialog Box"
48: End Sub
49: !-->
50: </SCRIPT>
51:
52: </BODY>
53:
54: </HTML>
```

Summary

VBScript, Microsoft's scripting language for the Internet, is designed to leverage the skills and investments of Visual Basic developers to the Internet. Compared with scripting languages such as JavaScript, VBScript is easier to learn and use. Various capabilities of VBScript can easily be used to develop sophisticated Web applications. VBScript can be used to create both client-side and server-side Web applications.

14

Fundamentals of VBScript

by Sanjaya Hettihewa

VBScript, a programming language for developing server-side and client-side Web applications, is a subset of Microsoft Visual Basic and is upwardly compatible with Visual Basic for Applications (VBA). VBA is used in Microsoft Office applications to build custom solutions using various Microsoft Office applications. If you are familiar with VBA or Visual Basic, you will feel right at home with VBScript.

VBScript is used by Web-page developers to add scripting, automation, and customization capabilities to Web pages and to develop richly interactive Web applications. If you're already familiar with Visual Basic or VBA, you'll be able to leverage your skills to the Internet using VBScript at the end of this section. Even if you're not familiar with Visual Basic or VBA, you'll still be able to develop Web applications using VBScript because the syntax of VBScript is easy to understand. This chapter covers the fundamentals of VBScript Web-application development.

You do not necessarily have to install VBScript. The VBScript engine is part of Internet Explorer and is installed on your system when you install Internet Explorer.

> **note**
>
> Visit Microsoft's VBScript Web site at `http://www.microsoft.com/`
> `VBScript/` for the most up-to-date information about VBScript.

Figure 14.1 shows a graphical representation of how client-side VBScript applications are executed by Web browsers. As you'll learn in the section "The Role of VBScript in Web-Page Development," VBScript applications are contained in HTML Web pages. When a VBScript-compatible Web browser downloads a Web page containing VBScript code, it executes that code whenever an object of the Web page triggers a VBScript subroutine contained in the VBScript code.

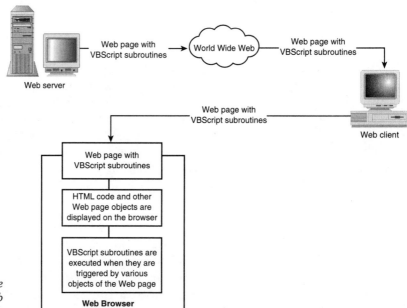

Figure 14.1.
How VBScript applications are executed by Web browsers.

The Structure of a VBScript Application

Before developing VBScript applications, you need to understand their structure. A typical VBScript application is composed of the following components:

- HTML code
- VBScript code delimiters
- VBScript subroutines

The HTML code can contain any number of valid HTML statements. Listing 14.1 contains valid HTML statements in every line of code except lines 23–42.

VBScript code delimiters separate VBScript code from the HTML code of a Web page. Lines 23–24 and 41–42 of Listing 14.1 are examples of VBScript code delimiters. Notice how the HTML comment tags (<!-- and -->) are used to enclose the VBScript source code. These tags prevent VBScript-challenged Web browsers from interpreting the VBScript source code as part of the text of the Web page and displaying it on the browser window.

A VBScript application is composed of one or more VBScript subroutines. VBScript subroutines are defined using the following syntax:

VBScript subroutines are contained between the two HTML tags <SCRIPT LANGUAGE="VBScript"> and </SCRIPT>. Certain events associated with various objects of a Web page trigger VBScript subroutines to perform certain tasks. For example, when a user submits a form, a VBScript subroutine can validate the data entered by the user before the data is sent to the Web server for processing.

See lines 25–30, 32–35, and 37–40 in Listing 14.1 for examples of VBScript subroutines.

Listing 14.1. A typical VBScript application.

```
 1: <HTML>
 2: <HEAD>
 3: <TITLE>VBScript Tutorial: Hello World!</TITLE>
 4: </HEAD>
 5:
 6: <BODY BGCOLOR="#FFFFFF" TEXT="#0000FF"
 7:       LINK="#B864FF" VLINK="#670000" ALINK="#FF0000">
 8:
 9: <B><FONT FACE="Comic Sans MS" SIZE=6 COLOR=RED>
10: VBScript Tutorial: <FONT></B>
11: <I><FONT FACE="Comic Sans MS" SIZE=5 COLOR=BLUE>
12:   "Hello World!" </I><P><FONT>
13:
14: <FORM>
15: <INPUT TYPE=BUTTON VALUE="Please click here for message box"
16:       NAME="BtnHello">
17: <INPUT TYPE=BUTTON VALUE="What time is it?"
18:       NAME="BtnTime">
19: <INPUT TYPE=BUTTON VALUE="What date is it?"
20:       NAME="BtnDate">
21: </FORM>
22:
23: <SCRIPT LANGUAGE=VBS>
24: <!-- To hide VBScript code from technologically challenged browsers
25: Sub BtnHello_OnClick
26:   titleString = "Windows NT Internet & Intranet Development"
27:   helloString = "Hello world! Welcome to the fun filled "
```

continues

Listing 14.1. continued

```
28:   helloString = helloString & "world of VBScript programming!"
29:   MsgBox helloString, 0, titleString
30: End Sub
31:
32: Sub BtnTime_OnClick
33:   timeString = "So, you want to know the time? The time is " & time
34:   MsgBox  timeString , 0, "Time Dialog Box"
35: End Sub
36:
37: Sub BtnDate_OnClick
38:   dateString = "Today's date is " & DateValue(date)
39:   MsgBox  dateString , 0, "Date Dialog Box"
40: End Sub
41: -->
42: </SCRIPT>
43:
44: </BODY>
45: </HTML>
```

The Role of VBScript in Web-Page Development

Before the appearance of client-side scripting languages such as VBScript, Web pages were mostly static entities. Interactivity in a Web page required the execution of a CGI application on the server and the display of the results of the CGI application on the Web browser. Although this method worked well for some applications, it tied up valuable network and system resources. VBScript allows Web-page developers to create multimedia-rich, interactive Web pages with great ease while conserving network bandwidth and Web-server system resources. The next sections discuss the role of VBScript in Web-page development.

Automating ActiveX Controls

ActiveX controls are powerful components that can be used to build sophisticated Web applications. By themselves, ActiveX controls are capable of performing limited tasks. For example, the Microsoft Forms 2.0 ComboBox ActiveX control is capable of displaying a list of items, and the Microsoft Forms 2.0 Image ActiveX control is capable of displaying a graphical image. VBScript is used to glue ActiveX controls together and develop more sophisticated Web pages. For example, a VBScript subroutine can allow a user to change the image displayed in a Microsoft Forms 2.0 Image ActiveX control when an image is selected using a Microsoft Forms 2.0 ComboBox ActiveX control.

Developing Dynamic Web Applications

VBScript is ideal for developing dynamic Web applications that immediately respond to user interactions. The Mr. Potato Head application discussed next is an example of a Web application that is better implemented with a client-side scripting language such as VBScript than with a server-side CGI application.

The application shown in Figure 14.2 is the CGI version of Mr. Potato Head. After a user selects various physical attributes of Mr. Potato Head, that information is transmitted to the Web server. A CGI application creates a graphics of Mr. Potato Head according to the physical attributes selected by the user and transmits the image to the Web browser, as shown in Figure 14.3. The CGI implementation of Mr. Potato Head is network intensive because data must be transferred between the Web browser and the Web server each time a user makes a selection. The CGI implementation is also processor intensive for the Web server because it must process a CGI request and create a Mr. Potato Head each time the user makes a selection. Browse `http://winnie.acsu.buffalo.edu/cgi-bin/potatoe-cgi` to experiment with the CGI version of Mr. Potato Head.

Figure 14.2.
Selecting the physical properties of Mr. Potato Head.

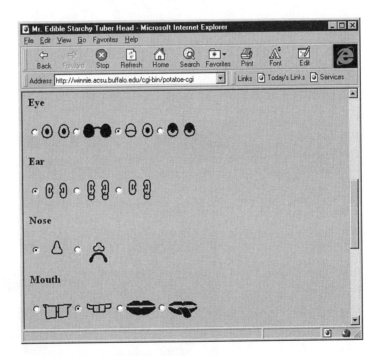

The ActiveX version of Mr. Potato Head, shown in Figure 14.4, addresses the limitations of the CGI version. As you can see, the ActiveX version is more interactive and easier to use because it allows the user to change the physical attributes of Mr. Potato Head on-the-fly without interacting with the Web server. Users can select physical attributes and drag-and-drop them on Mr. Potato Head. The ActiveX version of Mr. Potato Head is less processor intensive because it does not communicate with the Web server each time the user makes a change; it is less network intensive because all the processing is done locally. Browse the Web page at `http://www.microsoft.com/ie/most/howto/layout/eggplant/begin.htm` to experiment with the ActiveX version of Mr. Potato Head.

Figure 14.3.
An image of Mr. Potato Head created by a CGI application.

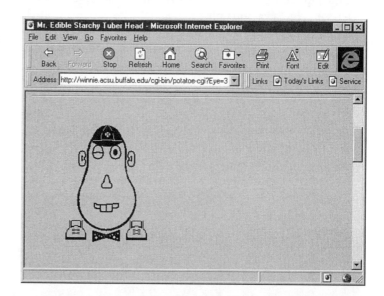

Figure 14.4.
The ActiveX version of Mr. Potato Head.

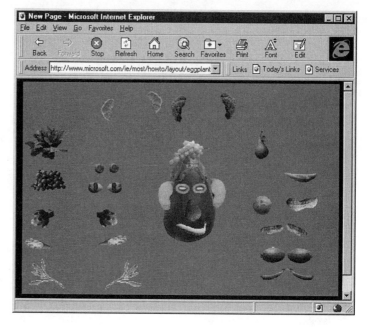

Error Checking

Error checking is a very important aspect of Web-application development. Lack of error checking usually results in flaky applications that are frustrating to use. Listed next are examples of how VBScript is used to perform error checking and to validate data entered by users:

- A VBScript application can be used to ensure that all required data-entry fields of an HTML form are filled in.
- A VBScript subroutine can be used to ensure that invalid data is not submitted for processing by a user. For example, a VBScript application can inform the user that the date he entered (45/67/1996, for example) is invalid—without the expense of establishing an HTTP connection to a server-side CGI application.
- VBScript can be used to verify that certain data is accurate before processing the data. For example, an online grocery-shopping application developed using VBScript can verify that the user really wants to order four eggs (because most people buy eggs by the dozen).

Manipulating Web-Browser Objects

VBScript applications can modify Web-browser objects such as the background color of the current Web page. This feature is particularly useful for creating sophisticated Web applications. For example, a VBScript subroutine of a multiframe Web application can change the contents of several frames when a user selects a URL or presses a button.

VBScript Programming Tips

When developing applications using VBScript (or any other programming language), you should create source code that is easy to maintain and read. Messy source code often leads to buggy applications that are hard to maintain and debug. The following tips will help you develop robust VBScript applications that are easy to maintain.

Indenting Source Code

Although indentation does not affect the way a VBScript application is executed, the lack of indentation can make an application extremely difficult to debug and maintain. You should indent control structures of applications as shown in Listing 14.2—particularly if it is a complex or large VBScript application. Also, do not be afraid to add blank lines between VBScript code segments to enhance readability and clarity.

Listing 14.2. Indentation makes it easier to read VBScript source code.

```
Sub BtnEvaluate_OnClick
 IF (OperatorBox.Value = "?") THEN
    MsgBoxString = "A valid operator is required to carry out "
    MsgBoxString = MsgBoxString & "an evaluation."
    MsgBoxString = MsgBoxString & chr(10)
    MsgBoxString = MsgBoxString & "Valid operators are: +, -, *"
    MsgBox MsgBoxString , 48 , "Invalid operator!"
 ELSE
    IF (OperatorBox.Value = "+")   THEN
       answer = CDbl(Operand1Box.Value) + CDbl(Operand2Box.Value)
    ELSEIF (OperatorBox.Value = "-")   THEN
       answer = CDbl(Operand1Box.Value) - CDbl(Operand2Box.Value)
    ELSEIF (OperatorBox.Value = "*")   THEN
       answer = CDbl(Operand1Box.Value) * CDbl(Operand2Box.Value)
    End IF
    MsgBox answer , 64 , "Results of calculation"
    Operand1Box.Value = answer
    Operand2Box.Value = 0
 END IF
End Sub
Sub AddDigit ( digit )
 REM Just in case there are any preceding zeros or spaces
 Operand1Box.Value = CDbl (Operand1Box.Value)
 IF ( OperatorBox.Value = "?") THEN
    IF ( Len ( Operand1Box.Value ) < 14 ) THEN
       Operand1Box.Value = Operand1Box.Value & digit
       Operand1Box.Value = CDbl (Operand1Box.Value)
    ELSE
       TooManyDigits
    END IF
 ELSE
    IF ( Len ( Operand2Box.Value ) < 14 ) THEN
       Operand2Box.Value = Operand2Box.Value & digit
       Operand2Box.Value = CDbl (Operand2Box.Value)
    ELSE
       TooManyDigits
    END IF
 END IF
End Sub
```

Using the Code-Continuation Character

The code-continuation character is used to split relatively long VBScript state-ments. Generally, if a VBScript statement is more than 80 lines long, you should use the code-continuation character to break the VBScript statement into two or more lines. This approach makes it easier to indent the VBScript application for easy reading, as shown in Figure 14.4. The code-continuation character is an underscore (_) placed at the end of the line to break a longer line, as demonstrated in lines 2–4 of Listing 14.3. Notice how the code-continuation character makes the VBScript source code easier to read by preserving the indentation of the VBScript code.

Listing 14.3. VBScript code with the code-continuation character.

```
 1: Sub OperatorBox_OnChange
 2:
 3:   IF (NOT((OperatorBox.Value = "+" ) OR _
 4:            (OperatorBox.Value = "-" ) OR _
 5:            (OperatorBox.Value = "*" ) OR _
 6:            (OperatorBox.Value = "?" ))) THEN
 7:     MsgString = "Do not type invalid characters "
 8:     MsgString = MsgString & "into the operator text box! "
 9:     MsgString = MsgString & chr(10)
10:     MsgString = MsgString & "The operator text box will now be reset."
11:     MsgString = MsgString & chr(10) & chr(10)
12:     MsgString = MsgString & "Valid input: +, -, *"
13:     MsgBox MsgString , 48 , "Invalid input detected!"
14:     OperatorBox.Value = "?"
15:   END IF
16:
17:  End Sub
```

Commenting Source Code

Commenting your source code can save hours or even days of application-development time. In the software-development industry, more time is spent maintaining existing applications than developing new ones. Commenting your source code makes it easier for you (or someone else) to understand your application and modify it without creating undue side effects. To insert a comment in VBScript applications, precede the comment with an apostrophe (') or the keyword Rem, like so:

```
' This is a comment
```

or

```
Rem This is a comment
```

Summary

VBScript is a powerful, lightweight scripting language for creating interactive, multimedia-rich, ActiveX-enhanced Web applications. Before client-side scripting languages such as VBScript were available, dynamic Web pages were created by server-side CGI applications. In some cases, the execution of server-side CGI applications is unnecessarily resource intensive. VBScript can be used in such cases to create dynamic content without any interaction with the Web server.

15

Interacting with Users

by Sanjaya Hettihewa

Virtually all VBScript applications interact with users browsing a Web site. Sometimes this interaction is indirect. For example, depending on the time of day, a VBScript application might greet the user with either "Good morning!" or "Good evening!" Although the greeting is displayed on the Web page by a VBScript application, this is not always obvious to the user, because the user did not do anything special to execute the VBScript application (other than viewing it with a Web browser). At other times, the interaction between a VBScript application and the user is very visible and direct—as in the case of an online calculator application.

This chapter demonstrates how to use features of VBScript to directly communicate with the user with the aid of Web-browser objects (HTML form elements, ActiveX controls, and so on) and message boxes. By the end of this chapter, you will be able to create richly interactive Web applications.

Obtaining User Input

There are several ways a VBScript application can obtain user input. Depending on the application and circumstances, you will have to select one or more of the following methods to obtain user input; these methods are discussed in detail in this chapter:

- Using the `InputBox` function to obtain text input from users.
- Using the `MsgBox` function to display a message to the user in a dialog box.
- Using data-entry objects of HTML forms such as textboxes, selection lists, and checkboxes.
- Using ActiveX controls when the application requires more control over various attributes of the data entry fields.

Using the `InputBox` Function

The `InputBox` function is used to obtain input from the user by presenting a dialog box. The syntax of the `InputBox` command is as follows:

```
InputBox(<Prompt>,<Title>,<Default>,<X>,<Y>)
```

Arguments of this command that are enclosed in pointed brackets can be replaced with the following values:

- `<Prompt>`—Dialog box prompt.
- `<Title>`—Title of dialog box.
- `<Default>`—Default input value.
- `<X>`—Horizontal position, in number of twips, from the left side of the screen. A twip is 1/20 of a printer's point, which is 1/1,440 of an inch.
- `<Y>`—Vertical position, in number of twips, from the top of the screen.

The VBScript application in Listing 15.1 demonstrates how the `InputBox` function is used to obtain user input.

Listing 15.1. Obtaining user input using the `InputBox` function.

```
 1: <HTML>
 2: <HEAD>
 3: <TITLE>Using The InputBox Function</TITLE>
 4: </HEAD>
 5: <BODY BGCOLOR="FFFFFF">
 6:
 7: <B>
 8:     <SCRIPT LANGUAGE="VBScript">
 9: <!--
10:
11:   UserInput = InputBox ("Please enter your name ", _
12:               "The InputBox function is used to obtain user input", _
13:               "Please type your name here", 300, 200)
14:
15:   TreeHeight = InputBox ("Please enter the height of your tree", _
16:               "The InputBox function is used to obtain user input", _
17:               "Please type the height of your tree here", 200, 200)
18:
19:   document.write "<PRE>"
20:
21:   For LoopCountVariable = 0 To (TreeHeight-1)
```

```
22:     document.write "Hello " & UserInput & "! "
23:     For AsterisksCountVariable = 0 To (TreeHeight-LoopCountVariable)
24:        document.write " "
25:     Next
26:     For AsterisksCountVariable = 0 To (LoopCountVariable*2)
27:        document.write "*"
28:     Next
29:     document.write "<BR>"
30:   Next
31:
32:   For LineCountVariable = 0 To  (TreeHeight / 3)
33:     For SpaceCountVariable = 0 To ( 7 + Len(UserInput) + (TreeHeight))
34:        document.write " "
35:     Next
36:     document.write "***<BR>"
37:   Next
38:
39:   document.write "</PRE>"
40:
41: -->
42:    </SCRIPT>
43: </B>
44:
45: </BODY>
46: </HTML>
```

The application in Listing 15.1 greets the user with his or her name and draws a tree next to the greeting (as shown in Figure 15.1). The VBScript application uses the InputBox function twice: once to obtain the user's name and once to ascertain the height of the tree.

Lines 19–39 of Listing 15.1 are responsible for greeting the user with the Web page shown in Figure 15.1. You might want to experiment with the VBScript code in lines 19–39 to learn how nested loops can be used to perform various repetitive tasks.

Figure 15.1.
The VBScript application greets the user with his or her name and draws a tree.

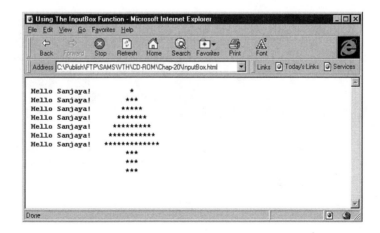

When the application in Listing 15.1 is executed, the user is greeted with the dialog box in Figure 15.2. This dialog box is generated by lines 11–13 of the VBScript application in Listing 15.1. Notice how the default value of the input box "Please type your name here" is displayed and highlighted in the input box.

Figure 15.2.
The VBScript applica-
tion asks for the user's
name.

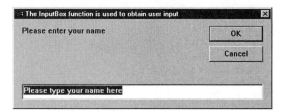

The user can type over the default value of the input box as shown in Figure 15.3. After the user types his or her name and presses the OK button, the dialog box in Figure 15.4 appears.

Figure 15.3.
The user types his or her
name.

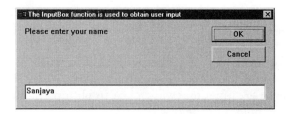

The dialog box in Figure 15.4 obtains the height of the tree that will be displayed on the Web browser. Lines 15–17 of Listing 15.1 are responsible for displaying the dialog box in Figure 15.4. Again, notice how the default value of the input box "Please type the height of your tree here" is displayed and highlighted.

Figure 15.4.
The VBScript applica-
tion asks for the height of
the tree.

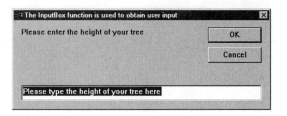

The user can type over the default value of the input box, as shown in Figure 15.5. After the user types the height of the tree, the VBScript application greets the user with the Web page shown in Figure 15.1.

Figure 15.5.

The user selects a tree
seven lines high.

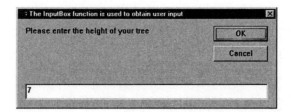

Using HTML Forms

Data-entry fields of HTML forms can be used by VBScript applications to interact with users. Listing 15.2 demonstrates how the application in Listing 15.1 is implemented using an HTML form for data entry. Use HTML forms for data entry when you are not certain your users have an ActiveX-enhanced Web browser such as Internet Explorer.

Listing 15.2. Obtaining user input using the `InputBox` function.

```
 1: <HTML>
 2: <HEAD>
 3: <TITLE>Using HTML Forms For Data Input</TITLE>
 4: </HEAD>
 5: <BODY BGCOLOR="FFFFFF">
 6: <B>
 7:     <FORM NAME="UserInput">
 8: <p>Please enter your name
 9: <INPUT LANGUAGE="VBScript" TYPE=text
10:        VALUE="Please type your name here" SIZE=30
11:        NAME="UserName"></p>
12: <p>Please enter the height of the tree
13: <INPUT LANGUAGE="VBScript" TYPE=text VALUE="7" SIZE=5
14:        NAME="TreeHeight"></p>
15:
16: <INPUT LANGUAGE="VBScript" TYPE=button VALUE="Please greet me!"
17:        ONCLICK="call GreetUser()" NAME="GreetButton"></p>
18:     </FORM>
19:
20:     <SCRIPT LANGUAGE="VBScript">
21: <!--
22: Sub GreetUser
23:
24:    document.open
25:    document.write "<BODY BGCOLOR=FFFFFF>"
26:
27:    Dim UserInput, TreeHeight
28:
29:    UserInput = Document.UserInput.UserName.value
30:    TreeHeight = Document.UserInput.TreeHeight.value
31:
32:    document.write "<PRE>"
33:
```

continues

Listing 15.2. continued

```
34:    For LoopCountVariable = 0 To (TreeHeight-1)
35:      document.write "Hello " & UserInput & "! "
36:      For AsterisksCountVariable = 0 To (TreeHeight-LoopCountVariable)
37:        document.write " "
38:      Next
39:      For AsterisksCountVariable = 0 To (LoopCountVariable*2)
40:        document.write "*"
41:      Next
42:      document.write "<BR>"
43:    Next
44:
45:    For LineCountVariable = 0 To  (TreeHeight / 3)
46:      For SpaceCountVariable = 0 To ( 7 + Len(UserInput) + (TreeHeight))
47:        document.write " "
48:      Next
49:      document.write "***<BR>"
50:    Next
51:
52:    document.write "</PRE>"
53:    document.write "</BODY>"
54:
55:    document.close
56:
57: End Sub
58:
59: -->
60:      </SCRIPT>
61: </B>
62: </BODY>
63: </HTML>
```

When the VBScript application in Listing 15.2 is first invoked, the Web page in Figure 15.6 is displayed. Notice how the GreetUser subroutine is attached to the OnClick event of GreetButton in lines 16 and 17 of Listing 15.2. When a user clicks GreetButton, the GreetUser subroutine is executed. The application in Listing 15.2 uses the document.open and document.close functions to display the user greeting when the user presses the Please greet me! button shown in Figures 15.6 and 15.7.

> # tip
>
> Notice how each of the data-entry fields of the Web page in Figure 15.6 contains default values. It is a good programming practice to include default data values to guide the user into entering valid data. Default data values also ensure that the application correctly executes even when a user forgets to fill in a data-entry field.

Figure 15.6.
The VBScript application in Listing 15.2.

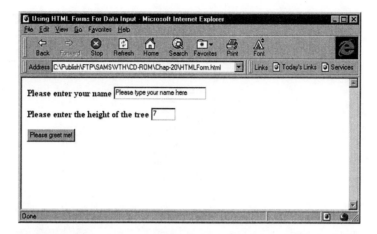

Figure 15.7.
The default values of the VBScript application are modified.

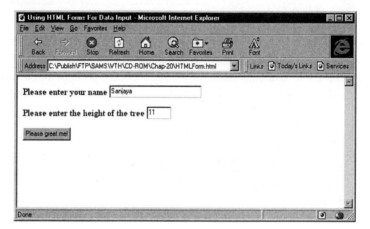

The user can change the default values of the field elements, as shown in Figure 15.7. When the user changes the default data-entry field values, the Please greet me! button is used to view the customized greeting generated by the VBScript application.

The VBScript application greets the user with the Web page shown in Figure 15.8. This Web page was dynamically generated by lines 22–57 of the VBScript application in Listing 15.2. Notice how the document.open and document.close functions are used to change the contents of the Web page without loading a new URL.

Figure 15.8.
*The VBScript applica-
tion greets the user.*

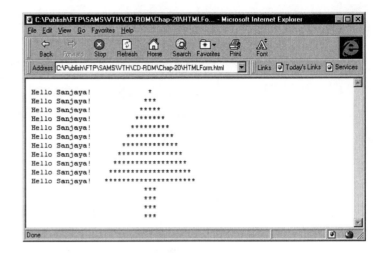

Using ActiveX Controls

The VBScript application in Listing 15.3 demonstrates how ActiveX controls can be used to obtain user input. ActiveX controls provide more control over various attributes of data-entry fields. Notice how the two ActiveX controls with object IDs UserName and HeightOfTree are defined in Listing 15.3 with attributes such as the font name, background color, and character size.

Listing 15.3. Obtaining user input using ActiveX controls.

```
 1: <HTML>
 2: <HEAD>
 3:     <SCRIPT LANGUAGE="VBScript">
 4: <!--
 5: Sub window_onLoad()
 6:   HeightOfTree.AddItem ("1")
 7:   HeightOfTree.AddItem ("2")
 8:   HeightOfTree.AddItem ("3")
 9:   HeightOfTree.AddItem ("4")
10:   HeightOfTree.AddItem ("5")
11:   HeightOfTree.AddItem ("6")
12:   HeightOfTree.AddItem ("7")
13:   HeightOfTree.AddItem ("8")
14:   HeightOfTree.AddItem ("9")
15:   HeightOfTree.AddItem ("10")
16:   HeightOfTree.AddItem ("11")
17: end sub
18: -->
19:     </SCRIPT>
20: <TITLE>Using ActiveX Controls For Data Input</TITLE>
21: </HEAD>
22: <BODY BGCOLOR="FFFFFF">
23: <B>
24: <p>Please enter your name
25:     <OBJECT ID="UserName" WIDTH=215 HEIGHT=24
```

```
26:        CLASSID="CLSID:8BD21D10-EC42-11CE-9E0D-00AA006002F3">
27:            <PARAM NAME="VariousPropertyBits" VALUE="746604571">
28:            <PARAM NAME="BackColor" VALUE="13828080">
29:            <PARAM NAME="Size" VALUE="5680;635">
30:            <PARAM NAME="Value" VALUE="Please type your name here">
31:            <PARAM NAME="FontCharSet" VALUE="0">
32:            <PARAM NAME="FontPitchAndFamily" VALUE="2">
33:        </OBJECT>
34: </p>
35:
36: <p>Please select the height of the tree
37:        <OBJECT ID="HeightOfTree" WIDTH=83 HEIGHT=24
38:         CLASSID="CLSID:8BD21D30-EC42-11CE-9E0D-00AA006002F3">
39:            <PARAM NAME="VariousPropertyBits" VALUE="746604571">
40:            <PARAM NAME="BackColor" VALUE="12184829">
41:            <PARAM NAME="DisplayStyle" VALUE="3">
42:            <PARAM NAME="Size" VALUE="2187;635">
43:            <PARAM NAME="MatchEntry" VALUE="1">
44:            <PARAM NAME="ShowDropButtonWhen" VALUE="2">
45:            <PARAM NAME="FontEffects" VALUE="1073741825">
46:            <PARAM NAME="FontHeight" VALUE="200">
47:            <PARAM NAME="FontCharSet" VALUE="0">
48:            <PARAM NAME="FontPitchAndFamily" VALUE="2">
49:            <PARAM NAME="FontWeight" VALUE="700">
50:        </OBJECT>
51: </P>
52:        <SCRIPT LANGUAGE="VBScript">
53: <!--
54: Sub GreetMeButton_Click()
55: call GreetUser()
56: end sub
57: -->
58:        </SCRIPT>
59:        <OBJECT ID="GreetMeButton" WIDTH=132 HEIGHT=32
60:         CLASSID="CLSID:D7053240-CE69-11CD-A777-00DD01143C57">
61:            <PARAM NAME="Caption" VALUE="Please greet me!">
62:            <PARAM NAME="Size" VALUE="3493;846">
63:            <PARAM NAME="FontEffects" VALUE="1073741825">
64:            <PARAM NAME="FontHeight" VALUE="200">
65:            <PARAM NAME="FontCharSet" VALUE="0">
66:            <PARAM NAME="FontPitchAndFamily" VALUE="2">
67:            <PARAM NAME="ParagraphAlign" VALUE="3">
68:            <PARAM NAME="FontWeight" VALUE="700">
69:        </OBJECT>
70: </B>
71:        <SCRIPT LANGUAGE="VBScript">
72: <!--
73: Sub GreetUser
74:
75:    document.open
76:    document.write "<BODY BGCOLOR=FFFFFF>"
77:
78:    Dim UserInput, TreeHeight
79:
80:    UserInput = UserName.Value
81:    TreeHeight = HeightOfTree.Value
82:
```

continues

Listing 15.3. continued

```
83:    document.write "<PRE>"
84:
85:    For LoopCountVariable = 0 To (TreeHeight-1)
86:      document.write "Hello " & UserInput & "! "
87:      For AsterisksCountVariable = 0 To (TreeHeight-LoopCountVariable)
88:        document.write " "
89:      Next
90:      For AsterisksCountVariable = 0 To (LoopCountVariable*2)
91:        document.write "*"
92:      Next
93:      document.write "<BR>"
94:    Next
95:
96:    For LineCountVariable = 0 To  (TreeHeight / 3)
97:      For SpaceCountVariable = 0 To ( 7 + Len(UserInput) + (TreeHeight))
98:        document.write " "
99:      Next
100:     document.write "***<BR>"
101:   Next
102:
103:   document.write "</PRE>"
104:   document.write "</BODY>"
105:
106:   document.close
107:
108: End Sub
109:
110: -->
111:     </SCRIPT>
112: </B>
113: </BODY>
114: </HTML>
```

As shown in Figure 15.9, the application in Listing 15.3 consists of three ActiveX controls: a textbox, combo box, and push button.

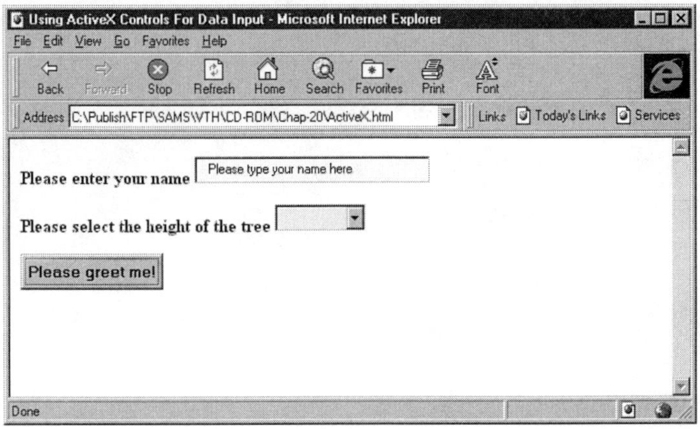

Figure 15.9.
*The ActiveX application
with its default values.*

Users can select various values using the ActiveX controls, as shown in Figure 15.10. After selecting values, users click the GreetMeButton ActiveX control defined in lines 59–69 of Listing 15.3.

Figure 15.10.
The default values of the ActiveX application are changed.

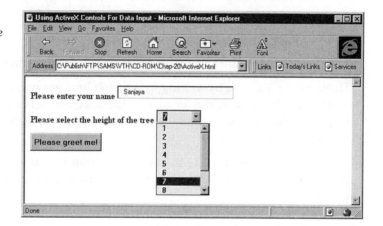

The output of the application in Listing 15.3 appears in Figure 15.11. When you compare Listing 15.3 with Listing 15.2, you will realize that the main difference between the two applications is the presence of ActiveX controls in Listing 15.3. Listing 15.3 uses ActiveX controls instead of HTML-form, data-entry controls for data input.

Figure 15.11.
Output of the ActiveX application in Listing 15.3.

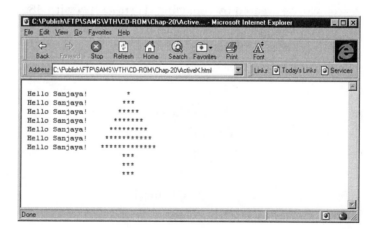

Displaying Messages

Virtually all VBScript applications display messages to the user. VBScript applications can display messages in the following ways:

- By writing to the Web-browser window
- By displaying the message in a message box
- By changing the properties of an HTML-form element or ActiveX control

Displaying messages by writing to the Web-browser window is very straightforward. All that's required is to use the document.write function. HTML-form elements and ActiveX controls can be used to display messages by using VBScript to set their properties.

Displaying messages using the MsgBox function is a more involved process. The next section demonstrates how the MsgBox function is used to display messages to the user.

Using the MsgBox Function

A message box can be displayed using the MsgBox command. Its syntax follows:

```
MsgBox <MessageBoxPrompt>,<ButtonStyle>,<Title>
```

By replacing <ButtonStyle> with various values shown in Table 15.1, a message box can be customized. For example, an OK dialog box with a warning message icon can be created by replacing <ButtonStyle> with 48.

Table 15.1. Message box codes.

Button Type	Button Description
0	OK
1	OK and Cancel
2	Abort, Retry, and Ignore
3	Yes, No, and Cancel
4	Yes and No
5	Retry and Cancel
16	Critical Message icon
32	Warning Query icon
48	Warning Message icon
64	Information Message icon
256	Second button is default

Button Type	Button Description
512	Third button is default
4096	Message box always appears on top of all other windows until the user responds to it

The VBScript application in Listing 15.4 demonstrates how messages are displayed using the MsgBox function.

Listing 15.4. Displaying messages using the MsgBox function.

```
1: <!--
2: © 1996 Sanjaya Hettihewa (http://www.NetInnovation.com/)
3: All Rights Reserved.
4:Permission is hereby given to modify and distribute this code as you wish
5: provided that this block of text remains unchanged.
6:  !-->
7:
8: <HTML>
9:
10: <HEAD>
11:    <SCRIPT LANGUAGE="VBScript">
12: <!--
13: Sub window_onLoad()
14:
15:    MessageBoxType.AddItem ("OK message box")
16:    MessageBoxType.AddItem ("OK / Cancel message box")
17:    MessageBoxType.AddItem ("Abort / Retry / Ignore message box")
18:    MessageBoxType.AddItem ("Yes / No / Cancel message box")
19:    MessageBoxType.AddItem ("Yes / No message box")
20:    MessageBoxType.AddItem ("Retry / Cancel message box")
21:
22:    MessageBoxIcon.AddItem ("Critical message icon")
23:    MessageBoxIcon.AddItem ("Warning query icon")
24:    MessageBoxIcon.AddItem ("Warning message icon")
25:    MessageBoxIcon.AddItem ("Information message icon")
26:
27:    MessageBoxButtonStatus.AddItem ("First button is default")
28:    MessageBoxButtonStatus.AddItem ("Second button is default")
29:    MessageBoxButtonStatus.AddItem ("Third button is default")
30: end sub
31: -->
32:    </SCRIPT>
33:
34:    <TITLE>Using MsgBox For Displaying Data</TITLE>
35: </HEAD>
36:
37: <BODY BGCOLOR="FFFFFF">
38: <B>
39:    <FORM NAME="MsgBoxOptions">
40: <p>Title of the message box
41:        <INPUT TYPE=text VALUE="Title of message box" SIZE=25
                NAME="MsgBoxTitle"></p>
```

continues

Listing 15.4. continued

```
42:        <p>Message box prompt
43:            <INPUT TYPE=text VALUE="Prompt of message box" SIZE=27
                    NAME="MsgBoxPrompt"></p>
44:        <INPUT TYPE=checkbox VALUE="ON" NAME="OnTop">
45:            Message box always appears on top of all other windows until the
            user responds to the message box
46:        </FORM>
47:
48:        <p>Please select type of message box
49:            <OBJECT ID="MessageBoxType" WIDTH=215 HEIGHT=24
50:             CLASSID="CLSID:8BD21D30-EC42-11CE-9E0D-00AA006002F3">
51:                <PARAM NAME="VariousPropertyBits" VALUE="746604571">
52:                <PARAM NAME="BackColor" VALUE="14022655">
53:                <PARAM NAME="DisplayStyle" VALUE="3">
54:                <PARAM NAME="Size" VALUE="5657;635">
55:                <PARAM NAME="MatchEntry" VALUE="1">
56:                <PARAM NAME="ShowDropButtonWhen" VALUE="2">
57:                <PARAM NAME="FontCharSet" VALUE="0">
58:                <PARAM NAME="FontPitchAndFamily" VALUE="2">
59:            </OBJECT></P>
60:
61:        <p>Please select icon of message box
62:        <OBJECT ID="MessageBoxIcon" WIDTH=215 HEIGHT=24
63:         CLASSID="CLSID:8BD21D30-EC42-11CE-9E0D-00AA006002F3">
64:            <PARAM NAME="VariousPropertyBits" VALUE="746604571">
65:            <PARAM NAME="BackColor" VALUE="14022655">
66:            <PARAM NAME="DisplayStyle" VALUE="3">
67:            <PARAM NAME="Size" VALUE="5657;635">
68:            <PARAM NAME="MatchEntry" VALUE="1">
69:            <PARAM NAME="ShowDropButtonWhen" VALUE="2">
70:            <PARAM NAME="FontCharSet" VALUE="0">
71:            <PARAM NAME="FontPitchAndFamily" VALUE="2">
72:        </OBJECT></P>
73:
74:        <p>Please select the status of buttons
75:        <OBJECT ID="MessageBoxButtonStatus" WIDTH=215 HEIGHT=24
76:         CLASSID="CLSID:8BD21D30-EC42-11CE-9E0D-00AA006002F3">
77:            <PARAM NAME="VariousPropertyBits" VALUE="746604571">
78:            <PARAM NAME="BackColor" VALUE="14022655">
79:            <PARAM NAME="DisplayStyle" VALUE="3">
80:            <PARAM NAME="Size" VALUE="5657;635">
81:            <PARAM NAME="MatchEntry" VALUE="1">
82:            <PARAM NAME="ShowDropButtonWhen" VALUE="2">
83:            <PARAM NAME="FontCharSet" VALUE="0">
84:            <PARAM NAME="FontPitchAndFamily" VALUE="2">
85:        </OBJECT></P>
86:
87: <p><INPUT TYPE=button VALUE="Please click here to see your message box!"
88:        NAME="MsgBoxButton"></p>
89:
90: </B>
91:
92:    <SCRIPT LANGUAGE="VBScript">
93: <!--
94: Sub MsgBoxButton_OnClick()
95:
```

```
96:    Dim MessageBoxStyleCode, MessageBoxString, ValidInput
97:
98:    MessageBoxStyleCode = 0
99:    ValidInput = 1
100:
101:   If MsgBoxOptions.OnTop.Checked Then
102:      MessageBoxStyleCode = MessageBoxStyleCode + 4096
103:   End If
104:
105:   Select Case MessageBoxType.Value
106:      Case "OK message box"
107:         MessageBoxStyleCode = MessageBoxStyleCode + 0
108:      Case "OK / Cancel message box"
109:         MessageBoxStyleCode = MessageBoxStyleCode + 1
110:      Case "Abort / Retry / Ignore message box"
111:         MessageBoxStyleCode = MessageBoxStyleCode + 2
112:      Case "Yes / No / Cancel message box"
113:         MessageBoxStyleCode = MessageBoxStyleCode + 3
114:      Case "Yes / No message box"
115:         MessageBoxStyleCode = MessageBoxStyleCode + 4
116:      Case "Retry / Cancel message box"
117:         MessageBoxStyleCode = MessageBoxStyleCode + 5
118:      Case Else
119:         MsgBox "I'm sorry but you have selected an " & _
120:                "invalid message box type." & _
121:                Chr(10) & "Please select a valid message " & _
122:                "box type using a" & Chr(10) & "pull down " & _
123:                "menu and try again.", 16, "Invalid Input!"
124:         ValidInput = 0
125:   End Select
126:
127:   Select Case MessageBoxIcon.Value
128:      Case "Critical message icon"
129:         MessageBoxStyleCode = MessageBoxStyleCode + 16
130:      Case "Warning query icon"
131:         MessageBoxStyleCode = MessageBoxStyleCode + 32
132:      Case "Warning message icon"
133:         MessageBoxStyleCode = MessageBoxStyleCode + 48
134:      Case "Information message icon"
135:         MessageBoxStyleCode = MessageBoxStyleCode + 64
136:      Case Else
137:         MsgBox "I'm sorry but you have selected an invalid " & _
138:                    "message box icon." & Chr(10) & "Please " & _
139:                    "select a valid message box icon using a" & _
140:                  Chr(10) & "pull down menu and try again.", 16, _
141:                    "Invalid Input!"
142:         ValidInput = 0
143:   End Select
144:
145:   Select Case MessageBoxButtonStatus.Value
146:      Case "First button is default"
147:         MessageBoxStyleCode = MessageBoxStyleCode + 0
148:      Case "Second button is default"
149:         MessageBoxStyleCode = MessageBoxStyleCode + 256
150:      Case "Third button is default"
151:         MessageBoxStyleCode = MessageBoxStyleCode + 512
```

continues

Listing 15.4. continued

```
152:     Case Else
153:       MsgBox "I'm sorry but the status of message box " & _
154:              "buttons you selected" & Chr(10) & "is invalid. " & _
155:              "Please select a valid message box button status " & _
156:              "using" & Chr(10) & "a pull down menu and try again.", _
157:              16, "Invalid Input!"
158:       ValidInput = 0
159:   End Select
160:
161:   If ValidInput Then
162:     MessageBoxString = _
163:              "The message box you are about to see is created " & _
164:              "using the following VBScript statement: " & CHR(10) & _
165:              Chr(10) & "MsgBox "  & Chr(42) & _
166:              MsgBoxOptions.MsgBoxPrompt.Value & Chr(42) & ", " _
167:              & MessageBoxStyleCode & ", " & _
168:              Chr(42) & MsgBoxOptions.MsgBoxTitle.Value & Chr(42)
169:     MsgBox MessageBoxString, 64, "Information"
170:     MsgBox MsgBoxOptions.MsgBoxPrompt.Value, _
171:              MessageBoxStyleCode, MsgBoxOptions.MsgBoxTitle.Value
172:   End If
173:
174: End Sub
175: -->
176:     </SCRIPT>
177:
178: </BODY>
179: </HTML>
```

The user interface of the application in Listing 15.4 is shown in Figure 15.12; virtually any type of message box can be created using the data-entry controls in this figure.

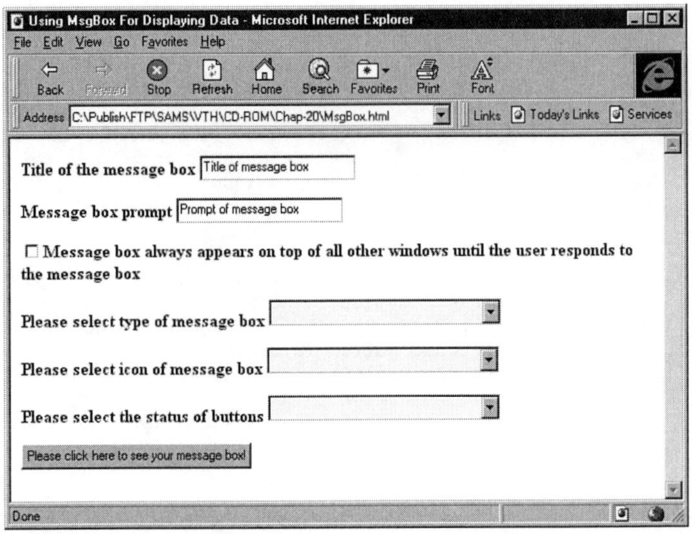

Figure 15.12.
The MsgBox *application.*

Change the values of the data-entry fields, as shown in Figure 15.13. Notice how the pull-down menus are used to select the characteristics of the message box being created. After specifying these characteristics, click the Please click here to see your message box! button.

Figure 15.13.
Data-entry fields of the MsgBox *application are used to choose the characteristics of a message box.*

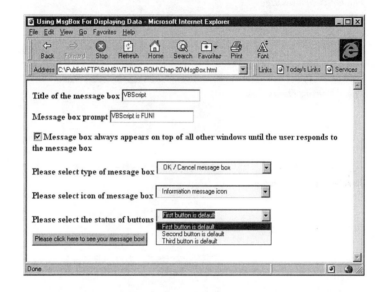

The Information dialog box in Figure 15.14 appears. This dialog box displays the actual VBScript statement used to generate a message box with the characteristics selected in Figure 15.13.

Figure 15.14.
The VBScript statement used to generate the message box selected in Figure 15.13.

After acknowledging the dialog box in Figure 15.14, the application in Listing 15.4 displays a message box with the characteristics selected in Figure 15.13 (as shown in Figure 15.15).

Figure 15.15.
Output of the ActiveX application in Listing 15.4.

Figures 15.16–15.19 show the types of message boxes that can be created using the MsgBox function.

Figure 15.16.
The Critical Message box.

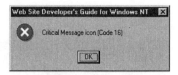

Figure 15.17.
The Warning Query box.

Figure 15.18.
The Warning Message box.

Figure 15.19.
The Information Message box.

Summary

Most Web applications interact with users to obtain and display information, and VBScript provides a rich set of tools for obtaining and displaying information to users. The user-interaction tips and techniques presented in this chapter can be used to develop richly interactive Web applications. VBScript can obtain user input from HTML-form data-entry elements, dialog boxes, and ActiveX controls. Use ActiveX controls to interact with users when you are certain your users have an ActiveX-enhanced Web browser, because ActiveX controls provide additional control over various attributes of data-entry objects. When interacting with users, you should validate user input before processing it.

C H A P T E R

16

VBScript Reference

by Weiying Chen

This chapter provides reference information for Visual Basic Scripting Edition (VBScript). It discusses the following:

- Variables and their data types
- Operators
- Constants
- Flow controls
- Sub routines and functions

> # note
>
> The VBScript features supported in Internet Explorer are dependent on the version of the VBScript.DLL installed on your system. If you try some of the programmatic statements discussed in this chapter and they do not work, it is likely that you have version 1 of the DLL installed on your system. You can download version 2 from the Microsoft Web site at http://www.microsoft.com/vbscript, which is available at the time of this writing. Version 3, which is currently in beta, will be available shortly.

Variables and Data Types

This section discusses variables and the data types recognized by VBScript.

Variables

A variable represents information in the program that can change as the script runs. A variable name

- Must begin with an alphabetic character
- Cannot contain an embedded period
- Must not exceed 255 characters

Also, variable names must be unique within the scope in which they are declared. The value of a variable declared outside a function or subprocedure is globally accessible throughout the script.

Declaring Variables

Variables can be declared explicitly with the Dim statement, as in the following:

```
Dim strVar
```

You can also declare several variables at once, like this:

```
Dim iTop, iBottom, iLeft, iRight
```

A variable can also be declared implicitly by simply assigning a value and beginning to use it, like this:

```
iNbr = 345
```

or this:

```
strVar = "The Big Apple"
```

However, this is not generally considered to be good programming practice because of the potential for introducing errors. To prevent the implicit declaration of a variable, use the Option Explicit statement, as in the following code:

```
Option Explicit
Dim MaxNbr
MaxNbr = 170
```

If the Option Explicit statement is placed at the beginning of your program and a variable is implicitly declared (by using it without first including it in a Dim statement), then an error is generated at runtime. (See Figure 16.1.)

Figure 16.1.
Runtime error generated by an undeclared variable.

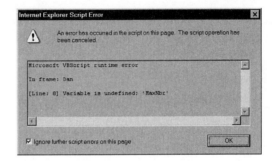

Variable Type Representation

A string literal is enclosed in quotation marks (" "), the most obvious way to differentiate string values from numeric values. Date literals and time literals can be represented by enclosing them in number signs (# #), like this:

```
StartDate = #01/01/95#
```

or this:

```
StartTime = #9:30#
```

The Scope of a Variable

The scope of the variable is controlled by where the variable is declared. Variables declared outside a procedure or function are *global*. A variable declared within a procedure or function is *local* to the procedure or function.

Scalars and Arrays

A variable can be a scalar or an array. A variable containing a single value is a *scalar* variable, as in the following example:

```
Count = Count + 1
```

A variable containing a series of values is an *array*. Arrays are declared in much the same way as scalar variables, except that the declaration of an array uses parentheses following the variable name, which can contain the number of elements in the array:

```
Dim AnArray(3)
```

An array declared in this way is called a *fixed-size array*. All arrays in VBScript start numbering at 0, so this array contains four elements. (In a zero-based array, the number of array elements is always one more than the number in parentheses.)

To assign data to an element of the array, use an assignment statement with an index into the array. For example, a value could be assigned to the third element of an array with the following statement:

```
A(2) = "Apple"
```

Data can be retrieved from an element using an index into the particular array element you want. For example:

```
strVar = A(8)
```

An array with multiple dimensions is declared by specifying the size of each dimension within the parentheses, separated by commas, as in the following:

```
Dim A(4, 10)
```

The first number indicates the rows, and the second number indicates the columns. An array can have up to 60 dimensions, although it is difficult to understand what an array with more than 3 or 4 dimensions represents.

An array can also be declared as a *dynamic array*, which means it can change size during the execution of the script. A dynamic array is declared by omitting the size within the parentheses with the Dim statements, like this:

```
Dim DynamArray()
```

However, when a dynamic array has been declared, you must use the ReDim statement to specify the array's number of dimensions and the size of each, like this:

```
ReDim DynamArray(9, 4)
```

This statement sets the initial size of the dynamic array to 10 rows and five columns. A subsequent ReDim statement can change the size for the array. However, if you change the size without using the Preserve keyword, any contents of the array will be lost. To add rows, for example, without losing the previously stored data, use a statement like the following:

```
ReDim Preserve DynamArray(9,5)
```

Although there is no limit to the number of times you can resize a dynamic array, if you make the size of a particular dimension smaller than it was, you will lose the data in the eliminated elements. In addition, if you resize a dimension in a multidimensional array, you can change only the last dimension. Further, you cannot change the number of dimensions without losing all the data in the array.

Data Types

Within VBScript, there is only one data type, the variant. However, this data type can be interpreted as several subtypes, depending on how the variable is used. For example, if the variable contains a string, it will be used as a string. If the variable contains all numeric characters, it will be used as a number. Data enclosed in quotes will be interpreted as a string. In addition to numbers and strings, a variable can be interpreted as one of the subtypes shown in Table 16.1.

Table 16.1. Data subtypes.

Subtype	Description
Boolean	Any variable that contains a number other than 0 can be interpreted as True in a Boolean expression. Any variable that contains a 0 can be interpreted as False.
Byte	An integer in the range of 0–255.
Currency	A number in the range of –922,337,203,685,477.5808 to 922,337,203,685,477.5807.
Date/Time	A number that represents a date between January 1, 100 and December 31, 9999.
Double	A double-precision, floating-point number in the range of –1.79769313486232E308 to –4.94065645841247E-324 for negative values or 4.94065645841247E-324 to 1.79769313486232E308 for positive values.
Empty	An uninitialized variable. Its value is 0 when used as a number or a zero-length string ("") when used as a string.
Error	An error number.
Integer	An integer in the range of –32,768 to 32,767.
Long	An integer in the range of –2,147,483,648 to 2,147,483,647.
Null	A variable intentionally initialized with no data.
Single	A single-precision, floating-point number in the range of –3.402823E38 to –1.401298E-45 for negative values or 1.401298E-45 to 3.402823E38 for positive values.
String	A variable-length string that can be up to approximately 2 billion characters in length.
Object	A variable containing an object.

Operators

VBScript has the full range of normal operators that you would expect, including comparison, arithmetic, logical, and concatenation operators. Operators within an expression are evaluated in the order of precedence. However, parentheses can be used to override this order and force some parts of an expression to be evaluated first.

For expressions that have more than one category of operator, the order of evaluation is as follows:

- Arithmetic
- Comparison
- Boolean (logical)

Comparison Operators

Comparison operators all have equal precedence. That is, they are evaluated from left to right in the statement in which they appear. These operators are shown in Table 16.2.

Table 16.2. Comparison operators.

Operator	Description
=	Equal to
<	Less than
>	Greater than
<=	Less than or equal to
>=	Greater than or equal to

Mathematical Operators

The mathematical operators are shown in evaluation order in Table 16.3.

Table 16.3. Mathematical operators.

Operator	Description	Example
^	Exponentiation	
-	Unary negation	
*	Multiplication	
/	Division	(x = 5 / 2 sets x equal to 2.5)
\	Integer division	(x = 5 \ 2 sets x equal to 2)

Operator	Description	Example
mod	Modulus (remainder) arithmetic	(x = 10 mod 3 results in x equal to 1)
+	Addition	
-	Subtraction	

Boolean Operators

Expressions that evaluate to true or false are referred to as *Boolean statements*. The Boolean operators combine Boolean expressions to produce a compound expression that also evaluates to true or false. In VBScript, the Boolean operators will also perform bitwise operations on algebraic expressions.

The Boolean operators in VBScript, in order of precedence, follow:

- NOT
- AND
- OR
- XOR
- EQV
- IMP

NOT

The NOT operator negates the value of a Boolean statement.

The truth table for the NOT operator is shown in Figure 16.2.

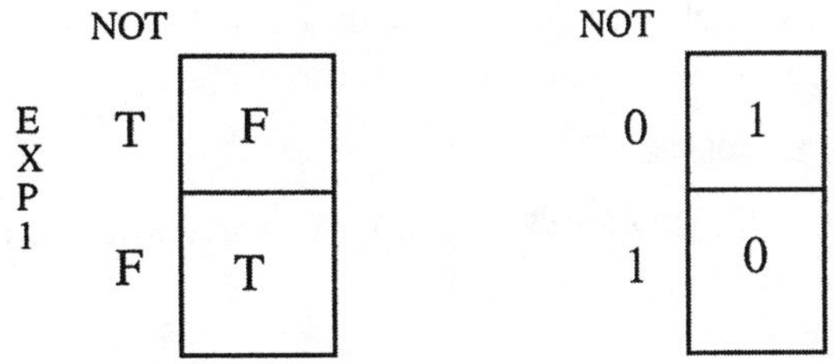

Figure 16.2.
The NOT truth table.

AND

The AND operator results in a true statement when both expressions are true, as in the following:

```
ANS = E1 AND E2
```

The truth table for the AND operator is shown in Figure 16.3.

Figure 16.3.
The AND *truth table.*

AND (EXP1 \ EXP2)	T	F
T	T	F
F	F	F

AND (EXP1 \ EXP2)	0	1
0	0	0
1	0	1

OR

The OR operator results in a `true` statement when either statement is true, as in the following:

```
ANS = E1 OR E2
```

The truth table for the OR operator is shown in Figure 16.4.

Figure 16.4.
The OR *truth table.*

OR (EXP1 \ EXP2)	T	F
T	T	T
F	T	F

OR (EXP1 \ EXP2)	0	1
0	0	1
1	1	1

XOR

The XOR (exclusive OR) results in a `true` statement when one, and only one, of the arguments is true, as in the following:

```
ANS = E1 XOR E2
```

The truth table for the XOR operator is shown in Figure 16.5.

Figure 16.5.
The XOR *truth table.*

XOR (EXP1 \ EXP2)	T	F
T	F	T
F	T	F

XOR (EXP1 \ EXP2)	0	1
0	0	1
1	1	0

EQV

The EQV operator results in a true statement when both expressions have the same truth value, both true or both false, as in the following:

```
ANS = E1 EQV E2
```

The truth table for the EQV operator is shown in Figure 16.6.

Figure 16.6.
The EQV truth table.

EQV	EXP2 T	F
EXP1 T	T	F
EXP1 F	F	T

EQV	EXP2 0	1
0	1	0
1	0	1

IMP

The IMP operator (implication) results in a true statement when the first expression implies the second, as in the following:

```
ANS = E1 IMP E2
```

The evaluation of this statement will result in ANS being set to false when E1 is true and E2 is false. In all other cases, ANS will be true.

The truth table for the IMP operator is shown in Figure 16.7.

Figure 16.7.
The IMP truth table.

IMP	EXP2 T	F
EXP1 T	T	F
EXP1 F	T	T

IMP	EXP2 0	1
0	1	1
1	0	1

String Concatenation

Strings can be concatenated using the string operators "&" or "+". (Microsoft does not recommend the use of "+".) The factors of the operation are strings or variants containing strings. The result is a string composed of the first string followed by the second string, as in the following code:

```
If
strClr1 = "Black" and strClr2 = "White"
then
strClrs = strClr1 & strClr2
sets the variable strClrs to "BlackWhite"
```

Constants

There are several constants defined within VBScript. You can also create user-defined constants with the Const statement.

Standard Constants

There are several constants defined within the language, such as colors and the days of the week. The valid color constants are shown in Table 16.4. The valid constants for days of the week are shown in Table 16.5.

Table 16.4. Color constants.

Color constants	Value	Description
vbBlack	&h00	Black
vbRed	&hFF	Red
vbGreen	&hFF00	Green
vbYellow	&hFFFF	Yellow
vbBlue	&hFF0000	Blue
vbMagenta	&hFF00FF	Magenta
vbCyan	&hFFFF00	Red
vbWhite	&hFFFFFF	White

Table 16.5. Weekday constants.

Day constants	Value	Description
vbSunday	1	Sunday
vbMonday	2	Monday
vbTuesday	3	Tuesday
vbWednesday	4	Wednesday
vbThursday	5	Thursday
vbFriday	6	Friday
vbSaturday	7	Saturday
vbFirstJan1	1	Use the week in which January 1 occurs (default)

Day constants	Value	Description
vbFirstFourDays	2	Use the first week that has at least four days in the new year
vbFirstFullWeek	3	Use the first full week of the year
vbUseSystem	0	Use the date format contained in the regional settings for your computer
vbUseSystemDayOfWeek	0	Use the day of the week specified in your system settings for the first day of the week

User-Defined Constants

Defining a constant allows you to give a meaningful name to take the place of a value that never changes. One of the benefits of defining and using constants is that if the value needs to change for some reason, you can easily change it at one place in the program, rather than having to hunt for every occurrence throughout the file.

In VBScript, constants are implemented as literal values assigned to constant names, using the Const statement and an assignment statement, like this:

```
Const MyString = "This is my string."
```

Or this:

```
Const MyAge = 49
```

Flow Control

VBScript provides four types of statements that can be used to control the flow of the program:

- If...Then...Else
- Do...Loop
- While...Wend
- For...Next

If...Then...Else

The If...Then...Else statement executes statements based on the truth value of the test condition. The syntax of this statement is as follows:

```
If <condition> Then
<statement block>
```

```
Else
<statement block>
End If
```

Listing 16.1 shows an example of the If… Then statement.

Listing 16.1. An example of the If . . . Then statement.

```
nbr = Document.Entry.Number.Value
if isNumeric(nbr) Then
if nbr > 170 Then
MsgBox "That number is too big to calculate."
Else
MsgBox "The factorial of " & nbr & " is " & Factorial(nbr)& "."
End If
Else
MsgBox "Enter a number."
End If
```

Do... Loop

The Do... Loop statement executes a block of statements while a truth condition is true, or until the truth condition becomes true. The condition can be tested after executing the block of statements once, or prior to executing the statement block, depending on the syntax used:

```
Do
<statement block>
[Exit Do]
<statement block>
End Do [Until ¦ While]
or
Do [Until ¦ While]
<statement block>
[Exit Do]
<statement block>
End Do
```

An example of the Do...End Do statement is shown in Listing 16.2.

Listing 16.2. An example of the Do . . . End Do statement.

```
Do
x = x + 1
document.write "<LI> A(x)"
End Do Until (x > 10)
```

While...Wend

The While...Wend statement executes a statement block as long as the test condition is true. The statement functions similar to the Do...While statement. Its syntax follows:

```
While <condition>
<statement block>
Wend
```

An example of this statement is shown in Listing 16.3.

Listing 16.3. An example of the While...Wend statement.

```
X = 0
While X < 10
document.write "<LI>" & A(X)
X = X + 1
Wend
```

For...Next

The For...Next statement executes a block of statements for a specified number of times. The syntax of this statement follows:

```
For <count> = <start> to <limit> Step <stepval>
<statement block>
Next
```

where

> count is the control variable.

> start is the initial value.

> limit is the maximum value.

> stepval is the increment added to count each time through the loop. count can be decremented each time, if stepval is a negative number.

In Listing 16.4, the For...Next statement executes five times, starting at 4. The STEP -1 statement causes the control variable to be decremented.

Listing 16.4. An example of a For...Next statement.

```
FOR X = 4 TO 0 STEP -1
IF ((DEST(X) = DEST2(X)) AND (ORG(X) = ORG2(X))) THEN
RSLT = DIST(X)
ORIGIN = ORG(X)
DESTINATION = DEST(X)
END IF
NEXT
```

Function and Sub Procedures

VBScript has two kinds of procedures, Sub and Function procedures. Sub procedures perform an action when called, without returning a value. Function procedures perform actions and return a value to the calling statement. Arguments are passed to functions and Sub procedures by value, which means that the Function or Sub procedure cannot change the value of the argument outside itself.

Function Procedures

Function procedures can return a value to the calling statement, like this:

```
x = Factorial(iNbr)
```

Functions must always be used on the right side of a variable assignment or in an expression, like this:

```
Temp = Factorial(iNbr)
```

or this:

```
MsgBox "The factorial of " & nbr & " is " & Factorial(nbr) & "."
```

Function procedures are defined by VBScript statements enclosed between the Function and End Function statements. A Function procedure can take arguments that are constants, variables, or expressions passed by the calling statement. If a Function procedure has no arguments, it must still contain an empty set of parentheses. All functions return the variant data type.

In Listing 16.5, the function calculates the factorial of an integer passed as an argument to the function. This listing provides an example of how a function returns its result.

Listing 16.5. An example of a Function procedure.

```
Function Factorial(iNbr)
' This function shows an example of recursion, which is supported by VBScript.
'However, this should be used cautiously, because it can cause stack overflow.
If iNbr = 1 Then
Factorial = 1
Else
Factorial = iNbr * Factorial(iNbr - 1)
End If
End Function
```

Sub Procedures

Sub procedures execute statements but do not return a value. Sub procedures are defined by VBScript statements enclosed between the Sub and End Sub statements. A Sub procedure can take arguments that are constants, variables, or expressions passed by the calling statement. If the Sub procedure has no arguments, it must still contain an empty set of parentheses. Here is an example:

```
Sub DisplayFactorial()
nbr = InputBox("Please enter an integer.", 1)
MsgBox "The factorial of " & nbr & " is " & Factorial(nbr) & "."
End Sub
```

InputBox is a built-in VBScript function that prompts a user for input. MsgBox is a built-in function, used here to display the result of the calculation of the Factorial function.

Procedure Arguments

Data is passed into a procedure through *arguments*. Arguments serve as place-holders for the data passed into the procedure. Parentheses must be included after the name of the procedure being defined. Any arguments placed within the parentheses are separated by commas. For example, in the following function, iRow and iCol are placeholders for the values passed in.

```
Function TableSize(iRow, iCol)
TableSize = iRow * iCol
End Function
```

Function arguments must follow the same rules for naming that variables do.

Calling a Sub Procedure

You can call one Sub procedure from another by typing the name of the procedure, along with the values of any arguments, separated by commas. Or, you can use the Call statement; however, if you do so, you must enclose the arguments in parentheses.

The following example shows these two methods for calling the same procedure. Although these are equivalent statements, notice that the parentheses are omitted in the call when the Call statement is not used.

```
Call AProc(arg_one, arg_two)
AProc arg_one, arg_two
```

Dialog Box Functions

There are two important built-in functions for getting input from the user and displaying messages to them:

- `InputBox`
- `MsgBox`

InputBox

The `InputBox` function displays a prompt in a dialog box and waits for you to input text or choose a button. If the user clicks OK or presses Enter, the `InputBox` function returns whatever is in the text box to the calling statement. If the user clicks Cancel, the function returns a zero-length string (`""`).

The syntax for this statement follows:

```
InputBox(prompt[, title][, default][, xpos][, ypos][, helpfile, context])
```

where the arguments to the statement call have the following meanings:

- `prompt` is a string expression displayed as the message in the dialog box. The maximum length of prompt is about 1,000 characters, depending on the width of the characters used. If `Prompt` consists of more than one line, you can separate the lines using a carriage return character (`Chr(13)`), a linefeed character (`Chr(10)`), or both (`Chr(13)` and `Chr(10)`).

- `title` is a string expression displayed in the title bar of the dialog box. If you omit the title, the name of the application is placed in the title bar.

- `default` is a string expression displayed in the text box as the default response if no other input is provided. If you omit the default, an empty text box is displayed.

- `xpos` is a numeric expression that specifies, in twips, the horizontal distance of the left edge of the dialog box from the left edge of the screen. (A twip is 1/20th of a pixel.) If `xpos` is omitted, the dialog box is horizontally centered.

- `ypos` is a numeric expression that specifies, in twips, the vertical distance of the upper edge of the dialog box from the top of the screen. If `ypos` is omitted, the dialog box is vertically positioned approximately one-third of the way down the screen.

- `helpfile` is a string expression that identifies the Help file to use to provide context-sensitive help for the dialog box. If `helpfile` is provided, `context` must also be provided.

- context is a numeric expression that identifies the Help context number assigned by the Help author to the appropriate Help topic. If context is provided, helpfile must also be provided. When both helpfile and context are supplied, a Help button is automatically added to the dialog box.

An example of using the InputBox for getting user input appears in Listing 16.6.

Listing 16.6. Getting user input.

```
Sub Display_OnClick
nbr = InputBox("Enter number: ", "Calculate Factorials")
If IsNumeric(nbr) Then
Call Fact(nbr)
Else
MsgBox "Enter a number!"
End If
End Sub
```

MsgBox

The MsgBox function displays a message in a dialog box, waits for the user to click a button, and returns a value indicating which button was clicked. The syntax for this statement follows:

MsgBox(prompt[, buttons][, title][, helpfile, context])

where the arguments have the following meanings:

- prompt is the string expression displayed as a prompt to the user. Prompts can be separated into multiple lines by inserting a carriage return (Chr(13)) in the prompt string. A linefeed character (Chr(10)) can also be used. The maximum prompt string is about 1,024 characters, depending on the width of the characters used.

- buttons is a numeric expression that defines the buttons and button style, the default button, and the mode of the message box. By adding values together from the following table, the expression can specify the number and type of buttons to display, the icon style to use, the default button, and the modality of the message box. (If this numeric expression is omitted, the default value for buttons is 0.)

By adding at most one value from each of the following four tables, you can specify the number and type of buttons, the dialog icon style, the default button, and the modality of the dialog box. Table 16.6 shows the dialog button values; Table 16.7 shows the dialog icon values; Table 16.8 shows the values required to set the button defaults; and Table 16.9 shows the values for dialog modality.

Table 16.6. Dialog buttons: number and style.

Value	Number	Description
vbOKOnly	0	Display OK button only
vbOKCancel	1	Display OK and Cancel buttons
vbAbortRetryIgnore	2	Display Abort, Retry, and Ignore buttons
vbYesNoCancel	3	Display Yes, No, and Cancel buttons
vbYesNo	4	Display Yes and No buttons
vbRetryCancel	5	Display Retry and Cancel buttons

If the dialog box displays a Cancel button, pressing the ESC key will have the same effect as clicking Cancel.

Table 16.7. Dialog icon style.

Value	Number	Description
vbCritical	16	Display Critical Message icon
vbQuestion	32	Display Warning Query icon
vbExclamation	48	Display Warning Message icon
vbInformation	64	Display Information Message icon

Table 16.8. Default dialog box button.

Value	Number	Description
vbDefaultButton1	0	First button is default
vbDefaultButton2	256	Second button is default
vbDefaultButton3	512	Third button is default
vbDefaultButton4	768	Fourth button is default

Table 16.9. Dialog box modality.

Value	Number	Description
vbApplicationModal	0	The user must respond to the message box before continuing work in the current application.
vbSystemModal	4096	All applications are suspended until the user responds to the message box.

> ## warning
>
> If the modality of a dialog box is set to vbSystemModal, the user will still be able to, for example, select and cut text in an open application. However, the dialog box will always remain on top.

- title defines a string expression displayed in the title bar of the dialog box. If title is omitted, the application name ("Visual Basic") is placed in the title bar.
- helpfile defines a string expression that identifies the Help file to use to provide context-sensitive Help for the dialog box. If a help file is provided, the context must also be provided. (This feature is not available on 16-bit platforms.)
- context is a numeric expression that identifies the Help context number assigned by the Help author to the Help topic. If a context is provided, a Help file must also be provided. When a Help file with context is provided, the user can press F1 to view the Help topic corresponding to the context. (This feature is not available on 16-bit platforms.)

MsgBox Return Values

If the MsgBox function is used on the right side of an assignment statement, as shown in the following code, the values shown in Table 16.10 may be returned:

```
rtnval = MsgBox(prompt, buttons, title, helpfile, context)
```

Table 16.10. MsgBox return values.

Value	Number	Description
vbOK	1	OK
vbCancel	2	Cancel
vbAbort	3	Abort
vbRetry	4	Retry
vbIgnore	5	Ignore
vbYes	6	Yes
vbNo	7	No

Listing 16.7 shows an example of how the InputBox and MsgBox functions can be used in your scripts.

Listing 16.7. InputBox and MsgBox uses.

```
<HTML>
<HEAD>
<TITLE>Calculate Factorials</TITLE>
<SCRIPT LANGUAGE="VBScript">
<!--
Sub GetNum_OnClick
nbr =  InputBox("Enter number: ", "Calculate Factorials")
If IsNumeric(nbr) Then
Result = Factorial(nbr)
MsgBox "The Factorial of " & nbr & " is " & Result,, "Factorial Result"
Else
MsgBox "Enter a number!"
End If
End Sub

Function Factorial(iNbr)
If iNbr = 1 Then
Factorial = 1
Else
Factorial = iNbr * Factorial(iNbr - 1)
End If
End Function
-->
</SCRIPT>
</HEAD>
<BODY>
<H1>Calculate a Factorial</H1>
Click the button to enter a number.
<P><INPUT NAME="GetNum" TYPE="BUTTON" VALUE="Factorial">
</FORM>
</BODY>
</HTML>
```

Output from this listing in Internet Explorer is shown in Figure 16.8.

Figure 16.8.
Output results:
the HTML page.

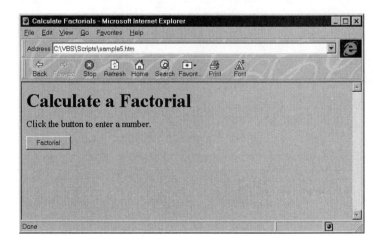

Figure 16.9 shows the input box that is displayed when the button on the browser page is clicked.

Figure 16.9.
The input box.

Figure 16.10 shows the message box that is returned as a result of the input.

Figure 16.10.
The MsgBox.

String Functions

The string functions provided by VBScript include the following:

```
Asc()
Chr()
InStr()
Lcase()
Left()
Len()
Ltrim()
Mid()
Right()
Rtrim()
Str()
StrComp()
String()
Trim()
Ucase()
```

Asc()

The Asc() function takes a single character or a string as input and returns the ASCII value. If a string is input, then the ASCII value of the first character in the string is returned. After the following code, A is equal to 65.

```
A = Asc("Apple")
```

Syntax: Asc(char ¦ string)

Chr()

The Chr() function takes a number as input and returns the character represented by that number. Its syntax follows:

```
Chr(number)
```

For example, a carriage return can be output in a text string with

```
document.write "This string has a " & Chr(13) & "carriage return embedded in
➥it."
```

InStr()

The InStr() function returns the position of the first occurrence of one string within another. The function takes as input an optional start position, the target string, the string to be found, and an optional numeric value that sets the search type. The syntax for the InStr() function follows:

```
InStr([start, ]string1, string2[, compare])
```

where

> start is an optional number indicating where the comparison is to begin
>
> string1 is the string being searched
>
> string2 is the string being sought
>
> compare is a number that indicates the comparison method.

The number may be:

0   exact character match

1   ignore case

The InStr() function returns the values shown in Table 16.11.

Table 16.11. **InStr** return values.

Function	Value
string1 is zero-length	0
string2 is not found	0
start > (Len(string1) - Len(string2))	0
string1 is Null	Null
string2 is Null	Null
Start Position	string2 is zero-length
string2 is found within string1	Position at which match is found

An example of how this function might be used is shown in Listing 16.8.

Listing 16.8. `Instr()` function.

```
string1 = "Boston Baked Beans!"
string2 = "Bak"
x = InStr(4, string1, string2)
```

The return value of the `InStr()` function is relative to position 1 of `string1`, regardless of the value of `start`. For example, in the previous listing, the return value will be 8.

Lcase()

The function `Lcase()` returns a string that has been converted to lowercase. Any lowercase and nonletter characters are unchanged. (If the string is `NULL`, then the function returns `NULL`.) The syntax for the `Lcase()` function follows:

```
Lcase(string)
```

For example, the following code sample would set the variable `str2` to `"much ado about 2"`:

```
str2 = Lcase("Much Ado About 2")
```

Left()

The function `Left()` returns a specified number of characters from the left side of a string. The function takes as input a string and a number representing the length. The syntax for the `Left()` function follows:

```
Left(string, length)
```

As an example, the following code would set the variable `str2` to `"The"`:

```
str2 = Left("The Big Apple", 3)
```

Len()

The `Len()` function takes as input a string and returns its length. Its syntax follows:

```
Len(string)
```

As an example, the following statement would set the variable `x` to `14`:

```
x = Len("Boston Blackie")
```

Ltrim()

The Ltrim() function takes as input a string and returns that string with any preceding spaces or tabs removed. Its syntax follows:

```
Ltrim(string)
```

The following statement would set variable str2 equal to "Bright Ideas":

```
str2 = Ltrim("              Bright Ideas")
```

Mid()

The Mid() function takes the following as input:

- A string
- A number representing the starting position
- An optional number representing the length

It then returns the specified string. The syntax for the Mid() function follows:

```
Mid(string, start [, length])
```

The following script statement would set the variable str2 to "Boy":

```
str2 = Mid("Little Boy Blue", 8, 3)
```

If the length is not provided or (length > (len(string) - start)), the function returns all characters from the start to the end of the input string.

Right()

The function Right() returns a specified number of characters from the right side of a string. The function takes as input a string and a number representing the length. The syntax for the Right() function follows:

```
Right(string, length)
```

The following script statement would set the variable str to "Apple":

```
str2 = Right("The Big Apple", 5)
```

Rtrim()

The Rtrim() function takes as input a string, and returns that string with any trailing spaces or tabs removed. Its syntax follows:

```
Rtrim(string)
```

The following script statement would set the variable str2 to "Bright Ideas":

```
str2 = Rtrim("Bright Ideas              ")
```

Str()

The str() function takes as input a number and returns a string representing a number.

> **note**
>
> The str() function does not work in version 2 of the VBScript.DLL. It should work in version 3.

StrComp()

The StrComp() function takes as input two strings and a control argument and returns a value indicating the result of the comparison. The control argument can be either 0, the default, or 1. If the control argument is 0, then the comparison is case sensitive. (The comparison is made on a bitwise basis.) If the control argument is 1, the comparison is case insensitive. The syntax of the StrComp() function follows:

```
StrComp(string1, string2, control)
```

The return values are shown in Table 16.12.

Table 16.12. The **StrComp** return values.

Value	Return Value
-1	string1 < string2
0	string1 = string2
1	string1 > string2
NULL	One of the strings is NULL.

Listing 16.9 would set k to -1.

Listing 16.9. **StrComp()** example.

```
x = "The Little Boy Blue"
y = "The Girl in Pink"
k = StrComp(x, y, 1)
MsgBox k
```

String()

The string() function takes as input a number and the decimal representation of an ASCII character and returns a string composed of the ASCII character repeated that number of times. The syntax of the string() function follows:

```
String(number, asciiID)
```

For example, the following code statement would set Str1 to a string of 10 spaces:

```
Str1 = String(10, 32)
```

Trim()

The Trim() function takes as input a string and returns that string with any leading or trailing spaces or tabs removed. Its syntax follows:

```
Trim(string)
```

The following script statement would set the variable str2 to "Bright Ideas":

```
str2 = Trim("           Bright Ideas              ")
```

Ucase()

The function Ucase() returns a string that has been converted to uppercase. Any uppercase and nonletter characters are unchanged. (If the string is NULL, the function returns NULL.) The syntax for the Ucase() function follows:

```
Ucase(string)
```

The following script statement would set the variable str2 to "MUCH ADO ABOUT 2":

```
str2 = Lcase("Much Ado About 2")
```

Math Functions

The math functions that are provided with VBScript include the following:

```
Abs()
Atn()
Exp()
Hex()
Int()
Fix()
Log()
Oct()
Rnd()
Randomize()
Sgn()
Sqr()
Sin()
Tan()
```

Abs()

The function Abs() takes a number as input and returns its absolute value. Its syntax () follows:

```
Abs(number)
```

For example, the following code sets x equal to 5:

```
x = Abs(-5)
```

Atn()

The Atn() function takes a number that represents the tangent of a right triangle and returns the corresponding angle in radians. The tangent of a right angle is the side opposite divided by the adjacent side. The syntax of the Atn() function follows:

```
Atn(tan)
```

For example, the following code sets x equal to 0.982793723247329:

```
x = Atn(3/2)
```

The results are in the range of the – /2 to /2 radians.(To convert degrees to radians, multiply degrees by /180. To convert radians to degrees, multiply radians by 180/ .)

Exp()

The Exp() function takes as input a number and returns the number e raised to that power. Its syntax follows: Exp(number)

For example, the following code sets the value of x to 20.08553692:

```
x = Exp(3)
```

If the value of the number exceeds 709.782712893, an error occurs. (The constant e is approximately 2.718281828.) See the "Log()" function section for more details.

Hex()

The Hex() function takes a number as input and returns its hexadecimal value. Its syntax follows:

```
Hex(number)
```

For example, the following code sets x to "A":

```
x = Hex(10)
```

> ### note
> The return value is a string that represents the hexadecimal value of an input number. To perform math operations, you must convert the string into a numerical value.

Int()

The `Int()` function takes a number and returns its integer portion. If the number is positive, the function truncates the trailing decimal. If the number is negative, the function returns the integer that is less than or equal to the input. The syntax of the `Int()` function follows:

```
Int(number)
```

For example, the following code sets x equal to -2:

```
x = Int(-1.25)
```

Fix()

The `Fix()` function also takes a number as input and returns its integer portion. However, if the input to `Fix()` is negative, `Fix()` returns the first negative integer greater than or equal to the number. The syntax of the Fix() function follows:

```
Fix(number)
```

For example, the following code sets x equal to -1:

```
x = Fix(-1.25)
```

`Fix(number)` is equivalent to `Sgn(number) * Int(Abs(number))`.

Log()

The `Log()` function returns the natural logarithm of the numeric argument, which must be greater than or equal to 0. Its syntax follows:

```
Log(number)
```

For example, the following code sets nbr to 1:

```
nbr = Log(2.71828182845905)
```

Oct()

The `Oct()` function takes a number as input and returns its octal value. Its syntax follows:

```
Oct(number)
```

For example, the following code sets x to "12":

```
x = Oct(10)
```

The return value is a string that represents the octal value of the input number. To perform math operations, you must convert the string into a numerical value.

Rnd()

The Rnd() function takes any numeric expression and returns a random number between 0 and 1. Its syntax follows:

```
Rnd(number)
```

The value of number determines how Rnd() generates a random number.

- If the number is less than 0, the function returns the same number every time, using the supplied number as the seed.
- If the number is greater than 0, the function returns the next random number in the generated sequence.
- If the number is equal to 0, the function returns the random number generated most recently.
- If a number is not supplied, the function returns the next random number in the sequence.

For any given initial seed, the same number sequence is generated because each successive call to the Rnd() function uses the previous number as a seed for the next number in the sequence. To generate a unique random number sequence, call Randomize without an argument to initialize the random-number generator with a seed based on the system timer. To produce random integers in a given range, use the following formula:

```
Int((upperbound - lowerbound + 1) * Rnd + lowerbound)
```

where upperbound is the highest number to be produced, and lowerbound is the lowest.

> **note**
>
> Calling Randomize() twice with the same value for the seed does not repeat the previous sequence. To repeat sequences of random numbers, call Rnd() with a negative argument immediately before using Randomize() with a numeric argument (see Listing 16.10).

Listing 16.10. A series of three random numbers.

```
Rnd(-1)
Randomize(3)
For I = 1 to 3
MsgBox Int((10 - 1) * Rnd)
Next
```

The code in Listing 16.10 will produce a series of three random numbers between 0 and 10. The sequence will be repeated each time the code is called.

Randomize()

Randomize() takes an optional numeric expression and initializes the random-number generator. Its syntax follows:

```
Randomize [(number)]
```

Randomize() uses the number argument to initialize the Rnd() function's random-number generator, giving it a new seed value. If the argument is omitted, the value returned by the system timer is used as the new seed value.

If Randomize() is not used, the Rnd() function (with no argument) uses the same number as a seed the first time it is called and thereafter uses the last generated number as a seed value.

note

To generate a unique sequence of random numbers, call Randomize() without an argument before calling the Rnd() function.

Sgn()

The Sgn() function takes a number as input and returns -1 if the number is negative and 1 if the number is positive. The syntax of the Sgn() function follows:

```
Sgn(number)
```

For example, the following code sets x equal to -1:

```
x = Sgn(-5)
```

Sqr()

The Sqr() function takes as input a numeric expression greater than or equal to 0 and returns its square root. The syntax of the Sqr() function follows:

```
Sqr(number)
```

For example, the following code sets x to 2:

```
x = Sqr(4)
```

> **note**
>
> Calling `Sqr()` with a negative number will result in an error.

Sin()

The `Sin()` function takes as input an angle in radians and returns its sine. The sine of an angle is the ratio of its opposite side divided by the hypotenuse. The result is within the range of −1 to 1. The syntax of the `Sin()` function follows:

```
Sin(radians)
```

For example, the following code sets x equal to `0.841471`:

```
x = sin(1);
```

Tan()

The `Tan()` function takes as input a number that represents an angle in radians and returns the ratio of the opposite side divided by the adjacent side. The syntax of the `Tan()` function follows:

```
Tan(radians)
```

For example, the following code sets x equal to `0.546302`:

```
x = tan(0.5)
```

Time and Date Functions

VBScript provides the following functions for manipulating dates and times:

```
Date()
DateSerial()
DateValue()
Day()
Hour()
Minute()
Month()
MonthName()
Now()
Second()
Time()
```

```
TimeSerial()
TimeValue()
Weekday()
WeekdayName()
Year()
```

Date()

The Date() function returns the current system date. Its syntax follows:

```
Date()
```

The following script statement sets x to the current date in the format mm/dd/yy:

```
x = Date()
```

DateSerial()

The DateSerial() function returns the date for a specified year, month, and day, based on the arguments passed in to the function. Its syntax follows:

```
DateSerial(year, month, day)
```

where

- year is a numeric expression or number from 100 to 9999.
- month is any numeric expression or number.
- day is any numeric expression or number.

To specify a date, such as December 31, 1991, the range of numbers for each DateSerial argument should be from 1 to 31 for days and 1 to 12 for months. You can also specify relative dates for each argument.

The following example uses numeric expressions instead of absolute date numbers. Here the DateSerial function returns a date that is the day before the first day (1 − 1) of two months after July (7 + 2) of 10 years after 1981 (1981 + 10); in other words, August 31, 1991:

```
DateSerial(1981 + 10, 7 + 2, 1 - 1)
```

For the year argument, values between 0 and 99, inclusive, are interpreted as the years 1900–1999. For all other year arguments, use a complete four-digit year (for example, 1800).

When any argument exceeds the normally accepted range for that argument, it increments to the next larger unit as appropriate. For example, if you specify 35 days, it is evaluated as one month and some number of days, depending on where in the year it is applied. If any argument is outside the range −32,768 to 32,767, or if the date specified by all the arguments falls outside the acceptable range of dates, an error occurs.

DateValue()

The DateValue() function takes as input either a string or a numeric expression that represents a date and returns a variant of subtype Date. The syntax of the DateValue() function follows:

```
DateValue(date)
```

The date argument is normally a string expression representing a date from January 1, 100 through December 31, 9999. However, date can also be any expression that represents a date, a time, or both a date and time, in that range.

If the date argument includes time information, DateValue doesn't return it. However, if date includes invalid time information (such as "92:65"), an error occurs. If date is a string that includes only numbers separated by valid date separators, DateValue recognizes the order for month, day, and year according to the Short Date format specified for your system. DateValue also recognizes unambiguous dates that contain month names, either in long or abbreviated form. For example, in addition to recognizing 12/30/1991 and 12/30/91, DateValue also recognizes December 30, 1991 and Dec 30, 1991.

If the year part of date is omitted, DateValue uses the current year from your computer's system date.

Day()

The Day() function takes as input any string or numeric expression that represents a date and returns a whole number from 1 to 31 representing the day of the month. (If date contains Null, Null is returned.) The syntax of the Day() function follows:

```
Day(date)
```

For example, the following script statements set X to #12/30/91# and Y to 30:

```
X = DateValue("December 30, 1991")
Y = Day(X)
```

Hour()

The Hour() function takes as input a string or numeric expression that represents a time and returns a whole number from 0 to 23 representing the hour of the day. (If time contains Null, Null is returned.) The syntax of the Hour() function follows:

```
Hour(time)
```

For example, the following script statements set L to 12:

```
K = "12:34:15"
L = Hour(K)
```

Minute()

The Minute() function returns a whole number from 0 to 59, representing the minute of the hour. The time argument is any expression that can represent a time. (If time contains Null, Null is returned.) The syntax for the Minute() function follows:

```
Minute(time)
```

For example, the following script statements set L to 34:

```
K = "12:34:15"
L = Minute(K)
```

Month()

The Month() function returns a whole number from 1 to 12, representing the month of the year. The date argument is any expression that can represent a valid date. (If date contains Null, Null is returned.) The syntax for the Month() function follows:

```
Month(date)
```

For example, the following script statements set Y to 12:

```
X = #12/30/1991#
Y = Month(X)
```

MonthName()

The MonthName() function takes as input a number or numeric expression that indicates the month and returns a string indicating the specified month. It also takes an optional Boolean expression that controls the abbreviation of the displayed month name. If this argument is omitted, the month name is not abbreviated. The syntax for the MonthName() function follows:

```
MonthName(month[, abbreviate])
```

Now()

The Now() function returns the current system date and time. (The parentheses are optional.) Its syntax follows:

```
Now()
```

For example, the following code sets DT equal to "2/15/97 4:54:09 PM" on the day I captured the return value:

```
DT = Now()
```

Second()

The Second() function takes a string or numeric expression that represents a time and returns a whole number from 0 to 59 representing the second of the minute. (If Null is passed as the expression, the function returns Null.)

Time()

The Time() function returns the current system time. Its syntax follows:

```
Time()
```

TimeSerial()

The TimeSerial() function takes a string or numeric expression that represents a time and returns data with the subtype of Date containing a specific hour, minute, and second. The syntax of the TimeSerial() function follows:

```
TimeSerial(hour, minute, second)
```

where the arguments have these meanings:

hour	Number between 0 (12:00 A.M.) and 23 (11:00 P.M.), inclusive, or a numeric expression
minute	Any numeric expression
second	Any numeric expression

To specify a time, the range of numbers for each TimeSerial argument should be in the range of 0 to 23 for hours and 0 to 59 for minutes and seconds. You can also specify relative times for each argument using any numeric expression that represents some number of hours, minutes, or seconds before or after a certain time.

For example, the following script statement sets x equal to "9:32:07":

```
TimeSerial(12 -3, 34 - 2, 16 - 9)
```

TimeValue()

The TimeValue() function takes a numeric or string expression that represents a time in a range from 0:00:00 to 23:59:59 and returns data with the Date subtype containing the time. Its syntax follows:

```
TimeValue(time)
```

For example, the following code sets x to "4:13:00":

```
x = TimeValue("4:13PM" )
```

Time can be entered using either a 12-hour or 24-hour clock. So, for example, "4:13PM" and "16:13" are both valid arguments. If the argument contains date information, TimeValue does not return it. However, if the date information is invalid, it will cause an error.

Weekday()

The Weekday() function takes a string or numeric expression and returns a whole number representing the day of the week. (If the date contains Null, Null is returned.) It also takes a constant as an optional argument that specifies the first day of the week. If this constant is omitted, Sunday is used as the first day of the week. The syntax of the Weekday() function follows:

```
WeekDay(day, constant)
```

Table 16.13 shows the values the firstdayoftheweek argument can take.

Table 16.13. FirstDayofTheWeek values.

Argument	Value	Description
vbUseSystem	0	Use NLS API setting
vbSunday	1	Sunday
vbMonday	2	Monday
vbTuesday	3	Tuesday
vbWednesday	4	Wednesday
vbThursday	5	Thursday
vbFriday	6	Friday
vbSaturday	7	Saturday

Table 16.14 shows the return values for the Weekday function.

Table 16.14. Weekday function return values.

Argument	Value	Description
vbSunday	1	Sunday
vbMonday	2	Monday
vbTuesday	3	Tuesday
vbWednesday	4	Wednesday
vbThursday	5	Thursday
vbFriday	6	Friday
vbSaturday	7	Saturday

WeekDayName()

The WeekDayName() function takes a numeric argument and returns the name of the day of the week. For example, the code in Listing 16.11 returns the name of the day of the week in the variable DayString:

```
DayString = WeekDayName(WeekDay(Now()))
```

Listing 16.11. WeekDay functions.

```
<HTML>
<HEAD>
<TITLE>Date Example</TITLE>
<SCRIPT LANGUAGE="VBScript">
<!--
Sub GetDay_OnClick
TheDate = DateValue(A_Date.Value)
TheWeekDay = WeekDayName(WeekDay(TheDate, vbUseSystem))
MsgBox "The day of the week for that date is " & TheWeekDay
End Sub
-->
</SCRIPT>
</HEAD>
<BODY>
<H1>What Day Did It Happen?</H1>
Enter a valid date and click the button.
<P><INPUT NAME="A_Date" TYPE="TEXT" SIZE="15">
<P><INPUT NAME="GetDay" TYPE="BUTTON" VALUE="What Day Is It?">
</BODY>
</HTML>
```

The output of Listing 16.11 is shown in Figure 16.11.

Figure 16.11.
Output of Listing 16.11.

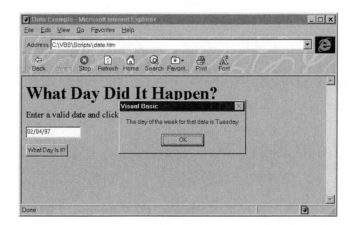

Year()

The Year() function takes as input any string or numeric expression that represents a date and returns a whole number representing the year. (If the date contains Null, Null is returned.) The syntax of the Year() function follows:

```
Year(date)
```

For example, the following statement sets x equal to the current year on the system:

```
X = Year(Now())
```

Boolean Functions

Boolean functions take any variable name and test its subtype. If the variant subtype matches the type being tested for, the function returns true; otherwise, it returns false. These functions include the following:

```
IsArray()
IsDate()
IsEmpty()
IsError()
IsNull()
IsNumeric()
IsObject()
```

IsArray()

The IsArray() function takes as input any variable name and returns true if the subtype of the variable is an array. Otherwise, it returns false. Its syntax follows:

```
IsArray(varname)
```

For example, if the following section of code is called, "False" will be displayed in the message box:

```
Dim nbr
 nbr = 5
 ans = IsArray(nbr)
 if ans then
 MsgBox "True"
 else
 MsgBox "False"
 End If
```

IsDate()

The IsDate() function takes as input any variable name and returns true if the subtype of the variable is an array; otherwise, it returns false. Its syntax follows:

```
IsDate(varname
```

For example, the following code sets ans to "True":

```
dt = #01/01/96#
ans = IsDate(dt)
```

IsEmpty()

The IsEmpty() function takes as input any variable name and returns true if the subtype of the variable is an array; otherwise, it returns false. The syntax of the IsEmpty() function follows:

```
IsEmpty(varname)
```

For example, the following code sets ans to "False":

```
dt = #01/01/96#
ans = IsEmpty(dt)
```

IsError()

The IsError() function takes as input a number or numeric expression and returns true if the subtype of the variable is an error; otherwise, it returns false. Its syntax follows:

```
IsError(varname)
```

IsNull()

The IsNull() function takes as input any variable name and returns true if the subtype of the variable is Null; otherwise, it returns false. Its syntax follows:

```
IsNull(varname)
```

IsNumeric()

The IsNumeric() function takes as input any variable name and returns true if the subtype of the variable is numeric; otherwise, it returns false. Its syntax follows:

```
IsNumeric(varname)
```

For example, the following code sets ans to "True":

```
nbr = 10348
ans = IsNumeric(nbr)
```

IsObject()

The IsObject() function takes as input any variable name and returns true if the subtype of the variable is an object; otherwise, it returns false. Its syntax follows:

```
IsObject(varname)
```

Conversion Functions

The conversion functions take numeric arguments and convert them from one subtype to another. The conversion functions provided by VBScript include the following:

```
CByte()
CCur()
CDbl()
CInt()
CLng()
CStr()
CvErr()
VarType()
```

CByte()

The CByte() function converts an expression in the range of 0 to 255 to the byte subtype.

CCur()

The CCur() function converts a numeric expression to the currency subtype. You can use the CCur() function to provide conversions from any other data type to a Currency subtype. The correct decimal and thousands separators are properly recognized based on the locale setting of your system.

CDbl()

The CDbl() function converts an expression in the range.

CInt()

The CInt() function takes a numeric expression and converts it into an integer subtype.

CLng()

The CLng() function takes a numeric expression and converts it into a long subtype.

CStr()

The CStr() function takes a numeric expression and converts it into a string.

CvErr()

The CvErr() function takes a valid error number and returns the subtype error.

VarType()

The VarType() function takes a variable name as input and returns its subtype. The documented return values and their meanings for this function are shown in Table 16.15.

Table 16.15. VarType() return values.

Value	Description
0	Empty
1	Null
2	Integer
3	Long
4	Single
5	Double
6	Currency
7	Date
8	String
9	OLE object
10	Error
11	Boolean
12	Variant
13	Non-OLE object
17	Byte
8192	Array

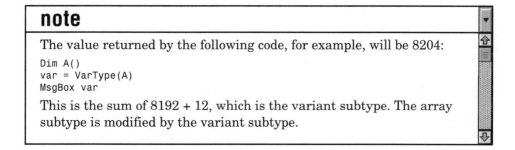

note

The value returned by the following code, for example, will be 8204:

```
Dim A()
var = VarType(A)
MsgBox var
```

This is the sum of 8192 + 12, which is the variant subtype. The array subtype is modified by the variant subtype.

Array()

The `Array()` function takes as input a series of values and returns a variant variable set to these values. Its syntax follows:

```
Array(val1, val2, ..., valn)
```

For example, the following script statements set `Name` equal to `"Dan"`:

```
x = Array("Andy", "Bob", "Carl", "Dan")
Name = x(3)
```

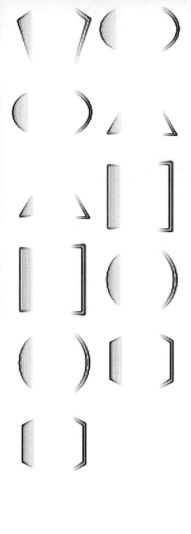

I N D E X

SYMBOLS

A

H

J-K-L

S

A V I A C O M   S E R V I C E

The Information SuperLibrary™

Bookstore	**Search**	**What's New**	**Reference**	**Software**	**Newsletter**	**Company Overviews**
Yellow Pages	**Internet Starter Kit**	**HTML Workshop**	**Win a Free T-Shirt!**	**Macmillan Computer Publishing**	**Site Map**	**Talk to Us**

You'll find thousands of shareware files and over 1600 computer books designed for both technowizards and technophobes. You can browse through 700 sample chapters, get the latest news on the Net, and find just about anything using our massive search directories.

All Macmillan Computer Publishing books are available at your local bookstore.

We're open 24-hours a day, 365 days a year.

You don't need a card.

We don't charge fines.

And you can be as **LOUD** as you want.

The Information SuperLibrary

http://www.mcp.com/mcp/   ftp.mcp.com

MACMILLAN COMPUTER PUBLISHING USA

A VIACOM COMPANY

Technical ---- Support:

If you need assistance with the information in this book or with a CD/Disk
accompanying the book, please access the Knowledge Base on our Web
site at **http://www.superlibrary.com/general/support**. Our most
Frequently Asked Questions are answered there. If you do not find the
answer to your questions on our Web site, you may contact Macmillan
Technical Support **(317) 581-3833** or e-mail us at **support@mcp.com**.

Laura Lemay's Guide to Sizzling Web Site Design

— *Laura Lemay & Molly Holzschlag*

This book is more than just a guide to the hottest Web sites. It's a behind-the-scenes look at how those sites were created. Web surfers and publishers alike will find this book an insightful guide to some of the most detailed pages. The latest Web technologies are discussed in detail, showing readers how the technologies have been applied. Readers also learn how they can implement those features on their own Web pages. The CD-ROM includes source code from the book, images, scripts, and more.

$45.00 USA/$63.95 CDN   *User Level: Casual–Accomplished*
ISBN: 1-57521-221-8   *400 pages*   *Internet-Web Publishing*

Web Publishing Unleashed, Professional Reference Edition

— *William Stanek, et al.*

Web Publishing Unleashed, Professional Reference Edition is a completely new version of *Web Publishing Unleashed*, combining coverage of all Web development technologies in one volume. The book now includes entire sections on JavaScript, Java, VBScript, and ActiveX, plus expanded coverage of multimedia Web development, adding animation, developing intranet sites, Web design, and much more! The book includes a 200-page reference section. The CD-ROM includes a selection of HTML, Java, CGI, and scripting tools for Windows/Mac, plus Sams.net Web Publishing Library and electronic versions of top Web publishing books.

$59.99 USA/$84.95 CDN   *User Level: Intermediate–Advanced*
ISBN: 1-57521-198-X   *1,200 pages*   *Internet-Web Publishing*

Web Programming Unleashed

— *Bob Breedlove, et al.*

This comprehensive tome explores all aspects of the latest technology craze—Internet programming. Programmers can turn to the proven expertise of the *Unleashed* series for accurate, day-and-date information on this hot new programming subject. This book gives timely, expert advice on ways to exploit the full potential of the Internet. The CD-ROM includes complete source code for all applications in the book, additional programs with accompanying source code, and several Internet application resource tools.

$49.99 USA/$70.95 CDN   *User Level: Accomplished–Expert*
ISBN: 1-57521-117-3   *1,056 pages*   *Internet-Programming*

HTML & CGI Unleashed, Professional Reference Edition

— *John December*

Readers will learn the logistics of how to create compelling, information-rich Web pages that grab readers' attention and keep users returning for more. This comprehensive professional instruction and reference guide for the World Wide Web covers all aspects of the development processes, implementation, tools, and programming. The CD-ROM features coverage of planning, analysis, design, HTML implementation, and gateway programming. The book covers the new HTML 3.2 specification, plus new topics such as Java, JavaScript, and ActiveX. It also features coverage of planning, analysis, design, HTML implementation, and gateway programming.

$59.99 USA/$84.95 CDN   *User Level: Accomplished–Expert*
ISBN: 1-57521-177-7   *900 pages*   *Internet-Programming*

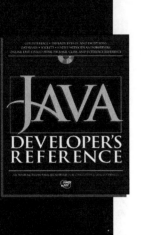

Java Developer's Reference

— Mike Cohn, et al.

This is the informative, resource-packed development package for professional developers. It explains the components of the Java Development Kit (JDK) and the Java programming language. Everything needed to program Java is included within this comprehensive reference, making it the tool that developers will turn to over and over again for timely and accurate information on Java and the JDK. The CD-ROM contains source code from the book and powerful utilities. The book includes tips and tricks for getting the most from Java and your Java programs. It also contains complete descriptions of all the package classes and their individual methods.

$59.99 USA/$84.95 CDN *User Level: Accomplished–Expert*
ISBN: 1-57521-129-7 *1,200 pages* *Internet-Programming*

Java Unleashed, Second Edition

— Michael Morrison, et al.

Java Unleashed, Second Edition is an expanded and updated version of the largest, most comprehensive Java book on the market. The book covers Java, Java APIs, JavaOS, just-in-time compilers, and more. The CD-ROM includes sample code, examples from the book, and bonus electronic books.

$49.99 USA/$70.95 CDN *User Level: Intermediate–Advanced*
ISBN: 1-57521-197-1 *1,200 pages* *Internet-Programming*

JavaScript 1.1 Developer's Guide

— Wes Tatters

The *JavaScript 1.1 Developer's Guide* is the professional reference for enhancing commercial-grade Web sites with JavaScript. Packed with real-world JavaScript examples, the book shows the developer how to use JavaScript to glue together Java applets, multimedia programs, plug-ins, and more on a Web site. The CD-ROM includes source code and powerful utilities.

$49.99 USA/$70.95 CDN *User Level: Accomplished–Expert*
ISBN: 1-57521-084-3 *600 pages* *Internet-Programming*

Visual Basic for Applications Unleashed

— Paul McFedries

Combining power and ease of use, Visual Basic for Applications (VBA) is the common language for developing macros and applications across all Microsoft Office components. With the format of the best-selling *Unleashed* series, users can master the intricacies of this popular language and exploit the full power of VBA. This book covers user interface design, database programming, networking programming, Internet programming, and stand-alone application creation. The CD-ROM is packed with the author's sample code, sample spreadsheets, databases, projects, templates, utilities, and evaluation copies of third-party tools and applications.

$49.99 USA/$70.95 CDN *User Level: Accomplished–Expert*
ISBN: 0-672-31046-5 *800 pages* *Programming*

Add to Your Sams.net Library Today
with the Best Books for Internet Technologies

ISBN	Quantity	Description of Item	Unit Cost	Total Cost
1-57521-221-8		Laura Lemay's Guide to Sizzling Web Site Design (Book/CD-ROM)	$45.00	
1-57521-198-X		Web Publishing Unleashed, Professional Reference Edition (Book/CD-ROM)	$59.99	
1-57521-117-3		Web Programming Unleashed (Book/CD-ROM)	$49.99	
1-57521-177-7		HTML 3.2 & CGI Unleashed, Professional Reference Edition (Book/CD-ROM)	$59.99	
1-57521-129-7		Java Developer's Reference (Book/CD-ROM)	$59.99	
1-57521-197-1		Java Unleashed, Second Edition (Book/CD-ROM)	$49.99	
1-57521-084-3		JavaScript 1.1 Developer's Guide (Book/CD-ROM)	$49.99	
0-672-31046-5		Visual Basic for Applications Unleashed (Book/CD-ROM)	$49.99	
		Shipping and Handling: See information below.		
		TOTAL		

Shipping and Handling: $4.00 for the first book, and $1.75 for each additional book. If you need to have it NOW, we can ship product to you in 24 hours for an additional charge of approximately $18.00, and you will receive your item overnight or in two days. Overseas shipping and handling adds $2.00. Prices subject to change. Call between 9:00 a.m. and 5:00 p.m. EST for availability and pricing information on latest editions.

201 W. 103rd Street, Indianapolis, Indiana 46290

1-800-428-5331 — Orders   1-800-835-3202 — FAX   1-800-858-7674 — Customer Service

Book ISBN 1-57521-257-9